W9-BVL-371

THE ONLY PLANE IN THE SKY

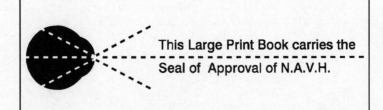

This Large Print Book carries the
Seal of Approval of N.A.V.H.

THE ONLY PLANE IN THE SKY

AN ORAL HISTORY OF 9/11

GARRETT M. GRAFF

THORNDIKE PRESS
A part of Gale, a Cengage Company

**LIBRARY OF CONGRESS CIP DATA ON FILE.
CATALOGUING IN PUBLICATION FOR THIS BOOK
IS AVAILABLE FROM THE LIBRARY OF CONGRESS**

ISBN-13: 978-1-4328-7721-7 (hardcover alk. paper)

Published in 2020 by arrangement with Avid Readers Press, an imprint of Simon & Schuster, Inc.

Printed in Mexico
Print Number: 01   Print Year: 2020

To my daughter, Eliza,
and to all the children affected by 9/11.
I hope this book helps you understand
the world in which you live.

CONTENTS

7

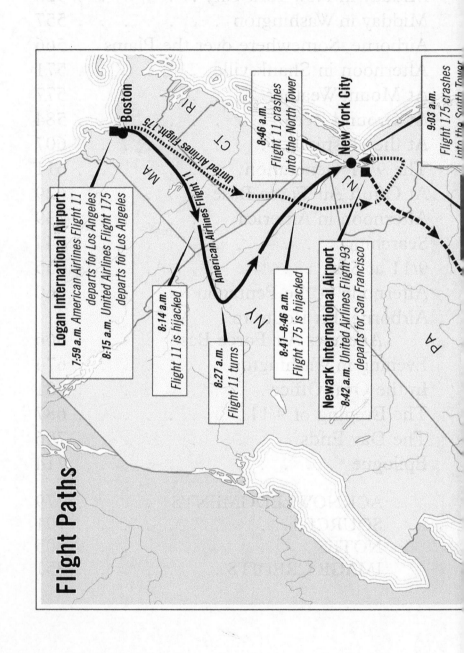

Flight Paths

Logan International Airport
7:59 a.m. American Airlines Flight 11 departs for Los Angeles
8:15 a.m. United Airlines Flight 175 departs for Los Angeles

8:14 a.m.
Flight 11 is hijacked

8:27 a.m.
Flight 11 turns

8:41–8:46 a.m.
Flight 175 is hijacked

Newark International Airport
8:42 a.m. United Airlines Flight 93 departs for San Francisco

8:46 a.m.
Flight 11 crashes into the North Tower

9:03 a.m.
Flight 175 crashes into the South Tower

United Airlines Flight 175

American Airlines Flight 11

Boston

New York City

RI
CT
MA
NY
PA
NJ

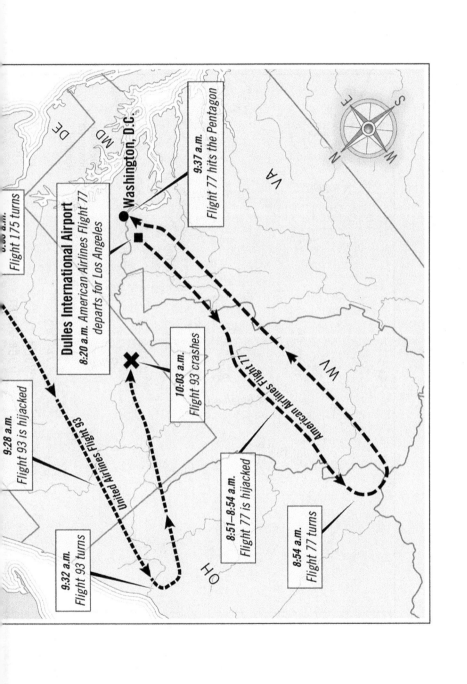

Dulles International Airport
8:20 a.m. American Airlines Flight 77
departs for Los Angeles

Washington, D.C.

9:37 a.m.
Flight 77 hits the Pentagon

Flight 175 turns

9:28 a.m.
Flight 93 is hijacked

9:32 a.m.
Flight 93 turns

United Airlines Flight 93

10:03 a.m.
Flight 93 crashes

American Airlines Flight 77

8:51–8:54 a.m.
Flight 77 is hijacked

8:54 a.m.
Flight 77 turns

DE

MD

VA

WV

OH

N
E
S
W

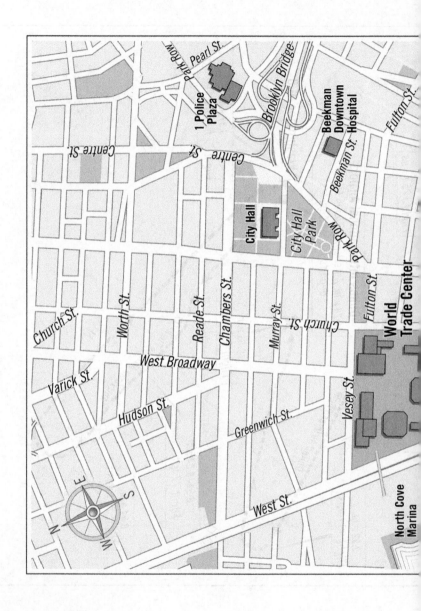

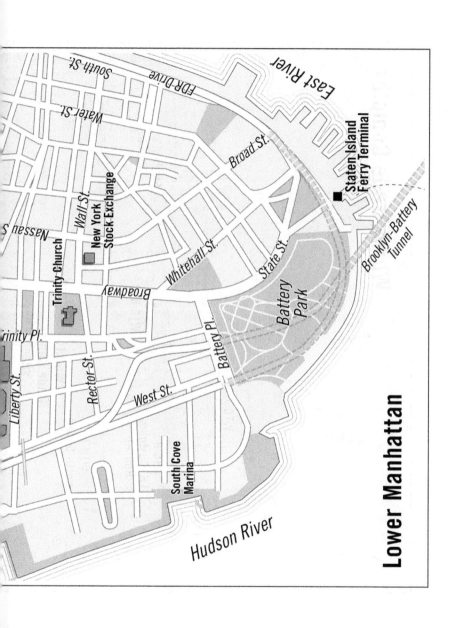

Lower Manhattan

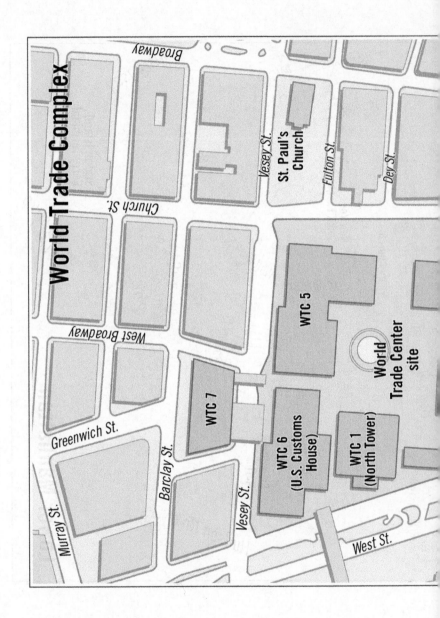

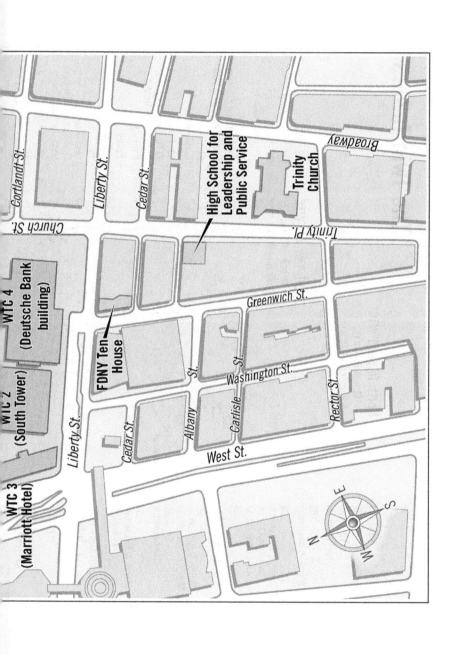

The Twin Towers

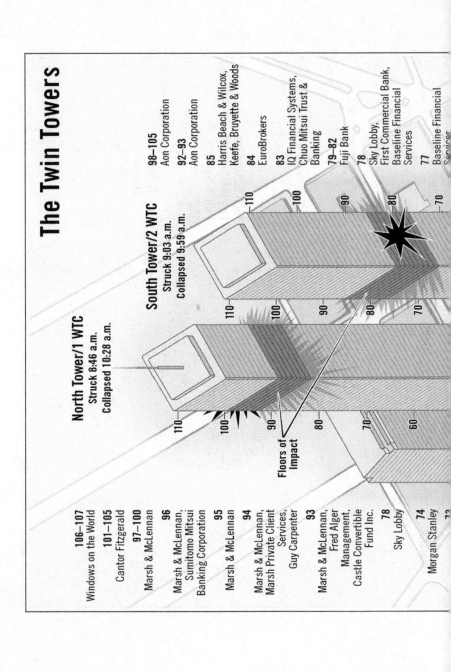

North Tower/1 WTC
Struck 8:46 a.m.
Collapsed 10:28 a.m.

South Tower/2 WTC
Struck 9:03 a.m.
Collapsed 9:59 a.m.

Floors of Impact

South Tower listing

98–105
Aon Corporation

92–93
Aon Corporation

85
Harris Beach & Wilcox,
Keefe, Bruyette & Woods

84
EuroBrokers

83
IQ Financial Systems,
Chuo Mitsui Trust &
Banking

79–82
Fuji Bank

78
Sky Lobby,
First Commercial Bank,
Baseline Financial
Services

77
Baseline Financial
Services

North Tower listing

106–107
Windows on the World

101–105
Cantor Fitzgerald

97–100
Marsh & McLennan

96
Marsh & McLennan,
Sumitomo Mitsui
Banking Corporation

95
Marsh & McLennan

94
Marsh & McLennan,
Marsh Private Client
Services,
Guy Carpenter

93
Marsh & McLennan,
Fred Alger
Management,
Castle Convertible
Fund Inc.

78
Sky Lobby

74
Morgan Stanley

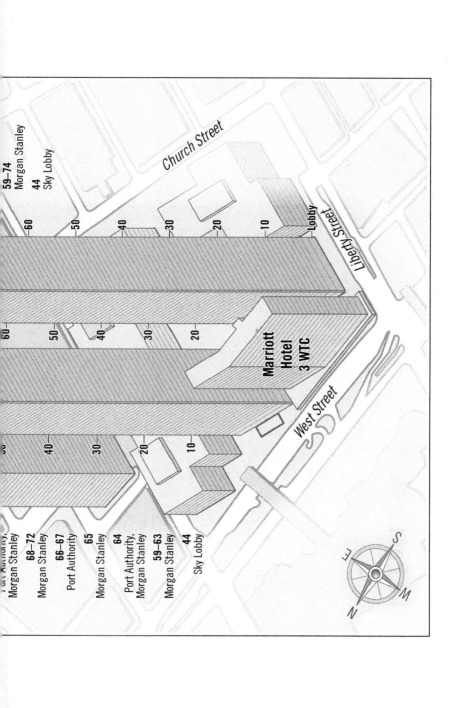

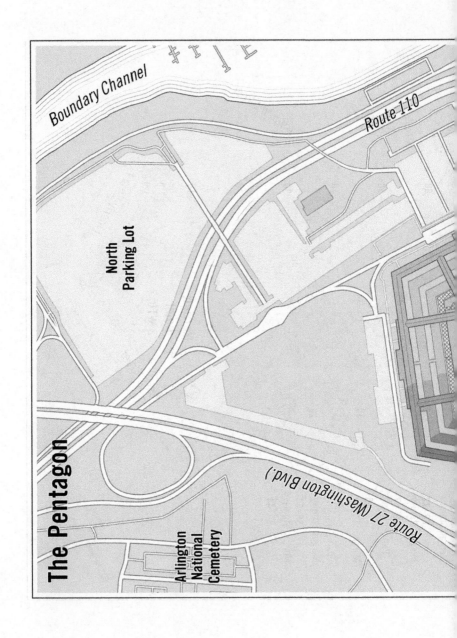

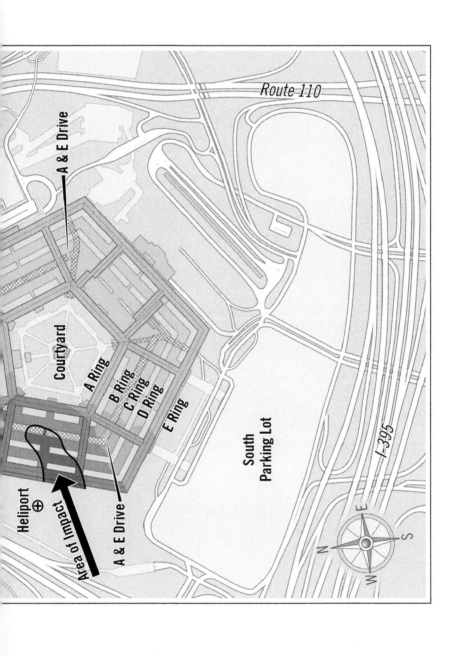

AUTHOR'S NOTE

Nearly every American above a certain age remembers precisely where they were on September 11, 2001. What began as an ordinary day became the deadliest terrorist attack in world history and the deadliest attack on the United States since Pearl Harbor, shocking and terrifying the global community, exposing us to unimaginable tragedy and evil, while also reminding us of the strength, bravery, and power of the human spirit. Heroes quite literally emerged from the ashes, and the hours and decisions that followed defined not just a generation but our modern era.

All told, 2,606 people died at the World Trade Center in New York City and another 125 at the Pentagon; 206 people died when their planes — American Airlines Flight 77, United Airlines Flight 175, American Airlines Flight 11, flight numbers now permanently retired and part of history — were hijacked and crashed into the centers of America's financial and military power; another 40 died in Shanksville, Pennsylvania, as brave passengers and crew wrestled control of United Flight 93 back from the hijackers. The 9/11 Memorial and Museum in New York City honors a precise tally of 2,983 casualties, including six killed in 1993, when the World Trade Center was attacked for the first time by the forerunners of the terror group that would ultimately bring these buildings down in just 102 minutes eight years later. The 9/11 victims represented not merely Americans but citizens of more than 90 nations.

The toll obviously stretched beyond the dead alone; more than 3,000 children lost a parent on 9/11, including some 100 children who were born in the subsequent months and would never meet their fathers. Upwards of 6,000 people were injured, and many more would face injuries — some physical, some psychological, some eventually fatal — stemming from the recovery work. Far beyond the official numbers, however, the attacks affected nearly every American alive that day — and hundreds of millions, if not billions, beyond our shores, as news of the attacks was broadcast the world over.

I've spent three years collecting the stories of those who lived through and experienced 9/11 — where they were, what they remember, and how their lives changed. The book that follows is based on more than 500 oral histories, conducted by me as well as dozens of other historians and journalists over the last seventeen years. I'm deeply grateful for their work and their understanding that history would want — and need — these stories recorded.

Collectively, these narratives help make sense of a day that we, as a country and as a people, are still trying to process. In her oral history of the day, Eve Butler-Gee, who on 9/11 was a clerk in the U.S. House of Representatives, remarked on how fascinated Americans are by their own memories of that day: "I've noticed we don't listen to each other's stories. We need to tell our story. Someone will start saying, 'Well, I was such-and-such,' and the other person will interrupt and talk over and say, 'Well, I was so-and-so.' The shock, in many ways, is still embedded in our memories that this thing happened on our shores, in the places where we felt the safest." Her observation rang true to me throughout this project, as every mention of 9/11 to friends or acquaintances immediately prompted people to pour out their own stories, often with heart-wrenching intimacy. This book is an attempt to listen, to hear others' stories, to know what it was like to experience the day firsthand, to wrestle with the confusion and the terror.

The Only Plane in the Sky is not meant to be a precise account of how and why September 11 occurred; groups like the 9/11 Commission devoted years of work and millions of dollars to provide those answers. Instead this book intends to capture how Americans *lived* that day, how the attacks in New York City, at the Pentagon, and in the skies over Somerset County, Pennsylvania, rippled across lives from coast to coast, from the Twin Towers to an elementary school in Sarasota, Florida, and how government and military officials on Capitol Hill, at the White House, in mountain bunkers, at air traffic control centers, and in the cockpit of fighter planes responded in an unprecedented moment to unimaginable horrors.

To construct this book, I worked for two years with Jenny Pachucki, an oral historian who has dedicated her career to stories of September 11 and who located for me about 5,000 relevant oral histories collected and archived around the country. We closely read or listened to about 2,000 of those stories to identify the voices and memories featured here. As part of that, I've drawn upon interviews and exhaustive work from the National September 11 Memorial & Museum and the 9/11 Tribute Museum (New York City), the Flight 93 National Memorial (near Shanksville, Pennsylvania), the September 11th Education Trust, the U.S. House of Representatives Historian's Office, C-SPAN, the Arlington County (Virginia) Public Library, the

Fire Department of the City of New York, the Historical Office of the Office of the Secretary of Defense, the U.S. Air Force, the U.S. Coast Guard, the 9/11 Commission, the Museum of Chinese in America (New York City), Columbia University, Stony Brook University, and other repositories, as well as a host of snippets and transcripts culled from news articles, magazine profiles, pamphlets, videos, documentaries, collections ranging from the trial exhibits of 9/11 conspirator Zacarias Moussaoui to a compilation published by America Online of its users' thoughts, posts, and memories of 9/11, and countless other books, including three that deserve specific mention for their usefulness: Mitchell Fink and Lois Mathias's terrific 2002 collection of oral histories, *Never Forget,* as well as two works focused on the 9/11 New York maritime boatlift, Mike Magee's *All Available Boats* and Jessica DuLong's *Dust to Deliverance.* To supplement those existing archival primary sources, I've also collected several hundred interviews, personal reflections, and stories myself, about 75 of which are featured here. I'm grateful to all who shared their stories.

Among these hundreds of memories collected as early as September 2001 and as recently as the spring of 2019, the chronologies and stories don't always line up neatly;

25

perspectives differ, and images blur with time. Traumatic memories especially are fallible. I've done my best to line things up according to the facts and timelines available. All interviews have been condensed and edited for clarity. Throughout the book, all titles, occupations, locations, and ranks are accurate to that moment. Additionally, for ease of reading and historical accuracy, I've edited some quotations to make verb tenses consistent and made minor factual corrections — for instance, where a speaker misremembered a name or title, such as calling the speaker pro tem the "president pro tem," or misstating what floor the sky lobbies in the Trade Center were on — and standardized some place names, code words, and other references that would otherwise be more confusing than illuminating.

While *The Only Plane in the Sky* is comprehensive, it is not complete. These stories capture only a single moment in time, and part of what makes 9/11 so poignant is learning how people fared in the days, weeks, months, and years thereafter. (Two key players on that day — Bernard Kerik, commissioner of the New York Police Department, and Speaker of the House Dennis Hastert — would both end up in prison, for instance.) As the nation united in solidarity after the attacks, it also descended into two wars that continue to this day and reshaped multiple corners of the world; thus 9/11 remains a daily presence in our national politics and our international geopolitics, and it fundamentally changed the way we live, travel, and interact with one another. As Rosemary Dillard, an American Airlines manager in D.C. whose husband, Eddie, was aboard one of the hijacked flights, said, "I still think that we all walk on eggshells. I don't think that the young people who will be [reading] this will know the same freedom I knew growing up."

Today, that new generation Dillard mentions barely remembers the day itself; 2018 marked the first year military recruits born after 9/11 were deployed to war zones in Iraq and Afghanistan, and the fall of 2019 will mark the entrance of the first college class born after the attacks. That passage of time makes remembering 9/11 all the more important. Indeed, to understand all that came after, we must first understand what it was like to live through the drama and tragedy that began under the crisp, clear blue skies of Tuesday, September 11, 2001.

ABOARD THE
INTERNATIONAL SPACE STATION

On August 12, 2001, NASA astronaut Frank Culbertson arrived at the International Space Station aboard the Space Shuttle Discovery. He would live and work aboard the Space Station for 125 days. On September 11, 2001, he was the only American off the planet.

Commander Frank Culbertson, astronaut, NASA: On September the 11th, 2001, I called the ground, and my flight surgeon Steve Hart came on. I said, "Hey Steve, how's it going?" He said, "Well, Frank, we're not having a very good day down here on Earth." He began to describe to me what was happening in New York — the airplanes flown into the World Trade Center, another airplane flown into the Pentagon. He said, "We just lost another airplane somewhere in Pennsylvania. We don't know where or what's happening."

I looked at the laptop that has our world map on it, and I saw that we were coming across southern Canada. In a minute we were going to be over New England. I raced around, found a video camera and a window facing in the right direction.

About 400 miles away from New York City, I could clearly see the city. It was a perfect weather day all over the United States, and the only activity I could see was this big black column of smoke coming out of New York City, out over Long Island, and over the Atlantic. As I zoomed in with a video camera, I saw this big gray blob basically enveloping the southern part of Manhattan. I was seeing the second tower come down. I assumed tens of thousands of people were being hurt or killed. It was horrible to see my country under attack.

We had 90 minutes to set up for the next pass across the United States. We set up every camera we could. I said, "Guys, we're gonna take pictures of everything we can see as we come across the U.S." An hour and a half later, we crossed Chicago. I was looking all around for any evidence of further attacks. I could see all the way to Houston. In a few minutes, we crossed Washington, D.C., directly over the Pentagon. I could look straight down and see the gash on the side of it. I could see the lights of the rescue vehicles, the smoke of the fires. Looking north, I could clearly see New York City and the column of smoke.

Every orbit, we kept trying to see more of what was happening. One of the most startling effects was that within about two orbits, all the contrails normally crisscrossing the United States had disappeared because they had grounded all the airplanes and there was nobody else flying in U.S. airspace except for one airplane that was leaving a contrail from the central U.S. toward Washington. That was Air Force One heading back to D.C. with President Bush.

SEPTEMBER 10TH

"GOOD DAYS AND BAD DAYS"

Monday, September 10th, in New York City began with the rededication of a Bronx firehouse, home to Engine 73 and Ladder 42. Mayor Rudolph "Rudy" Giuliani, Fire Commissioner Thomas Von Essen, and Chief of Department Peter Ganci listened as Fire Department Chaplain Father Mychal Judge offered a homily for the renovated firehouse.

Father Mychal Judge, chaplain, FDNY: Good days. And bad days. Up days. Down days. Sad days. Happy days. But never a boring day on this job. You do what God has called you to do. You show up. You put one foot in front of another. You get on the rig and you go out and you do the job. Which is a mystery. And a surprise. You have no idea when you get on that rig. No matter how big the call. No matter how small. You have no idea what God is calling you to. But he needs you. He needs me. He needs all of us.

Across the country, Monday was a regular workday, the beginning of fall, the first full week after Labor Day, and for many communities the first day of school after the quiet summer doldrums of August. Reporters and news broadcasters filed back into their offices, as did government officials and business professionals, bringing cities back to life. Many anticipated a slow start to the season.

Tom Brokaw, anchor, NBC News: I'd been off most of the summer. A friend called up to ask how it was to be back. I said, "I'm doing fine, but there's no news. It's hard to get cranked back up." It looked like it was not going to be a terribly stimulating autumn. Social Security reform was the hot topic. The economy was winding down.

Mary Matalin, aide to Vice President Dick Cheney: There was a sense of "Okay, now back to business." We had economic issues at the time. We were on the front end of a recession.

Matthew Waxman, staff member, National Security Council, White House: This was an administration that was interested in Great Power politics. A great deal of effort was focused on U.S.-Russian arms control and the strategic relationship questions about how to manage a rising China. These were the central questions. Two possible regional crises that week we were worried about were Burundi and Macedonia.

Monica O'Leary, Cantor Fitzgerald, North Tower, 105th floor: On September 10th, in the afternoon — my guess is around two o'clock — I was laid off. I don't know the exact time, but I know I thought to myself, *Oh, I can be home in time for* General Hospital. When I got laid off, I was on the 105th floor. I was upset. I was crying. Eventually, when I calmed down, the woman for HR gave me the choice: "Do you want to go back to the desk and get your stuff, or do you want to go home?" I said, "Oh, no, no, no. I want to go say good-bye to everybody." I went around and started kissing everybody good-bye. They were all great. This guy, Joe Sacerdote, stood up in the back row, and he yelled, "It's their loss, Monica!"

Lyzbeth Glick, wife of United Flight 93 passenger Jeremy Glick: I was on maternity leave from a teaching job at Berkley, a business college in New York. On that Monday morning, September 10, Jeremy helped me pack up the car — he was going to California on business and was booked on a flight that night. We live in Hewitt, New Jersey, and I was going up to my parents' house in the Catskill Mountains while he was away. He packed me up, and then he headed down to Newark for a meeting. He called me at around five o'clock and said there had been a fire in Newark, and he didn't feel like arriving in California at two in the morning. He decided to go home, get a good night's sleep, and catch the first flight out Tuesday morning.

From May to October 2001, Vanessa Lawrence and Monika Bravo were supposed to be two of a total of fifteen artists in residence on the 91st and 92nd floors of the World Trade Center's North Tower, as part of the Studio Scape program run by the Lower Manhattan Cultural Council. Both were inspired by the Towers and had begun to incorporate them into their art.

Vanessa Lawrence, artist, North Tower, 91st floor: Because I was living in a basement where I just saw people's feet, I thought it would be amazing to paint from such a high view — seeing different weather patterns, changing skies, changing light.

35

Monika Bravo, artist, North Tower, 91st floor: The reason I applied was because I wanted to film. I had this image in my mind — the Twin Towers above and only clouds underneath. The thing I missed most from my native Colombia were the clouds and the mountains. We have a lot of clouds all the time, and for me, the cloud is like home.

Vanessa Lawrence: I loved that skyline. Every morning coming in, there was something special. Again at night, seeing them lit up, just the lights on them. It was a really special skyline.

Monika Bravo: I told everybody throughout the summer, "If you see something coming — a storm — let me know. I'm always going to have a camera ready." The afternoon of September 10th, around 2:55 p.m., the storms happened.

Vanessa Lawrence: I grabbed my watercolors because I could see this storm coming. It was amazing watching it way out, looking out across Brooklyn and out on the horizon. I remember watching this dark cloud going down to the ground, and all the colors in it and everything. There's one of my favorite paintings I did.

Monika Bravo: I started filming. The storm

was coming from New Jersey south, through the Verrazzano Bridge and the Statue of Liberty. You see these clouds moving very fast — and there's a moment that is really, really incredible in the film. You see one drop hitting the window, then in a second all these water drops hitting the window. The storm is there. It's with you.

Vanessa Lawrence: Watching it coming, coming, coming, coming, and then — nothing. We were in this thick cloud and the rain.

Monika Bravo: The video is the witness of the last people standing, the last night before these towers cease to exist and everything and everybody that was inside. You see people in the South Tower coming in, working. You see people alive. You can see boats going. You see the city of Brooklyn lighting up. You see the movement of the bridges. It's alive. You see the life of the city from the last night you could see it from that perspective.

I filmed for many hours, until 9:00 or 9:30 p.m. probably. The storm was very long, the whole afternoon. I filmed in different places, in time lapse, in slow motion. It was beautiful. Then, at one point, my cell phone rang. I was married then, and this person called me: "Are you going to come home?" I said, "Oh no, beautiful thunderstorm." I said to him, "Why don't you come over and bring me some cigarettes." He said, "No, I'm not going to bring you anything. You come home." So I said, "All right, all right." I actually took the tape out of the camera. I left my computer because it was raining a lot. I was looking for a place to put it — I found an old file cabinet made out of wood. I remember thinking, *Is this going to be safe?* And then, *This is the World Trade Center. Nothing can happen to this building.*

TUESDAY BEGINS
"AN EASY DAY"

Around the world, September 11th began as any other weekday. Congress was reengaging after its summer recess. In Herndon, Virginia, at the Federal Aviation Administration's (FAA) national command center, Ben Sliney prepared for his first day running the nation's airspace. Nearby, in Langley, Virginia, Gina Haspel began her first day at the CIA's counterterrorism center. In Washington, D.C., FBI Director Robert Mueller — who had started in his new post just one week earlier, on September 4 — was scheduled to appear at 8:00 a.m. for his first briefing on the FBI's unfolding investigation of a terror group known as al-Qaeda and its bombing of the USS Cole *the previous fall. Far from America's shores, the captain of the U.S. Navy's aircraft carrier USS* Enterprise *was just finishing a long tour enforcing the no-fly zone over Iraq and looking forward to returning home.*

In New York City it was primary day; New Yorkers would choose the candidates vying to replace the man who had run their city for eight years, Rudy Giuliani. Millions of residents, work-ers, schoolchildren, and commuters awoke and began preparing for the day, many boarding trains, ferries, subways, and buses to make their way into Lower Manhattan. The FDNY's director of fire education safety was particularly excited that Tuesday: he was set to launch a new toy, modeled on a New York firefighter, and had chosen the day carefully. The date, after all, seemed perfect for firefighters: 9-1-1.

Lt. Joseph Torrillo, director of Fire Education Safety, FDNY: Fisher-Price had a line of children's toys called "Rescue Heroes" that kids loved. They had a police officer called Jake Justice, a lifeguard called Wendy Waters, an ambulance attendant called Perry Medic. They wanted a New York City fire-fighter — they were going to call him Billy Blazes. They would give me one dollar for every Billy Blazes sold around the world, money I would use in my public education program. They wanted to do a big press conference and introduce this new Rescue Hero to the world. I was scratching my head with the executives, and I said, "9-1-1 is the emergency phone number in New York City. Why don't we have a 9-1-1 Day in New York?" So on 9/11 at nine o'clock in the morning, every TV station in New York City was waiting for me at Rockefeller Center to introduce this new Rescue Hero.

Herb Ouida, World Trade Centers Association, North Tower, 77th floor, and father of Todd Ouida, Cantor Fitzgerald, North Tower, 105th floor: As we did every morning, my son Todd and I left our home together to travel to work, because Todd was working at the World Trade Center for Cantor Fitzgerald. When we got down to Hoboken, I said to Todd, "Why don't you take the ferry with me, it's a beautiful day?" He said, "No, Dad, it's too cold." I told him, "Have a great day, sweetheart." Those were my last words to Todd.

Richard Eichen, consultant, Pass Consulting Group, North Tower, 90th floor: I used to take the train every day to the Trade Center. I was sitting next to a friend — we belonged to the same golf club — and we were talking about how bad the food was. That was my biggest care in the world that day.

Ted Olson, solicitor general, U.S. Department of Justice: My wife, Barbara, was supposed to travel Monday, and my birthday was Tuesday. She decided that she was not going to go Monday. She did not want to be gone on the morning of my birthday, she

41

wanted to be there when I woke up. I left for work very early in the morning — before 6:00 — and she left shortly after to go to the airport. I heard from her before she boarded. This plane was scheduled to leave at 8:10 in the morning. We always called one another a lot during the day, sometimes very briefly. She called me at 7:30 or 7:40, before she got on the plane.

Rosemary Dillard, base manager, American Airlines: My husband, Eddie, had just acquired a house in L.A. and was going out to work on the house to get it in order so he could rent or sell it. We were driving out to Dulles, because Flight 77 was nonstop to L.A., and we were laughing. I remember him getting out, and he reminded me, "Before you go to work, get gas." He kissed me. My last words to him were, "Be home by Thursday."

Laura Bush, first lady of the United States, White House: I'd spent most of the morning going over the briefing that I was supposed to give that day to the Senate Education Committee. I was giving a briefing on the results from a summit that I'd had earlier in the summer on early childhood education. It was about nine months into George being president, and I was really hitting my stride as first lady.

42

Ada Dolch, principal, High School for Leadership and Public Service (HSLPS), New York City: It was primary election day. Our school building was going to be used for the very first time as a voting site.

Fernando Ferrer, Bronx borough president and candidate for New York City mayor: Hard primary campaign. My wife and I went to vote. It was all very nice, and our tracking polls gave me reason to be in a very good mood that day.

Sunny Mindel, communications director for the mayor of the City of New York, Rudy Giuliani: On September 11th, I was facing what I thought would be an easy day.

William Jimeno, officer, Port Authority Police Department (PAPD): I remember waking up and making a decision. I'm a big bowhunter — I like to deer hunt — and the weather was going to be great. I was going to possibly take a "P-day," which is a personal day at the Port Authority Police. I said, "No, I'm going to save it for a later time."

The storm of September 10th that swept across the Northeast, marking the passage of a strong cold front, preceded a high-pressure system of dry Canadian air that gave rise to a unique — and memorable — meteorological phenomenon known as "severe clear," cloudless skies that made an enduring impression on all who would witness what transpired in the hours ahead.

Ben Sliney, national operations manager, FAA Command Center, Herndon, Virginia: That was my first day on the job as national operations manager. When I got up that morning and looked at the Weather Channel and saw that the entire East Coast was going to be severe clear, I anticipated it would be a pretty good first day.

Melinda Murphy, traffic reporter, WPIX TV, New York City: We would fly for the morning show from 7:00 a.m. to 9:00 a.m. I had 14 hits [TV appearances] a morning — people still remember me as the "Chopper Chick." The sunrise that morning was incredible. We actually commented about how gorgeous the World Trade Center towers looked, reflecting this red sunrise — this crimson, gorgeous reflection like you've never seen ever.

Vanessa Lawrence, artist, North Tower, 91st floor: I was getting to the World Trade Center at six o'clock. The sun started coming up. I remember a beautiful sunrise. Walking in, you could see the red coming up through the windows.

Katie Couric, anchor, *The Today Show* :
It was the perfect fall day, a little touch of autumn in the air. It was one of those back-to-school September days, full of possibilities, and, in its own way, a new beginning.

Bruno Dellinger, principal, Quint Amasis North America, North Tower, 47th floor: The sky was so pure. The air was so crisp. Everything was perfect.

Capt. Jay Jonas, Ladder 6, FDNY: It's like the air was scrubbed clean.

Richard Paden, trooper, Aviation Unit, Pennsylvania State Police: A really nice morning, weather-wise. As pilots we say "Clear Blue and 22" when it's blue skies and not a cloud in the sky.

Lt. Col. Tim Duffy, F-15 pilot, Otis Air Force Base, Cape Cod, Massachusetts: One of the prettiest days I've ever flown — literally there was not a cloud in the sky and visibility was probably better than a hundred miles. It was crystal clear.

Sen. Tom Daschle (D-South Dakota), Senate Majority Leader: One of the most beautiful days of the year.

Jeannine Ali, controller, Morgan Stanley, South Tower, 45th floor: There has never been as brilliant of a blue sky as there was that day.

Hillary Howard, weather anchor, WUSA-TV, Washington, D.C.: The sky was extraordinarily blue.

Lt. Jim Daly, Arlington County (Virginia) Police Department: A gorgeous blue.

Joyce Dunn, teacher, Shanksville-Stonycreek School District, Pennsylvania: So blue.

Brian Gunderson, chief of staff for House Majority Leader Richard Armey (R-Texas): Deep blue.

Michael Lomonaco, executive chef, Windows on the World, North Tower, 106th floor: Deep, deep blue.

Eve Butler-Gee, chief journal clerk, U.S. House of Representatives: Cobalt blue.

Katie Couric: Cerulean blue.

Mike Tuohey, ticket agent, Portland International Jetport, Maine: The bluest of blues.

Julia Rogers, page, U.S. House of Representatives: One of those days that you wish you could put in a bottle.

President George W. Bush began his morning in Sarasota, Florida, where he was set to read to elementary school students as part of his push for the No Child Left Behind legislation. His new administration was still finding its legs after a rocky transition period shortened by the bitter Bush v. Gore *Florida recount and the controversial Supreme Court decision that declared him the winner of the 2000 election — a decision many still disputed in September 2001.*

Gordon Johndroe, assistant press secretary, White House: The day started off very normally — the president went for a run, and I took the press pool out with the president. I remember I got stung by a bee, and I asked [White House physician] Dr. [Richard] Tubb if he had something he could give me for the swelling. He said, "Yeah, we'll get you something when we get to the airplane."

Sonya Ross, reporter, Associated Press: It was a garden-variety trip. It was low-ranking staff, and a lot of the top journalists didn't come. It was a scrub trip.

Mike Morell, presidential briefer, Central Intelligence Agency: I walked into his suite for the president's morning intelligence briefing; he was surrounded by breakfast foods and hadn't touched any of it. The second intifada was well under way then, and the briefings at that time were very heavy on Israeli-Palestinian stuff. There was nothing in the briefing about terrorism. It was very routine.

Andy Card, White House chief of staff: The president was in a great mood. He had that George W. Bush strut that morning.

B. Alexander "Sandy" Kress, senior education adviser, White House: Those were probably the last carefree moments he had in his term.

Andy Card: I remember literally telling him, "It should be an easy day." Those were the words. "It should be an easy day."

CHECKING IN

"YOU'LL MISS YOUR PLANE"

As America's day began, two men arrived for their early-morning connection to Boston at the Portland International Jetport in Portland, Maine. They checked in at 5:43 a.m. Over the course of the morning, seventeen men checked in to their flights at Boston's Logan International, Washington's Dulles International, and Newark International. While some were selected for extra screening or had their checked bags searched, no one gave the knives they carried onboard a second look — they were allowed under the security regulations at the time. The men made their way onto carefully selected cross-country flights, targeting four planes amid the nearly 40,000 domestic flights scheduled for that Tuesday.

Mike Tuohey, ticket agent, Portland International Jetport: Everybody was in a good mood, it was a gorgeous day, and things were going like clockwork.

49

Vaughn Allex, ticket agent, Washington Dulles International Airport, Virginia: These two guys came running in the front door looking around and didn't know which way to go.

Mike Tuohey: I saw these two fellows standing there looking around. I looked at the tickets — I go, "Whoa, first-class tickets." You don't see $2,400 tickets anymore. There were less than 30 minutes prior to the flight [when they arrived]. The younger fellow was standing off to the right. I was asking the standard questions — has anybody given you anything to carry on board the plane, have your bags been out of your control since you packed them? He was shaking his head, smiling at me, so it's OK.

Vaughn Allex: We just finished the morning check-in. The counter was clear. I said to the other agent, "Here are the passengers that are running late, but I think that we can get them on."

Mike Tuohey: I said, "Mr. Atta, if you don't go now, you will miss your plane."

8:00 A.M. IN NEW YORK CITY

"A REALLY HAPPY FEELING"

The World Trade Center had the two tallest buildings in New York City, iconic fixtures on the skyline for nearly 40 years. Reaching more than 1,300 feet into the sky, the 110-story twin buildings — the North Tower, known as One World Trade, and the South Tower, known as Two World Trade — anchored a 16-acre complex of seven buildings in the heart of Lower Manhattan's financial sector. Nestled between them was Three World Trade, which held a 22-story Marriott Hotel. Four other buildings surrounded the site: Four World Trade, a nine-story building occupied primarily by Deutsche Bank; Five World Trade, also a nine-story office building; Six World Trade, an eight-story building occupied by the U.S. Customs House for New York and other government agencies; and Seven World Trade, a 47-story building that included New York's Office of Emergency Management. Beneath the complex was a shopping mall that housed eateries and about 80 retail stores.

The World Trade Center site was owned by the Port Authority of New York and New Jersey, a governmental agency created in 1921 that also oversees New York's airports — LaGuardia, Kennedy, and Newark — the Port Authority Bus Terminal in New York City, the PATH commuter train system, as well as the tunnels and bridges between the two states. It has its own Port Authority Police Department (PAPD), which in 2001 consisted of 1,331 officers, all of whom were cross-trained in basic firefighting. In July 2001, real estate mogul Larry Silverstein purchased the lease for World Trade Center buildings One, Two, Four, and Five.

As Tuesday, September 11, 2001, began, the 50,000 people who worked across the World Trade Center complex began to arrive. Each floor of the North and South Towers represented a full acre of office space. On an average day, 70,000 visitors would pass through for meetings, shopping, a meal at the Windows on the World restaurant atop the North Tower, or to soak in views from the public observation deck atop the South Tower. For all of them, it was just another morning.

Dan Potter, firefighter, Ladder 10, FDNY: My wife worked at One World Trade Center, and she had a business engagement with other bosses on the 81st floor. I made her an asparagus omelet for breakfast. Then she went to walk to work.

Jean Potter, Bank of America, North Tower, 81st floor: I would leave the house every day and say to him the last line of this movie, *The Story of Christ:* "Just remember, Jesus said I am always with you." That's how I would leave him in the morning as I would go to work.

Dan Potter: Then I would begin my day. I was studying for the lieutenant promotion exam coming up in October. I walked across to the Trade Center — I had a pickup parked at the bottom of Two World Trade Center. We had spaces down there, provided for the firefighters assigned to Ten House [the station near the Towers that housed Ladder 10 and Engine 10].

Jared Kotz, Risk Waters Group, New York City: I was an employee of Risk Waters Group, which was holding the technology conference at Windows on the World on September 11th. My job that morning was to make sure all of our publications were unloaded and put on display racks.

William Jimeno, officer, PAPD: It was a normal routine day. We got a little coffee, went out on post, and I remember standing, looking at the entrance of the bus terminal at 42nd and Eighth Avenue — what we call "the rush." The rush is where everybody from New Jersey, Connecticut, other parts of New York take buses into the terminal. It's a steady flow of thousands of people coming into Midtown Manhattan.

Michael Lomonaco, executive chef, Windows on the World, North Tower, 106th floor: My usual hours were from 8:30 in the morning until 10:00, 10:30 at night. That morning my wife and I got up a little bit early because we were voting in the primaries. There was no one at the polls. It wasn't that busy.

My reading glasses were in need of repair. When I hit the street in front of Tower Two, I thought, *Wow, it's really early. It's not even 8:15. I bet I can get the optometrist to see me, and I can have my glasses this afternoon.* I made a detour to the Trade Center Concourse level and I went straight for Lens-Crafters. A minute later, I was standing at the counter, asking, "I need new lenses for my glasses."

Judith Wein, senior vice president, Aon Corporation, South Tower, 103rd floor: My husband and I, we got off the bus right when it got to Pearl and Frankfort. We would walk up the block, following the Brooklyn

Bridge coming down, and at City Hall Park we would say good-bye. He would go to his place, and I would walk down to the Trade Center. The weather was so nice. You had a really happy feeling. I turned and smiled to him. He said later that stuck in his mind, because for hours he didn't know whether I was alive or not.

Vanessa Lawrence, artist, North Tower, 91st floor: I was hesitant to go make this phone call to my friend Amelia, who was coming to see the studio. I thought, *I need a break.* About 8:30, I went down. You came down the elevator and then through a door to use the pay phone. I called her. I went and got a juice. Coming back, one of the security guards started chatting to me: "How are you doing?" I'm like, "Good. Good." I was so anxious to get back up and paint. It's like, "Got to go," and walked on the elevator, went up.

Richard Eichen, consultant, Pass Consulting Group, North Tower, 90th floor: You got in the elevators and went up to the 78th floor, the Sky Lobby. Then you had to go to another elevator bank, and then get up to the 90th floor. The elevator going up to 78 was so fast you could actually feel it, and your ears would pop.

David Kravette, bond broker, Cantor Fitzgerald, North Tower: The offices were on the 105th floor. It took about five, ten minutes just to go upstairs — two elevator rides up. But when you got up top the views were spectacular. You could see the world.

Jared Kotz: I got up to the 106th floor and was greeted by some of my colleagues. Paul Bristow walked up to me and said, "Jared, I was here early. I saw the magazines, so I pulled them out of the boxes and set them up on a display rack. Is this what you wanted?" I said, "Yeah, this is great! Paul, thanks very much." If Paul hadn't been there early and set up the magazines, I probably would have still been there when the plane hit. Then I realized of all the things that had arrived, we were missing one of our titles. I offered to go back to our office and pick up some copies. I bid farewell to everyone and thought I would see them in an hour or less. I headed down the elevator. The elevator stopped at the floor below the Windows on the World. It was Cantor Fitzgerald's office. One gentleman got on the elevator, another stood there in the hallway, discussing something with him. I'll never forget his face.

Dan Potter: I drove over to Staten Island. I remember going into the American Legion Hall. You got your study material for the

56

lieutenant's exam and then you went and sat at a desk. You had an hour to do usually 50 questions.

Joe Massian, technology consultant, Port Authority, North Tower: I was working on floor 70. I remember sitting at my desk for a minute with my backpack on. After about five or ten minutes — this is probably about 8:30 a.m. — I decided to take my backpack off and lay it on my desk.

David Kravette: I had a meeting at eight o'clock. They're running late. At 8:40, I get a call from the [ground-floor] lobby: "Your visitors are here." One of the guys came without a wallet, no ID at all. Someone had to go down and sign for him. There was a girl who sat behind me, a desk assistant who was very helpful, but she was eight-and-a-half-months pregnant. I said to myself, *I'm not going to make her go down.* I went downstairs. I see my client. I go, "Which one of you knuckleheads forgot your ID?"

Joseph Lott was scheduled to speak at the Risk Waters conference at Windows on the World. He spent the night of the 10th at the Marriott Hotel between the two towers, known as Three World Trade Center.

57

Joseph Lott, sales representative, Compaq Computers: The shirt I was going to wear — a white shirt — was pretty wrinkled from laying in the suitcase, so I put on a green shirt. I went down to breakfast. My colleague Elaine Greenberg was there. We sat and had breakfast, and we went over some changes to the slides. She said that she had gone to a vacation home in Massachusetts, and while she was there she saw a tie and bought it for me. It was a stunning tie. I said, "This is such a nice gesture — I'm going to put this on." She said, "Well, not with that shirt. You're not going to put on a red and blue tie with a green shirt." As we left the restaurant at the Marriott, I said, "I'm going to go back and change and put on that white shirt. It will look better with this tie. Go on ahead without me."

I set up an ironing board and ironed the white shirt. I put that shirt on with my new tie. As I was waiting to go from the seventh floor back down to the lobby, I felt a sudden movement in the building.

Jared Kotz: I walked into the office and called my London colleagues to let them know that everything but one box had arrived. I could see the time was 8:46. I remember thinking, *Gee, I have plenty of time to get back downtown before the event starts.* I was talking to one of my colleagues in London when I heard the plane go over.

THE HIJACKINGS
"WE HAVE SOME PLANES"

The drama of September 11th began not in New York but in the skies over Massachusetts. That morning, 92 people — 11 crew joined by 81 passengers — boarded American Airlines Flight 11, scheduled to fly nonstop from Boston's Logan Airport to Los Angeles International Airport. At 7:59 a.m., its pilot, Capt. John Ogonowski, accelerated down the runway and launched his Boeing 767 into the sky. Among the 81 passengers were five men set on ensuring Flight 11 never made it to its destination.

Sixteen minutes later, on another Logan runway, Capt. Victor Saracini also accelerated his plane, United Airlines Flight 175, another Boeing 767, scheduled nonstop to Los Angeles. He and First Officer Michael Horrocks were carrying a light load that day, just 65 people — 9 crew and 56 passengers — including, again, five hijackers.

Over the next 32 minutes, both planes were hijacked and flown toward New York, confusing air traffic controllers.

8:09 A.M.

The final routine transmission from American Airlines Flight 11 came just 10 minutes into its flight.

> **AA11:** Boston Center, good morning, American 11 with you passing through one-niner-zero for two-three-zero.
>
> **Boston Sector:** American 11, Boston Center, roger, climb, maintain level two-eight-zero.

8:13 A.M.

Shortly after American Airlines Flight 11 made its final normal transmission, it ceased responding to air traffic control. Garbled radio messages and frantic telephone calls from passengers and crew spread word of the drama above.

> **Boston Sector:** American 11, turn 20 degrees right.
>
> **AA11:** Turning right, American 11.
>
> **Boston Sector:** American 11, climb, maintain flight level three-five-zero.
>
> **Boston Sector:** American 11, climb, maintain flight level three-five-zero?

Boston Sector: American 11, Boston?

Boston Sector: American one-one — the American on the frequency — how do you hear me?

Boston Sector: American 11, if you hear Boston Center, ident?

8:19 A.M.

About 20 minutes after takeoff, and just minutes after the hijacking, Betty Ong, a 45-year-old flight attendant aboard American Airlines Flight 11, used an in-seat AT&T air-phone to call the airline's reservations line, reaching agent Winston Sadler at American's Southeastern Reservations Office in Cary, North Carolina. The call would last 25 minutes. Ong had chosen to fly on Flight 11 that day so she could meet her sister to plan their trip to Hawaii for the following week.

Betty Ong: Um, the cockpit's not answering. Somebody's stabbed in business class, and, um, I think there is Mace — that we can't breathe. I don't know, I think we're getting hijacked.

Winston Sadler: Which flight are you on?

62

Betty Ong: Flight 12.*

Winston Sadler: And what seat are you in? *[Silence]* Ma'am, are you there?

Betty Ong: Yes.

Winston Sadler: What seat are you in? *[Silence]* Ma'am, what seat are you in?

Betty Ong: We just left Boston, we're up in the air.

Winston Sadler: I know.

Betty Ong: We're supposed to go to L.A. and the cockpit's not answering their phone. . . .

Winston Sadler: OK, but what seat are you sitting in? What's the number of your seat?

Betty Ong: OK. I'm in the jump seat right now. That's 3R.

Winston Sadler: OK. Are you the flight attendant? I'm sorry, did you say you're the flight attendant?

Betty Ong: Hello?

Winston Sadler: Hello, what is your name?

Betty Ong: Hi, you're gonna have to speak up. I can't hear you.

* In her panic, Ong gave the wrong flight number.

Winston Sadler: What is your name?

Betty Ong: OK, my name is Betty Ong. I'm Number 3 on Flight 11.

Winston Sadler: OK.

Betty Ong: The cockpit is not answering their phone and there's somebody stabbed in business class and there's — we can't breathe in business class. Somebody's got Mace or something.

Winston Sadler: Can you describe the person, that you said someone is, what, in business class?

Betty Ong: I'm sitting in the back. Somebody's coming back from business. If you can hold on for one second, they're coming back. *[Inaudible]* Anyone know who stabbed who?

Unidentified flight attendant: *[Inaudible]* I don't know, but Karen and Bobby got stabbed.

Betty Ong [back to Sadler]: Our, our Number 1 [flight attendant] got stabbed. Our purser is stabbed. Ah, nobody knows who stabbed who and we can't even get up to business class right now because nobody can breathe. Our Number 1 is, is stabbed right now. And our Number 5. Our first-class passenger that, ah first ah class galley flight attendant and our purser has been stabbed and we can't get to the cockpit, the door won't open. Hello?

Winston Sadler: Yeah, I'm taking it down, all the information. We're also, you know, of course, recording this, um, at this point?

Realizing the severity of the situation, Sadler then followed protocol and patched the call from Flight 11 in to American Airlines operations agent Nydia Gonzalez, connecting the three of them together.

Nydia Gonzalez: This is operations. What flight number are we talking about?

Winston Sadler: Flight 12.

Nydia Gonzalez: Flight 12, OK.

Betty Ong: No, we're on Flight 11 right now. This is Flight 11.

Winston Sadler: This is Flight 11. I'm sorry, Nydia.

Betty Ong: Boston to Los Angeles.

Winston Sadler: Yes.

Betty Ong [to Sadler]: Our Number 1 has been stabbed, and our 5 has been stabbed. *[To her fellow passengers:]* Can anybody get up to the cockpit? Can anybody get up to the cockpit? *[To Sadler:]* We can't even get into the cockpit. We don't know who's up there.

Winston Sadler: Well if they were shrewd, they would keep the door closed, and —

Betty Ong: I'm sorry?

Winston Sadler: Would they not maintain a sterile cockpit?

Betty Ong: I think the guys are up there. They might have gone there — jammed their way up there, or something. Nobody can call the cockpit. We can't even get inside.

[Silence]

Betty Ong: Is anybody still there?

Winston Sadler: Yes, we're still here.

66

Betty Ong: OK. I'm staying on the line as well.

Winston Sadler: OK.

8:21 A.M.

While Winston Sadler stayed on the line with Betty Ong, Nydia Gonzalez used a second line to call American Airlines' Systems Operations Center, where she reached manager Craig Marquis and relayed word of the hijacking. The recording of this second telephone call, with Marquis, does not capture Ong's side of the conversation, where she relayed additional information to Gonzalez.

Craig Marquis: American Airlines emergency line, please state your emergency.

Nydia Gonzalez: Hey, this is Nydia at American Airlines calling, I am monitoring a call in which Flight 11, the flight attendant, is advising our reps that the pilot, everyone's been stabbed.

Craig Marquis: Flight 11?

Nydia Gonzalez: Yeah. They can't get into the cockpit is what I'm hearing. . . .

Craig Marquis: OK, uh, uh, I'm assuming they've declared an emergency? Let me get [air traffic control] on here, stand by. . . .

Nydia Gonzalez: OK.

Craig Marquis: Anything else from this flight attendant?

Nydia Gonzalez: Uh, so far what I've gotten: the Number 5 flight attendant's been stabbed, but she seems to be breathing. The Number 1 seems to be stabbed pretty badly, she's lying down on the floor, they don't know if she is conscious or not. The other flight attendants are in the back. And that's as far as I know. It seems like the passengers in coach might not be aware of what's going on.

Craig Marquis: These two passengers were from first class?

Nydia Gonzalez [back to Ong]: Hey, Betty? Do you know any information as far as the [inaudible] of the men there in the cockpit with the pilots? Were they from first class? [Back to Marquis:] They were sitting in 2A and B. They are in the cockpit with the pilots.

68

Craig Marquis: Who's helping them? Is there a doctor on board?

Nydia Gonzalez [to Ong]: Is there a doctor on board, Betty, that's assisting you guys? You don't have any doctors on board. OK. So you've gotten all the first-class passengers out of first class?

Craig Marquis: Have they taken everyone out of first class?

Nydia Gonzalez [to Marquis]: Yeah, she's just saying that they have. They're in coach. What's going on, honey? OK, the aircraft is erratic again. Flying very erratically. She did say that all the first-class passengers have been moved back to coach, so the first-class cabin is empty. What's going on on your end, Craig?

Craig Marquis: We contacted air traffic control. They are going to handle this as a confirmed hijacking, so they're moving all the traffic out of this aircraft's way.

Nydia Gonzalez: OK.

Craig Marquis: He turned his

transponder off, so we don't have a definitive altitude for him. We're just going by — they seem to think that they have him on a primary radar. They seem to think that he is descending. . . .

Nydia Gonzalez: What's going on, Betty? Betty, talk to me. Betty, are you there? Betty? *[Inaudible]* Do you think we lost her? OK, so we'll like — we'll stay open. We — I think we might have lost her.

8:2 4 A.M.

Back in Boston, air traffic controllers received what appeared to be a call from Flight 11, as the cockpit microphone was keyed three times. They later realized that the hijackers apparently had tried to speak over the intercom to the passengers on board but instead used the air traffic control frequency.

Boston Sector: Is that American 11 trying to call?

Mohamed Atta, hijacker: *[Indistinct noise]* We have some planes. Just stay quiet and we'll be OK. We are returning to the airport.

Boston Sector: And, uh, who's trying to call me, here? American 11, are you trying to call?

Mohamed Atta: Nobody move, everything will be OK. If you try to make any moves, you will injure yourself and the airplane. Just stay quiet.

Following the confusing radio call, air traffic controllers conferred among themselves to figure out what was transpiring. Boston air traffic control contacted other controllers who oversaw planes at higher altitudes, a post known as Athens 38, who might have had radio contact with Flight 11.

Unknown Boston air traffic controller: Hey, 38?

Athens Sector 38: Yes.

Unknown Boston air traffic controller: You guys heard anything from American?

Athens Sector 38: No.

Unknown Boston air traffic controller: OK, we think there might be somebody in the cockpit right now taking it over.

Mohamed Atta [to passengers aboard Flight 11]: Nobody move please. We are going back to the airport. Don't try to make any stupid moves.

8:33 A.M.

Fearing the worst, air traffic controllers asked for local fighter aircraft to intercept and escort the flight, the standard protocol at the time for hijackings.

Cape Cod, Massachusetts, air traffic control: Cape Approach.

Dan Bueno, air traffic control, Boston Sector: Hey Cape, ah, Dan Bueno calling from Boston Center. Hey, we've got a situation with American 11, a possible hijack.

Cape Cod air traffic control: American 11?

Dan Bueno: Yes sir, departed Boston going to LAX. Right now he's out to Albany. Like to scramble some fighters to go tail him.

Cape Cod air traffic control: Well, OK. Well, we'll talk to Otis [Air Force Base] here.

8:34 A.M.

Nydia Gonzalez [to Craig Marquis]: They think they might have a fatality on the flight. One of our passengers, possibly in 9B, Levin or Lewis, might have been fatally stabbed.

8:37 A.M.

Still not fully understanding the situation on board American Airlines 11 but realizing it was grave, FAA Boston Center alerted a military unit known as the Northeast Air Defense Sector (NEADS), part of the North American Aerospace Defense Command (NORAD). That morning, NORAD had scheduled its biggest annual exercise — a scenario aimed at repelling a Russian nuclear attack — that added to the confusion as military bases and commanders across the country struggled to comprehend what was real and what was part of the exercise.

Joseph Cooper, air traffic control, Boston Center: Hi, Boston Center, TMU [Traffic Management Unit], we have, ah, a problem here, we have a hijacked aircraft headed toward New — New York, and we need you guys to, we need

73

someone to scramble some F-16s or something up there to help us out.

Sgt. Jeremy Powell, Northeast Air Defense Sector (NEADS), Rome, New York: Is this real-world or exercise?

Joseph Cooper: No. This is not an exercise, not a test.

8:38 A.M.
Air traffic control called United Flight 175, the other Boston-to-Los Angeles flight, which had taken off at 8:15 a.m. and was a few miles behind American Airlines Flight 11, to warn it about the hijacking. The flight crew responded normally.

New York Center: OK, United 175, you have him at your 12 o'clock, now five, 10 miles.

United Airlines Flight 175: Affirmative, we have him. He looks about 20, say about 29, 28 thousand [feet].

New York Center: OK, thank you. United 175 [Indistinct] turn 30 degrees to the right, I want to keep you away from this traffic.

74

United Airlines Flight 175:
Thirty degrees to the right, United 175, heavy.

8:40 A.M.
Shortly after, NEADS called Otis Air Force Base on Cape Cod, Massachusetts, and ordered two alert pilots to scramble to intercept American Airlines Flight 11.

Sgt. Jeremy Powell, Northeast Air Defense Sector (NEADS), Rome, New York: This is Huntress placing Panta four-five, four-six on battle stations — I repeat battle stations — time one-two-four-one [1241 Greenwich Mean Time, 8:41 a.m. ET]. Authenticate Hotel Romeo, all parties acknowledge with initials. Command Post.

8:44 A.M.
American Airlines 11 flight attendant Madeline "Amy" Sweeney, filling in for a sick colleague aboard the hijacked plane, placed a telephone call to the American Airlines Flight Services Office at Logan Airport. She spoke with services manager Michael Woodward, who was also a friend.

Madeline "Amy" Sweeney, American Airlines 11 flight attendant: The flight has been hijacked. This flight is Flight 11 from Boston to L.A. The plane is a 767. I am in the back with Betty Ong, AA flight attendant. A man in business class has had his throat slashed and is presumably dead. Number 1 flight attendant has been stabbed and Number 5 flight attendant has been stabbed. There is a bomb in the cockpit. I can't make contact with the cockpit, can you do it? We have paged for a doctor or nurse for the flight attendants. The coach passengers don't know what's happening.

The hijackers are of Middle Eastern descent. One spoke good English and one didn't.
It is a rapid descent. Something is wrong. I don't think the captain is in control.
I see water.
I see buildings.
We're flying low.
We're flying very, very low.

76

Oh my God.
We're flying way too low.

INSIDE AIR TRAFFIC CONTROL
"DASH MARKS IN A PILE OF CLUTTER"

As the hijackings began on the East Coast, civilian air traffic controllers at the FAA struggled to comprehend the sudden and unprecedented threat to the 4,000 airplanes still in the air. As they rushed to contact and scramble fighter aircraft from Otis Air Force Base in Massachusetts and Langley Air Force Base in Virginia, military units in charge of the nation's air defense confronted a threat they'd never imagined: an attack coming not from outside the U.S. but from within its own borders. A decade after the end of the Cold War, they found the tools at their disposal scattered and insufficient. Caught off guard, they improvised a response.

After American Airlines Flight 11 initially checked in with air traffic controller Peter Zalewski, the first warning that something had happened in the air came when the pilots ceased to respond to radio calls.

Peter Zalewski, air traffic controller, Boston Center, Nashua, New Hampshire: When American Airlines Flight 11 came to me, the pilot said, "Boston Center, this is American 11, climbing to flight level two-three-zero."

I called him many, many times: "American 11, how do you hear? American 11, this is Boston Center. Do you hear me?" I'm calling and calling, and I'm like, *My God! Maybe they're drinking Dunkin' Donuts coffee up there.* Honestly, that's what I was thinking. Then there's these transmissions. The first transmission from the aircraft, it's garbled to me. I don't understand it. Then there was a second one — a voice. I remember him saying, "Nobody move, please. We're going back to the airport." I will never forget that feeling up the back of my neck. It was like this adrenaline or something. I felt fear. I'm like, *Oh, my God! The plane's being hijacked.*

Colin Scoggins, airspace and procedures specialist and military specialist, FAA, Boston Center: I came in at about 8:25 in the morning, and as soon as I walked to the front door someone came to me and said that there was a hijack going on. We'd worked hijacks in the past, and they were usually uneventful.

Peter Zalewski: I yell at [the supervisor]: "John, get over here. This plane is being hijacked — absolutely." I go, "It's Middle Eastern voices — positive." I could tell by the second time — I was used to working Egypt Air, Saudi, Turkish, all of them: "It's Middle Eastern voices."

Colin Scoggins: Mohamed Atta, the pilot on American 11, the lead terrorist, stated something about "more planes," that they had more planes. It was definitely plural. That's when things really started to ramp up.

Ben Sliney, national operations manager, FAA Command Center, Herndon, Virginia: I was the national operations manager on 9/11. That is a position located in the Washington area that has overarching authority over the nation's airspace. That was my charge: the safe and efficient operation of the nation's airspace.

Col. Bob Marr, commander, NEADS, Rome, New York: There was a huddle of people around one of the radar scopes. I saw that huddle and thought, *There's got to be something wrong.*

Maj. Gen. Larry Arnold, commander of the 1st Air Force, NORAD, Tyndall Air Force Base, Florida: We had a major North

American Air Defense exercise that morning, a command post exercise. There was a team of people that introduced scenarios that you have to react to and respond to. As we were winding up the [exercise] briefing my executive officer, Lt. Col. Kelley Duckett, handed me a slip of paper. Bob Marr had called and said there was a hijacking in the Boston Center Area.

Ben Sliney: My experience with hijackings — and our protocol — was that we cooperate.

Lt. Col. Dawne Deskins, mission crew commander, NEADS, Rome, New York: At this point our mind-set was the 1970s-vintage hijack. We didn't have a huge concern this aircraft was going to crash.

Maj. Gen. Larry Arnold: I said, "Bob, go ahead and scramble the aircraft."

Maj. Joe McGrady, F-15 pilot, Otis Air Force Base, Cape Cod, Massachusetts: A scramble order was issued. I ran to our jets. I started up. We realized we did not have any weapons. They filled up our jets with gas. Even though we were "Winchester" — which means we had no weapons — we took off.

Lt. Col. Tim Duffy, F-15 pilot, Otis Air Force Base, Cape Cod, Massachusetts: When we took off, I left it in full afterburner the whole time. We were supersonic going down to Long Island, and my wingman, "Nasty" [Maj. Dan Nash], called and said, "Hey Duff, you're super," and I said, "Yeah, I know, don't worry about it." I wanted to get there.

Col. Bob Marr: At Mach One, it would take them 16 minutes to get there — that's 10 miles a minute.

Lt. Col. Kevin Nasypany, mission crew commander, NEADS, Rome, New York: Almost simultaneously, we brought in more surveillance technicians to look at the scope.

Staff Sgt. Larry Thornton, NEADS: The area was so congested, the hijacked flight was incredibly difficult to find. We were looking for little dash marks in a pile of clutter on a two-dimensional scope.

Master Sgt. Joe McCain, NEADS: We picked up a search track going down the Hudson Valley, straight in from the north toward New York. The plane was fast and heading in an unusual direction with no beacon [transponder]. We watched that track until it faded over New York City.

Lt. Gen. Tom Keck, commander, Barksdale Air Force Base, Shreveport, Louisiana: We were in the midst of this big annual exercise called GLOBAL GUARDIAN. They loaded all the bombers, put the submarines out to sea, put the ICBMs at nearly 100 percent. It was routine, you did it every year. A captain said, "Sir, we had an aircraft hit the World Trade Center." I started to correct him, saying, "When you have an exercise input you have to start by saying, 'I have an exercise input.' That way it doesn't get confused with the real world." Then he pointed me to the TV screens in the command center. You could see smoke pouring out of the building. Like everyone else in aviation that day, I thought, *How in a clear-and-a-million day could someone hit the World Trade Center?*

THE FIRST PLANE

"THIS WILL BE THE WORST DAY OF OUR LIVES"

At 8:46 a.m., American Airlines Flight 11 roared south through the sky over Manhattan, traversing the length of the island, surprising citygoers, before it crashed into the North Tower, known as One World Trade Center, at about 465 miles per hour.

William Jimeno, officer, PAPD, at the Port Authority Bus Terminal: A shadow came over 42nd and Eighth Avenue. It completely covered the street for a split second.

Chief Joseph Pfeifer, Battalion 1, FDNY: In Manhattan, you rarely hear planes because of the tall buildings. We all looked up. In almost disbelief, we saw the plane pass, and it was flying so low. Our eyes followed it as it passed behind the buildings, and then it re-appeared. It aimed right into the building.

Juana Lomi, paramedic, New York Beekman Downtown Hospital: I was standing outside, and I heard a rumbling sound — it sounded like a truck, but it was too loud.

Cathy Pavelec, administrator, Port Authority, North Tower: I worked in One World Trade Center, on the 67th floor. I had a window office that faced north. I glanced out the window and I saw the plane — it was a little bit over to my right and I noticed that it was very low. I had worked in the World Trade Center since before it had officially opened, and we'd seen a million things over the years. As I watched, the plane got closer and closer and closer. I was in complete disbelief.

Bruno Dellinger, principal, Quint Amasis North America, North Tower, 47th floor: Everybody's heard plane engines, except very few people have heard the sound of plane engines when they're at full strength, full force, flying up in the sky. That is a horrifying sound. I still remember it very clearly — the sound of the engines flying at full force toward the World Trade Center.

Cathy Pavelec: I watched the fuselage disappear into the building.

Ian Oldaker, staff, Ellis Island: At 9:00 a.m., every morning, was the first staff boat from Battery Park over to Ellis Island. I

85

stopped at Au Bon Pain and got a croissant. I was continuing down Broadway. Then I heard the largest POP. I turned around, and I saw glass — lots of glass — in the sky. It was really bright out, and it was reflecting off the glass and the sky. Light shimmering everywhere.

NYPD Sgt. Mike McGovern was with Chief of Department Joseph Esposito, just pulling into One Police Plaza, the department headquarters, a few blocks from the World Trade Center.

Sgt. Mike McGovern, aide to the chief, NYPD: We heard a tremendous explosion or bang. We thought it was something above us, because we were directly under the Brooklyn Bridge. We pulled up to the checkpoint at police headquarters and there was a cop manning his post. We find out after the fact this particular cop, Pete Crane, was a pilot. He said into the radio, "Central, be advised that a 767 just struck the North Tower of the World Trade Center." Chief Joe jumped out of the car and he said, "What did you say?"

Joe Esposito, chief of department, NYPD: I said, "How did you know it was a 767?" He said, "I'm a pilot." I said, "Are you sure?" He said, "I saw —." I said, "Okay."

Sgt. Mike McGovern: We turned the car around and went.

86

Peter Johansen, director of operations, New York Waterways ferries: Honestly, I think most people felt it was a navigation accident. The reason I say that is our ferry continued around to Pier 11, the Wall Street terminal, and there were about a hundred people on board. Every single one of them got off and went to work that morning. As they're walking off, there are envelopes and letters floating down from the sky.

Brian Conley, resident, Lower Manhattan: It looked like a ticker-tape parade.

Chief Joseph Pfeifer: I told everybody to get in the rigs because we were going down there. I picked up the department radio and told them a plane hit the World Trade Center, and to transmit a second alarm. That was done immediately. That was the first official report.

Jared Kotz, Risk Waters Group: One of my friends came out of an office, yelling, "Which building is the conference in?" I thought, *Gee, what are you so excited about? You've got plenty of time to get down there.* I yelled, "It's One World Trade Center." He replied, "No, no! Which building is it? Is it the one with the tower on it?" I walked down to the south side of my office and looked out to verify that indeed it was the Tower with the radio tower. At that moment, I realized something terrible had happened. I saw a large gaping hole and the sky full of what could only be described as confetti — millions of sheets of white paper, floating like confetti in the sky, floating east from the World Trade Center.

Ian Oldaker: I heard the fire engines. I went east to see what was going on back there. It was much more exciting than eating my croissant.

Flight 11 hit between the 93rd and 99th floors, exploding 10,000 gallons of jet fuel into the offices of the investment firm Fred Alger Management, on the 93rd floor, and Marsh & McLennan, which occupied floors 93 up to 100. At Fred Alger Management, 35 people died; at Marsh & McLennan, 295. The crash immediately destroyed all exits from the floors above, leaving trapped 702 employees and visitors at the bond trader Cantor Fitzgerald on the top floors, from 100 to 105, all of the employees, conference-goers, and diners on the 106th and 107th floors at Windows on the World, as well as one engineer for NBC, William Steckman, working on the 110th floor to operate the broadcast antenna that topped the tower. The crash released a jet-fuel-based fireball that shot down at least one elevator shaft and exploded through the lower floors and the tower's West Street lobby. Thick, black smoke engulfed the upper floors and light northwest winds carried the smoke over the roof of the South Tower.

Robert Leder, executive, SMW Trading Company, North Tower: Our office was on the 85th floor. I was looking out the window, facing the Empire State Building, when I saw the plane come into the building. There was such a dramatic change of atmospheric pressure. The building swayed from the impact, and it nearly knocked me off my chair. Our ceiling imploded. Some of our walls began to implode.

Richard Eichen, consultant, Pass Consulting Group, North Tower, 90th floor: I'm one of five survivors from the 90th floor of the North Tower. I didn't have the key to my office, and that's what saved my life. I was waiting outside, reading the *Times* — a section on Dell computers, I mean, the random things that you remember — leaning against the wall with my briefcase, my coffee cup on the floor, eating a bagel, waiting for these guys to show up.

All of a sudden, I heard the loudest sound, "Bang," I've ever heard. Hugely, immensely loud. Then all of a sudden I heard, "Boom boom boom boom boom boom boom." Which I now think was the airplane tearing out the girders inside, followed by another "Boom!" Everything exploded in flames. The ladies' room door actually burst out against its hinges, and out came a fireball — it singed the second wall. That's how far out it came.

Harry Waizer, tax counsel, Cantor Fitzgerald, North Tower: I was in the elevator at 8:46 in the North Tower when the first jet hit the Trade Center. My office was on the 104th floor. I had gone up to the Sky Lobby on 78, and I'd made the transition over to the local elevators — I was somewhere between 78 and 104.

Jean Potter, Bank of America, North Tower, 81st floor: I was thrown out of my chair — like thrown. It was this horrible loud explosion, and the building started rocking back and forth, and smoke filled the air immediately. We fortunately were right by a staircase because our floor was fully involved with fire. I heard of maybe four or five survivors from above us.

Vanessa Lawrence, artist, North Tower, 91st floor: I had literally put one foot out of the elevator on the 91st and was thrown to the side. Smoke and debris blasted down the corridor, the building shook.

David Kravette, bond broker, Cantor Fitzgerald, ground-level lobby of the North Tower: All of a sudden jet fuel blasted out of the central elevator bank and mushroomed everywhere. People were — 20 yards from me — lifted on this fireball and thrown through those lobby windows and incinerated.

Cathy Pavelec, administrator, Port Authority, North Tower, 67th floor: I ran around the floor yelling, "A plane crashed into the building. We have to get out of here."

Vanessa Lawrence: I don't remember hearing anything. My memory is in silence and slow motion, but I know it was all happening very quickly and very loud.

Richard Eichen, consultant, Pass Consulting Group, North Tower, 90th floor: I saw off my left shoulder an Asian man coming toward me — he looked like he had been deep-fried. He had his arms out, and his skin was hanging like seaweed. He was begging me to help him. He said, "Help me, help me," and then did a face-plant right between my legs. He died between my legs. I looked down, and that's when I saw my shirt was full of blood. I didn't know before that I had been hurt.

You could smell fuel. I had no idea what

happened. I could see in the elevator shaft — floor-to-ceiling flames. It looked like a shower curtain shimmering. It's funny the things that you do in the situation — I put my bagel down in the entranceway and said, "I have to remember when it's over, I have to pick up the bagel and throw it away."

Robert Leder, executive, SMW Trading Company, North Tower, 85th floor: The first thing that came to my mind was to call my wife. I told her that the World Trade Center had been hit by a plane. She didn't believe me. Right after I spoke with her, I opened a door to see what was going on, and this black billowing smoke came straight at us. I shut the door right away. The whole office reeked of jet fuel.

Vanessa Lawrence: When the blast hit, the first thing that came into my head was, *Did I leave my tote by an electrical socket?* It was that horrible thing, *Oh, my God! How am I going to explain this?* Even going down the stairs, it was still, *Was this me? What if this is my fault?*

Anthony R. Whitaker, World Trade Center (WTC) commander, PAPD, North Tower ground-level lobby: I saw two people out of the corner of my left eye. They were on fire. They ran toward me, and then they ran right past me. They issued no sound. All their clothes were burnt off, and they were smoldering.

David Kravette: One of the girls who worked with me, Lauren Manning, was coming into the lobby when that fireball came down, and it took her through the glass. She was burned over 80 percent of her body and survived. If I was 20 yards further along in my walk, I would be dead or severely burned. There was no fire afterwards. It literally exploded out, burned itself out, and disappeared within seconds. It was three, four, five seconds at most.

Harry Waizer: The elevator started to fall. It burst into flames. I had a briefcase, a cloth briefcase, in my hand, and I was using it to try to beat out the flames. I was burned on my legs and on my arms. The elevator initially was plummeting, then an emergency system kicked in, because it started gliding. As it was going, I got hit in the face by a fireball that came in through the gap between the elevator doors and the body of the elevator. I have this impression of this orange ball coming at my face and a sensation — I can't call it a burning — of it making contact and then it was gone.

David Kravette: It's a comedy of errors that I'm alive. Everyone else in my office upstairs that day perished. They were all trapped. There was no way out.

Meanwhile, hundreds of feet below the impact zone, people were still going about their day. The World Trade Center complex was so massive that those in the underground shopping concourses didn't feel the plane hit and did not realize something terrible had transpired until they saw others fleeing.

Alan Reiss, director of the World Trade Center, Port Authority: We went down to have coffee and a bagel at Fine and Shapiro, a deli-restaurant right near where the A train and E train entrance was. I was sitting with my back to the Concourse when my colleague Vicki [Cross Kelly] said, "Something must have happened. People are running like crazy on the Concourse — they're panicked." I figured that there was probably someone with a gun or some holdup. I hadn't heard anything, didn't feel anything, smell anything.

Michael Lomonaco, executive chef, Windows on the World, inside the underground shopping complex underneath the Towers: They took me into the examining room at LensCrafters and did the examination. The doctor examined my old glasses.

The optometrist left me in the examining room, closed the door. He came back in — burst through the door, really. He looked pale. He said, "Something happened. We've got to get out of here."

Across the 16 acres of the World Trade Center site, neighbors in the South Tower, Two World Trade Center, watched the disaster unfolding in the North Tower. For some occupants of the Towers, the 2001 attack was the second terrorist attack on the complex they had experienced; in 1993, a small group of Islamic extremists had exploded a car bomb in the parking garage beneath the North Tower, hoping it would topple the building. The explosion killed six and injured around 1,000 and provoked numerous security and fire safety improvements in the complex — some of which saved lives on 9/11.

In the initial aftermath of the collision, many occupants reasoned that the incident would be similar to the '93 bombing; there wasn't necessarily mass panic or initial concern — even from some above the impact zone, who figured they could evacuate from the roof or just wait for firefighters to extinguish the fire below. Occupants in the South Tower were quickly reassured by an official building-wide announcement over the P.A. system that their building was not affected and were told to remain at their desks. Similarly, guests in the Marriott Hotel between the two towers realized something had happened but continued to go about their day.

Robert Small, office manager, Morgan Stanley, South Tower, 72nd floor: The explosion on 9/11 felt very similar to the explosion in '93. I said to myself, *Jeez, not again.*

Elia Zedeño, financial analyst, Port Authority, North Tower, 73rd floor: The building shook. I thought, *This is it — I am going down,* and immediately I thought, *Earthquake.* But, instantaneously, it was, *Earthquake. 1993.* There was no pause, thinking, *What could it be?* Nothing like that. It was, *Earthquake. No, 1993.* I immediately thought, *In 1993 I didn't have my keys to get home. Today I am going to have my keys.*

Herb Ouida, World Trade Centers Association, North Tower, 77th floor, and father of Todd Ouida, Cantor Fitzgerald, North Tower, 105th floor: When the building shook I knew immediately from the 1993 bombing experience to leave. No one could have dissuaded me. I knew, though, my son Todd was on the 105th floor.

96

Harry Waizer, tax counsel, Cantor Fitzgerald, North Tower, 78th floor sky lobby: I was in shock. I got off the elevator. I was remarkably calm. I had my bag still with me. I walked over between two of the larger elevator banks, put it down, and said, "I can't carry this right now," and "I'll get it back later."

Michele Cartier, Lehman Brothers, North Tower: I was working on the 40th floor for Lehman Brothers. Everybody started clearing the floor, and we began our descent. Nobody knew exactly what was going on. There was no indication that this was a terrorist attack. We pretty much thought you'd go back outside, you'd come out, you'd come back upstairs, and you would go back about your business.

Jared Kotz, Risk Waters Group: One of my colleagues, Samara Zwanger, had the phone number for David Rivers, one of our editors, who was in the conference at Windows on the World. He told her that nobody knew what had happened. There had been a huge explosion, all the windows had fallen out, all the ceilings had come down, and everyone had been knocked to the ground, but everyone was okay, and everyone was going to be evacuated.

Constance Labetti, accountant, Aon Corporation, South Tower, 99th floor: Our boss, Ron Fazio, knew he had to get us out of there. He said, "Go to the staircase." I returned to my desk to grab my sneakers because I had 99 flights to descend. I started to climb down on the steps. I still had my heels on, and my sneakers in my hand. I remember hearing the PA announcement come on — the PA announcement said, "Do not evacuate. Stay where you are. We have no structural damage. There's structural damage to Tower One, which we're evacuating, but Tower Two go back to your workstations." I caught up to a couple in the staircase — maybe the 90th floor, 92nd floor. I said to them, "Could you wait a moment while I put my sneakers on?" They said, "Of course, we'll wait." I was trembling so much that I couldn't tie my sneakers. I remember the man saying to me, "Just tie your sneakers. Don't worry. Don't worry." I tied my sneakers, then we continued on down.

Judith Wein, senior vice president, Aon Corporation, South Tower, 103rd floor: It was a wide staircase, and we were going down two abreast. There was a little space in the middle. Every once in a while I saw somebody go up — come up. They would mumble, "Oh, I left such-and-such on my desk." I'm always wondering in retrospect: *Did they ever come back down?*

Robert Small, office manager, Morgan Stanley, South Tower, 72nd floor: People on my floor started to leave. A friend of mine and I started to watch it on television in one of the boardrooms. We walked north, looking out the windows, and you could see the smoke, you could see the flame. We started trying to guess what was falling. Was it a book? Was it a piece of paper? Was it a drape? Was it a chair? After a few minutes, we saw people jumping, falling, landing. That wasn't good. After a few of those, we decided not to watch. Let's go back, call our families, let them know we're okay — still thinking everything was in the North Tower. Nothing was going to happen at the South Tower.

Michael Lomonaco, executive chef, Windows on the World, in the shopping complex under the Towers: I got out into the corridor. There was an official from the Port Authority motioning with the arms. He was telling people, "Run! Get out!" I exited out onto Liberty Street, crossed over to Church Street. I turned and looked back to see what had happened. I could see the horrific fire in Tower One. I thought maybe there had been an explosion.

Frank Razzano, guest, Marriott Hotel: I remember hearing a big bang. I got up out of bed. I opened the drapes on the windows on the Liberty Street side of the building. I saw papers fluttering down to the ground. I said to myself, *Well, must've been a big wind that must've blown off the harbor and blew a pane of glass out in one of the buildings.* I turned around, closed the drapes, and got back in bed.

Michael Lomonaco: I thought, *Oh my god — everybody at work.* I thought, *What's happening on 106?* Then the next thought was, *Okay, I'm going to stay calm. They'll go down the fire stairways.* I had complete optimism that people were coming down.

News of the crash reverberated across the city as New Yorkers struggled to understand what had happened. The attack interrupted primary day across New York City, as voters planned to choose a successor to Mayor Rudy Giuliani. The confusion was especially pronounced in Lower Manhattan, one of the most densely packed areas of the United States, as the crash was felt or witnessed by hundreds of thousands of people in nearby apartment buildings, offices, hospitals, transit terminals, schools, and across the financial district surrounding Wall Street, just blocks away.

One of the schools closest to the World Trade

Center — just three blocks south of the complex — was the High School for Leadership and Public Service (HSLPS), one of New York City's small specialty schools, home to about 600 students and 40 faculty.

Ada Dolch, principal, HSLPS: At about 8:45, the lights in the lobby went out. Within 10 seconds, the lights went right back on, and immediately after that there was this very loud bang, this very loud explosion.

Heather Ordover, English teacher, HSLPS: We all heard the scream of the engines, like a bomb in a war movie — then the flash. The kids ran to my back window. I ran to my back window. We saw burning paper, smoke, falling debris. I ran back to the front of the room, yelling to the kids to sit down and write about what they'd just seen — anything to get them away from the windows.

Keturah Bostick, student, HSLPS: One of the teachers, Mr. Donnelley, ran into our classroom, saying, "Did you see that?" Everyone screamed, "What?" He responded, "The airplane went right into the tower, and we saw everything." A few seconds later, Mr. Bronsnick came on the loudspeaker and said that the crash was being controlled by the firemen and didn't affect us and that it would still be a full day of school.

Razvan Hotaranu, student, HSLPS: There were papers everywhere, like the Yankees parade, and a lot of ash.

Ada Dolch: Through the radio we could hear that something was going on at the World Trade Center. I knew that that's where [my sister] Wendy worked [for Cantor Fitzgerald]. The words out of my mouth were very clear: "God, please take care of Wendy. I have to take care of the kids in the school."

Fernando Ferrer, candidate for New York City mayor: The Twin Towers loomed large in the consciousness of the city. In 2001, it was even a part of the political and governmental dialogue of New York, because at that time they were on the brink of being sold. I had made a specific proposal that the proceeds of the sale of the Twin Towers would go toward a fund for affordable housing in New York City.

We were on our way to Manhattan, coming down from the northeast Bronx, on the Bruckner Expressway to the Triborough Bridge toll plaza. My young assistant, Kalman Yeger, got a call from his wife, and I heard his end of the conversation: "There's a fire in the World Trade Center?" Kalman told all kinds of jokes, good sense of humor. I thought he was kidding. "Fire in the Trade Center? Oh, there goes my housing plan!" Then he said, "No! This is for real."

Jillian Volk, preschool teacher, Lower Manhattan: I was on the corner of Church and Thomas, at work, about a five-minute walk from the Trade Center. My fiancé, Kevin Williams, worked in Tower Two for a small investment banking firm on the 104th floor. I felt something: my classroom shook. One of my students looked at me and said, "It's thundering." I knew it wasn't thundering. A woman came running into the hallway and said a bomb had gone off in the Trade Center. I panicked. I called Kevin, hoping I would get an answer. He picked up his line and told me a plane had gone into Tower One, and he had to go because they were being evacuated. He wasn't panicked or anything.

Howard Lutnick, CEO, Cantor Fitzgerald, North Tower: It was my son Kyle's first day of kindergarten. As I walked him upstairs, an administrator grabbed me and said, "Your office is looking for you. A plane has hit the building." I jumped in the car, and as I got down there, I saw that huge, black, billowing smoke. The guy driving my car started crying.

Jimmy Maio, driver for Howard Lutnick: We had a clear shot from the 40s on down, on Fifth Avenue, right at the World Trade Center. I knew all our people were above where that smoke was coming out of and would have no shot of getting out.

Andrew Kirtzman, City Hall reporter, NY1: I was scheduled to host election night coverage on New York 1 that night, so I slept in that morning. The telephone rang, and it was my mother. She was incredibly agitated. All she said was, "Can you believe it?" I was like, "What?" She said, "Turn on the television." It became apparent this was a catastrophe. I bolted out of bed and I had to decide — this sounds ridiculous — whether to take a shower. For months afterwards, I felt guilty about running into the shower. I took the fastest shower I've ever taken, got dressed, grabbed a pen, a reporter's notebook, and my reporter's press pass, put it around my neck, and went bolting out of my apartment.

Rudy Giuliani, mayor, New York City: I was having breakfast at the Peninsula Hotel right off Fifth Avenue, 55th Street. We were beginning to stand up to leave the table. My staffer Denny Young came over and said, "A twin-engine plane had hit the North Tower of the World Trade Center." I went to the men's room because I thought I'd be at the crash site a long time.

Andrew Kirtzman: I hailed a cab, jumped into it, and screamed, "Take me to the World Trade Center!"

Rudy Giuliani: We rushed down in my SUV. One of the things that has always remained in my memory is we were passing Saint Vincent's Hospital, in the Village, and I saw many doctors and nurses and attendants in the street with stretchers. It was the first time a feeling registered with me: *This looks like a war zone. It must be worse than I thought. They must know something that hasn't been conveyed to me about how bad this is.*

Outside the Towers, the sound and sight of the crash prompted an immediate call to arms by firefighters, police, paramedics, EMTs, and other first responders. For nearly 400 of them, it would be their last. At 8:58 a.m., en route to the scene, Chief Esposito issued an order for a Level 4 mobilization to the World Trade Center, the NYPD's highest level of alert, summoning nearly 1,000 officers to the disaster site. That same minute, an NYPD helicopter, hovering over the Towers, reported that roof rescues — which had been successful following the 1993 bombing — would be impossible due to the volume of heat and smoke. Minutes later, Chief

Esposito ordered that given the conditions no helicopters should attempt to land on the roof. Although they don't know it, the fate of everyone above the 91st floor in the North Tower was already sealed.

Sal Cassano, assistant chief, FDNY: On the morning of September 11th, I was at headquarters in Brooklyn. Sitting with me was Chief of Department Peter Ganci, Chief of Operations Dan Nigro, Donald Burns, Jerry Barbara. Jerry was killed. Donald was killed. Peter was killed.

Dan Nigro, chief of operations, FDNY: I heard a loud sound; I thought someone had dropped something heavy in the office above me. The next thing I heard was Pete Ganci shouting, "Look out the window, a plane hit the World Trade Center!" We decided to go together — Pete Ganci and I — in his car, so we could talk strategy on the way there. We flew over the Brooklyn Bridge and arrived in about five minutes at the base of the North Tower.

Tracy Donahoo, transit officer, NYPD: I had graduated from the police academy in May. It was my second day actually on patrol, in uniform, with a senior officer, in an actual job. My post was Broadway-Nassau, one block away from the World Trade Center, standing on the northbound 4 and 5 platform. We heard over the radio, "10-13, an airplane hit the World Trade Center." We were like, *What?* We heard it again: "10-13 10-13! A plane hit the World Trade Center!" We ran up the stairs. A "10-13" means everyone run to the aid of whoever or whatever is going on.

William Jimeno, officer, PAPD: Our police desk said all officers had to come back to the police desk. I met up with Dominick Pezzulo — he was a great guy — and he goes, "Willy, something must be really bad for them to call us all back to the police desk."

Capt. Jay Jonas, Ladder 6, FDNY: I could start to see from our firehouse in Chinatown the black plume of smoke going across the sky. I said, "Everybody get their gear on. Let's get going." Engine 10 transmitted a second alarm and a "10-60" signal, which is massive casualties.

Lt. Mickey Kross, Engine 16, FDNY: Our computer went off, and we got the ticket: "Respond to Manhattan, Box 8-0-8-7, One World Trade Center. Signal 3:3." That's a third alarm. It was Engine 7, Engine 55, Engine 3, Engine 16 — that's my company — Ladder 5, Rescue 4. It said: "Respond to lobby command post, One World Trade Center." It's Incident 103 — one hundred and third incident in Manhattan of that date.

William Jimeno: Inspector Lawrence Fields, who was the commanding officer at the bus terminal for the Port Authority police, came in and said, "We've commandeered a bus on Ninth Avenue — we need the following people to get on the bus."

Dan Nigro: As we approached Manhattan, we discussed what we were going to do when we got there. Chief Ganci transmitted a fifth alarm. It was already a third-alarm assignment, which would be approximately 14 engines and maybe seven ladder companies. The fifth alarm would give us a couple of additional chiefs, eight additional engines, and six additional truck companies.

Francine Kelly, registered nurse and nurse manager, Saint Vincent's Catholic Medical Center, New York City: Other staff and physicians at Saint Vincent's literally said they were walking into the emergency department, looking down Seventh Avenue, when they saw the World Trade Center get hit. Within two minutes, we were already calling our disaster code.

Jeff Johnson, firefighter, Engine 74, FDNY: We knew we were going to something pretty catastrophic.

Capt. Jay Jonas: It looked fake, to be honest. The sky was so blue and the sun was glistening off the metal of the exterior of the World Trade Center. You saw an airplane-shaped hole in the North Tower with fire and smoke coming out of the building, under pressure. It was boiling out. I still can't believe how bad it looked.

Meanwhile, uptown, FDNY Fire Education director Joseph Torrillo was heading to his press conference in Midtown Manhattan for the 9:00 a.m. unveiling of the Billy Blazes Rescue Hero.

Lt. Joseph Torrillo: I was driving over the Brooklyn Bridge. I could see the North Tower, and I was like, *Whoa!* I could see about 10 floors of fire all around the top of the building. Now, as a firefighter, as an engineer, that's an uncontrollable fire. Three college fire cadets were sitting in the back seat of my car to help at the press conference. Joe Broadbent, one of the fire cadets, said to me, "What do you think is going on?" I said to him, "Everybody on the top of the building is going to die." I said, "The building is going to collapse."

As I got to the other side of the Brooklyn Bridge, I said to myself, *This press conference ain't happening today.* I knew all the firefighters in Engine 10 — Ladder 10 — who I spent the bulk of my career with — were going to be the first ones in that building, and they're going to need as much help as they could get.

Dan Nigro: I said, "Pete, this will be the worst day of our lives."

In both the North and South Towers, office workers began to evacuate, while far below first responders arrived, took stock of the scene, and formulated plans for rescues. Almost immediately, heroes began to emerge inside the buildings, while spouses, family members, and friends tried to figure out whether their loved ones at the World Trade Center had been affected.

Lila Speciner, paralegal, Port Authority, North Tower, 88th floor: Our colleague Frank DeMartini saved our lives. He was running all over the floor looking for people, gathering people. He came barging into the office and said, "You got to leave. Staircase" — whatever-it-was, I don't even remember, A, B, or C — "it's open and it's clear." Frank told us all, "Move!" We walked in a very orderly fashion. After we left the floor, there was still plenty of smoke and milling around and what have you. But everybody left. He stayed on the 78th floor lobby. He stayed because there was someone in the elevator, trapped, banging on the door.

Edna Ortiz, wife of Pablo "Paul" Ortiz, superintendent of construction, Port Authority, North Tower: Mr. DeMartini and Paul were going office to office trying to let them out, because doors had jammed. The people they rescued remember them using crowbars to try to get the doors open.

Joe Massian, technology consultant, Port Authority, North Tower, 70th floor: We made our way into a stairwell. At this point, it reminded me of an elementary fire drill — very calm, very collected, nobody pushing, nobody shoving.

Harry Waizer, tax counsel, Cantor Fitz-gerald, North Tower: I don't know whether to think of it as an incredible sense of calm or a sense of unreality, but I was entirely focused. I did not have a clue how badly I was hurt. I thought, *I have to get downstairs, I have to get to the lobby, and I have to get to help.*

Vanessa Lawrence, artist, North Tower, 91st floor: We had gone down the stairs. I remember the first few floors being filled with smoke and debris. The sprinklers were on. It was dark. Then I remember going down stairs further, and lights were on and people were coming out of their offices. The sprinklers were strong — I had my flip-flops on, and I took them off because I was slipping all over the place.

Richard Eichen, consultant, Pass Consulting Group, North Tower, 90th floor: I said, "Okay, I better figure out how badly I'm hurt." I felt that my face was all bloody. The left side of my head was open, and I could put my hand in there — I could feel my skull. I could actually feel the bone. It stung but didn't really hurt, cause I think I was in shock. Then I said, "Okay, I've got to do something here."

Harry Waizer: As I was walking down, I caught a glimpse of my arm and saw a blackened flap of skin hanging down. It was almost matter-of-fact, telling myself: *Okay, you don't want to look at that again, just look at the feet, look at the steps, keep walking.*

John Abruzzo, staff accountant, Port Authority, North Tower, 69th floor: I'm a C5-C6 quadriplegic, so I'm able to function and get around on my wheelchair. I remember the building suddenly swayed, and that it swayed in one direction only. I looked out the north windows and debris was raining down. I must have been in a state of shock. The thing that brought me out of it was my supervisor shouting some expletive. He was outside my cubicle saying we had to evacuate.

Peter Bitwinski, assistant manager, Accounts Payable, Port Authority, North Tower, 69th floor: I have known John for a long time. Our desks were side by side for many years in Accounts Payable, so needless to say, he was a close friend of mine. I said, "John, where's your [evacuation] chair?"

John Abruzzo: I had been there in 1993 when the World Trade Center was bombed. Different job, same floor. A group of Port Authority employees and two fellows from Cantor Fitzgerald, plus some other folks from Deloitte & Touche, were all there to help evacuate me. It took us six hours to get out. After the 1993 bombing, the World Trade Center purchased these evacuation chairs.

Peter Bitwinski: He seemed to be in shock. He didn't even respond to me. So again I said, "John, do you know where your chair is?"

John Abruzzo: They made it clear I was going with them, one way or the other.

Joe Massian: Back then, two-way pagers were big. Pagers were working. People were getting news through pagers of what happened: a plane crash. I didn't realize it wasn't a small plane.

Edna Ortiz: I received a phone call. It was Paul, and what he told me was that something had happened, but he didn't know what it was, and if I turned on the television, not to worry because he was okay. I said, "All right." He said, "I'll get back to you. I'll call you as soon as I can."

Joe Massian: We continued to file down. Occasionally you would hear, "Move left." And "move left" meant that you would all push to the left side of the stairwell and actually look at the wall, because somebody was coming down who was burnt.

Edna Ortiz: I turned on the television and saw what had happened. I picked up the phone and called him back. When he answered the phone, he asked me what happened, and I explained to him that it was a plane. He said, "Okay. There are things I got to do here, so I have to go right now. I'll talk to you as soon as I can." He hung up. I called him and asked what he was doing. He told me he was getting people out. I asked him when he was done to get out too.

Genelle Guzman, office assistant, Port Authority, North Tower: I worked in the Tunnels, Bridges, and Terminals Division on the 64th floor. I thought that it probably was an earthquake because back home in my country, in Trinidad, I had experienced an earthquake with that shaking. I came back to my cubicle and other coworkers were leaving. They said, "I don't know what's going on but we think some plane hit the building." My supervisor came over and he said, "Genelle, we've got to leave. Grab your bag. That's it. We're out of here. A plane hit the building."

Pasquale Buzzelli, engineer, Port Authority, North Tower: I remember I was up late, watching *Monday Night Football,* so I was a little late getting into work. I didn't get in until probably close to 9:00. I worked on the 64th floor. It was during the express [elevator] part of that trip that I felt what was the plane hitting the building, the impact. The elevator shook violently. The lights flickered. At my office, I went right over to my boss, Pat Hoey, at the time. I said, "Pat, do you know what happened?" He was like, "I don't know. I'm trying to find out." The floor was well lit. The phones were functioning, computers were on. Everything seemed pretty normal. So right away I phoned my wife, Louise — she was at home, seven-and-a-half-months pregnant.

Louise Buzzelli, Riverdale, New Jersey, and wife of Pasquale Buzzelli, Port Authority, North Tower, 64th floor: It was tough sleeping through the night because I was at the end of the pregnancy, and I would be up half the night, tossing and turning. The morning was probably my best time to actually sleep. It was about 8:30, quarter to 9:00, and the phone rang.

Pasquale Buzzelli: She goes, "What's the matter? Is everything okay?" I said, "No, everything's fine. I'm here at work." I said, "Don't be alarmed. Turn the television on and tell me what you see. Something happened to the building."

Louise Buzzelli: I got up out of bed. Right away I turned on the television and I didn't have to search at all — any station I went on, I saw the top of his building on fire. I said, "Oh, my gosh, Pasquale! Your building is on fire! Why are you calling me?"

Pasquale Buzzelli: She said, "They're saying that a plane hit the building."

116

Louise Buzzelli: He promised he was going to be leaving and he would call when he got downstairs. That's when we hung up.

Pasquale Buzzelli: Whatever was happening, the fire was above, there was nothing below, and not thinking of a collapse, I thought I was okay. Eventually, we were going to get out, so it wasn't an issue. We were not on fire here, there was no smoke here. There was never a decision of, "Hey, let's leave." Part of that was because we probably wanted to keep the stairwell clear so we could allow access, have the firemen reach the point of impact. Why clutter the stairs even more?

First responders flooded into the World Trade Center within minutes, many summoned by escalating alarms, but others simply saw what had transpired and, knowing the city faced an unprecedented calamity, made their way to the site. As the morning unfolded, rescue efforts encompassed not just the Twin Towers but the whole World Trade Center site, including the 22-story Marriott Hotel sandwiched between the two towers and the 48-story office building, known as Seven World Trade Center, that housed commercial tenants like Salomon Brothers, as well as numerous government offices for agencies like the Secret Service, the IRS, and New York City's emergency command center, its Office of Emergency Management.

The neighboring 39-story skyscraper known as the Deutsche Bank building was also affected. Given the scale of the tragedy, numerous specialty and elite rescue units were being dispatched, including the NYPD's Emergency Service Unit and the FDNY's special rescue units.

Scott Strauss, officer, Emergency Service Unit, Truck 1, NYPD: The Emergency Service Unit, or the ESU, is the SWAT and rescue team for the City of New York. We handle every kind of crisis, any large-scale event, from bomb jobs, hostage jobs, barricaded perpetrators, people jumping off of buildings, people jumping off of bridges. We cut people out of cars. We handle hazardous material incidents, weapons of mass destruction incidents. We're the answer to the city police's problems. If the precinct cops can't handle the situation, they'll give us a call.

Det. David Brink, Emergency Service Unit, Truck 3, NYPD: We started making our way down to the Trade Center. I saw the building burning. I looked over to my colleague Mike Garcia, and I go, "I guess we're going to get a lot of work in today."

Scott Strauss: Every police officer was working their way down to the Trade Center.

118

Traffic was terrible. There were civilians directing traffic, trying to get the emergency vehicles through.

David Norman, officer, Emergency Service Unit, Truck 1, NYPD: There was a lot of debris falling from the building. Stuff was raining down on top of us when we initially pulled up. We gathered our equipment, donned our self-contained breathing apparatus, donned our rope rescue gear, our medical gear, and elevator equipment — things like that.

Det. David Brink: The equipment that day probably went around 70 pounds. When we were walking toward the Towers, our arms were hanging heavy from all the equipment that we had on us.

Det. Steven Stefanakos, Emergency Service Unit, Truck 10, NYPD: You could imagine the madness of the scene.

Det. Sgt. Joe Blozis, crime scene investigator, NYPD: There were thousands of people running. The fright was etched in their faces.

Dr. Charles Hirsch, chief medical examiner, City of New York: I will never forget seeing an airplane engine in the middle of

West Street and then an amputated hand next to it.

Alan Reiss, director of the World Trade Center, Port Authority: A detective, Richie Paugh, and I went out onto the plaza. We saw the gash in the Tower and people jumping. It really wasn't safe to be out there, but we see a wheel of a plane, and this detective said, "That's evidence. We have to take it back with us." I said, "Are you crazy?" Richie said, "No, that's it," and drags this thing back into the Port Authority police desk.

Tracy Donahoo, transit officer, NYPD: People were all streaming out of the building. My mind-set was, *The fire department's gonna get here. They're gonna go upstairs, they're gonna put out this fire, and that's the end of the day.* As we know, it wasn't that at all. It escalated.

Anthony R. Whitaker, WTC commander, PAPD, North Tower lobby: I ordered the cop at the desk to begin a full-scale evacuation of the entire complex.

Alan Reiss: I spoke to the people up in Windows on the World, who I knew, telling them, "We're going to see if we can get the fire department up there. But take a napkin, wet it with the water from a flower vase, and cover your face to breathe through it." I didn't think we were going to make it up there. I had my real doubts.

Jay Swithers, paramedic, FDNY: A lot of patients were coming out of the plaza, and immediately the EMS crews on the scene were giving them triage tags we use to identify who should go first. They start out with green, which are people who are walking wounded, who could basically stay. Then it goes to yellow, which are people that basically will need an ambulance, but they're not serious at the time. The next one is immediate — immediate is a red code. A lot of patients were hysterical, crying. The Millennium Hotel became very helpful. They were bringing out nicely padded chairs from the lobby — their beautiful chairs — for patients to sit down.

Capt. Jay Jonas, Ladder 6, FDNY: I was heading toward the [ground-floor] lobby command post when I ran into Ladder 3 and Capt. Paddy Brown. Paddy was almost a larger-than-life type of person, very highly respected by everyone in the fire department. He served two tours of duty in Vietnam as a marine, got his discharge, and became one of the most highly decorated firemen in the history of the fire department. He's very well-liked, very well-known, very compassionate guy. He said, "Jay, don't even report into the command post — they're just going to send you upstairs." I almost said, "All right, I'll go upstairs with you." Instead I said, "Let me check in first. I'll meet you upstairs."

I reported into the command post. I was standing there waiting to get orders, and I saw Commissioner Von Essen talking to Pete Hayden, who was the deputy chief running the fire. I heard Hayden say to Von Essen, "We're not putting this fire out. This is strictly a rescue mission."

Jeff Johnson, firefighter, Engine 74, FDNY: As soon as we got into the Marriott Hotel, there were a number of companies and civilians in the lobby of the hotel. We asked a chief what we should do. He said, "Well, we have to check these reports of people in the Marriott." There were a considerable amount of firemen in the building at the time. They looked like bumblebees. We took the elevator up to the 18th floor. We went up the south stairwell to the highest floor we could find. It is considered a 22-story building. The gym was on 22. As we were searching the area, I happened to look into one particular area, and it was a spa. A Jacuzzi — a big one. In the Jacuzzi was part of the landing gear from the plane.

Anthony R. Whitaker: All that morning, I don't think I really had a good understanding of what was going on. Whatever it was, it was bigger than us.

Al Kim, vice president of operations, TransCare Ambulance: We had no idea the scope of what was going on above us. The buildings are so large and the footprint so big, and you're at the base of it, you can't crane your neck back far enough to see really what's going on.

Thomas Von Essen, commissioner, FDNY: Nothing could have ever really prepared us for what happened — or how fast the events would unfold.

The Second Hijacking

"UNITED 175, DO YOU READ NEW YORK?"

The second plane, United Airlines Flight 175, also en route to Los Angeles from Boston, was hijacked minutes before American Airlines Flight 11 crashed into the World Trade Center. United Airlines Flight 175 had nine crew and 56 passengers aboard. Moments before the American plane hit Tower One, the pilots of United 175 heard the distress call from American Airlines Flight 11 and reported it to air traffic control.

8:41 A.M.

United Airlines Flight 175: New York UAL 175 heavy.

Air traffic control: UAL 175 go ahead.

United Airlines Flight 175: We figured we'd wait to go to your center. We heard a suspicious transmission on our departure from BOS — sounds like someone keyed the mike and said "Everyone stay in your seats."

Air traffic control: OK. I'll pass that along.

United Airlines Flight 175: It cut out.

8:51 A.M.
Ten minutes later, air traffic control tried to pass along routine instructions to the flight. It never responded again.

New York Center: United 175, recycle your transponder and squawk code of one-four-seven-zero.

New York Center: United 175, New York?

New York Center: United 175, do you read New York?

New York Center: Delta 1489, do you read New York?

Delta Flight 1489: Delta 1489, go ahead.

New York Center: OK, just wanted to make sure you read New York. United 175, do you read New York?

9:00 A.M.
In the final minutes of the flight, United Flight 175 passengers phoned family members and left voice mails of care and concern. Brian

Sweeney, a 38-year-old former F-14 pilot in the Gulf War, left a voice mail for his wife, Julie, back in Massachusetts. Peter Hanson, 32, traveling with his wife, Sue Kim, 35, and their two-and-a-half-year-old daughter, Christine, called his father. Christine would be the youngest victim on September 11th.

Brian Sweeney, passenger, United Flight 175: Hey Jules, this is Brian. Ah, listen. I'm on an airplane that's been hijacked. If things don't go well, and it's not looking good, I just want you to know I absolutely love you, I want you to do good, have good times — same with my parents. I'll see you when you get here. I want you to know that I totally love you. Bye, babe. I hope I call you.

Peter Hanson, passenger, United Flight 175: It's getting bad, Dad. A stewardess was stabbed. They seem to have knives and Mace. They said they have a bomb. It's getting very bad on the plane. The plane is making jerky movements. I don't think the pilot is fly-

126

ing the plane. I think we are going down. I think they intend to go to Chicago or someplace and fly into a building. Don't worry, Dad. If it happens, it'll be very fast. Oh my God, oh my God, oh my God.

9:01 A.M.
Below, on the ground, confusion spiraled at air traffic control, as various sectors tried to piece together the rapidly changing events — even to understand that a second flight had been hijacked — and muster a response.

Peter Mulligan, FAA New York Center: Do you know if anyone down there has done any co-ordination to scramble fighter-type airplanes?
Controller at FAA Command Center, Herndon, Virginia: *[Indistinct]* still think the airplane's in the air?
Peter Mulligan: No, we have several situations going on here. It is escalating big, big time, and we need to get the military involved.

FAA Command Center: Why, what's going on?

Peter Mulligan: Just get me somebody who has the authority to get military in the air, now.

9:02 A.M.
Learning that a second plane had been taken over, New York air traffic control called other FAA offices to try to spot United Flight 175 as it approached Manhattan.

New York Center: Hey, can you look out your window right now?

New York Terminal Radar Approach Center (TRACON), Long Island: Yeah.

New York Center: Can you see a guy at about 4,000 feet, about five east of the airport right now, looks like he's —

New York TRACON: Yeah, I see him.

New York Center: Is he descending into the building also?

New York TRACON: He's descending really quick too, yeah.

New York Center: Well that's —

New York TRACON: Forty-five hundred feet now, he just

128

dropped 800 feet in like one sweep.

New York Center: That's another situation. What kind of a plane is that, can you guys tell?

New York TRACON: I don't know. I'll read it out in a minute.

New York TRACON: *[Indistinct]*.

New York TRACON: Another one just hit the building.

New York Center: Wow.

New York TRACON: *[Indistinct]* Oh my god. . . . Another one just hit it hard.

New York Center: Another one just hit the World Trade.

New York TRACON: The whole building just, ah, came apart. . . . *[Indistinct]* Oh my god.

New York Center: Holy smokes. All right. I guess you guys are going to be busy.

THE MILITARY GEARS UP
"A HOST OF POTENTIAL PROBLEMS"

Across the eastern United States, those in charge of the nation's airspace — both the military air defense units and civilian air traffic controllers — dealt with the confusion sparked by a second hijacking, even as they were unsure about the fate of American Airlines Flight 11.

Colin Scoggins, air space and procedures specialist and military specialist, FAA, Boston Center: Somehow it was determined that American 11 was still in the air, so I was the one who made the call to Northeast Air Defense Command and advised them that American 11 was still in the air. Of course, I was incorrect.

Lt. Col. Kevin Nasypany, mission crew commander, NEADS, Rome, New York: We also had the indication — misinformation that we received through FAA channels —

130

that Flight 11 never crashed and was heading toward Washington.

Maj. Gen. Larry Arnold, commander of the 1st Air Force, NORAD, Tyndall Air Force Base, Florida: I wanted to scramble our Langley aircraft right then — F-16s out of North Dakota were on alert at Langley Air Force Base in Virginia.

Ben Sliney, national operations manager, FAA Command Center, Herndon, Virginia: While we were trying to get information, New York Center starts to have a problem also. They were having a problem with an aircraft — it was United 175, it turns out.

Maj. Gen. Larry Arnold: I said, "Bob [Marr], we need to get those [Langley fighters] over Washington, D.C., in case we are under attack." Other airplanes now are being called "possibly hijacked" by the FAA.

Col. Bob Marr, commander, NEADS, Rome, New York: We are looking at a host of potential problems.

Capt. Craig Borgstrom, F-16 pilot and squadron operations commander, Langley Air Force Base: The guy from the sector asked me, "How many can you get airborne right now?" I told him I had two on battle stations. He said, "That's not what I asked — how many total airplanes can you send up?" I said, "I'll give you three." He said, "Then go."

In the air throughout the Northeast, confused airline pilots tried to decipher the chaos engulfing the country and air traffic controllers below.

Chuck Savall, pilot, Midwest Express Flight 73: I was the captain of the Midwest Express flight from Milwaukee to Newark. We descended toward Newark on a normal and beautiful morning. We heard another airline pilot on the radio say, "We heard something about a plane hitting the World Trade Center." We were 25 miles away in the air. I looked out the window. We saw the flames and smoke.

Gerald Earwood, pilot, Midwest Express, Flight 7: I was flying Milwaukee to New York LaGuardia. We started down to 18,000 feet and saw the smoke coming off the first tower that had been hit. We thought it was an air-conditioning unit that was on fire.

As the two Midwest flights approached New York — just two among dozens of planes then inbound to the region's three busy airports, each of which in 2001 served about 1,000 flights a day — they found themselves in the midst of the still-unfolding attacks, as United Flight 175 turned off its transponder and made a left turn toward Manhattan.

Gerald Earwood: I was ordered to take evasive action to avoid colliding with United 175. I witnessed the disaster straight-on. We were descending to 4,000 feet on arrival for LaGuardia. The smoke from the first World Trade Center tower was obscuring LaGuardia Airport. I asked the controller, "We cannot see the airport?" Three times I called them. There was no chatter, no talk, no anything. Then he came back screaming at us, "Midex 7, are you with me?" I said, "Roger, we are descending down to 4,000 feet." He ordered a hard left turn and started screaming, "Turn left, immediately — now, now, immediately!" I have never had a controller scream like that, be that excited.

Col. Bob Marr, commander, NEADS, Rome, New York: As we're watching the television, we see another aircraft come into view and hit the second tower of the World Trade Center.

Frank Loprano, chief of aeronautical operations, Newark Airport, Port Authority: I had picked up binoculars and was looking at the Trade Center. I just put the binoculars down on the desk, and the second building erupted in flames. I picked up the direct line to the control tower and said, "Newark is closed. We're launching bombs."

Ben Sliney, national operations manager, FAA Command Center, Herndon, Virginia: We were discussing shutting down all the traffic on the East Coast to deal with New York's problem. We were shutting all that traffic down when, right before our eyes, United 175 came onto the television screen.

Gerald Earwood: As we are coming out of the right turn, we heard an aircraft announce on the frequency, "We saw an airplane hit the World Trade Center." I looked up and saw the impact of United 175.

Lt. Col. Kevin Nasypany, mission crew commander, NEADS, Rome, New York: It was an "Oh, shit" mode. That's the best way to describe it — disbelief. We're under attack. We figured if there's two, there might be more.

Lt. Col. Tim Duffy, F-15 pilot, Otis Air Force Base, Cape Cod, Massachusetts: They say the second aircraft hit the World Trade Center — so confusion in my cockpit: *The second aircraft?*

Ben Sliney: When United 175 struck the

building, I told them to ground-stop every plane in the country, regardless. No one could take off.

Within minutes, New York had closed its airports and begun redirecting inbound aircraft to other locations.

Lt. Col. Tim Duffy: We were about 60 to 70 miles outside Manhattan, and I could see the Towers burning. Right then, I looked up and said, "Okay, obviously everything just changed." From my personal mind-set we took off to go help somebody, then looked up to see it burning, and said, "Okay, now people are dying." You switch into combat mind-set.

Susan Baer, general manager, Newark International Airport: I called the manager of JFK and said, "Have you heard anything?" As I'm speaking to him, the second plane hit the South Tower, which we saw — the impact, the smoke. I said, "The Trade Center's been hit again. I'm closing the airport. You should do the same."

Chuck Savall, pilot, Midwest Express Flight 73: At that point, we had to figure out our Plan B: How much fuel did we have and where could we go? Our initial thought was going to look at LaGuardia. Our dispatchers were watching this on CNN. They told us to get as far from the East Coast as we possibly could, so that is what we did. We headed for Cleveland.

Lt. Col. Tim Duffy: They came back on and said, "NORAD took control of all the airspace in the country. Proceed directly to Manhattan and set up Combat Air Patrol." I said, "OK, got that." It was a very surreal experience — flying over Central Park at 1,000 feet and 500 knots, trying to identify possible targets. That was just wrong. You should never be doing this over Manhattan.

At 9:24 a.m., the fighters at Langley Air Force Base were scrambled. Initially, not realizing the threat they were facing, the fighters were sent east toward the Atlantic Ocean, following standard policies intended to intercept incoming Russian bombers.

Capt. Craig Borgstrom, F-16 pilot and squadron operations commander, Langley Air Force Base: Shortly after takeoff, they changed our heading more northwesterly toward D.C. and gave us "max-subsonic." That's as fast as you can go without breaking the sound barrier. I've never heard it before in my short career, but I don't think anyone's heard that order before.

THE SECOND PLANE

"CENTRAL, WE'RE UNDER ATTACK"

The Aon Corporation occupied floors 92, 93, and 98 to 105 of the South Tower. At 8:59 a.m., Sean Rooney, the vice president of Aon's risk management services, located on the 98th floor, called his wife, Beverly Eckert, and left a voice-mail message.

Sean Rooney, vice president, Aon Corporation, South Tower, 98th floor: Hey, Beverly, this is Sean, in case you get this message. There has been an explosion in World Trade One, that's the other building. It looks like a plane struck it. It's on fire at about the 90th floor. And it's, it's — it's horrible. Bye.

Sean called back at 9:01 a.m. and again got Beverly's voice mail. The recording captured an announcement in the background; it was the

137

Port Authority reassuring occupants of the South Tower that they were not in danger.

> **Sean Rooney:** Hi honey, this is Sean again.
>
> **Port Authority announcement:** May I have your attention, please.
>
> **Sean Rooney:** Looks like we'll be —
>
> **Port Authority announcement:** Repeating this message:
>
> **Sean Rooney:** — in this tower for a while. Um, it's —
>
> **Port Authority announcement:** The situation occurred in Building One, if the —
>
> **Sean Rooney:** It's secure here.
>
> **Port Authority announcement:** — conditions warrant on your floor you may wish to start an orderly evacuation.
>
> **Sean Rooney:** I'll talk to you later, bye.

Two minutes after the Port Authority's announcement, television viewers across the country who had tuned in to see the dramatic live footage of the crash at the North Tower watched as United Airlines Flight 175 appeared on their screens. The attacks interrupted the final minutes of morning news shows, broad-

casting the horror in New York City into the homes of millions of people sitting down to breakfast, racing to get kids to school, or readying themselves for a September Tuesday at work.

Jane Clayson, anchor, *The Early Show*, CBS: It was a fairly light news day. We were finishing a segment with the woman who runs *Gourmet* magazine. We were about to close the show.

Katie Couric, anchor, *The Today Show*, NBC: I was in the back room, where you could go between segments to work on what's next, take a break, or drink a cup of coffee. Matt Lauer was doing an interview with somebody who had written a book about Howard Hughes. I looked up at the monitor, and I saw the World Trade Center was on fire. I thought, *Oh wow.* I looked at the time and was like, *Thank God it's before nine o'clock when most people get to work.* Right away, Matt cut that interview short, and I scurried back in next to him and started to try to decipher what had happened.

Deena Burnett, at home in San Ramon, California, wife of United Flight 93 passenger Tom Burnett: I was awakened by the three children running into my room,

139

normal for most mornings. They came in a little before 6:00 a.m., and I immediately got up and out of bed. Anna Clare and our two five-year-old twins, Halley and Madison, told me what they wanted for breakfast. I turned on the television. I noticed that on every station there was a news report about the World Trade Center. I thought, *My goodness, air traffic control must be terribly messed up.*

Jane Clayson: The first witnesses kept saying it was a commercial jet. My co-anchor Bryant Gumbel and I kept asking, "Are you sure?" I was thinking to myself, *This must have been an accident.* "You're certain it wasn't a small plane?" Witness after witness said, "I am positive it was a commercial jet."

Katie Couric: The first glimpse of it, I don't think I appreciated how massive the fire was because it looked like it was coming out of the side of the building. Smoke was obscuring a lot of the gaping hole that was there. I remember my hand was shaking like a leaf. Al Roker was very helpful because he knew a lot about the structure of the building, because he had been in local news there when that first bomb went off in the basement in '93.

Deena Burnett: The phone rang, and it was

140

my mom, who said, "Deena, have you seen the television? They're saying this is an American Airlines flight that's gone into the Towers. Tom's in New York, isn't he?" I said, "Don't worry, Mom. He'd be flying United or Delta." I reassured her: "Mom, don't worry. Planes crash all the time and Tom's never on them."

Katie Couric: We were talking, we were getting eyewitness accounts, and then of course the really chilling, and shocking, visual was when that second plane was flying toward the building. It felt like it was in suspended animation.

Jane Clayson: We saw it live. As it rounded the corner, there were people in the studio pointing to monitors. You could see it coming. You could hear gasps throughout the studio. Then it exploded into that building. There was silence. We all looked at one another.

Katie Couric: Matt said, "This is obviously something deliberate." I remember thinking, *Well, don't say that yet.* If you remember the Oklahoma City bombing, everybody assumed that was the work of Muslim extremists. I was very cautious about calling it that. I was sort of paralyzed, but I wanted to be careful about characterizing it a certain way, but

Matt said right away, "This is a terrorist attack."

Peter Jennings, anchor, ABC News: I simply put my hands in the air and told everybody in the newsroom to stay quiet, because we didn't know what was happening. Our suspicions were instant. Rather than risk saying something foolish, I let the audience absorb it.

At 9:03 a.m., traveling at about 590 miles per hour, United Flight 175 crashed into the South Tower — Two World Trade Center — hitting at an angle, its lower left wing slicing into the 77th and 78th floors, which housed the Sky Lobby, used to transfer from express to local elevators, and its upper right wing hitting the 85th floor. Most of the impact zone, floors 78 to 83, was occupied by Fuji Bank, where employees had evacuated after the attack on the North Tower, only to return to their offices when told by the Port Authority that the incident was under control. Fuji Bank ultimately lost 23 employees and visitors in the attack.

Only a single stairway in the South Tower, Stairwell A, survived the crash. Fewer than 20 people would escape from the impact zone or above.

Stanley Praimnath, Fuji Bank, South Tower, 81st floor: I was watching toward

142

the direction of the Statue of Liberty and something caught my eye — a plane, and this plane is getting closer.

Steven Bienkowski, Aviation Unit, NYPD: Our helicopter was on the southwest side of the South Tower. I glanced over my shoulder, and there came a United Airlines aircraft right at us, a little bit underneath where we were — I do mean underneath us — it probably missed us by about 300 feet.

James Cowan, Harbor Unit, NYPD: The second plane came in so tight the NYPD helicopter pilot took evasive action and pulled up.

Steven Bienkowski: It proceeded to fly right through the building, right in front of us. I must have gone numb. I don't remember hearing an explosion, although it must have been extremely loud. It was all I could handle to watch that happen.

Melinda Murphy, traffic reporter, WPIX TV, New York City: We had gone back to our newsroom for the postmortem of our show. We had video monitors up — the television was always on. I saw the buildings on fire. My photographer ran to the assignment desk and said, "You've got to launch the helicopter." I got in a cab and called my husband. I said, "Listen, I'm going to be really late tonight." Just as we pulled up to the 30th Street heliport, the second plane hit. It was this unbelievable scene. The fire was right outside our window. In my ear, they were like, "We have to go live, are we ready to go live?" I wasn't even ready to say "Oh my God" out loud, much less talk about it on camera. But I did.

Robert Small, office manager, Morgan Stanley, South Tower, 72nd floor: I called my wife. There was this sudden *swoosh, bang, boom.* It was the most violent ride I'd ever been on. The plane came in over us. We were on floor 72 and it hit floor 78. I was thrown onto my desk, and then thrown back about two or three times. Stuff came off the walls, shelves came down. I pick up the phone and my wife's screaming, "What happened?" I said, "Something exploded." She said, "Get out of there!" I said, "Okay. I'll call you later." There was no "I love you. If I don't see you again —"

Michael McAvoy, associate director, Bear Stearns: I was in my office in downtown Brooklyn, with a clear view of the World Trade Center. The smoke was thick and black. I walked back to my desk to call my buddy Jimmy, my best friend for over 30 years. He worked for Cantor Fitzgerald in

Tower One on the 104th floor. No answer. *Maybe, just maybe, he took the day off and went golfing. Man, I hope so.* After the second plane hit, I ran back to my desk and called my mom. She told me that my brother John, a New York City fireman with Ladder 3 on 13th Street, had worked the night tour, so he was still in the firehouse when the planes hit. I called his firehouse. No answer.

Charles Christophe, attorney, Broadway: I called my office and the receptionist told me that my wife [Kirsten L. Christophe] called and said that the first tower was hit. I don't know if she saw or she knew — because her office was on the 104th floor in the South Tower. She told my receptionist that she was safe and there was nothing to worry about, and she would call me later. I went back to my office at 225 Broadway. I was waiting for her call and trying to make calls. She was not answering. And we heard the second explosion.

Louise Buzzelli, Riverdale, New Jersey, and wife of Pasquale Buzzelli, Port Authority, North Tower, 64th floor: A lot of phone calls started coming in. At first, nobody wanted to ask me the question. One particular phone call I remember was from his cousin, Ralph. He's like Pasquale's brother. He goes, "Don't worry. Pasquale's going to get out. It's okay." He said, "Did you hear from him?" I said, "Yeah. We spoke. He said that they were going to be leaving." As I was on the phone with him, we both saw the second plane hit at the same time. He was seeing it live from his building, and I saw it right on the television.

Judith Wein, senior vice president, Aon Corporation, South Tower, 103rd floor: I walked my way down from 103 to 78, met up with my colleagues, and we were standing around in the Sky Lobby, waiting our turn to get in the big cattle car elevators to go down. When the second plane hit, I basically went flying to the total opposite end. I thought, *So is this how it ends? Is this what life is — going to work, getting there like 7:00 in the morning, leaving at 5:00, taking an hour and a half each way to commute, and not having much of a life? Is this what it's all about?* I landed on my arm, which got smashed. I had three cracked ribs, a slightly punctured lung. I had abdominal bleeding. But I was okay. The arm broke my fall. Later, the doctor asked, "What landed on you?" I said, "Me."

Stanley Praimnath: I'm scared I'm going to get sucked out by the air pressure. I'm holding on to all this mangled furniture.

Jean Potter, Bank of America, North Tower, 81st floor: We made our way into the Sky Lobby. That's when the South Tower was hit. There was this other huge explosion you could see out the window. I saw fireballs and paper and it's like, *Oh God what is this? What now?* We got back onto our original staircase and started descending.

Joe Esposito, chief of department, NYPD: All the debris is coming down. We looked up and it reminded me of the old cartoon with the Road Runner when the Coyote is watching everything come down on him. The safe — or whatever the Road Runner would throw at him — would come down. It was getting bigger and bigger. The debris is getting bigger and bigger as it's getting close to us.

Lt. Mickey Kross, Engine 16, FDNY: It reminded me of those movies — those old Godzilla movies — where the monster would come out of the ocean, and everybody would be running and screaming and tripping and falling down.

David Norman, officer, Emergency Service Unit, Truck 1, NYPD: One of the landing wheels from the aircraft fell, burning, right in front of us. It was almost like the size of a Volkswagen landing in the street.

Bernie Kerik, commissioner, NYPD:
Debris and body parts and the plane and the building — it was all coming down right on top of us. I'm yelling at my staff to get aviation to close down the airspace. I'm screaming at these guys to get me air support. They're looking at me like, "Is there a fucking number to call for an F-16?"

Frank Razzano, guest, Marriott Hotel:
The next thing I heard was a huge explosion, and this time I got up, I opened the drapes, I looked out the window, and I saw fireballs falling into the street. Cars were on fire. I turned on the television. I saw on TV that they were reporting that two planes had hit the World Trade Center. My thought was, *This is very unfortunate. But this is going on basically 60 to 70 stories above me. It's got nothing to do with me. I've got a case that's going to trial in approximately one week. I've got a lot of work to do.* My thought at that moment was, *The fire department would come down, they'd put out the fire and, while this is a tragic incident, that'd be that.* I turned on my heels, and I went into the bathroom. I took a shower, I shaved, and I got dressed.

Fernando Ferrer, candidate for New York City mayor: We hear the report: a second plane hit Tower Two. I said, "Let's go back to

148

the Bronx. This is no accident." Kalman [Yeger, my assistant] said, "No, we got a campaign schedule." I repeated, "This is not an accident!" He said, "No, we got to head downtown! We got to — !" I said, "There is no more campaign."

Dan Potter, firefighter, Ladder 10, FDNY, at the study session for the lieutenant's exam in Staten Island: I start going through the questions. Somebody came busting through the doors and says, "Holy shit, two planes hit the Trade Center." Harvey Harrell's phone rang next to me, real quick, and I heard him say, "Two planes. Another plane hit the Trade Center." Harvey Harrell died in the Trade Center. He was from Rescue 5 in Staten Island. He called from the American Legion Hall back to the firehouse, "Don't let that truck leave till I get there." It was close. He was off duty, and he told them, "I want to get on the truck with you."

Bill Spade, firefighter, Rescue 5, FDNY: I heard them say on the radio, basically, "We have a huge fire. Send me four more Rescues." To have four Rescues responding at the same time for the same fire was unprecedented. As I made my way up West Street — it's only a short distance between there and the Trade Center — body parts were everywhere. I remember trying to go around them and I couldn't. I said a little prayer. I said, "I'm going to run over them," and I did.

Joe Esposito: I go on the radio. I immediately say, "Central, we're under attack. A second plane has just hit the second tower. We are under attack."

At home in Riverdale, New Jersey, Louise Buzzelli, seven-and-a-half-months pregnant, waited for word on her husband, Pasquale, in the North Tower.

Louise Buzzelli: I never left the television. I remember from the day before, he had his work shirt hung over the bedpost. I would always say to him, "Can you please pick up your things?" That day, I just wanted to feel him, and I took the shirt and put it on. We have a cross in our room, and I grabbed the cross, and I was praying to God that this would be over, and he could get out and this would all be something that we could get past and the world could get past.

Pasquale Buzzelli, engineer, Port Authority, North Tower, 64th floor: We actually watched a replay of the second plane hitting — it was a snowy picture — on one of the televisions in the conference room. That's when we knew that this was no accident.

150

Louise Buzzelli: He did call me one more time after the second plane crashed into the second building. I thought he was now downstairs, so I was like, "Oh, thank God." I was like, "Oh, did you make it down? Are you okay? Where are you?" He's like, "No, we're still here." I got so angry at him.

Pasquale Buzzelli: She said, "What are you still doing there? Get out!" I said, "I know, Louise." I said, "We're fine here. We're going to be leaving soon." She kept saying, "Get the hell out!"

The second attack transformed — and compli-cated — the already massive rescue effort at the World Trade Center. At 9:10 a.m., the NYPD declared an unprecedented second Level 4 mobilization, summoning another 1,000 officers and supervisors to the scene. The FDNY similarly called a second fifth alarm, dispatch-ing hundreds more firefighters, including 23 engines and 13 ladder companies. That number doesn't include numerous fire companies, firefighters, EMTs, and paramedics who contin-ued to self-dispatch, and because the attacks took place around the time of the standard 9:00 a.m. shift change, many trucks were "riding heavy," that is, carrying firefighters from both the night and day tours. PAPD officers flooded into the area around the World Trade Center,

151

even as other colleagues moved to close the bridges and tunnels into New York City, part of a precautionary security procedure known as OPERATION OMEGA. PAPD's superintendent, Fred V. Morrone, began climbing up the North Tower Stairwell B at 9:11 a.m. to assess the damage above.

City officials struggled to organize a response to the attacks, in part because New York's $13 million emergency command center was housed on the 23rd floor of Seven World Trade Center, and it was evacuated soon after the attacks — there was no backup location. The city's leaders, including Mayor Rudy Giuliani, who quickly made his way to the area, instead improvised a response plan as they worked out of makeshift command posts.

Dan Nigro, chief of operations, FDNY: The horror of the day had just multiplied exponentially.

Capt. Jay Jonas, Ladder 6, FDNY, awaiting orders in the North Tower's ground-floor lobby command post: I'm standing there. It was very loud — as you can imagine, the acoustics in the lobby of the World Trade Center weren't really good, a lot of echoes — and all of a sudden it got very quiet. One of the firemen from Rescue 1 looked up and said, "We may not live through today." We looked at him, and we looked at each other, and we said, "You're right." We took the time to shake each other's hands and wish each other good luck and "Hope I'll see you later," which is especially poignant for me because we all had that acknowledgment that this might be our last day on earth and we went to work anyway.

Juana Lomi, paramedic, New York Beekman Downtown Hospital: Now things started getting worse. I said, "Listen, guys, anybody you cannot quick triage — not breathing properly, chest pain, leg fractures, anything on the leg that they can't run — they're going to go on the ambulance. Nobody else is going on the ambulance. They're going to run. They're going to use their legs or whatever."

Monsignor John Delendick, chaplain, FDNY: The look on [Chief of Department] Peter Ganci's face was really amazing because Ganci usually had two looks when he was at a fire. The first would be a look of defiance, saying, "We got you. We got you." The second one was more of a jovial thing. Once things were settling down, and the fire was dark and down, he would joke a lot. He'd walk around, talk to people. This was a real look of fear. I never saw this on him before.

Bernie Kerik, commissioner, NYPD: Mayor Giuliani made a comment to me, like, "We're in uncharted territory. The city has never experienced anything like this."

Det. David Brink, Emergency Service Unit, Truck 3, NYPD: I was trying to cinch up my belt from my rope rescue gear. I felt a pat on my shoulder, I looked up, and it was Rudolph Giuliani. He said, "Be careful going in there." I said, "Thanks."

Thomas Von Essen, commissioner, FDNY: I remember seeing Ray Downey, the head of Special Operations, in the lobby, and he said, "These buildings can collapse." He said it in passing — not that these buildings will collapse in 40 minutes and we have to get everybody out, or not that they'll collapse by tomorrow, or not that they necessarily will collapse at all — just that they *can* collapse. That was the first sense I had of the enormity of this.

Capt. Jay Jonas, Ladder 6, FDNY: I was thinking that Chief [Pete] Hayden was going to send me over to the other building, because nobody was there yet. I said, "Another plane has hit the second tower." He closed his eyes, nodded his head, and said he knew. He said,

"Take your guys upstairs here and do the best you can for search and rescue."

Across the region, even as the massive NYPD and FDNY mobilizations activated additional units, off-duty first responders and those who lived outside of Manhattan realized the magnitude of the disaster and began to make their way downtown. At 9:29 a.m., FDNY issued a full "recall," bringing all of its employees back to work. Ultimately, 60 of the FDNY personnel killed on 9/11 were supposed to be off-duty that morning.

Dan Potter, firefighter, Ladder 10, FDNY, in Staten Island: I ran to the front of the American Legion building. I could look right across the water and see the Trade Center. I saw the column of smoke coming out. There was a phone right there, and I dialed the phone real quick to see if I could get ahold of Jean. It went right into her voice mail. I ran right to my truck, and I raced back.

Lt. Chuck Downey, FDNY: I was home, off-duty. I responded from Long Island, from Commack. The roads were really tough getting in.

Capt. Joe Downey, Squad Company 18, FDNY: I was also home that day. I started

155

getting phone calls from my mom — she wanted to see if we were working. She knew my dad [Ray Downey, head of FDNY Special Operations] was there because he went to work that morning, but she didn't know if we were working. My company in Lower Manhattan would be one of the first two units coming in. My company was wiped out that day.

Joe Graziano, firefighter, Ladder 13, FDNY: We got on a truck and it seemed like the city opened up for us. We got down there in no time. There were six of us, and I was the only one who came back.

John Napolitano, father: I knew my son [firefighter Lt. John P. Napolitano] was with a rescue company and that he'd probably be going in. I wanted to tell him, "Don't be a hero." After several attempts trying to get through to him — busy, busy, busy, busy — I called my house to see if my wife spoke to my son. I said, "The phone's busy, and I want to tell him don't take any chances if he's going to go down there." My wife was crying and she said, "He's already there."

LIVE, ON AIR

"*IS IT* WAR OF THE WORLDS?"

As radio and TV stations interrupted their regular programming with footage of New York, word spread nationally of the attacks and transfixed the country. It was a shocking way to wake up for those not on the East Coast, and uncharted territory for broadcasters covering the event.

Bob Edwards, anchor, *All Things Considered,* National Public Radio (NPR): I went into the studio and started doing our entire program live. I concentrated on words I was trying not to say. I didn't want to use the word "terrorism." I thought about the Oklahoma City bombing — how people speculated that Arabs were responsible.

Preston Stone, resident, North Dakota: I woke to a friend's voice on my answering machine — his speech was halting and anxious, and he was saying something about a car bomb at the State Department. I learned

157

about the attacks in-depth from NPR. Bob Edwards was hosting, and I clearly remember his long pauses in response to the scenes being described to him by reporters in the field.

Bob Edwards: I was also trying not to say things like "Holy shit!" In situations like this, your gut reaction is to use crude words that people say in everyday life, but you can't say them into that microphone.

Anne Worner, resident, Texas: I was out for my morning walk. Just as I got back into the house, the phone rang. My girlfriend called in hysterics, saying, "We are at war, we are at war. Turn on your television!" Shaking, I went into the living room and turned on the TV. I cried and cried, sitting there watching the coverage.

Jason Fagone, resident, Ohio: I was on a long-distance cycling trip with some college friends that month, biking down the East Coast from Maine to Pennsylvania. We were somewhere in New England on the morning of September 11th. We happened to be close to a Best Buy, so we went there and watched the news on the TVs in the Best Buy. Every TV in the store was tuned to CNN or another live news feed, dozens of TVs showing the Twin Towers and the dark gray smoke. The employees let us sit on the floor and watch. They were watching too.

Rosemary Dillard, Washington, D.C., base manager, American Airlines, and wife of Flight 77 passenger Eddie Dillard: I arrived at my American Airlines management job at Ronald Reagan Airport and went to a meeting. Early in the meeting, we heard screams from the Admirals Club nearby. We went to see what the commotion was and returned to the meeting after seeing a sketchy TV news report. About 15 minutes later, we heard screams again and saw that United Airlines Flight 175 had hit the South Tower of the World Trade Center. The meeting was adjourned and I walked to my office.

Katie Couric, anchor, *The Today Show*, NBC: During a break when Matt [Lauer] was doing an interview, I ran into that back workspace and called my parents and told them to get into the basement. It felt like the world was coming to an end. I felt like, "Is it *War of the Worlds*?"

At Emma Booker Elementary School, Sarasota, Florida

"EVERYONE'S PAGER STARTED GOING OFF"

A thousand miles south of New York, President George W. Bush had arrived at Emma Booker Elementary School in Sarasota, Florida. At 8:55 a.m. he began what he thought was going to be a quick stop before heading back to Washington for lunch and the evening's congressional picnic at the White House.

Karl Rove, senior advisor, White House: We were standing outside the elementary school. My phone rang. It was my assistant Susan Ralston, saying that a plane had hit the World Trade Center — it wasn't clear whether it was private, commercial, prop, or jet. That's all she had. The boss was about two feet away. He was shaking hands. I told him the same thing. He arched his eyebrows like, "Get more."

Dave Wilkinson, assistant agent in charge, U.S. Secret Service: Eddie Marinzel and I were the two lead agents with the

160

president that day. The head of the detail was back in Washington. We heard, "There's an incident in New York."

Andy Card, chief of staff, White House: We were standing at the door to the classroom, when a staffer came up and said, simply, "Sir, it appears that a twin-engine prop plane crashed into one of the World Trade Center towers." We all said something like "What a tragedy." Then the principal opened the door and the president went into the classroom to meet the students.

Brian Montgomery, director of advance, White House: Mark Rosenker, the head of the White House Military Office, said to me, "Dr. Rice needs to talk to the president." There was this group of students, all young ladies in uniforms, and teachers, all oblivious to all of this.

Natalia Jones-Pinkney, student, Emma Booker Elementary: Everyone had their hair done and new bows and everything.

Sandra Kay Daniels, second-grade teacher, Emma Booker Elementary: Our principal introduced him to the children, and he shook a couple of the kids' hands and introduced himself, tried to lighten the room up a little because the kids were in awe. They were like little soldiers, quiet, struck by the sight of the president. He said, "Let's get started with reading." The story was *My Pet Goat* from our reading series.

Brian Montgomery: The president was very gracious and greeted them, and then said, "I need to go take an important telephone call." He went into the holding room and went directly to the STU-III, the secure telephone.

Ari Fleischer, press secretary, White House: There's always a secure telephone waiting for the president, but in the nine months he'd been president, I don't think we'd ever used one before an event like that.

Dave Wilkinson: We're asking ourselves, *Is there any direction of interest toward the president?* That's the phrase, "direction of interest." Or is this just an attack on New York?

Sandy Kress, senior education advisor, White House: I was back in the media room. There was some buzz about the first plane, people were watching it on a TV. Then there was a stampede across the media room as they saw the second plane hit.

Rep. Adam Putnam (R-Florida): I was brand new — a freshman congressman. We'd gone into the media center to wait for the president and the children to read together in the other room. We were clustered around the TV and watched the second plane hit.

Col. Mark Tillman, presidential pilot, Air Force One: We were all getting ready, based on the estimated departure time. All of us had already shown up at the plane.

Master Sgt. Dana Lark, superintendent of communications, Air Force One: There were two TV tuners, worldwide television tuners at my workspace on Air Force One. They were like old-school rabbit ears — UHF and VHF frequencies. We didn't have the ability to tune into CNN, Fox, or anything else. It was the *Today Show,* the strongest signal that day, and they're showing pictures of the Towers, smoke billowing out. I saw the second airplane strike. *Oh shit.* I dropped everything and ran downstairs to get Colonel Tillman: "You've got to come see this."

Col. Mark Tillman: It didn't make any sense. It's a clear-and-a-million day.

Staff Sgt. William "Buzz" Buzinski, security, Air Force One: We protect the plane 24 hours a day, even after the president has left. One of the advance Secret Service agents had told us about the first plane. Then, about 17 minutes later, I saw the same guy sprinting across the tarmac. He said, "Another plane hit the Towers." I knew instantly it was terrorism. We started to increase security around the plane — made it a tighter bubble.

Staff Sgt. Paul Germain, airborne communications system operator, Air Force One: Big airplanes just don't hit little buildings. Then, as soon as that second plane hit, that switchboard lit up like a Christmas tree.

Col. Mark Tillman: Everything started coming alive. We were hooked into the PEOC — the White House bunker — and the JOC — the Joint Operations Center — for the Secret Service. They're all in the link now.

Andy Card: I was thinking that we had White House people there — my deputy, Joe Hagin, and a team were in New York preparing for the UN General Assembly. I was thinking that Joe was probably at the World Trade Center — that's where the Secret Service office was, in the basement.

Mike Morell, presidential briefer, Central Intelligence Agency: I was really worried that someone was going to fly a plane into that school. This event had been on the schedule for weeks, anyone could have known about it. Eddie Marinzel, the lead Secret

Service agent, wanted to get the hell out of there as fast as possible.

Rep. Adam Putnam: There's some debate within the staff that I can hear about how the president needs to address the nation. They're saying, "We can't do it here. You can't do it in front of fifth-graders." The Secret Service is saying, "You're doing it here or you're not doing it at all. We're not taking the time to do it somewhere else."

Dave Wilkinson: We're beginning to get the motorcade up and running, getting the motorcycle cops back, we're ready to evacuate at a moment's notice. All of a sudden it hits me: *The president's the only one who doesn't know that this plane has hit the second building.* It was a discomfort to all of us that the president didn't know. The event was dragging on, and that's when Andy Card came out.

Andy Card: A thousand times a day, a chief of staff has to ask, "Does the president need to know?" This was an easy test to pass. As strange as it sounds, as I was standing there waiting to talk to the president, I was reflecting on another time that I'd had to be the calm one: I'd been acting chief of staff to President George H. W. Bush when he threw up on the Japanese prime minister. I was all business in that moment. He'd refused to get in the ambulance — he didn't want anyone to see the president get in the ambulance — and in the limo, he's still sick and he's getting sick on me. In the hotel, I take out my laminated "in case of emergency" card. I went down my checklist. I was telling people, "He's not dying, he's still the president." My job that day was to be calm, cool, and collected. Not the same magnitude, of course, but I knew my job on 9/11 was to be calm, cool, and collected.

Karl Rove: I remember Andy Card pausing at the door, before he went in, it seemed like forever, but it was probably just a couple heartbeats. I never understood why, but he told me, years later, that he needed to spend a moment formulating the words he wanted to use.

Ellen Eckert, stenographer, White House: There are six stenographers who work for the White House Press Office. One of us always travels with the president. I always said I typed fast for a living all over the world. That morning was uneventful until Andy walked in.

Andy Card: I knew I was delivering a message that no president would want to hear. I decided to pass on two facts and an editorial comment. I didn't want to invite a conversation because the president was sitting in front of the classroom. The teacher asked the students to take out their books, so I took that opportunity to approach the president. I whispered in his ear, "A second plane hit the second tower. America is under attack." I took a couple steps back so he couldn't ask any questions.

Mariah Williams, student, Emma Booker Elementary: I remember him being all happy and joyful. Then his expression changing to very serious and concerned.

Lazaro Dubrocq, student, Emma Booker Elementary: I can remember seeing his expression change dramatically.

Andy Card: I was pleased with how the president reacted — he didn't do anything to create fear.

Gordon Johndroe, assistant press secretary, White House: Having been in that room — and it wasn't an issue until the Michael Moore documentary [*Fahrenheit 9/11*] — it would have been odd if he'd jumped up and ran from the room. It didn't seem like an eternity in the room. He finished the book and went back into the hold room.

Karl Rove: When the president walked back into the staff hold, he said, "We're at war — give me the FBI director and the vice president."

Ellen Eckert: As we walked out of the classroom, everyone's pager started going off.

Rep. Adam Putnam: Matt Kirk, our White House liaison, said to Rep. Dan Miller, the other congressman traveling with the presidential party, and me, "We might be the only plane back to D.C. today." We went and got in our vehicle in the motorcade. You could see the windows and hatches of the motorcade open up, the visible expression of the armaments that are always around the president.

Karl Rove: Eddie Marinzel came up to the president — he was sitting in one of those tiny elementary school chairs — and Eddie said, "We need to get you to Air Force One and get you airborne." They'd determined this might be an effort to decapitate the government.

Dave Wilkinson: We ended up with a compromise — Andy Card said we have a whole auditorium full, waiting for the next event. There was no imminent threat there in

Sarasota, so we agreed the president could give a statement before we left.

Brian Montgomery: He went to the auditorium. I remember looking at the students when he said, "America is under attack," and these girls, their faces were saying, *What's he telling us?*

David Sanger, White House correspondent, *New York Times*: I'll never forget the look on his face. He was ashen. He must have known his presidency had changed forever, that it would be measured from that moment forward by what he said, how he said it, and how well he could calm the nation.

Andy Card: He gave a very brief statement, he started off and I cringed right away. He said, "I'm going back to Washington, D.C." I thought, *You don't know that. We don't know that. We don't know where we're going.*

Gordon Johndroe: I told the press we'd be leaving right for the motorcade. We had this joke, mostly with the photographers — no running. No running to catch the president. This time, I told them, "Guys, we're going to have to run. We're going to have to run to the motorcade." Going down the highway, our 15-passenger van was barely keeping up.

Dave Wilkinson: The motorcade left there, and in a very aggressive fashion we got to the aircraft. Intelligence information is always sketchy. When we were riding was the first time we hear there's something vague about a threat to the president. That ratcheted things up.

Rep. Adam Putnam: On the motorcade back, there are all these protesters — it was still all about the recount — signs like, "Shrub stole the election."

Andy Card: In the limo, we were both on our cell phones — he was frustrated because he couldn't reach Don Rumsfeld. It was a very fast limo ride.

Dave Wilkinson: We asked for double motorcade blocks at the intersection. Double and triple blocks. Not just motorcycle officers standing there with their arms up, but vehicles actually blocking the road. Now we're worried about a car bomb. The whole way back, we were using the limos as a shell game, to keep the president safe.

Col. Mark Tillman: As the motorcade's coming in, I've got the 3 and 4 engines already running.

Andy Card: When the limo door opened, I

was struck that the engines on Air Force One were running. That's normally a protocol no-no.

Buzz Buzinski: I was on the back stairs watching as they pull up, wondering, *What's the president thinking? What's Andy thinking?* You could feel the tension. We'd been attacked on our soil. You could see it on their faces — Andy Card, Ari Fleischer, the president.

Mike Morell: They re-searched everyone before we could reboard, not just the press. They searched Andy Card's briefcase, he was standing right in front of me in line. They went through my briefcase — which was filled with all these classified materials — but I wasn't going to object that day.

Eric Draper, presidential photographer: Andy Card said at the top of the stairs, "Take the batteries out of your cell phone. We don't want to be tracked." That brought up: "Are we a target?" I wasn't thinking of that.

Col. Mark Tillman: President Bush comes up the stairs in Sarasota. We watched him come up the stairs every day with that famous Texas swagger. That day, no swagger. He was trucking up the stairs. As soon as the passengers are on board, I fired engines 1 and 2.

Rep. Adam Putnam: There was one van, maybe a press van, that was parked too close to the plane's wing. I remember a Secret Service agent running down the aisle; they opened the back stairs, and he ran down to move the truck. He never made it back on board. They didn't wait for him.

Andy Card: We were starting to roll almost before the president gets into the suite.

Arshad Mohammed, White House correspondent, Reuters: My notes say we took off at 9:54 a.m.

Gordon Johndroe: That thing took off like a rocket. The lamps were shaking because they'd fired up the engines so much.

Karl Rove: The pilot stood that thing on its tail — nose up, tail down, like we were on a roller coaster.

Ellen Eckert: We were climbing so high and so fast I started to wonder if we'd need oxygen masks.

Staff Sgt. William "Buzz" Buzinski: You could see fear and shock. People couldn't believe what they had seen.

Col. Dr. Richard Tubb, presidential physician, White House Medical Unit: The people who are the permanent, apolitical staff — the medical unit, the flight crew, the military aide — they were all well-versed in their emergency action plans, irrespective of who the president was, but we didn't have the relationship yet with the political staff. Over time, you build those relationships, and there hadn't been that much time. That particular transition was so abbreviated, and ugly as the 2000 campaign was, it was even harder. Those guys were still trying to put their government together.

Andy Card: President Bush took office on January 20, 2001 — but the responsibility of being president became a reality when I whispered in his ear. I honestly believe as he contemplated what I said, he realized, "I took an oath: *Preserve, protect, and defend the Constitution.* It's not cutting taxes, it's not No Child Left Behind, it's not immigration, it's the oath." When you pick a president, you want to pick a president who can handle the unexpected. This was the unexpected.

Eric Draper: Soon after we got on board, I see the president pop out of the cabin. He's heading down the aisle. He says, "OK, boys, this is what they pay us for."

First Reactions in D.C.

"THAT'S A STRANGE ACCIDENT"

The attacks in New York interrupted business across Washington, D.C., as officials at the White House, on Capitol Hill, and elsewhere puzzled over what to make of the odd events unfolding up the East Coast.

Gary Walters, chief usher, White House: It was a little bit before 9:00 a.m. when Mrs. Bush came downstairs — I met her at the elevator. As we were walking out, I remember we were talking about Christmas decorations.

Laura Bush, first lady: My Secret Service agent, the head of my detail, Ron Sprinkle, leaned over to me as I got into the car and said, "A plane has hit the World Trade Center."

Brian Gunderson, chief of staff for House Majority Leader Richard Armey (R-Texas): As we walked into our morning staff meeting, I could see on the TV screen — like any congressional office, there were a lot of TV screens around — that a plane had struck one of the World Trade Center towers. We assumed it was a small plane. I thought it was going to be more along the level of like a bad school shooting somewhere — the kind of event that dominates national news, but it doesn't really change what Congress does that day.

Condoleezza Rice, national security adviser, White House: I thought, *Well, that's a strange accident.* I called the president. We talked about how odd it was. Then I went down for my staff meeting.

Adm. James Loy, commandant, U.S. Coast Guard: There was almost a hopeful tone in the early broadcasting, "We're not exactly sure how this happened or why this happened, but, boy, it happened, and it's tragic."

Ted Olson, solicitor general, U.S. Department of Justice: I heard of the disaster occurring at the World Trade Center. There's a television in the back of my office. I turned it on and watched with horror the film being replayed, the airplanes crashing into the World Trade Center. *Barbara's plane, could that be one of those planes?* I made a mental

175

calculation. *Oh, thank goodness, it can't be her plane.* There wasn't enough time for that airplane to have gotten to New York.

Sen. Tom Daschle (D-South Dakota), Senate Majority Leader: Sen. John Glenn, a dear friend, came by. I said, "Did you see that? A pilot flew into the World Trade Center." He said, "Pilots don't fly into buildings. That wasn't a pilot."

Matthew Waxman, staff member, National Security Council, White House: I had started about six weeks earlier as Condi Rice's executive assistant. At about nine o'clock, we would have a daily Situation Room meeting for the national security adviser and all the senior directors. It was during that meeting that the second plane hit.

Mary Matalin, aide to Vice President Dick Cheney: I was with the vice president when the second plane hit, and we knew instantly that this was not an accident.

Condoleezza Rice: It was the moment that changed everything.

Matthew Waxman: We went into full crisis response mode.

176

Rep. Porter Goss (R-Florida), chair, House Intelligence Committee: I was upstairs in the committee room, which was then up in the House attic, with a few senators and congressmen. Sen. Bob Graham and I were hosting a breakfast meeting for Mahmud Ahmed, the head of the Pakistan intelligence service. We'd been in Pakistan the week before and had invited him to Washington to continue the conversation. He was actually sitting there in our inner sanctum when my staff handed me a note saying a plane hit the Trade Towers. Then we got the second report. Ahmed turned absolutely ashen and was escorted out of the room. I think before we even left the room, the words "al-Qaeda" had appeared in our discussion.

Mary Matalin: We went right into work mode. While we were in his office making calls to New York, making calls to the president, making calls wherever they needed to be made, the Secret Service barged into his office.

Dick Cheney, vice president: Radar caught sight of an airliner heading toward the White House at 500 miles an hour.

Lewis "Scooter" Libby, chief of staff to Vice President Dick Cheney: We learn that a plane is five miles out and has dropped below 500 feet and can't be found; it's missing. You look at your watch and think, *Hmmm, five miles out, 500 miles an hour. Tick, tick, tick.*

Dick Cheney: My Secret Service agent said, "Sir, we have to leave now." He grabbed me and propelled me out of my office, down the hall, and into the underground shelter in the White House.

Mary Matalin: My jaw dropped and the jaws of my colleagues dropped because we had never seen anything like that.

Condoleezza Rice: The Secret Service came in and they said, "You have got to go to the bunker." I remember being driven along, almost propelled along. We had no idea where it was safe and where it wasn't. We didn't think the bunker of the White House was safe at that point.

Dick Cheney: They practice this — you move, whether you want to be moved or not, you're going.

Mary Matalin: There was a call to evacuate — initially we were ordered to evacuate to the mess, which is the lowest floor accessible in the West Wing. We all sat around there for some minutes. Then out of nowhere came this call: "Run, run, run, they're headed for the White House, run for your life!" I was in a purple pencil skirt and red patent leather Charles Jordan spiked heels. Not the best outfit to run for your life in.

Gary Walters: The Secret Service officers started yelling, "Get out, get out, everybody get out of the White House grounds." I remember early on, the chaos. People running, screaming. Fear was in my mind.

Rafael Lemaitre, staff, Office of National Drug Control Policy, White House: I wasn't sure where to go. All I knew is that I should run away from the White House, and I sure as hell wasn't getting on Metro [the subway] either. I briskly walked northbound on 17th Street. An image I'll never forget was of a blind homeless man, standing on his regular corner near the Farragut North Metro exit, begging for change. He seemed oblivious to the fact people were rushing the opposite way of the regular morning rush hour pedestrian traffic. He was still asking for change. It was an absurd image.

Christine Limerick, housekeeper, White House: The look on the faces of the Secret Service agents who were told that they had to stay — I will never forget that because we had at least the opportunity to flee.

Ian Rifield, special agent, U.S. Secret Service: We were fairly confident that plane was going to hit us. The supervisor in the [Secret Service's] Joint Operations Center basically said, "Anybody who survives the impact, we'll go to an alternate center, and we'll continue." It wasn't a joke.

James Davis, supervisory special agent, FBI Headquarters, Washington, D.C.: There was this overwhelming feeling that we were on the run. They evacuated the building; it was so frustrating because agents want to do something. I stayed behind and realized suddenly I was all alone on the fifth floor. It's just me. I wondered if our building was going to be hit next; I thought, *I wonder if this is going to hurt?*

At the White House, Secret Service agents hustled the vice president and other top aides into the bunker underneath the North Lawn, a facility known as the Presidential Emergency Operations Center (PEOC) that dates back to World War II and is meant to protect the president from an incoming attack.

Dick Cheney: A few moments later, I found myself in a fortified White House command post somewhere down below.

Commander Anthony Barnes, deputy director, Presidential Contingency Programs, White House: Vice President Cheney arrived in the bunker, along with his wife. The PEOC is not a single chamber; there are three or four rooms. The operations chamber is where my watch team was fielding phone calls. Then there's the conference room area where Mr. Cheney and Condi Rice were — that's the space that had the TV monitors, telephones, and whatever else.

Mary Matalin: It took a while for everybody to actually get to that area. It hadn't been used for its intended purpose — which was to be a bomb shelter — since its inception.

Commander Anthony Barnes: Shortly thereafter, I looked around and there was Condi Rice, there was [White House Communications Director] Karen Hughes, there was Mary Matalin, there was [Transportation Secretary] Norm Mineta. Mr. Mineta put up on one of the TV monitors a feed of where every airplane across the entire nation was. We looked at that thing — there must have been thousands of little airplane symbols on it.

Mary Matalin: The vice president was squarely seated in the center. It was emotional, but it was really work, work, work. We were trying to locate first and foremost all the planes. Identify the planes. Ground all the planes.

Commander Anthony Barnes: Things really began to happen very fast.

Matthew Waxman: I was still in the Situation Room, and I got a message saying Condi Rice had requested I come down to work with her in the PEOC. I wasn't really sure what it was like above ground in the White House. I wasn't sure anybody had shut the national security adviser's office. During the day, there are open safes and highly classified information sitting on her desk or my desk. Perhaps the scariest moment for me was when I went back up to check on the office, standing by myself in the national security adviser's office, realizing the White House had been totally evacuated. For all I could tell, I might have been alone in the West Wing. That was the moment at which it most hit me that perhaps I was in some grave personal danger.

Commander Anthony Barnes: Every one of my guys in the watch room have at least two phones to their ears. I was talking to the Pentagon Operations Center on one line. I had a line to FEMA [Federal Emergency Management Agency], and people are asking us for directions on what to do and how to do it.

Matthew Waxman: The TV feeds would occasionally go down. The vice president was pretty ticked off about that. There were technical glitches that day. One of my jobs was to stand with a phone in my hand to make sure that there was an open line between the PEOC and some of the other national security officials. So that if the vice president or the national security adviser needed to speak to one of them, we had a direct line out with me at one end and a counterpart on the other.

Commander Anthony Barnes: That first hour was mass confusion because there was so much erroneous information. It was hard to tell what was fact and what wasn't. We couldn't confirm much of this stuff, so we had to take it on face value until proven otherwise.

A few miles from the White House, across the Potomac River, the military's leadership at the Pentagon — including the Office of the Secretary of Defense and the service branches' Joint Chiefs of Staff — realized the nation was at war.

Waxman, left, with Cheney in the bunker.

Donald Rumsfeld, secretary of defense: I was at a breakfast with congressmen and someone came in and said that a plane had hit a World Trade Tower. The breakfast ended, and I came back for my intelligence briefing. I was sitting there when someone said that a second plane had hit the other tower.

Col. Matthew Klimow, executive assistant to the vice chair of the Joint Chiefs of Staff, Gen. Richard Myers, Pentagon: My first inclination was to turn around and draw the draperies shut in the office, thinking maybe there'd be a bomb blast. I was worried about flying glass. Every time I think about that I think of how futile it would have been if the plane had hit my part of the building.

Victoria "Torie" Clarke, assistant secretary of defense for public affairs: We went in to talk to the secretary, who was at his stand-up desk. We were saying, "Here's what's going on, and what we know. The command center is going to start getting spun up." He said something like, "Well, let's take a look at my schedule, maybe we will have to move something." His special assistant said, "Everything is coming off your schedule — this is your schedule today."

Joe Wassel, communications officer, Office of the Secretary of Defense: We all started thinking, *What's next? What are we doing? What can be done?* We had a discussion and my coworker actually said, "We could be next," meaning the Pentagon.

Staff Sgt. Christopher Braman, chef, U.S. Army: My wife called about 9:25, frantic on the telephone, and told me a plane had hit the Trade Center in New York. I remember reading that morning there was an Afghan Northern Alliance general that was assassinated over the weekend. I told my wife, "You know I bet you that had something to do with it." Then I realized my wife didn't want to hear that — she just wanted to know

185

I was OK. I told her, "Not to worry. I love you."

AMERICAN AIRLINES FLIGHT 77
"BLIP, BLIP, BLIP. GONE."

At 8:20 a.m. American Airlines Flight 77, a decade-old Boeing 757, had taken off from Dulles International Airport, outside Washington, D.C., en route to Los Angeles. It carried six crew and 58 passengers, just a third of its capacity. The last routine communication from the plane came at 8:51 a.m., and by 8:54 it had deviated from its intended course, turned south, and then headed back toward Washington.

Ted Olson, solicitor general, U.S. Department of Justice: One of the secretaries rushed in and said, "Barbara's on the phone." I jumped for the phone, so glad to hear Barbara's voice. Then she told me, "Our plane has been hijacked." I had two conversations — my memory tends to mix the two of them up because of the emotion of the events. We spoke for a minute or two, then the phone was cut off. Then she got through again, and we spoke for another two or three or four minutes. She told me that she had been

187

herded to the back of the plane. She mentioned that they had used knives and box cutters to hijack the plane. We then both reassured one another — this plane was still up in the air, this plane was still flying. This was going to come out OK. She said, "I love you." She sounded very, very calm.

Dan Creedon, departure controller, TRACON, Reagan National Airport, Washington, D.C.: We were trying to juggle big decisions. There was some sketchiness and some miscommunication back and forth, and some slowness in realizing that we were dealing with an additional hijack, because by gosh, we already had two.

Ted Olson: I was in shock and horrified. I reassured her that I thought everything was going to be OK. I was pretty sure everything was not going to be OK. After the first conversation, I had called our command center at the Department of Justice to alert them there was another hijacked plane, that my wife was on it, and she was capable of communicating. I wanted to find out where the plane was. She reported to me that she could see houses. We segued back and forth between expressions of feeling for one another and this effort to exchange information. Then the phone went dead.

Ben Sliney, national operations manager, FAA Command Center, Herndon, Virginia: There had never been a situation where hijackers ever flew the plane, which created the biggest paradox for us on that day, trying to figure out what was going on — how could a hijacker force the pilot, either by holding a gun or a knife to his or her head, force them to fly into the building?

Maj. Gen. Larry Arnold, commander of the 1st Air Force, NORAD, Tyndall Air Force Base, Florida: Our fighter aircraft were getting close to Washington, D.C., when American 77 came back on radar scope. I think the tape showed that it was about three minutes before it hit the Pentagon.

Dan Creedon: I'll never forget — it was a military transport out of Andrews Air Force Base. Gofer Zero-Six was the call sign. He was making a left turn out of Andrews, going right over Washington National Airport, southeast of the Pentagon, when American 77 was acquired by the Dulles approach controller. I said to the guy working the C-130 out of Andrews, "Hey, you'd better call traffic on that guy because these two guys are head to head." He said, "Traffic, at 11 o'clock, four miles, do you see anybody out there?"

Lt. Col. Steven O'Brien, pilot, C-130 known as "Gofer Zero-Six," Minnesota Air National Guard: I noticed an aircraft at about our 10 o'clock position, higher than us. I could see that he was descending. He made a fairly steep, banked turn in front of us.

Dan Creedon: The pilot came right back and said, "Yes, sir, an American seven-five-seven turning southeast bound." I'll never forget — I was like, "What?" Maybe I was the slowest guy on the planet that day, but I really didn't understand that was a hijacked aircraft until it hit the Pentagon.

Lt. Col. Kevin Nasypany, mission crew commander, NEADS, Rome, New York: I got a report that Reagan Tower thought there was an aircraft coming in, about six miles outside. I was looking at the scope, and the D.C. airspace was very similar to New York or the Boston area — a lot of aircraft.

Ted Olson: I called some people, maybe because I had to share the dread that was living inside me. I called my mother and I called my son.

Danielle O'Brien, air traffic controller, Washington Dulles International Airport, Virginia: I noticed the aircraft. It was

190

an unidentified plane to the southwest of Dulles, moving at a very high rate of speed. The speed, the maneuverability, the way that he turned, we all thought in the radar room — all of us experienced air traffic controllers — that it was a military plane. You don't fly a 757 in that manner. It's unsafe.

Lt. Col. Steven O'Brien: They requested that we follow this airplane. I don't think they said "chase," but "do you think you could turn and follow this airplane?" That was strange. I had never had a request like that in all my entire career of flying. It was very, very strange, but I still matter-of-factly said, "Sure, we can follow that airplane." It became a losing proposition because this airplane was going faster. We could still see the glint off the wingtips.

Ted Olson: I dreaded the realization that what had happened to the airplanes in New York was going to happen to her plane.

Lt. Col. Dawne Deskins, mission crew commander, NEADS, Rome, New York: I had the scope focused in on the D.C. area and got blips of this aircraft that appeared to be going in a turn around D.C. I probably got six or seven radar returns on it before it faded and was gone. I got this feeling in the pit of my stomach.

Danielle O'Brien: We waited, and we waited. Your heart was beating out of your chest waiting to hear what's happened.

Robert Hunor, contractor, Radian, Inc., Pentagon courtyard: National Airport is right next to the Pentagon, so there's a huge amount of aircraft traffic going overhead. I remember when we walked outside it was dead silent. We were talking, and I was like, "They must have shut down the airport." All of a sudden I heard a faint sound — like an engine spooling up. You could hear the plane flooring its throttles. I had begun to say, "I thought that they shut the airport," and then the plane hit.

Mike Walter, senior correspondent, *USA Today Live:* I was stuck in traffic [near the Pentagon]. I rolled down the window. That's when I heard the jet. I looked up and saw its underbelly, then it banked, and it began to dive. It was unbelievable.

Craig Bryan, engineering technician, Pentagon Navy Annex, Arlington, Virginia: I can still hear the jet engine. The throttle was wide open; it was screaming.

Lt. Col. Kevin Nasypany: I see one blip, two blips, radar only, blip, blip, blip. Gone.

Lt. Col. Steven O'Brien: We saw this huge fireball. I reported to air traffic control — I said something to the effect, "That airplane's down. It's crashed."

Dennis Smith, maintenance inspector, Pentagon Building Manager's Office: There was a big, giant ball of fire, red and black. The heat hit us like from a barn fire. Then parts started flying out of the sky.

Ted Olson: After the second phone call, we kept watching television. Not too long later, we could see over the television screen smoke coming from the Pentagon. I knew in my heart that it was her flight.

Gary Walters, chief usher, White House: I heard a loud muffled thud. I looked over the tree canopy to my right in the direction of the Pentagon, and I could see the big plume of black smoke with flames in the middle of it.

Rosemary Dillard, Washington, D.C., base manager, American Airlines, and wife of Flight 77 passenger Eddie Dillard: My administrative manager came up to me, grabbed me, and said, "Rosemary, one of those was our crew — it was Flight 77." I turned and looked at her and said, "It couldn't have been Flight 77 — I just put

Eddie on Flight 77. It cannot be Flight 77." She had the name of the crew. I knew the kids, the flight attendants. I went in and contacted my regional manager and my VP, and I called my friend who works in scheduling to see what plane it was. It was Flight 77.

Lt. Col. Steven O'Brien: We proceeded on a little bit farther — that's when the silhouette of the Pentagon became apparent. Then I realized that it had crashed into the Pentagon. And I know no pilot would ever do something like that. Things were really going haywire.

Danielle O'Brien: The Washington National Airport controllers came over our speakers and said, "Dulles, hold all of our inbound traffic. The Pentagon's been hit."

The Third Plane

"PLANE INTO PENTAGON. WE NEED ALL HELP."

Across the Potomac from Washington, D.C., the riverbank in Arlington, Virginia, is dominated by the massive concrete Pentagon, the global headquarters of the U.S. military and the offices of the secretary of defense. It is also the largest low-rise office building in the world, and home to a daily population of workers and visitors of around 35,000, all protected by its own police force, which was known in 2001 as the Defense Protective Service.

In September 2001, the building was undergoing its first full-scale renovation since its construction during World War II. Each of its five wedges was being updated with new bomb-proof windows, better wiring, and better fire-suppression systems. Staff and personnel had just started to move back into the renovated parts of "Wedge 1."

At 9:37 a.m., American Airlines Flight 77 crashed into Wedge 1, the western side of the Pentagon, at 530 miles per hour, skimming so low over the nearby highways that it knocked *down five streetlights. The force of the impact sent the plane through the first three of the Pentagon's five rings of corridors, penetrating the building the length of more than a full football field. Instantly, 400,000 square feet of the Pentagon erupted in flames.*

Robert Hunor, contractor, Radian, Inc., Pentagon courtyard: The plane hit between the second or third floor, E-Ring. The innermost ring is A, and the outermost ring is E. There's five — everything is five: five floors, five rings, five sides. The fireball — you could feel the heat on your face. It didn't sound like an explosion in the movies. It sounded like a dumpster being dropped off a truck at 2:00 in the morning. It was really, really loud, and then the fireball was about five stories high — as tall as the building. We stared in disbelief.

Scott Kocher, contractor, SAIC, Pentagon: We were standing there watching the events at the Trade Center when all of a sudden there was a loud boom. It sounded like somebody had dropped a large safe on the floor above us. I'd say not more than 60 seconds to two minutes later, there was a report on the news saying that the Pentagon had been rocked by an explosion. Obviously

196

we all turned and looked at each other, because we were in the Pentagon.

Lt. Michael Nesbitt, Defense Protective Service, Pentagon: All of a sudden the wall shook. It was pretty loud. I've been in this building at all hours and heard crashes and bangs. I've heard it all. I looked at the burning towers on TV and said, "Oh no, oh no." We had been hit, although I had no idea it was a plane.

Steven Carter, assistant building manager, Pentagon: The fire alarm system for the building was sounding in a massive area of Wedge 1 — there was smoke and fire and water flow from the sprinkler system. I thought possibly it had been a truck bomb or briefcase bomb. The number of fire alarms coming in showed 355 alarms and climbing, so I was leaning more toward a truck bomb.

The plane hit an area of the Pentagon that primarily housed the army's personnel offices and the Navy Operation Center. Inside the affected offices — transformed instantly into fiery, smoke-filled infernos — personnel struggled to escape.

Sheila Denise Moody, accountant, Resource Services Office: September 11th,

2001, was my first day here at the Pentagon. There was also another lady who started work with me that same day, Louise. She and I were both laying out our personal items and getting acquainted with the job.

Louise Rogers, accountant, Resource Services Office, Pentagon: Our office was in the section that had been completed with renovations. Everything was brand new, nice, and neat.

Sheila Denise Moody: Louise came to my desk and told me about the World Trade Center. She left my cubicle and went around to the front of the office, toward the portion of the offices that faced the window, and went to fax some paperwork.

Louise Rogers: I started the fax machine — put the papers in the fax, dialed the number — and at the exact moment that I hit the start key, the plane hit.

Sheila Denise Moody: A burst of hot air hit my face. The burst was so strong — it had so much force — that it forced me to close my eyes. When I opened my eyes there was a ball of fire shooting right to the right of me. I was in shock. The building was shaking — there was debris and things falling from the ceiling. The ceiling opened up, and I was covered in some liquid. To this day I still really don't know what it was.

Louise Rogers: At first, I thought I'd blown up the fax machine. It's like the initial stage of shock — I thought, *My God, what did I do?* Then I realized it wasn't me. I smelled the jet fuel. Being around the air force for 30-some years in one way or another, I recognized jet fuel when I smelled it.

Lt. Col. Rob Grunewald, information management officer, U.S. Army, Pentagon: We had no idea about New York. We were in an enclosed conference room. We hadn't seen or heard anything about the events unfolding. At 9:38 I felt a low rumble, the floor began to shake, and then there was an explosion. A big fireball came through the ceiling, and the wall in front of me fractured. The ceiling — one of those Styrofoam-type ceilings — exploded into a million pieces, and the room instantaneously went dark.

Lt. Col. Ted Anderson, legislative liaison officer, U.S. Army, Pentagon: It was a loud roar — the building literally shook — and there was a sucking sound, which I believe was the oxygen escaping as the jet fuel poured into the corridors right down the hall from us and ignited, taking all of the oxygen out of the air. Our ceiling caved in. The lights went out, but the phone was still working. I was on the phone with my wife. I was a little stunned, just for an initial second, and then I said, "Listen, we have been bombed. I have to go." I hung up the phone. I screamed for everybody in the office to get out. I got up and moved, and that was the last time I was ever in that cubicle.

John Yates, security manager, U.S. Army, Pentagon: I didn't hear a thing. Suddenly there was this tremendous explosion, and I remember a ball of fire coming from my left. I was blown through the air, and when I landed the room was black. Totally black. There was furniture strewn everywhere. It was hot — the smoke came down to within a foot of the floor. I don't know how long that took — maybe a minute? Two minutes? I didn't have a concept of time.

Philip Smith, branch chief, U.S. Army, Pentagon: I was standing in front of a copy machine making some photocopies to prepare for a meeting. That copy machine is probably what saved my life, because it was between me and the incoming flight of the plane. Within a few feet of where I was there, two teammates were killed. They were in cubicles that were just eight or ten feet from me.

John Yates: It was pure black. You were in a

black room, you didn't know where you are. What's the first thing you do? You put your hands out to try to find where you are. Everything I touched burned me.

Lt. Col. Rob Grunewald: Now we had a problem. There were a dozen or so of us in this room, and the room was instantly dark, no lights, no windows. Nobody knew what happened.

Similar to the experience at the World Trade Center, the massive scale of the Pentagon and its unique shape meant that while many occupants felt the explosion, most didn't immediately realize either what happened or the gravity of the situation. For staff in the other parts of the building, including Secretary of Defense Donald Rumsfeld, the impact was felt — though few guessed what had caused it.

Joe Wassel, communications officer, Office of the Secretary of Defense: Something had struck the building. The first words out of my mouth were "That wasn't good." I got up and started walking pretty briskly — but walking — to the secretary of defense's office.

Donald Rumsfeld, secretary of defense: We were sitting in my office when the plane hit the building. The building shook and the tables jumped. I assumed it was a bomb.

Victoria "Torie" Clarke, assistant secretary of defense for public affairs: I thought there must have been a car bomb. What's extraordinary to me is that we knew that two commercial airliners had hit the Trade Center, a terrorist attack, and smart people were guessing it was al-Qaeda. Yet when something bad happened here, it didn't occur to us that it was another airliner. That's how unfathomable it was. It never occurred to us that it was another plane.

Col. Matthew Klimow, executive assistant to the vice chair of the Joint Chiefs of Staff, Gen. Richard Myers, Pentagon: There was pandemonium in the corridors. People were running down the halls yelling. Then, on the conference call, we were notified by Pentagon security that a plane had hit. I immediately told General [Hugh] Shelton [chairman of the Joint Chiefs], who was on his way to Europe, and was on the other phone, "Sir, we've been hit here by an airplane. Turn your airplane around and get back to the United States."

William Haynes, general counsel, Department of Defense: All of a sudden things really sped up.

Adm. Edmund Giambastiani, senior military assistant, Office of the Secretary of Defense: The secretary opened his door and asked me what the hell was happening. I said it sounded like an explosion, and it sounded like it was in the building, and he needed to get out of there.

Aubrey Davis, officer, Protective Service Unit, Defense Protective Service, Pentagon: The secretary came out the door and asked what was going on. I told him we were getting a report that an aircraft had hit the Mall side of the building. He looked at me and immediately went toward the Mall. I said, "Sir, do you understand, that's the area of impact, the Mall." He kept going, so I told Officer [Gilbert] Oldach to come on. I saw Mr. Kisling, Joe Wassel, and Kevin Brown sitting in the personnel security office, and I waved for them to come with us.

Donald Rumsfeld: I went out to see what was amiss.

On the other side of the Pentagon, away from the secretary of defense's suite, officials, including the Defense Protective Service, the Arlington County Police Department, and the Arlington County Fire Department — which had responsibility for emergencies at the Pentagon

— launched a massive rescue effort, evacuated the building, tended to the injured, and secured a sensitive military installation, even as FBI agents rushed to examine the largest crime scene in the history of the capital region.

Jennifer Meyers, dispatcher, Arlington County Emergency Communications Center: I recall the message on my work pager said, "Plane into Pentagon. We need all help."

John Jester, chief, Defense Protective Service, Pentagon: I immediately ran down to the Operations Center to assess what was going on. The alarms went off, the phones were ringing.

Lt. Michael Nesbitt, Defense Protective Service, Pentagon: Chief Jester came in and told me to get on the "Big Voice" [P.A. system] and tell people to evacuate. I said, "All personnel in the Pentagon need to evacuate. You need to evacuate now."

Lt. Col. Ted Anderson, legislative liaison officer, U.S. Army, Pentagon: I started barking orders to get out of the building. Here I am, dressed for legislative business with Congress — I've got on a nice suit with a striped shirt, tie, and suspenders — and

I'm screaming at full-bird colonels and general officers to move out of the building, barking orders, screaming. They listened. They tried to get out of the Mall entrance, but the guards mistakenly thought that they were under attack from outside, so they secured that entrance. They had taken out most of their small arms, machine guns, etc. It looked like they were preparing to defend the doors there. So I started moving people toward the center of the Pentagon. This all took place within two minutes.

Capt. Randall Harper, Defense Protective Service, Pentagon: People were hollering, "Get out, get out. Run for your life." I was told by people in the Center Court that they saw people run out there on fire.

John F. Irby, director, Federal Facilities Division, Real Estate and Facilities Directorate, Washington Headquarters Services, Pentagon: You could see the terror on people's faces as they left.

Lt. Robert Medairos, Arlington County Police Department: Pretty much everything in that first half hour was chaos. Everybody was coming from everywhere to help.

Mike Walter, senior correspondent, *USA Today Live:* I remember the soundtrack of that day, it was this siren. It was as if it was looped — it was sirens, sirens, sirens.

The iconic Twin Towers presided over New York's skyline for nearly thirty years.

On September 10, 2001, cameras placed on the 91st floor of the North Tower by artist-in-residence Monika Bravo captured an intense thunderstorm passing through New York City. Bravo later titled the video "Uno nunca muere la vispera"—"you cannot die on the eve of your death."

A view of the North Tower after American Airlines Flight 11 was flown into the building at 8:46 a.m. on September 11, 2001.

One of the 92 people onboard American Airlines 11 was Betty Ong, a flight attendant who called the airline's reservation line to report the hijacking.

North Tower survivor Richard Eichen's temporary building identification pass. Not having the key to his office on the 90th floor that morning saved his life.

By 9:00 a.m., nearly every news channel was broadcasting live footage of the North Tower on fire. Viewers and anchors alike were shocked at 9:03 a.m. to see United Airlines Flight 175, the second hijacked flight of the day, crash into the South Tower.

Within 20 minutes of the first crash, both of the Twin Towers were in flames, and it was clear that the crashes were deliberate. In the North Tower, floors 93 to 99 were directly impacted; in the South Tower, floors 78 to 83 saw widespread devastation.

President Bush was in the middle of a press event at Emma Booker Elementary School in Sarasota, Florida, when he was informed that America was under attack.

Vice President Cheney, in Washington, initially watched the events unfold from his White House office; moments later, he was rushed out by Secret Service.

Sep. 12, 2001, 17:37:19   impact

Sep. 12, 2001, 17:37:22   #3 impact zoomed

Sep. 12, 2001, 17:37:23   #4 impact

At 9:37 a.m., American Airlines Flight 77 crashed into Wedge 1 of the Pentagon in Arlington, Virginia. Security cameras captured the resulting impact. The date on the surveillance camera was mistakenly set a day off to read September 12.

The stairwells of both towers filled up as the morning unfolded, with workers heading down and firefighters heading up.

Mike Kehoe, who would ultimately survive the day, was one of many firefighters who made their way up the stairs in the North Tower to evacuate the higher floors.

AP photographer Richard Drew captured one of the most horrifying images of 9/11 at 9:41 a.m., a photo from the North Tower that came to be known as "The Falling Man." The man has never been positively identified.

At 9:59 a.m., the South Tower of
the World Trade Center collapsed.
The North Tower followed at
10:28 a.m., 102 minutes after
the first plane hit the building,
shocking onlookers who did not
believe it was possible for the
Towers to completely fall.

New York Mayor Rudolph Giuliani immediately made his way downtown, passing St. Vincent's Hospital with his team.

After the Twin Towers fell, lower Manhattan was enveloped in ash and smoke, forcing thousands to leave Manhattan on foot over the Brooklyn Bridge.

About 30 minutes after it was hit, Wedge 1 of the Pentagon collapsed. Nearly everyone rescued from the wreckage was found within that half hour.

As military and civilian workers rushed to help, firefighters struggled to fight the raging inferno inside the building.

Secretary of Defense Donald Rumsfeld was in a different wedge of the Pentagon when the attack occurred, but quickly made his way to the crash site to evaluate the damage and offer assistance.

The FBI also made their way to Arlington to secure evidence and debris for the eventual investigation into the day's events.

The White House bunker, known as the PEOC, filled up throughout the morning.

By midmorning, Vice President Cheney and Secretary of State Condoleezza Rice had been secured and brought to the bunker, where they coordinated with officials on Capitol Hill and elsewhere, many of whom were fearful another attack was imminent.

As officials in Washington gathered on the ground, President Bush and White House Chief of Staff Andrew Card found themselves aboard Air Force One with little idea of where to go.

After the towers collapsed in New York, taking citizens out of the city by water was one of the only viable options for officials to sanction.

As thousands of people lined piers trying to escape, ferries and private boats were commandeered as shuttles, resulting in the largest maritime evacuation since World War II.

A little bit after 10:00 a.m., United Airlines Flight 93 crashed into the soft ground of an old mine in Shanksville, Pennsylvania, after passengers thwarted the hijackers' suspected plan to attack Washington, D.C.

Responders from Somerset County immediately rushed to the scene, forced to improvise their response to an unprecedented event.

As teams arrived at the crash site, they were horrified to realize that there was no one to rescue, bringing efforts to a brief standstill.

Teams of FBI agents and responders shifted their attention to recovering evidence from the impact zone.

One of the only intact remains of United Flight 93.

NASA astronaut Frank Culbertson was the only American not on planet Earth for September 11. He documented the view of New York post-attack from the International Space Station.

On Capitol Hill

"THERE BEGAN THE CHAOS"

Across Capitol Hill, morning meetings were interrupted by the news alerts that an emergency situation was also unfolding at the Pentagon. Staff, representatives, and senators quickly realized that what appeared as a tragic accident in New York had spread into their own backyard — and that they themselves, under the dome of the U.S. Capitol, might be a target.

John Feehery, press secretary to Speaker Dennis Hastert (R-Illinois): Amid all the tumult, we were called down to the Speaker's office. The sergeant at arms gave us a briefing. It was a very strange, surreal experience because the sergeant at arms was telling us that everything was going to be fine, and then we turned on the TV and saw another plane hit the World Trade Towers. It was one of those mornings when everything was jumbled up.

Brian Gunderson, chief of staff for House Majority Leader Richard Armey (R-Texas): All of a sudden, one of the plain-clothes policemen — he was part of the Speaker's security detail — stood up and said, "Look!" He pointed out the window. He apparently saw, if not the fireball, at least the column of smoke rising in the distance from the Pentagon.

Brian Gaston, policy director for House Majority Leader Richard Armey (R-Texas): The meeting broke up right then and there.

Tish Schwartz, chief clerk, House Judiciary Committee: I froze. You could literally see the smoke billowing up. Everybody was numb: *Oh my God, what's going on?* There were no bells going off, there was no panic, screaming, anything like that. Everybody was very calm, but stunned, and in disbelief. The word "surreal" is used a lot, but that's what it was.

Sen. Tom Daschle (D-South Dakota), Senate Majority Leader: And there began the chaos.

Rep. Dennis Hastert (R-Illinois), House Speaker: I had two phones on my desk — a secure phone to the White House and this regular old red phone that I took all my calls on. All of a sudden, I see the red phone flashing, and I said, "Well, they probably put the call through on the red phone." I picked it up, figuring it was the vice president. There was a guy on the other end of the line, "What are you guys doing up there on Capitol Hill . . . taxes are too high . . . pollution all over the country," on and on, ranting and raving. I said, "Whoa, wait a minute. Who is this?" He said, "Never mind, who is this?" I said, "This is the Speaker of the House — I think you have the wrong number."

Rep. Porter Goss (R-Florida), chair, House Intelligence Committee: I raced down the stairs to brief the Speaker. I found him in his office staring down the Mall at the smoke from the Pentagon. I said we had to evacuate immediately. He agreed, saying, "On the way out, I want to open the House for a quick session and a prayer."

Rep. Dennis Hastert: I decided to cancel Congress.

Rep. Porter Goss: We walked onto the House Floor about 10 minutes before 10, and the parliamentarian said we couldn't open the House yet because the call was for 10:00 a.m. I turned around to say something to the Speaker, but he wasn't there. He was being removed by security to a secure location.

Rep. Dennis Hastert: All of a sudden, two of my security guys — one on each side of me — picked me up and whisked me away. I said, "What's going on?" They said, "We think there's a fourth plane and we think it's headed for the Capitol."

Rep. Porter Goss: I told the parliamentarian, "We're doing this now, because we're going to evacuate." There was no question we had to get out of there.

Father Gerry Creedon, guest chaplain, House of Representatives: The House chaplain, Reverend Dan Coughlin, advised me that I would do the opening invocation, and then Congress would be dismissed. I got a piece of paper and wrote — using his shoulder as a desk — a new prayer. Porter Goss said to me, "I don't care what your prayer is, as long as it's brief." I read the prayer, the gavel was hit, and the House was dismissed.

Rep. Dennis Hastert: People were told to get out — run. There were 5,000 people that work in or around the Capitol.

Sen. Tom Daschle: There was a mad

scramble, literally running out of the Capitol building. I saw young staff, I even saw Sen. Robert C. Byrd, carrying a couple of books, and having some difficulty walking quickly, but nonetheless evacuating.

Julia Rogers, page, U.S. House: I was really scared. You could sense the tension in the police officers. They weren't their normal selves. You could see the fear on their faces and in their eyes, and that further frightened me.

Rep. Porter Goss: There we were, standing at the bottom of the steps of the Capitol wondering if the building would be there the next time we came back.

Brian Gunderson: I remember seeing a network news crew, and the producer was frantically telling his crew to get that camera pointed at the Capitol Dome. He had assumed — as we all did at that time — that there might be another jetliner heading for the Capitol, and he thought it was important that his camera was in a position to get the shot of that jet smashing into the Capitol Dome.

Tyler Rogers, page, U.S. House: One of the page responsibilities is delivering flags — when you fly them over the Capitol, the pages

211

pick them up and deliver them to the members' offices. We have these big mail carts full of flags. One of our colleagues was on flag duty that morning, and she had her cart full of flags. She was told to evacuate and she didn't have anywhere to put the flags. She's rolling down the street with this gigantic thing. She was one of the smallest pages, but she has this gigantic cart full of flags. She was like, "I can't leave these. I couldn't ditch them."

Rep. Dennis Hastert: I was whisked down the elevator. The next thing I know, I'm in the back of a Suburban, headed to Andrews Air Force Base. It was bizarre. I remember this car was just going a hundred miles an hour, very fast.

Brian Gunderson: There were very elaborate plans, of course, for the Speaker, because the Speaker's in the line of presidential succession. The majority leader is not. His security detail very quickly hustled him out of the Capitol, then they got into his official vehicle and left. But he didn't have any particular place to go. There was no assigned relocation position.

Rep. Porter Goss: There wasn't any plan. You've now taken 535 of the most important

212

people in the country and put them out on the lawn.

Rep. Martin Frost (D-Texas), chair, House Democratic Caucus: No one told us to either stay or to leave. That was the interesting thing. Each of us acted on our own. My instant reaction was to get away from the Capitol. We were as much in the dark as anyone else.

FLIGHT 93 IN PERIL

"I'M ON AN AIRPLANE
THAT'S BEEN HIJACKED"

The day's chaos then jumped to the skies over Ohio. The fourth — and, as it turned out, final — attack of September 11th unfolded aboard United Airlines Flight 93, a Boeing 757 aircraft scheduled to fly from Newark International Airport to San Francisco. The flight had pushed back from the gate at 8:01 a.m. — its final passenger, Mark Bingham, had only barely made the flight, boarding at 7:55. Due to airport congestion, Flight 93 sat on the runway in Newark for 41 minutes and took off at 8:42 a.m., much later than scheduled. It carried 40 people — seven crew and 33 passengers.

Unlike the other three hijacked planes, there were only four terrorists aboard Flight 93; the person believed by U.S. officials to be the fifth intended hijacker, Mohammed al-Qahtani, was turned away by immigration authorities in early August when he tried to enter the U.S. in Orlando.

United Airlines dispatcher Ed Ballinger messaged the planes he was overseeing at 9:19 a.m. to warn of possible cockpit intrusions: "Beware any cockpit intrusion — two a/c [aircraft] hit World Trade Center." Flight 93's pilot, Capt. Jason Dahl, sent a message back at 9:26 a.m.: "Ed, confirm latest mssg plz." Two minutes later, First Officer LeRoy Homer transmitted a brief radio call, where he can be heard shouting, "Mayday! Mayday! Get out!"

John Werth, air traffic controller, Cleveland Air Route Traffic Control Center: United 93 came onto my scope, and called, and I acknowledged him. It was nothing out of the ordinary. He checked in, "Good morning Cleveland," the usual. The next transmission we got from United was unintelligible. It sounded like a life-and-death struggle. It was some screaming and some guttural sounds.

The first official report of trouble arrived from the plane at 9:36 a.m. — one minute before American Airlines Flight 77 hit the Pentagon — when a flight attendant phoned United's San Francisco maintenance office to say they had been hijacked. In the following minutes, as word spread through air traffic control, passengers and crew members used the in-seat Airfones and their cell phones to call their airline authorities and loved ones — and learned, to their horror, about what had already occurred on the ground below.

John Werth, air traffic controller, Cleveland Air Route Traffic Control Center: I looked at my partner, who sits to the right of me. He had this pretty wide-eyed look on him. I said, "Dave, did that garbled radio transmission sound the same to you as it did to me?" He stared at me and nodded his head. I said, "We better find out who it is," because we had probably seven or eight aircraft on the frequency at the time. I suspected it was either United 93 or Delta 1989. Right after that happened, United 93 had gone down about 300 feet on his altitude readout.

Stacey Taylor Parham, air traffic control specialist, Cleveland Air Route Traffic Control Center: That flight all of a sudden started descending, and then it climbed. It just left its flight path and left its altitude.

John Werth: I asked the flight in front of United 93, "Did you hear an aircraft transmission that sounded like screaming?" He said, "Yes, we heard that." A small business jet also said he heard it.

Deena Burnett, San Ramon, California, wife of United Flight 93 passenger Tom Burnett: The phone rang and it was Tom's mother. Her first question was, "Do you know where Tom is?" The phone rang in on call-waiting, and I said, "Oh, let me go — that may be him." I saw on the caller ID that it was Tom's cell phone. I was relieved, thinking that if he was on his cell phone, he was in the airport somewhere and was fine. I said, "Tom, are you okay?" He said, "No, I'm not. I'm on an airplane that's been hijacked. It's United Flight 93." He told me what was going on. "They've already knifed a guy. I think one of them has a gun." I started asking questions, and he said, "Deena, just listen." He went over the information again and said, "Please call the authorities," and hung up. I felt a jolt of terror run through my whole body. It was as if I'd been struck by lightning.

Alice Ann Hoagland, at home in Los Gatos, California, mother of United Flight 93 passenger Mark Bingham: The call came in at 6:37 in the morning, and a family friend answered it. We were all still in bed because we have young babies in the family and we were all trying to get some sleep. I heard our friend pad down the hall past my room to rouse my sister-in-law, Cathy, out of bed. I heard Cathy say on the phone, "Well, we love you too, Mark. Let me get your mom." Cathy saw me, and she said, "Alice, talk to Mark. He's been hijacked." She also handed me a slip of paper that said "93 United." She had written this down while he was talking to her. I'm a flight attendant for

United Airlines.

I took the phone and he said, "Mom, this is Mark Bingham." I knew he was a little flustered because he used his last name. He said, "I want to let you know that I love you." I spoke to Mark for about a total of three minutes. He said, "There are three guys on board who have taken over the plane, and they say they have a bomb."

Deena Burnett: As I was explaining Tom's phone call to the FBI, the phone rang in again on call-waiting, and I said, "I have to go." The FBI agent said, "Call me back." I clicked over and the first thing Tom said was "They're in the cockpit." I told him about the World Trade Center. He hadn't known about it yet. He relayed that information to the people sitting around him. He said, "Oh, my God, it's a suicide mission." He started asking questions: "Who's involved? Was it a commercial airplane? What airline was it? Do you know how many airplanes are involved?" He was really pumping me for information about what was going on, anything that I knew.

Lyzbeth Glick, wife of United Flight 93 passenger Jeremy Glick: I must have gotten up just after the first plane hit, because the first thing I did was turn on the TV and saw the World Trade Center. I was about to get some breakfast in the kitchen when I heard the phone ring, and I heard my parents scream, "Oh my God, Jeremy!" I went into the room and all color had drained from their faces. I started to panic. I said, "Oh, my God, that wasn't Jeremy's flight, was it?" They said, "No. He's okay, for now." They added "for now" because Jeremy had told them that the plane had been hijacked. They handed the phone to me. He sensed panic in my voice, and we started saying "I love you." We must have said it for 10 minutes straight until it calmed us down. Then he explained to me what had happened.

Lisa Jefferson, Verizon Airfone supervisor: I was stopped by a representative who told me that she had a gentleman on her phone, and his plane was being hijacked. I immediately went over.

Deena Burnett: A news reporter came on saying that the Pentagon had been hit, and I started wailing. I mean, really wailing, making a noise that I did not know I could make, thinking it was Tom's plane that had hit the Pentagon.

Alice Ann Hoagland: Tom Burnett was in 4B, Mark was in 4D. It was Tom who told Deena, "Well, some of us are going to do something." Tom and Mark were seated right behind two of the hijackers, two of the murderers, who happened to be seated in 3C and 3D. The other two terrorists were seated in 6B and 1B, so that means that Tom and Mark were between everybody.

Lyzbeth Glick: Then Jeremy started asking me what was happening in New York and did they crash planes into the World Trade Center? I guess he had heard it from one of the other passengers. I hesitated for a minute, then I said, "Honey, you need to be strong, but yes, they are crashing planes into the World Trade Center."

Deena Burnett: The phone rang again and it was Tom and he said, "Deena." I said, "Tom, you're okay," thinking that he had survived the plane crash at the Pentagon. He said no. I said, "They just hit the Pentagon." I could hear people talking and spreading the news in the background and I could hear their concern and I could hear people gasping as if they were surprised and shocked. Tom came back on the phone and said, "I'm putting a plan together. We're going to take back the airplane." I asked, "Who's helping you?" He said, "Different people, several people. There's a group of us. Don't worry. We're going to do something." Then he said, "I'm going to call you back," and he hung up.

Lauren Grandcolas, United Flight 93 passenger, in a voicemail message to her husband: Honey, are you there? Jack, pick up sweetie. Okay, well I just wanted to tell you I love you. We're having a little problem on the plane. I'm fine. I just want you to know that I love you more than anything. Please tell my family I love them, too.

Linda Gronlund, United Flight 93 passenger, in a voicemail message to her sister: Elsa, it's Lin. Um, I only have a minute. I'm on United 93. It's been hijacked by terrorists who say they have a bomb. Apparently, they, uh, flown a couple of planes into the World Trade Center already and it looks like they're going to take this one down as well. [*Sobbing*] Mostly, I just wanted to say I love you and I'm going to miss you. I don't know if I'm going to get the chance to tell you that again.

CeeCee Lyles, United Flight 93 flight attendant, in a voice-mail message to her husband,

Lorne: Hi baby. Baby — you have to listen to me carefully. I'm on a plane that's been hijacked. I'm on a plane, I'm calling from the plane. I want to tell you that I love you. I love you. Please tell my children that I love them very much — and I'm so sorry babe. I don't know what to say — there's three guys. They've hijacked the plane. I'm trying to be calm. We've turned around and I've heard that there's planes that have flown into the World Trade Center. I hope to be able to see your face again, baby. I love you, bye.

Lisa Jefferson, Verizon Airfone supervisor: I took over the call from Flight 93. I said, "My name is Mrs. Jefferson. I understand your plane is being hijacked, so could you please explain to me in detail exactly what's happening?" I asked him if anyone was hurt. The flight attendant next to him said yes — there were two people laying in first class on the floor, the pilot and the copilot, and their throats had been slashed. He asked me if I knew what they wanted — money, ransom, or what? I told him I didn't have a clue.

Lyzbeth Glick, wife of United Flight 93 passenger Jeremy Glick: Jeremy said he didn't think he was going to make it out. He told me he loved me and our daughter, Emerson, very much, and he needed us to be happy. He sounded very sad. He kept saying, "I can't believe this is happening to me."

Lisa Jefferson: I asked the caller his name, and he told me, "Todd Beamer, from Cranbury, New Jersey."

John Werth, air traffic controller, Cleveland Air Route Traffic Control Center: Then the plane started a rapid descent south of Akron.

Lisa Jefferson: The plane took a dive and he said, "Oh, my God! We're going down! We're going down!"

Mahlon Fuller, Pittsburgh watch supervisor, FAA: A fellow who was working approach control, Paul Delfine, said, "Mal, I need you real bad." I could tell by the tone of his voice there was something very wrong. I ran over to the radar scope and he pointed: "This airplane's been hijacked over Cleveland. We don't know where he's going." The airplane was going very fast and it was headed directly for the center of the Pittsburgh airport. Without thinking about it, I said, "Evacuate the facility."

Chuck Savall, pilot, Midwest Express Flight 73: We knew how bad things were. I made an announcement to the passengers to let them know that we would try to get them on the ground safe. On the way to Cleveland, we were heading right for Flight 93. Our courses were pretty much head-on. They made us do an emergency descent and land in Pittsburgh.

Col. Matthew Klimow, executive assistant to the vice chair of the Joint Chiefs of Staff, Gen. Richard Myers, Pentagon: We knew Flight 93 was heading to Washington, but no one knew where it was.

Lt. Col. Kevin Nasypany, mission crew commander, NEADS, Rome, New York: We had heard that there was a possible other hijack out in Pennsylvania. I had one of the control teams take the Langley aircraft — the F-16s — and start moving them northwest of D.C. We had thrown basically a 30-mile circle around D.C. and made it a restricted area — no fly.

John Werth, air traffic controller, Cleveland Air Route Traffic Control Center: Because of the miscommunications somewhere along the line, I think we may have been the only ones who actually knew where he was.

Ben Sliney, national operations manager, FAA Command Center, Herndon, Virginia: We had a report from a small, private aircraft pilot who saw a United jet waggling his wings. That threw a lot of ambiguity into this situation, because that is a universal signal the pilot has lost radio and is unable to communicate. Even at that late junction, minutes before the aircraft hit the ground in Pennsylvania, we were still wondering whether it was truly hijacked.

Deena Burnett, at home in California, wife of United Flight 93 passenger Tom Burnett: He called back about five minutes till seven. He asked, "Is there anything new?" I said no. He was very quiet this time, very calm. He had been very calm and collected through the other conversations, but he was very solemn in this conversation. He asked, "Where are the kids?" I said, "They're fine. They're sitting at the table. They're asking to talk to you." He said, "Tell them I'll talk to them later."

THE WORLD TRADE CENTER EVACUATION

"TIME WAS STANDING STILL"

As the fateful 9:00 a.m. hour ticked by, the New York Fire Department launched the biggest response in its history, drawing resources from across its five boroughs. Thousands of other first responders and government officials arrived on the scene as well, from local, state, and federal agencies.

Thomas Von Essen, commissioner, FDNY: Inside the [North Tower ground-floor] lobby, I think we knew less of what was going on than people outside or in the street, or the people watching TV.

Chief Joseph Pfeifer, Battalion 1, FDNY: We tried every possible means of communication that day. But even cell phones weren't working. Each of the systems we tried failed. I felt very frustrated. It was almost like the closer you were, the less you knew. The helicopters were up, but we had no means to

226

communicate with them. We tried a number of times. We were the least informed.

Steven Bienkowski, Aviation Unit, NYPD: People saw the helicopter, and I'm sure many of them were thinking that we were going to be able to save them. In fact, we weren't able to do anything. We were as close as you could possibly be, and still we were helpless, totally helpless.

Chief Joseph Pfeifer, inside the ground-floor lobby of the World Trade Center: Groups of firefighters were coming in. We would brief them, tell them the plan, and send them up. One of the engine companies that came in was Engine 33, which was my brother Kevin's. I told him we thought the lowest level of fire was at floor 78. I told him we didn't have any elevators available. Then we spent a couple seconds looking at each other, with a real feeling of concern for each other. Then he knew what he had to do. I watched him walk away, and that was the last time I saw him.

William Jimeno, officer, PAPD: Sergeant [John] McLoughlin ran up to us and said, "I need volunteers to go in with us, and I need people who know how to use Scott Air-Packs," the breathing apparatuses that the firefighters use. Port Authority police officers are cross-trained not only for law enforcement but firefighting. I don't know which of us said it first — either Dominick Pezzulo, Antonio Rodrigues, or me — but one of us said, "We just graduated. We know how to use it." Sergeant McLoughlin said, "That's good, that's four of us, we're going to go." We started running toward the building. I remember thinking to myself, *Wow, this is bad.*

James Luongo, inspector, NYPD: As I hit Vesey between Church and Broadway, the first thing that struck me was the amount of women's shoes. I couldn't understand it. Then I realized women had run out of their shoes — the high heels and what have you. There were women's shoes all over.

Sgt. Anthony Lisi, Emergency Service Unit, Truck 6, NYPD: Sergeant [Tom] Sullivan stopped us and said, "We have hundreds of firemen and cops in the building already, doing rescue work. I want you to stop, take off that gear, and put on your heavy vest and helmet, and grab weapons, because we're getting word that they're shooting civilians as they're running out of the building." We were, over our radio, getting reports of shots fired at the Trade Center. It winds up it was police officers who were shooting out the windows so more people could run out faster. There were shots fired — but by good guys, not bad guys.

Sharon Miller, officer, PAPD: Before we got out of the car — me, Richie Rodriguez, Jimmy Nelson, and Jimmy Parham — we all held hands and we said, "We're going in together, we're gonna come out together."

Lt. Mickey Kross, Engine 16, FDNY: I huddled the guys together because I knew this was going to be a tough day. I got into a little huddle, like football players do. I says, "Come here." I says, "Just treat this like a fire. We'll stick together. Watch each other's back."

Capt. Jay Jonas, Ladder 6, FDNY: I walked over to my crew, and I says, "Okay, guys. Here's the deal. It's a raw deal, but this is what we have to do." I said, "We have to go upstairs in this building for search and rescue." Then I said — and I forgot I made this one statement, but all my guys swear that I said it — they said I said, "They're trying to kill us, boys. So let's go." And they did, to their credit. I don't think anybody would have looked down on them if they ran up West Street. As we were about to hit the stairway, Sal D'Agostino said to me, "Hey, Cap, I wonder where the air force is?" I says, "Yeah, I wonder how many thousands of fires I've been to in my career and I've never hit a stairway wondering where the air force was." We were hoping they had our backs.

William Jimeno, officer, PAPD: In the midst of all this chaos, all this disaster, inside that World Trade Center, there were people helping each other. I remember seeing a black gentleman with a white gentleman, carrying this blond woman who had a severe cut on her leg. I remember thinking to myself, *Will, if these normal civilians can be this brave, we as rescue workers, we need to be three steps above them, because they're counting on us.*

James Luongo, inspector, NYPD: There were a bunch of people who came out of the building on Vesey Street. They were a little disoriented about which way to go. I started yelling to them to come to me. They were looking around. Finally, a woman heard my voice. She touched the people next to her, she pointed to where me and Dennis and Sergeant Boodle were — and with that, debris came down and killed all of them. With all the things I saw that day, that, to me, was the worst because those people were so close, but yet they didn't make it.

William Jimeno: As we walked into the Port Authority police desk [at the base of the Tow-

230

ers], I remember being stunned by a piece of the fuselage that our detectives had brought in. Your mind is trying to register — even though you know that a plane had hit — why is there a piece of the plane here?

James Luongo: Quite a few people came to the site looking to go in because their loved ones were there. I remember one woman standing on the corner by Vesey and West, and I told her that she had to leave. She said, "I'm not leaving." We were back-and-forth like this for a second or two. I said, "I hope he's worth your life because you're not going to be able to get to him." She said, "He *is* worth my life." She looked to walk past me. I stopped her, and she pushed me. I grabbed her and picked her up to walk with her. She was hitting me as I was walking away. "Let me in! Let me go! I gotta go there!"

William Jimeno: Christopher Amoroso, someone that we had worked with and really liked — good, good cop — said, "Sarge, can I hook up with you guys?" Sarge said, "Yeah, Chris, you can." Christopher had an injury over his left eye, and we asked him what happened. "Something hit my eye, probably a piece of concrete. We've got to keep working." Sergeant McLoughlin had asked another officer, Anthony Rodrigues, to meet us up at Tower Two. Unfortunately for Anthony,

231

one of the victims that fell from the building hit too close to him — he had human remains on his body. He said, "Sarge, I can't work in this." Sarge told him, "Go change your uniform and meet us up by Tower Two." At that point, we became five.

Inside both towers — each now fatally stricken, their seemingly impregnable structures burning, melting, and weakening under temperatures that reached 1,800 degrees Fahrenheit — thousands of evacuating office workers rushed to exit their building, even as firefighters and police officers worked their way inside to provide aid.

Richard Eichen, consultant, Pass Consulting Group, North Tower, 90th floor: I got to a neighboring office and met Charlie Egan — their systems administrator — and he was annoyed because the explosion knocked off his servers. He was going to stay until midnight, bringing his servers all back up. I remember going with Charlie into the server room and saying, "Look, if it means anything I'll stay with you, and together we'll get these things back up." He was really annoyed. Then he said, "I better call the building." He called down there and goes, "Hi this is so-and-so, Clearstream Banking." I think he gave his name. "There are five of us here, we're on the 90th floor." The office building said, "Stay there, we know where you are." Meanwhile, we're looking out the window, and we can see large chunks of the building falling. Huge chunks of the building — the size of like trucks falling — and it's like, *Well, I really don't think that's a viable option.*

Herb Ouida, World Trade Centers Association, North Tower, 77th floor, and father of Todd Ouida, Cantor Fitzgerald, North Tower, 105th floor: I thought my son Todd was on the stairs. Todd called his mother immediately when the plane hit. He said to her, "Mommy, don't worry. You're going to hear there was an explosion at the World Trade Center. I'm going to the stairs." She said, "What about Daddy?" Todd said, "I just spoke to him. He's all right." Todd had not spoken to me. Here was a kid who had suffered as a child from anxiety disorder, panic attacks, and at the moment of greatest danger, he's protecting his mother. He was 25 years old.

Judith Wein, senior vice president, Aon Corporation, South Tower, 103rd floor: I was literally walking over bodies. So many people died at that moment of impact — the way they landed maybe, they broke their necks or something. Some other guy came up — we later found out his name was Welles

Crowther, and he had been a volunteer fireman upstate — and he asked where there was a fire extinguisher. I pointed to where it was, and he went to get it. He was running different places and trying to put out fires. He had a red bandana on his face. He was calm and commanding: "This is what we have to do. This is what needs to be done." He directed people to the only open working staircase — the only one that went all the way down. He stayed up there and helped and didn't make it out.

Bruno Dellinger, principal, Quint Amasis North America, North Tower, 47th floor: Suddenly I felt the urge to go, and I dropped everything and left.

Stanley Praimnath, Fuji Bank, South Tower, 81st floor: I crawled the entire length of the loans department, the lounge, the computer room, the communication room. That's as far as I can go. I can't go any further because one lousy sheetrock wall stood firm.

Brian Clark, executive vice president, EuroBrokers, South Tower: Our offices occupied the entire 84th floor. Everything was destroyed. I started down with this group of six people following me with my flashlight. We only went three floors, down to the 81st

234

floor, [when] I was distracted by this banging noise. I heard, "Help, I'm buried. I can't breathe."

Stanley Praimnath: This man behind the wall was saying, "I can hear your voice! Bang on the wall, I'll know where you are." He said, "Climb over the sheetrock wall." I said, "I can't." He said, "You've got to think of your family. If you want to live, you must do it."

Brian Clark: Suddenly he said, "Can you see my hand?" He was waving his hand down by the floor. I shined my flashlight on it and followed it up the arm to see his two eyes through this hole in the wall. He scrambled up, I missed him the first time, but the second time he jumped I caught him and heaved him up and over the wall. We fell back down on the ground, him on top of me. He gave me this big kiss. And I said, "I'm Brian." He said, "I'm Stanley."

Stanley Praimnath: He said, "Come on, buddy, let's go home."

More than 1,100 people were trapped above the impact zones across both the North and South Towers. As conditions worsened and smoke and fire permeated the upper floors, they dialed 911, emergency services, and the Port

Authority's World Trade Center command post, hoping to speed rescuers to their aid, not realizing how dire their situation actually was. For 24 minutes, 32-year-old Melissa Doi — trapped on the 83rd floor of the South Tower — spoke to a 911 operator, waiting for a rescue that would never come.

Melissa Doi, financial manager, IQ Financials: It's very hot, everywhere on the floor.

911 operator: Okay, I know you don't see it and all, but I'm, I'm . . . *[stumbles over words]* I'm gonna, I'm documenting everything you say, okay? And it's very hot, you see no fire, but you see smoke, right?

Melissa Doi: It's very hot, I see . . . I don't see, I don't see any air anymore!

911 operator: Okay . . .

Melissa Doi: All I see is smoke.

911 operator: Okay, dear, I'm so sorry, hold on for a sec, stay calm with me, stay calm, listen, listen, the call is in, I'm documenting, hold on one second please . . .

Melissa Doi: I'm going to die,

aren't I?

911 operator: No, no, no, no, no, no, no, say your — ma'am, say your prayers.

Melissa Doi: I'm going to die.

911 operator: You gotta think positive, because you gotta help each other get off the floor.

Melissa Doi: I'm going to die.

911 operator: Now look, stay calm, stay calm, stay calm, stay calm.

Melissa Doi: Please God . . .

911 operator: You're doing a good job ma'am, you're doing a good job.

Melissa Doi: No, it's so hot I'm burning up.

Christine Olender, assistant general manager of Windows on the World, in a phone call to the Port Authority Command Center: We're getting no direction up here. We're having a smoke condition. We have most people on the 106th floor — the 107th floor is way too smoky. We need direction as to where we need to direct our guests and our employees, as soon as possible.

Officer Steve Maggett, PAPD: Okay. We're doing our best. We've got the fire department, everybody, we're trying to get up to you, dear. All right, call back in about two or three minutes, and I'll find out what direction you should try to get down. Are the stairways, A, B, and C all blocked off and smoky?

Christine Olender: The stairways are full of smoke — A, B, and C. And my . . . and my electric . . . my fire phones are out.

Officer Steve Maggett: Oh, yeah, they're . . . all the lines are blown out right now. But everybody is on their way, the fire department . . .

Christine Olender: The condition up on 106 is getting worse.

Officer Steve Maggett: Okay, dear. All right, we are doing our best to get up to you right now. All right, dear?

Christine Olender: But where . . . where do you want to [inaudible] can you at

least . . . can you at least
direct us to a certain tower
in the building. Like what
tower . . . like what
area . . . what quadrant of
the building can we go into,
where we are not going to get
all this smoke?

Officer Steve Maggett: Unless
we find out what exactly . . .
area is the smoke . . . where
most . . . most of the smoke
is coming up there, and we can
kind of direct that. As I
said, call back in about two
minutes, dear.

Christine Olender: Call back
in two minutes. Great.

*Back inside the stairwells of the North and
South Towers, civilians and rescuers mixed in
single-file lines, each group tired and sweaty
from the exertions behind and ahead. As one
group descended to evacuate, the others
continued to climb, determined to help anyone
still trapped.*

Richard Eichen, consultant, Pass Consulting Group, North Tower, 90th floor:
The five of us went out. My coworker Lucy
sat down and said, "I'm not going anywhere."

I said, "Lucy, we're not leaving anybody behind. We've got to get out of here. We're starting to burn." I put her hands on my shoulders. She stood behind me, I put her hands on my shoulders, and held her hands so she wouldn't let go. I said, "Come on." I said, "I'm hurt. I need help. I don't want to die by myself. I need help." I did that to get her to go. Then together we went out. We actually caught stairwell A, which it turned out was the only viable staircase up there.

Lt. Mickey Kross, Engine 16, FDNY: We were ordered to the 23rd floor [in the North Tower] to report in to some other command post. We entered Stairway B, which was the core stairway in the building. As we were going up, the people in the building were coming down and, actually, it was very smooth.

Stephen Blihar, officer, Emergency Service Unit, Truck 10, NYPD: We made it to the ninth floor [of the North Tower], and I remember filling a coffee pot with water and grabbing some plastic cups for everybody, because by that time, we were hot and sweaty, and I knew we were going up at least another 70 floors.

David Norman, officer, Emergency Service Unit, Truck 1, NYPD: There were people waiting on floors on the way up. We were informing them, "You need to leave. You need to continue flowing down the staircase. Don't obstruct the staircase flow. Continue to move."

Capt. Jay Jonas, Ladder 6, FDNY: You had a row of firemen going up the stairs, and you had a row of civilians coming down the stairs.

Lt. Mickey Kross: We carry a lot of equipment. We carry 60, 70 pounds of equipment with us, on average. It's a little slow going up the stairs, and it was hot that day. We stopped about every five floors and took a little breather.

Peter Bitwinski, assistant manager, Accounts Payable, Port Authority, North Tower, 69th floor: We encountered maybe 20 to 25 firemen. It's one of the sadder memories I have of that day. They were walking up with full equipment, these big metal picks, and they were sweating like crazy.

Cathy Pavelec, administrator, Port Authority, North Tower, 67th floor: As they walked past us — both of my brothers are firemen in New Jersey — I was very careful to say "Hello, thank you, God bless you" to every single one of them. They were huffing and puffing, and these were big strong guys.

Herb Ouida, World Trade Centers Association, North Tower, 77th floor, and father of Todd Ouida, Cantor Fitzgerald, North Tower, 105th floor: The stairways were much better lit this time than in the '93 bombing, and unlike '93, there was no smoke coming up because the explosion was above us. New Yorkers were very brave that day — people helped each other. We were saying "Déjà vu." We were trying to encourage each other and say, "Oh we've been through this before." We didn't realize this was different. None of us realized the building was going to collapse.

David Norman: When we got to floor 31, we found probably about a half dozen or more firefighters, one or two civilians on that floor dealing with chest pains, exhaustion, and stuff like that. We looked at each other and said, "We already have a triage set up here for us. This was our mission. Why don't we stay here?"

Sharon Miller, officer, PAPD: We stopped on the 27th floor. That's when I said to my supervisor, PAPD Captain Kathy Mazza, "Hey, Kat, I really love my job but this is getting bad." I said, "I'm really not ready to die yet." She goes, "Oh, don't worry about it. We'll be fine." I said, "Well, how about a hug?" And we hugged! Then she goes, "All right, that's enough of that!"

Judith Wein, senior vice president, Aon Corporation, South Tower, 103rd floor: I walked down with another man. He actually had a severed arm, which we didn't know about because he was wearing a suit. It kept his arm in. He was holding onto the lower part of his arm, but I didn't think anything of that.

Bruno Dellinger, principal, Quint Amasis North America, North Tower, 47th floor: The heat was quite intense in the stairwell. There were some people who took their shirts off. The intensity of the warning signs — the fire alarms were in full force — like stroboscopic lamps and the fire alarm's sound was pounding you all the time.

Judith Wein: We're walking down the stairs, and around [floor] 40, some rescue workers came in, and they said we should sit and rest. The two others went to sit on the stairs, and I went to sit down. I had my tush sticking out, getting ready to sit, and something inside me said, *Don't sit.* It almost felt like somebody had an arm or a hand on my back, pushing me up. It was a weird feeling, just *Don't sit.* I said, "Look. If you guys are tired, you sit, but I can't sit." Because I didn't sit, they got up and we walked. The rescue workers walked us through somebody's office to an internal elevator which was working, and so we went from about 40 down to the lobby. I was told, later, that we were the last group of people to go down in that elevator.

Elia Zedeño, financial analyst, Port Authority, North Tower, 73rd floor: Most of my journey down the stairs was in this complete state of non-emotion. I saw people injured, but I had no reaction. I remember moving to the side and letting them walk in front of us. I remember a woman who was screaming and screaming and screaming. I couldn't really completely understand what she was saying, but there was a man helping her, and he had blood on his forehead, and all he kept saying to her was "We were the lucky ones, we were the lucky ones." He kept repeating that. I was thinking, *What in the world did this woman see?*

Peter Bitwinski, assistant manager, Accounts Payable, Port Authority, North Tower, 69th floor: We started to make our way down the staircase with John Abruzzo in the evacuchair. We had to get a routine going, so we decided two people on the bottom would hold the evacuchair, with two people at the top. We had eight people who were actively taking him down, four people at a time.

John Abruzzo, staff accountant, Port Authority, North Tower, 69th floor: We wanted to make time, but they were not absolutely sure how the chair worked or how it would handle. I don't think the manufacturer even thought about the chair going down 69 flights.

Peter Bitwinski: We kept switching our team. The two guys holding the handles on top of the evacuchair would move to the bottom of the evacuchair after five flights. Then after you were on the bottom, you would move off the chair, and two other guys would take your place. You'd be free of chair duty for five or 10 floors.

John Abruzzo: The firemen cheered us on, encouraging us. "Keep on going," they said. "You're doing a good job, keep going."

Marcel Claes, firefighter, Engine 24, FDNY: I just kept climbing. I knew it was going to be a hard day, but I kept thinking about putting water on the fire.

Bruno Dellinger: While I was walking down, they were going up to their deaths.

And I was walking down to live. I will never forget this.

Lila Speciner, paralegal, Port Authority, North Tower, 88th floor: That will stay with me forever. They were going where we were running from.

Despite the fact that an incident had occurred within the buildings, not many companies formally evacuated their staff; many of the early evacuees had made the decision on their own to leave. In the South Tower, however, Morgan Stanley's efforts likely saved scores or even hundreds of lives. The company, which occupied floors 59 to 74, as well as a few other, scattered lower floors, had invested heavily in evacuation equipment and training following the 1993 bombing, and its vice president of security, a former British paratrooper–turned–Vietnam veteran named Rick Rescorla, ignored the Port Authority's initial announcement that those in the South Tower could remain at their desks. Instead, the retired colonel immediately began working to ensure everyone escaped.

`Rick Rescorla, vice president of security, Morgan Stanley, in a phone call to his best friend, Dan Hill:` The dumb sons of bitches told me not to evacuate. They said it's just Building One. I told them I'm getting my people the fuck out of here.

Jeannine Ali, controller, Morgan Stanley, South Tower, 45th floor: On September 11th, our Security Department were the ones that got all of the Morgan Stanley employees out of the offices. With bullhorns, our security was saying, "Evacuate the building now." I remember them saying, specifically, "You have to evacuate the building now."

Robert Small, office manager, Morgan Stanley, South Tower, 72nd floor: As we're going down, we get down to the 40s and we run into Rick Rescorla — I knew him through the fire safety training. He was always a jovial Scottish guy — always fun, had the brogue. He wasn't fun that day. I tried to be humorous passing him, saying, "Hey, I'm the last man off 72. You don't have to go check it. Everyone's gone." He goes, "Just get out. Just go. Just get out." His tone was dead-on serious. I'd never seen him that serious before.

Barbara Fiorillo, manager, Mercer Consulting, South Tower, 54th floor: We heard voices of people directing the flow of traffic — there were very strong male voices: "Speed up, slow down, speed up, slow down." It turns out that we were in the same elevator bank as Morgan Stanley, and they had worked at the tower in the first bombing. They had enormous training and experience. The voice directing the traffic was such a calming effect.

Robert Small: We came across a man, a big man — I hate to use the word "fat," but he was. He was huge, and he was struggling on the stairs and he was holding on to the banister with both hands. I offered him some water. He said, "I can't take your bottle of water." I dropped my bag, opened it up, and he saw that I had dozens of bottles. He took a couple. We sat there with him and were talking. He didn't say who he was or what floor he had started on. He didn't have it in him. I said, "When you're ready we'll go together, and James and I will get you down." He said, "No, no, no, do me a favor. If you see anybody — rescue or firemen — let them know where I am." I felt bad leaving him. We left him three, four bottles of water, and we said good-bye.

Rick Rescorla, in a phone call to his wife, Susan: I don't want you to cry. I have to evacuate my people now. If something happens to me, I want you to know that you made my life.

Ultimately, only eleven Morgan Stanley staff — out of more than 2,700 in the South Tower — died on September 11th. Rescorla and two of his fellow security personnel were among those eleven.

Richard Eichen, consultant, Pass Consulting Group, North Tower: As you got lower and lower you got into more and more people. I was afraid that it was getting congested — I wasn't afraid of the buildings falling. I was afraid of panic.

Vanessa Lawrence, artist, North Tower: If the flow stopped for too long, people shouted out, "Don't worry! People congestion!"

Bruno Dellinger, principal, Quint Amasis North America, North Tower: It taught me something about human beings in distress. We were receiving from everywhere around us warning signs that this was a very, very dangerous situation. The moment we got those messages something inside — a defense mechanism — kicked in and stopped us from panicking.

Robert Small, office manager, Morgan Stanley, South Tower: As we're into maybe the 20s we came across two women — one helping the other. The one doing all the help was also burdened with bags. She was helping a woman who she said was four months pregnant. "Okay. Let us help you. Let us carry the bags." She let us carry the bags, but now the pregnant woman wanted to stop. We gave her some water. She says she's hot. I took some water out, I made a little rag, sponging her back and her neck, making her feel a little bit better. She was finally ready to go. No sooner did we get a couple of floors down than she wanted to stop. Like football coaching — when you tell a kid to do a push-up, you always try to get one more out of them — I told her, "Give me one more floor, then we'll stop. I'll give you water. Give me one more floor." And we did.

Constance Labetti, accountant, Aon Corporation, South Tower, 99th floor: I would start to cry, and I'd start to tremble, and I heard my father's voice. My father had been dead since 1985 — and I heard his voice, clear as day, telling me that I was not going to die in this building. I straightened up and kept walking down the steps. A few minutes later, I heard my uncle — who kind of took over being my dad when my dad passed away. My uncle passed away in '99, and he used to call me "Kiddo." I heard my uncle's voice in my left ear telling me,

"Kiddo, just take one step at a time." And I did.

Richard Eichen, consultant, Pass Consulting Group, North Tower, 90th floor: When we finally got down to the 20s, we saw our first firefighter coming up. At this point Lucy was lying on a landing. She pretty much passed out. The firefighter said, "We've set up a station a couple of floors down." We carried her spread-eagle. I carried her legs. He carried her under her armpits. The two of us carried her down the stairwell maybe two floors. When we got to the aid station, they asked me if I was okay and I said, "Yeah, I'm fine." I met Lt. Glenn Wilkerson — who unfortunately didn't make it out. We were about three feet from each other, and he said, "What's it like up there?" I told them what it was like.

Robert Small: We got down to the fifth floor. Everything's fine. The ladies are fine. All of a sudden we heard, "New York City Police. Anybody here?" So we called out. It was a female officer and — I'm assuming — a male detective, because he was in a suit. She and the detective wanted to help us out. I was very adamant, saying, "Don't need your help." I said, "I've been coming down since 72. I got this far — five more flights." We told them about the gentleman upstairs and Rick on the 44th floor and they headed up. You could hear them floor by floor — opening doors, screaming out if anyone needed assistance, and then slamming the doors and going up to the next level. I know she didn't make it. It always bothered me that she didn't make it, because if she did help us, would that have kept her out?

Richard Eichen: They had given Lucy some oxygen. She was coming around and she was feeling better and at some point she said, "All right, I'm ready." "Lucy, are you sure?" "Yeah. I'm ready." "Okay." So we got up, I took her hand. We go back in the stairwell. We continued going down.

Lt. Mickey Kross, Engine 16, FDNY: We encountered a group of people who were nonambulatory. We started to assist these people, trying to get them down. Me and Andy [from Engine 1] had somebody between us — a woman — and she was going very slowly, one step at a time. I wanted to get out of that building. It was like time was standing still.

Frank Lombardi, chief engineer, Port Authority, North Tower: Water was starting to run into the stairwells — the sprinkler systems must have been turned on — and we had to watch our footing to make sure that we wouldn't slip.

Richard Eichen: It was pretty deep water — mid-calf to below the knee. All the water had gone down and collected there. It's like, *Wow, this is like a sinking ship. What the hell?* Finally, a few more stairs, and we got into the lobby.

Linda Krouner, senior vice president, Fiduciary Trust, South Tower: We got to the ground level. We got out of the elevator and looked out at the plaza area. My first thought was, *This is Britain during the Blitz,* because that's really what it looked like.

Robert Small: We got down to the main level. We were being escorted. It was like Hansel and Gretel with the breadcrumbs — a human line of police and rescue and you name it. They said, "Come this way. Exit to the north."

Constance Labetti, accountant, Aon Corporation, South Tower, 99th floor: We got to the lobby and my coworker Jules and I had to rest for a moment because we were perspiring terribly. We had walked down 100 flights of steps. People were coming up to me, hugging me, and telling me, "Thank you, thank you," and hugging me as they walked by me, and I said to Jules, "What? Why? What are they doing that for?" She said, "Connie, you don't know what you were saying? You were saying, 'We're not going to die in this building. Just take it one step at a time.' " I was repeating what my father and my uncle were telling me, and I didn't even know it.

At the High School for Leadership and Public Service — a block south of the South Tower — students and teachers tried to figure out an evacuation plan. Eventually, the occupants of the school and its neighbor, the High School of Economics and Finance, fled four blocks south, along with thousands of other people in Lower Manhattan, to Battery Park, at the tip of Manhattan.

Robert Rosado, student, HSLPS: Ms. Ordover asked us to write about what we thought had happened while she went online.

Heather Ordover, English teacher, HSLPS: The lead photo on CNN's web page was what we couldn't see from my classroom: the north side of the North Tower with an enormous gaping hole.

Ada Dolch, principal, HSLPS: Panic was beginning to set in. People were streaming into our lobby. Parents started coming in, "I

254

want my child." I stood up on the table in the lobby and said, "Ladies and gentlemen, I am the principal of the school." I said, "No one is allowed to go upstairs." There was this sense of, *I got to take care of my chickadees,* and all my kitties were upstairs safe.

Razvan Hotaranu, student, HSLPS: I knew that whatever happened I needed to get home fast. I knew my mom must've been very worried for me.

Ada Dolch: When the second tower was hit, our building really shook — a piece of the plane fell in front of our school building. Debris was falling on our rooftop. We could see flying paper on fire.

Keturah Bostick, student, HSLPS: I knew I was going to die. It seemed like there was no hope in the world. I found some friends, we all prayed and told each other that we loved each other. Next I pulled out a paper and started to write a letter to my family members telling them how much I loved them.

Ada Dolch: Where would we go? Where can you congregate with a lot of children? I said, "Oh, I know where we're going. We're going to Battery Park." We initiated an evacuation plan. I had my assistant principals go floor by floor and evacuate all the students. I stood at the outside door and simply said to them, "Hold each other's hands. Stay together." I would say to them, "You should pray. This is a good time to be praying, and to ask God for mercy that we will be safe."

Rosmaris Fernandez, student, HSLPS: I led the group to Battery Park.

Keturah Bostick: We ran, thinking that the worst was over, and after that nothing else could go wrong.

Tim Seto, student, HSLPS: We walked toward Battery Park. There was all this debris on the ground — newspapers, ashes, and burned stuff. The Towers looked like two smoldering cigarettes, pointed upward.

Heather Ordover: A student and I picked up pieces of honeycomb insulation. I picked up someone's insurance policy, burnt in half and charred around the edges.

Ada Dolch: The kids were in total shock. They were very scared. They were catatonic.

Heather Ordover: We hustled them down to the edge of Battery Park. I stood, on a bench, with Liz Collins, a math teacher. The kids rallied around us.

Dan Potter, firefighter, Ladder 10, FDNY: As I get off the Verrazzano Bridge, there was a bus lane and police vehicles were shooting through it. I got right behind them. A cop was standing right in front of me, so I held my badge out the window, and he flagged me through. We were in a convoy of police vehicles, doing about 70 miles an hour, between two barriers all the way through.

Jean Potter, Bank of America, North Tower: We were going down, but, again, there was smoke. Everything was lit. The staircase was lit. Smoke in the air, the smell of jet fuel. We were making our way down pretty quickly, and then it started to bottleneck a little bit. We started seeing firemen come up in the 20s. That's when I saw [FDNY Capt.] Vinnie Giammona. I grabbed his arm and said, "Vinnie, be safe." I knew that he was not going to make it out.

Dan Potter: I didn't think that these towers were going to collapse. This was the massive, biggest fire I've ever seen, but as you're calculating, you don't really know the extent of the damage. I was convinced that we'll get up there and put it out.

Jean Potter: We're getting down to like 11, 10, and on like 8, I started yelling at people to move. I don't ordinarily yell — I'm a very soft-spoken individual — but I started screaming at people, "Move it! Move it! We're almost out of here! Move it! Move it!" The lobby was completely devastated. There was glass all over.

Dan Potter: When I got up West Street, just about Rector Street, I noticed police starting to put some barriers out. I noticed body parts in the street. There were big pieces and smaller pieces. I looked up at the Trade Center and I could see the flames, see the firemen. I wondered, *Where is she? Where could she possibly be?* I thought, *She's got to be up on the roof.* I was convinced at this point that she's up on the roof. I was going to do the best I could to get a team together and get up there.

Jean Potter: They took us down into the Concourse. I'm so grateful I kept my shoes on because the water was ankle deep and there was broken glass all over. There was a human chain of emergency workers yelling at us, "Run! Run! Ruuuun!" When do they tell you to run in an emergency? It was so horrifying.

Richard Eichen: When we got into the lobby it was really scary. It looked like someone dumped a barbecue on it — it was covered in ash. I remember hearing the water dripping, dripping, dripping.

Jeannine Ali, controller, Morgan Stanley, South Tower: They were directing people out, up through Borders and out toward Five World Trade. There was a fireman — he couldn't have been more than 19 years old — with a hose on his shoulder. I remember looking at him and saying to him, "There is nothing you can do. Don't go in there." He said, "Lady, it's my job. I have to do it."

Linda Krouner, senior vice president, Fiduciary Trust, South Tower: I got out and crossed the street. The first thing that hit me was the sounds. There were so many sounds. There were sirens and people screaming. It was like you were in the middle of one of those action movies with everything coming apart at the same time — fire engines, the ambulances, the police, and people shouting.

Richard Eichen: As we got closer to the door, there were security guards helping guide people out. I think they were some of the bravest people — unsung heroes of 9/11 — because they could have run away. This was way beyond their pay grade. But they stayed.

Ralph Blasi, director of security, Brookfield Properties, owner of the World Financial Center and 1 Liberty Plaza: I have the greatest admiration for the private security officers, guys who are only making about $25,000 a year. We had often asked security guards, prior to 9/11, what they would do if a bomb went off and they saw a couple dead bodies. The consensus was always that they would run. But on September 11th, I had 60 guards working with me and not one ran. With the two towers burning, standing with bullhorns, keeping people moving out of the Towers, they never blinked.

JUMPING

"THE SUN WAS SHINING ON THEM"

Amid the catastrophe at the World Trade Center, no sight left as powerful an impression on rescuers, officials, and evacuees as the developing tragedy of victims — trapped without escape on the Towers' upper floors, caught amid rising, unbearable temperatures and deadly smoke — who fell or chose to jump.

Wesley Wong, assistant special agent in charge, FBI New York: This fireman said something to me that I didn't understand — he said, "Watch out for the falling bodies." I remember crossing West Street and thinking, *What did he say about falling bodies?* I said, "It's a fire." As I got close to the building this fireman from behind yelled, "Run! Here comes one!" I froze and I looked up over my right shoulder, up into that beautiful bright blue sky. I saw a fellow spread-eagle, coming out of the sky. He had on navy blue dress pants, a white shirt, and a tie. Dark hair. I couldn't believe what I saw.

Det. David Brink, Emergency Service Unit, Truck 3, NYPD: There were a lot of bodies that were coming down. I saw daisy chains of four people holding hands, just leaping out of the buildings. I kept looking up, saying, "I want to help you guys. Hold on. Please hold on," but I knew there was nothing I could do. I felt so helpless and powerless.

Dr. Charles Hirsch, chief medical examiner, City of New York: It was a sight and sound that I'll never forget. The awful sound of people impacting.

Gregory Fried, executive chief surgeon, NYPD: You'd hear this *whoosh,* and then it would go crash, and then all of a sudden you'd hear a splat. One of the cops said to me, "What was that?" I looked at him and said, "That was a person."

Quentin DeMarco, officer, PAPD: The clothes of the jumpers sounded like a flag or a sail in a windstorm.

Bill Spade, firefighter, Rescue 5, FDNY: There were motion-detector doors that opened up into the North Tower. These doors kept opening and closing with the bodies that were coming down.

Peter Moog, officer, NYPD: I did see one jumper actually hit a fireman on the corner near Vesey and West. I later found out that the fireman was Danny Suhr. He played for the fire department football team. I coach our team, and I've played, so I knew Danny. He was one of the first firemen to get killed.

William Jimeno, officer, PAPD: The one that struck me the most — it's almost like my eyes could zoom in up to him — it was a blond gentleman wearing a pair of khakis and a light pink shirt, collared shirt, and when he jumped, he jumped almost like he was on a cross, like Jesus. He jumped, looking up in the air, and he went down.

Stanley Trojanowski, firefighter, Engine 238, FDNY: I must've blessed myself between 40 and 50 times, once for each jumper.

Bill Spade: We've seen death at other things, but this time it was something different. There were so many, so many.

Sgt. Mike McGovern, aide to the chief, NYPD: I had blood splatter on the cuffs of my pants from the people jumping and landing on the ground.

Rudy Giuliani, mayor, New York City: All of a sudden I saw a man at a window, must have been the 100th floor, 101st, 102nd floor, North Tower. He threw himself out the window. I froze, stopped, and watched him come all the way down. It was a totally shocking experience, unlike any I've ever had before. I leaned over to the police commissioner and said, "This is much worse than we thought. It's off the charts." We had practiced a lot of things — anthrax, sarin gas, airplane crashes, building collapses, hostage situations, derailed trains, West Nile virus. I was pretty confident that we were the most prepared place in the United States for any emergency — maybe in the world. This was beyond anything that anybody had imagined.

Bernie Kerik, NYPD commissioner: I've been in this business 26 years, and I've done everything under the sun. I've been involved in gun battles. I've had partners who were killed. But I've never felt as helpless as I did on that morning. You couldn't yell to these people and ask them to stop, or make them stop.

Melinda Murphy, traffic reporter, WPIX TV, airborne over New York Harbor: Our camera's pretty strong. I said, "What's that dripping off the building?" It looked like something was dripping. Chet's like, "I don't know." So we zoom in and we could see people jumping. We were on live TV and I remember going, "OK, that's it, zoom out, zoom out." I didn't want anybody to see it.

Sunny Mindel, communications director for the mayor of the City of New York, Rudy Giuliani: I remember seeing colleagues from the police department's press operation surrounded by television cameras with their lenses trained upward on people jumping. The first thing you learn when you do what I do is you never obscure the lens of a camera. That's a violation of the First Amendment — to interfere with the press. I was so riveted to this moment of people making this decision to jump that my gut instinct was: *This is an invasion of the most intimate moment ever.* My hands started to go up to block the lenses. But then I thought, *No, this has got to be recorded for history.* I just stood there.

THE FAA MAKES HISTORY

"WHEN IS THIS GOING TO COME TO AN END?"

At 9:42 a.m., five minutes after the Pentagon attack, the FAA issued an unprecedented order: Every plane in the country must land immediately. Beyond the massive disruption in the airspace over the United States, more than a hundred transatlantic flights were diverted to small airports in Newfoundland, Nova Scotia, and elsewhere in Canada. Pilots, flight crews, and passengers all tried to understand what had happened in the United States, hungry for information wherever they could find it.

Ben Sliney, national operations manager, FAA Command Center, Herndon, Virginia: I said, "That's it!" I said, "I'm landing everyone!" I remember a colleague putting his hand out to grab my shoulder, and he said, "Wait a minute! Do you want to think about that?" I said, "I've already thought about it, and I'm going to do it."

266

Dan Creedon, departure controller, TRACON, Reagan National Airport, Washington, D.C.: As soon as Flight 77 hit the Pentagon, it was obvious that no one should get near Washington. We could not trust any crew.

Ben Sliney: I walked down to the middle of the floor, and everyone came over to me. I said, "We're going to land everyone at the nearest airport regardless of destination."

Maj. Gen. Larry Arnold, commander of the 1st Air Force, NORAD, Tyndall Air Force Base, Florida: Boston Center had stopped all takeoffs, then the Department of Transportation stopped all flights, and then my boss declared SCATANA, which stands for Security Control of Air Traffic and Air Navigation Aids. It means the military is taking control of all the navigation aids and of the airspace.

Lt. Col. Kevin Nasypany, mission crew commander, NEADS, Rome, New York: I feel I'm still so far behind in what's happening, the whole situation. It's a catch-up situation, and I don't like being in a catch-up situation — never have, never will.

Terry Biggio, operations manager, Boston Air Route Traffic Control Center: The controllers were telling the pilots, "You're gonna have to land." We told them, "You're not leaving our airspace — you gonna have to pick an airport, get a hold of your company, tell us where you're gonna go, and tell us where you're gonna land."

Kristie Luedke, chief of air traffic control training, Johnstown–Cambria County Airport, Pennsylvania: Cleveland Center said, "We are bringing everybody in. Everybody's landing."

Gerald Earwood, pilot, Midwest Express Flight 7: Every plane was considered a threat. We were asked probably 15 or 20 times, "Are you still with us?" It was total mass confusion.

Maj. Gen. Larry Arnold: The only thing I can equate it to is when I was at Da Nang. Da Nang became known as "Rocket City" by attacks by the North Vietnamese and Vietcong. I was there during three of those attacks. If I could explain to you how it was on 9/11: *we were under attack.* You don't know when it's going to end. You're getting calls — turned out to be 21 aircraft or 22, we were never sure whether it was 21 or 22 — but we were keeping track, writing with grease pencils every time one was called "potentially hijacked," meaning something was going on

268

with this aircraft. I felt like we were under attack, like it was when I was hearing the rockets coming in when I was at Da Nang: *When is this going to come to an end?*

Ben Sliney: When the order came out to land at the nearest airport regardless of destination, I expected some pushback. Out of 4,500 aircraft in the air, I only got one request to land at an airport that was not the nearest one. I refused the request.

Dan Creedon: To put 4,500 aircraft on the ground in places where they were not supposed to go — at the same time that the military is trying to get airborne and control the chaos — is an incredible feat of air traffic controllers and air traffic managers coordinating that.

George "Bill" Keaton, air traffic controller, Cleveland Center: A couple times that day my voice did crack a little bit on frequency when I was working and it bothered me that the professionalism slipped a little bit. But it was a very emotional time. I saw people in the aisles crying.

Ben Sliney: To give some perspective, I believe 700 landed within the first 10 minutes, and 3,500 within the first hour.

Terry Biggio: They did an incredible job, under warlike conditions, with unbelievable precision.

Ben Sliney: I do not think the aviation industry got the thanks that they deserve from the American public.

Rick Greyson, passenger, ATA Airlines, Chicago to Orlando: About 30 or 40 minutes into the flight, after level off, I heard the engines throttle back to idle and felt the plane making a very rapid descent. The captain came on the PA and announced that "due to a national emergency, all airspace in the United States had been shut down" and that we would be "landing in Louisville very shortly." My teenage daughter read the look on my face and said, "Dad! What is it?" I told her I didn't know, but told her to lower her window shade. I guess I was expecting incoming nukes and wanted to protect her from the flash. Silly, how one's mind thinks of such things, as though that would have done a damned bit of good!

Bob Schnarrenberger, flight attendant, US Airways, Pittsburgh to London: Our lead flight attendant came through the cabin. She said, "Bob, I need you to tighten down the galleys, put everything away, lock up all your carts, finish your service in 45 minutes."

She left for the back of the airplane, and I'm thinking: *Okay, what's going on?* I pried and she took me aside and told me there was a critical situation in the U.S. and that the U.S. was "under siege." Those were her words. I can remember them as if it was just yesterday.

We were diverted to a little town called Stephenville in Newfoundland. There were five other jumbo jets on the ground there from all over. We were the last one that landed.

Jackie Pinto, passenger, Milan to Newark: The pilot made an announcement that we were going to be delayed, our landing was going to be delayed. Then things progressed, and he made an announcement and said, "We're not going to be landing in Newark today." That, of course, was peculiar, but I didn't think anything odd. As soon as we landed, they made the announcement that we landed in Gander, Newfoundland, which I had never heard of.

Gerald Earwood: We were the next-to-last aircraft to land at LaGuardia. They put us on a taxiway, pointing at the World Trade Center, watching the World Trade Center burn.

THE TRADE CENTER RESCUE CONTINUES

"YOU'RE GOING TO GET OUT!"

At the World Trade Center, the first crowds to evacuate the damaged buildings emerged onto the adjacent plazas and streets to find horrors anew. Few realized, though, that the clock was ticking and they had mere minutes to escape the scene.

Michael Jacobs, investment banker, May Davis Group, North Tower, 87th floor: Everyone from my company got out but one — Harry Ramos — and he died a hero's death. Harry was the nicest guy you'd ever want to meet. He was helping my coworkers get down, and on the way, they came across an obese man who had given up. Harry and another of our workers, Hong Zhu, started down with him. They got as far as 30-something, but the guy gave up again. The firemen yelled, "Come on, get up, get up." The firemen walking up the stairs told Hong and Harry, "If he won't go, you guys get the hell out." Hong got scared. He said, "Come on Harry, let's go." Harry said, "No, I'm going to stay with him." He did. Hong got out. They haven't found Harry.*

Howard Lutnick, CEO, Cantor Fitzgerald, North Tower: I stood at the door off of Church Street. People were coming out, and I was yelling at them to run. I would ask them what floor they were coming from. Someone would scream, "55!" and I would scream, "We're at 55!" because I kept wanting to get numbers higher up the building, from my office's floors, 101 through 105. I got to the 91st floor.

Jimmy Maio, driver for Howard Lutnick: There was nothing we could do. I wasn't so concerned for our safety because I thought the deed had been done.

Elia Zedeño, financial analyst, Port Authority, North Tower, 73rd floor: I saw debris all along the outside perimeter of the building. I was looking and thinking, *Oh my*

* The man Harry Ramos waited with was Victor Wald, a 49-year-old New York stockbroker with Avalon Partners and father of two. Wald had only started working at Avalon in late August. Later, Ramos's and Wald's families would request that their names be placed together on the 9/11 Memorial.

God, this is more than what I thought. My eyes start to focus a little bit more. I realized I was looking at bodies.

Joe Massian, technology consultant, Port Authority, North Tower, 70th floor: I remember stepping out of the building. My coworker Larry and I were helping our colleague, Theresa — each of us had one of her arms. I remember taking a minute, looking back and up. I said to Larry, "You've got to see this! Hollywood could never make this in a movie."

Constance Labetti, accountant, Aon Corporation, South Tower, 99th floor: The debris, the blocks of concrete, the fires. I saw shoes and briefcases. We thought we were in a war zone. We all gasped. We couldn't believe what we were seeing.

Harry Waizer, tax counsel, Cantor Fitzgerald, North Tower, 104th floor: Once I lay down in the ambulance, I did start to feel something. I literally did not feel pain before then. I started feeling chilled pain. I started trembling. I was shaking, chattering.

Bruno Dellinger, principal, Quint Amasis North America, North Tower, 47th floor: What we went through will haunt us until the end of our lives.

274

Near the base of the World Trade Center, New York City's leaders continued to search for an acceptable command post from which to oversee the rescue effort and formulate the city's response.

Sgt. Mike McGovern, aide to the chief, NYPD: We ended up — the chief, the mayor, the police commissioner, the first deputy, the commissioner of operations, ended up in this office building on the corner of West Broadway and Barclay.

Rudy Giuliani, mayor, New York City: The police commissioner and I discussed the actions he had taken. He said, "I closed the tunnels and the bridges. Nobody else can be allowed into Manhattan." I said, "Are we covering our priority targets?"

Joe Esposito, chief of department, NYPD: The order was: *Evacuate all high-rises, protect all your sensitive locations, high-risk locations.* We didn't know where the next shoe was going to drop.

Sunny Mindel, communications director for the mayor of the city of New York, Rudy Giuliani: There was a tremendous sense of urgency, but nobody was panicked. Everybody had seen some pretty mind-

275

staggering things, but everybody was doing what they needed to be doing.

Joe Esposito: [The mayor] was desperately trying to get on the phone and talk to Washington.

Rudy Giuliani: They got the White House on the phone, and it was Chris Hennick, who was the deputy political director for President Bush. I asked Chris how he was. He said, "Okay." I said, "Do we have air cover?" He said, "It has already been requested and it was sent out. You should see the planes in five or 10 minutes." I said to him, "Can I talk to the president?" He said, "You can't; we're evacuating the White House right now," which was a very eerie feeling. I said, "Has the Pentagon been attacked?" I had heard that rumor. Chris said — I'll always remember how he answered it because it was a very military answer — he said, "Affirmative."

Bernie Kerik, commissioner, NYPD: I've known the mayor for about 11 or 12 years, and I've never seen him look as worried or concerned about anything as much as he did when he was on the phone with the White House. He put the phone down and he said, "Well, that's not good at all. They've hit the Pentagon and they're evacuating the White House." It was a clear signal that this was no longer just about New York City. It was about the United States.

Michele Cartier, Lehman Brothers, North Tower, 40th floor: I tried calling my brother James on his cellular, but he didn't pick up. I tried calling my parents, and I think their line was busy. I called my sister Marie at her job. I said, "Marie, I'm evacuating the building. They don't know if it's a plane or a bomb, but I'm leaving. You have to get in touch with James. He's in the other building." We're all worrywarts for each other. We're a very tight-knit family. James was assigned to work at Aon Corporation.

John Cartier, brother of James Cartier, electrician, who was working in the South Tower: He was on assignment for a company called P. E. Stone, had a contract to do some form of electrical work for Aon. Jimmy was there, working on the 105th floor of the South Tower, along with a few other coworkers from P. E. Stone.

Michele Cartier: When I made it to the last step I remember feeling really good, like, "All right! This is the last step, everybody!" Then I look out into the plaza, and I pretty much see a war zone.

John Cartier: I'm Michele and James's

older brother. I'm one of seven kids. I was working at the old *New York Post* building on the East Side, by the FDR Drive, and Jimmy called to let me know that a plane had hit Tower One, and that Michele was in there, and we needed to figure out a plan, get together, and handle the situation. I said to him, "All right. I'm going to leave now. I'm going to get to you." I rode my motorcycle downtown, and I got to within about a block and a half of the Trade Center.

Michele Cartier: I was out there talking with my coworkers Barbara and Rob about how we're going to get home. "Do you think the trains are running?" I'm babbling and babbling, and I see my brother John a few steps away. I remember screaming out, "John-o!" I hugged him. When I saw John, I was safe again. I knew everything would be okay.

John Cartier: In the midst of thousands and thousands of people evacuating, through the doings of my brother James calling me, getting me down there, I look out and here comes my sister. She just pops out of the crowd. The odds of that happening are probably — you're better off hitting the Lotto.

Michele Cartier: John filled me in on what had been going on as I was walking down the stairs. He talked about the second plane hitting. I said, "Second plane? Where was the first one?"

Above the impact zone, victims phoned friends and family members, sharing final thoughts and love. Melissa Harrington Hughes, director of business development for a communications network service who was only in New York for a one-day business trip and became trapped in the North Tower, called her father in Massachusetts.

Bob Harrington, father: She was a little hysterical and I couldn't understand what she was saying, so I said, "Slow down a minute and tell me what the problem is so I can help you out." I said, "You get to the stairwell and get out of that building as fast as you can." I told her that I loved her. She said, "I love you too, Dad," and she said, "You have to do me a favor. You have to call Sean and tell him where I am and tell him that I love him."

`Minutes later, Melissa Harrington Hughes called her husband, Sean, still asleep in San Francisco, and left him a voice mail:` Sean, it's me. I just wanted to let you know I love you and I'm stuck in

279

this building in New York. There's lots of smoke and I just wanted you to know that I love you always.

John Cartier: We had four phone calls from Jimmy. One was to me and three went to my sister Maria that were intermittent and cut off. The last phone call that we received from him was 20 minutes before the collapse. We know that my brother was alive at that point. He said that he was with a lot of people and he was on the 105th floor. True to form, he told my sister, "Tell Mommy and Daddy that I love them, and that we're going to try to get down." That was the last time we heard from him.

Mary Maciejewski, wife of Jan Maciejewski, waiter, Windows on the World, North Tower, 106th floor: Jan's normal shift was lunch, so he'd get there at 10:30 a.m. But the Friday before, his manager called and asked if he could work breakfast. My office is about 10 blocks away. The minute I got to my desk — I work on the 46th floor — people were screaming and running to the windows. Then my phone rang, and it was Jan. He told me that there was smoke, awful smoke, and that they were in touch with the fire department, who told them not to move, that they were going to come and get them. I told him to go wet a napkin and put it over his face so he could breathe. He told me there was no water anywhere so he was going to go get some from the flower vases. Then the second building was hit, and they decided to evacuate my building. Jan told me to hang up and get out, so I would be safe, and to call him back on his cell phone when I got outside. But there was no connection.

Howard Lutnick, CEO, Cantor Fitzgerald, North Tower: We have speakerphones in each office — all of the offices across the country were connected to each other all day. The other offices heard the New York office saying, "We need help. We need help. We need help." It wasn't screams. There was nowhere to go. Couldn't go down. Couldn't go up.

Stephen Larabee, Cantor Fitzgerald, L.A. office: My son Chris worked for Cantor Fitzgerald in New York. He called me right after the airplane hit the building. It was very early in Los Angeles. He said, "Dad, did you hear our building was hit by an airplane?" I said, no, I hadn't. Having been in that building before, I wasn't terribly concerned because I'd seen small aircraft flying by, and that's what I surmised had happened. I said, "Well, take care of yourself, get out of the building, evacuate with everybody else, and give me a call after that's done." I hung up the phone and walked to get coffee.

A couple of people in our trading room were either hooked up to CNN or CNBC, one of those stations, and started talking real loud. Then we realized what had happened. We had a speaker system that went to all our branch offices, and somebody in our New York office said, "Does anybody know we're here? Is anybody coming to get us?" Then we all realized how horrible this thing was. Frank Harrison in our Chicago office said, "You guys, get on the floor, stay low, cover if you can with anything, don't let the smoke get you." There was some crowd noise, then it was static. The speaker system went dead.

Howard Lutnick: My brother, Gary, was in the building. Later that night, when I spoke to my sister, she told me that she spoke to my brother. She had said to him, "Oh, my God. Thank God you're not there." He said, "I am here, and I'm going to die. I wanted to tell you I love you." He said goodbye.

Beverly Eckert, wife of Sean Rooney, VP of risk management, Aon Corporation, South Tower, 98th floor: It was about 9:30 a.m. when he called. When I heard his voice on the phone, I was so happy. I said, "Sean, where are you?," thinking that he had made it out and that he was calling me from the

282

street somewhere. He told me he was on the 105th floor. I knew right away Sean was never coming home.

There was a building in flames underneath him, but Sean didn't even flinch. He stayed composed, talking to me the way he always did. I will always be in awe of the way he faced death. Not an ounce of fear — not when the windows around him were getting too hot to touch, not when the smoke was making it hard to breathe.

I wanted to use the precious few minutes we had left to talk. He told me to give his love to his family, and then we began talking about all the happiness we shared during our lives together, how lucky we were to have each other. At one point, when I could tell it was getting harder for him to breathe, I asked if it hurt. He paused for a moment, and then said, "No." He loved me enough to lie. In the end, as the smoke got thicker, he kept whispering "I love you," over and over.

Terri Langone, wife of FDNY firefighter Peter Langone: My husband called to let me know, "Turn on the TV, Ter. We think a plane crashed into the Towers." Then he proceeded to talk to me like it was any other day. Then he said, "Keep the TV on and watch. I'm not going to be home anytime soon." That was that. That was the last time I spoke to him. I'm one of the fortunate ones to have spoken to him that day.

John Cartier: You've got to look at the small gifts that we were given as a family. There's a lot of families out there who didn't get a last word or a last phone call. One of the other young ladies who lost her husband said it best. She said, "We were the lucky of the unlucky to have those last words."

Dan Nigro, chief of operations, FDNY, inside the ground-floor lobby of the North Tower, at the FDNY command post: I said to Chief Ganci, "I am going to quickly walk around and see what the damage looks like." When I got to the center of Vesey Street, I could see clearly the north side of the South Tower. The corner of the building was taken out. We didn't see that when the plane hit, it sliced right through the tower. I wanted to get back to say to Pete, "I think we have less time than we might have thought we had. The South Tower looks terrible."

Jean Potter, Bank of America, North Tower: I came out [of the World Trade Center] at 9:55. I looked at my watch. There's flaming debris all around me. I walked one block, and I saw one of my [apartment building's] doormen. I said,

"Richard, what happened?" I turned around — the sight of the Towers flaming was unbelievable. My doorman said a plane hit the World Trade Center. Then I was trying to get contact with Dan and my family because, I thought, *If anybody sees this, they're going to think I'm dead.*

Melinda Murphy, traffic reporter, WPIX TV: The Towers were on fire. My photographer Chet had been a firefighter. He said, "The buildings are going to fall." I remember being really mad, vehemently saying, "They are not, they are not going to fall down!" He said, "They are going to fall. They're going to pancake down."

Dan Nigro: I heard somebody call out to me, a civilian employee of the fire department. He said, "Chief, my wife works on the 92nd floor of the South Tower and I can't get in touch with her." It was one of those instances where you really have your hands full with what you are doing, but I thought, *Let me stop for a minute.* I felt so bad for him. I knew his wife had given birth about three months before. I said, "No one's phone is working. I am sure she got out before this even happened, and she's probably already a few blocks away, so when the phones start working again you'll be able to contact her. Don't worry."

285

Stopping to talk to this person inadvertently saved me and my aide, who was with me — and is also my nephew — from certain death. We were walking to go through the South Tower lobby, and whatever time it took me to say those few words would have been enough time to put me in a place where I would not have been able to get away.

Bill Spade, firefighter, Rescue 5, FDNY: We were right in front of Stairway C [in the North Tower]. The people were coming down, and we kept telling people, "You're almost out, you've almost made it out."

Lila Speciner, paralegal, Port Authority, North Tower: We got down to the Concourse level. The sprinklers were on. Everything was soggy, wet, whatever, but we started to smile because, okay, we were done.

William Jimeno, officer, PAPD: We bumped into another group of Port Authority police officers — a classmate of mine, Walwyn Stuart. He actually had his first little girl while we were in the academy. We punched each other's fists, and we said, "Be safe." They started walking away. That would be the last time we saw any of those Port Authority police officers.

Lt. Gregg Hansson, Engine 24, FDNY:
There was a chief on the 35th floor [in the North Tower] with us. Over his radio came a "Mayday" to get out of the building — a "Mayday" basically means to run. We didn't, at the time, have any understanding why that order was given, and it didn't make sense to us. Within seconds, the South Tower collapsed.

The First Collapse

"SOMETHING WASN'T RIGHT"

At 9:59 a.m. less than an hour after it was the second building hit, the South Tower, weakened by fires fueled by thousands of gallons of jet fuel, collapsed.

Dan Potter, firefighter, Ladder 10, FDNY: I ran into the Engine 10 firehouse, at the base of the World Trade Center, and Captain Mallory grabbed me and said, "Sign into the book, because it's total recall, they're calling all firefighters back here." I remember signing the book and putting on my gear. Other firefighters were also starting to run in now. One of them was Pete Bielfeld — I figured he and I would team up. As we go toward the front of the firehouse, I said, "Pete, let me go grab a tool first. Stand here. Let me go grab a rescue tool." I turned around, ran back for that. He didn't wait for me. As I was going out the front [of the firehouse], there was a firefighter standing in the door. I don't know who he was. I remem-

288

ber him standing there, looking up, and he saw the top of the tower twist. As I was going by, he clotheslined me — he sticks his arm out and it catches me. He goes, "Holy shit, here it comes."

Dan Nigro, chief of operations, FDNY: No one has heard a high-rise building collapse before, but as soon as I heard it, I knew what it was.

Donna Jensen, resident, Battery Park City: It was this *rat-tat-tat-tat-tat-tat-tat-tat,* this snapping sound in perfect rhythm, this loud, cracking, snapping sound.

John Cartier, brother of James Cartier, electrician, who was working in the South Tower: At first, it was a faint sound, and then it came closer and closer.

Capt. Sean Crowley, NYPD: We're talking to [NYPD officer] Glen Pettit at the intersection of Liberty and West when we hear a rumble.

Edward "Eddie" Aswad Jr., officer, NYPD: I'm looking at the building, and Sean's facing me. The next thing you hear is, "It's going!" I look up and see this black cloud of smoke.

Capt. Sean Crowley: I was looking away from the building, toward Eddie. I saw his face, and he goes, "Fucking run," or something like that. He turned around and ran toward where our cars were parked, which was right in front of Three World Financial Center, underneath the walkway. I never saw Glen again.

William Jimeno, officer, PAPD, inside the lobby of the South Tower: Everything started shaking. I looked back toward the lobby, and I saw a fireball the size of my house coming. Sergeant [John] McLoughlin yelled, "Run!" I said to myself, *What did I get myself into?* As I was running, I could see a light in front of me. I remember thinking, in a split second, *Wow, I should run toward the light, maybe it will take me outside.* Then I remembered we promised we would not leave each other. I saw Dominick run, he turned to the left, so I started to follow him. At that point, all I felt was my body go up in the air and get slammed.

John Cartier: The sound was so deafening.

Michele Cartier, Lehman Brothers, North Tower, 40th floor: This high-pitched sound, and I didn't know what that was, but it was so eerie, like your fingernails-on-a-chalkboard type of thing.

Bruno Dellinger, principal, Quint Amasis North America, North Tower, 47th floor: I heard a sound that today I cannot remember. It was so powerful, such a huge sound that I blocked it. It scared me to death. I blocked it, and I cannot bring it back up to consciousness.

Howard Lutnick, CEO, Cantor Fitzgerald, North Tower: The loudest sound I'd ever heard.

Gregory Fried, executive chief surgeon, NYPD: I can't even give you an analogy.

Bill Spade, firefighter, Rescue 5, FDNY: Like six or eight subway cars pulling into the station at the same time with their brakes.

Det. Steven Stefanakos, Emergency Service Unit, Truck 10, NYPD: Like a thousand freight trains crashed.

Kenneth Escoffery, firefighter, Ladder 20, FDNY: Like an incoming missile.

James Dobson, paramedic: Like an avalanche.

Gulmar Parga, marine engineer, fireboat John D. McKean, FDNY: Like a giant chandelier, all the glass breaking.

Catherine Leuthold, independent photo-journalist: Like 30,000 jets taking off.

Sharlene Tobin, financial consultant, One New York Plaza: Like a machine gun.

Joe Massian, technology consultant, Port Authority, North Tower, 70th floor: A pop and then a sift — like taking a bag of sugar and pouring it into a container.

Al Kim, vice president of operations, TransCare Ambulance: I told everyone, "Incoming! Run!"

Constance Labetti, accountant, Aon Corporation, South Tower, 99th floor: We really thought that the end of the world was upon us.

The collapse of the South Tower instantly trapped guests, staff, and rescuers inside the Marriott Hotel, located between the Twin Towers, as wreckage pounded the roof.

Frank Razzano, guest, Marriott Hotel: I was standing there watching the TV. I said to myself, *Jesus Christ, if I leave this building* *today without my stuff, they're never going to let me back in this building tonight.* I started packing all my documents and getting everything ready to go, thinking, *I wonder if I can get a bellman to come up and help me take all this stuff down?* At that point the building shook, as if you were in an earthquake. I looked out the window, and what had been a bright sunny day suddenly turned pitch black. It was as if a curtain of concrete and steel had come falling down, like the curtain at a play. I could literally see it coming down, past the window — almost in slow motion — turning everything pitch black.

Jeff Johnson, firefighter, Engine 74, FDNY: The entire building started to shudder. It was lights out. I fell down.

Frank Razzano: It was as if the building was being hit by artillery fire. You could feel the building breaking up around you.

Jeff Johnson: We immediately called for the other members of our crew. It's a military thing. We called, "Pat?" "Yeah." "John?" "Yeah." "Lieu, it's Jeff." We had us four, and then we called Ruben, and we didn't get an answer. We kept screaming, "Ruben? Ruben?"

Frank Razzano: I yelled out into what was

left of the hallway, "Is anybody there?" I hear a voice that said, "Come this way." The room was located almost right next to the fire staircase. Right at the base of the doorjamb, in some rubble, was a New York City fireman. I learned later that his name was Jeff Johnson. I said, "Are you okay?" He said to me, "Are you okay?" I said, "Yeah, I'm fine. How are you? Is there anything I can do to help you?" He said, "No, I'm fine. I want you to go down the fire stairs."

Jeff Johnson: Immediately in front of us was a complete wall of debris.

Frank Razzano: When I got to the fourth-floor landing and began to walk down the stairs to where the third-floor landing would be, it was blocked with rubble. I began trying to move rubble away and create an opening. I got enough rubble out of the way that I could squeeze through. On the third-floor landing were three men and the banquet manager of the hotel.

Jeff Johnson: We gave immediate "Maydays" on the radio that as a unit we were missing a member. Nobody was answering us. We did hear somebody calling out on the radio a "Mayday." He was a fireman, and he didn't know where he was. "I'm trapped, but I don't know where I am." That's the most heart-wrenching and worst-case scenario.

Frank Razzano: Within a few minutes, Jeff Johnson came down. He was with another fireman now, that he had met coming down the stairs. Jeff looked around. An I-beam was leaning up against the landing on the third floor and was wedged on a ledge on the second floor. Jeff climbed down the I-beam, walked along the ledge, came back, and yelled up to us, "Each of you are going to have to climb down the I-beam and walk along the ledge and go back into the building. We have got to find a way out."

I also recall him saying, "Look, nobody's coming. Nobody is coming for us. Any of the firemen or rescue people who are tasked at getting people out of the building — they are dead. If they were in the street, they are dead. If they were in the buildings, they are dead. Nobody is coming to get us. We have to get out on our own."

The unprecedented collapse — the first time a high-rise building had ever fallen — was witnessed by millions around the world, on television, and in person across the New York region, including by those who had already evacuated from the World Trade Center and Lower Manhattan.

Beverly Eckert, wife of Sean Rooney, VP of risk management, Aon Corporation, South Tower, 98th floor: I suddenly heard this loud explosion through the phone. It reverberated for several seconds. We held our breath. I know we both realized what was about to happen. Then I heard a sharp crack, followed by the sound of an avalanche. I heard Sean gasp once as the floor fell out from underneath him. I called his name into the phone over and over.

Cathy Pavelec, administrator, Port Authority, North Tower, 67th floor: I ran into a woman on the street who I knew from my office, Denise. We started up the ramp to go to the Brooklyn Bridge, but then I saw all these fighter planes. I didn't know if they were ours or not. I said to Denise, "We can't go on a bridge. We can't go on a landmark." I really thought that the planes belonged to somebody other than us. We turned around to get off the bridge. We heard a noise, we looked up, and we saw Tower Two collapse.

Robert Small, office manager, Morgan Stanley, South Tower, 72nd floor, now on the Brooklyn Bridge: It looked like a Fourth of July sparkler. It swayed to one side and fell within itself. Then it was gone. You can see the glitter from the metal and the glass as this big gray cloud formed.

Michael McAvoy, associate director, Bear Stearns, Brooklyn: In seconds, it was gone. People screamed again. I looked at my coworker Brian and said, "Holy shit, 20,000 people just died."

Monica O'Leary, former employee, Cantor Fitzgerald, North Tower: I remember standing there with my neighbor John, saying, "Where the hell did that go? Where the hell did that go? Where did the building go? Where'd they go?"

Judith Wein, senior vice president, Aon Corporation, South Tower, 103rd floor: My heart dropped. I thought of everybody who was still up there. It was their end.

Melinda Murphy, traffic reporter, WPIX TV: When the building fell it became a personal story for me because my husband worked a couple of blocks away. It became, "Oh my God, my husband may not be alive." On camera, I was fine. As soon as they told me I was clear, I was a mess.

Peter Jennings, anchor, ABC News: We went into silent mode. It was not necessary for us to add our own anxiety or shock. It was all evident for everybody. Throughout my entire career, I have always been conscious that there are times when some people on television talk too much. Silence or natural sound on occasion is infinitely more powerful and relevant.

Aaron Brown, anchor, CNN: The hardest words I've ever spoken on TV in 25 years were these: "The United States is under attack." It took me too long, perhaps a half hour too long, to utter those words. They were there, I assure you. I knew what it was.

Cathy Pavelec: We stood there for a minute and then the cloud started to come after us. For the first time that day, I really thought we were going to die.

Richard Grasso, chairman and CEO, New York Stock Exchange: When the South Tower was coming down, my head of security came racing across the floor. He was uncharacteristically shaken. He said, "We're learning the city's gone code black." Which means the mayor's dead, the police commissioner's dead, and the fire commissioner's dead. At that point, I turned to my colleague and said, "Ring the bell — we're closed."

Inside the Cloud
"THIS IS NOT MY DAY, I'M NOT DYING HERE"

The South Tower collapsed at an estimated speed of nearly 124 miles an hour, and later estimates held that the winds generated from the collapse of the World Trade Center peaked as high as 70 miles per hour, driving the accompanying cloud of debris scores of blocks away as the hurricane-force wind spread devastation throughout Lower Manhattan.

Rudy Giuliani, mayor, New York City: I heard someone yell, "The tower is coming down." I heard a big noise, saw the desk shaking. My first impression of "The tower is coming down" was that the radio tower on the top of the building had come down. I certainly didn't have the impression that the whole building had come down.

Rosmaris Fernandez, student, HSLPS: I could not believe that the World Trade Center was coming down. I stared at the buildings coming down in amazement until I came to

299

my senses and realized that it was time to run.

Ada Dolch, principal, HSLPS: That was the moment when I said, "OK, this is the end." I saw this tsunami wave of dust and debris coming in our direction. It was coming fast. It felt like pins and needles on your back. It was beyond frightening.

Heather Ordover, English teacher, HSLPS: I remember seeing the solid-as-a-wall smoke coming down Trinity Place right at Battery Park.

Jean Potter, Bank of America, North Tower: I remember thinking, *Maybe I am going to die. Maybe it is my time. How do I outrun this?* I was in such a state of shock. A police officer took me by the hand and dragged me into a subway station — the Dey Street subway station — and we kept going deeper and deeper.

Dan Potter, firefighter, Ladder 10, FDNY: There was a blue tarp out in front of the firehouse — I guess they were going to use it for triage. There was a Chinese man on it, and he had a broken leg. When the Towers started coming down, I grabbed him as best I could and started pulling him back.

Det. David Brink, Emergency Service Unit, Truck 3, NYPD: We went under one of the overhangs by Building Six. It was like when you were doing one of those school drills back in the day with the nuclear threats from Russia. They would tell you to duck and cover and go under your school desk. The only thing we really had to duck and cover under was these overhangs.

Howard Lutnick, CEO, Cantor Fitzgerald, North Tower: I looked over my shoulder, and there was this big, giant, black tornado of smoke chasing me. I dove under a car, and the black smoke went *foosh.*

Jan Khan, New York Metropolitan Transportation Council, North Tower: A hurricane-type wind blew us to the floor.

Lt. Joseph Torrillo, director of fire education safety, FDNY: As I was running that air caught the back of my helmet, and I saw my helmet fly away. My helmet was flying faster and higher, and I could see it as I was running. It was like *The Wizard of Oz.* At that point, as the building came down lower and lower, the air pressure was so strong — they estimate almost like a tornado force — the air pressure lifted me off of my feet and I was flying through the air.

Tracy Donahoo, transit officer, NYPD: It hit so hard I went flying. I don't know how far I went, I went flying — I could feel myself in the air. I landed on my knees and on my hand. It was dark. It was so black in there. You couldn't see anything and I couldn't breathe. I was choking.

Ian Oldaker, staff, Ellis Island: The smoke came right up the street, like fingers. It was really gray and dirty. We couldn't see the Towers, so we didn't know what had fallen.

Linda Krouner, senior vice president, Fiduciary Trust, South Tower: There was this gigantic cannonball of dust approaching me along these streets. I started running because I wanted to avoid this gargantuan ball of debris approaching me — a little bit like the Indiana Jones cannonball.

Joe Massian, technology consultant, Port Authority, North Tower: My fear was that the buildings would begin to domino, and I'd get caught between the two dominoes. I believe my picture was taken right when I passed the church. You can see the tree line in the photo.

Gregory Fried, executive chief surgeon, NYPD: Your brain couldn't adjust to the

concept of the World Trade Center coming down on you.

Ian Oldaker: We started running south. We ran right up to the water. There's a guardrail there — a big iron handrail. A lot of people ran up with us. There were a couple of hundred people right on this handrail. You're looking in, and you're looking down, and it's, "Hudson. Smoke. Hudson. Smoke." A lot of people looked down really temptingly at that water.

James Filomeno, firefighter, Marine 1, FDNY: We were docked near the pier. I was watching people running toward us like a herd of cattle. I watched debris coming down on them. People were jumping headfirst onto the deck and screaming. People were trying to hand me their kids: "Take my baby. I don't want to stay here. Take the baby." People fell in the water. It was horrible.

James Cowan, Harbor Unit, NYPD: We were yelling for people in the water to answer us. There were dozens of people in the water.

Vanessa Lawrence, artist, North Tower: I only just got out of the building when it was coming down. I started running across the road to the subway, and the big blast came up. As soon as I put my foot down on the sidewalk, the building was down, and I couldn't see anything.

Chief Joseph Pfeifer, Battalion 1, FDNY: I heard all the crashing and the steel and then the street went totally black. As a firefighter, you expect blackness inside a burning building. Outside in broad daylight, you don't.

Bruno Dellinger, principal, Quint Amasis North America, North Tower: In about five seconds, darkness fell upon us with an unbelievable violence. Even more striking: there was no more sound. Sound didn't carry anymore because the air was so thick.

Melinda Murphy, traffic reporter, WPIX TV, airborne over New York Harbor: This incredible dust cloud came up, and it looked like all of Lower Manhattan was gone.

Dan Potter, firefighter, Ladder 10, FDNY: Then it started — the rain of the debris. Everything hitting around you. I dove to the floor, covered myself up. I figured: *This is it.* The force buckled the metal doors of the firehouse. They blew out every window. The ambulance that was up in the front there was crushed.

Dr. Charles Hirsch, chief medical examiner, City of New York: The pummeling by debris seemed to go on forever. It was probably a minute or so.

Edward Aswad Jr., officer, NYPD: I could feel stuff going up my legs, the soot and the debris.

Lt. Joseph Torrillo, director of fire education safety, FDNY: I got hit over the head with a piece of steel, and my whole head was split open. Huge chunks of concrete were hitting my body. Every time another chunk hit me, I could hear my bones snapping.

William Jimeno, officer, PAPD: I felt a lot of pain, I grabbed my helmet, and I grabbed for my radio, which was on my left lapel, and I was yelling "8-13!," which is Port Authority police code for "officer down." "8-13! 8-13! Officers down! 8-13! Jimeno, we're down! Our team is down!" We were getting pummeled with debris. I was trying to fight for my life. At one point, something hit my left hand, my radio went flying. A big piece of concrete must have hit my helmet, it came flying off — ripped the chin strap right off — and I covered my head. As fast as this was happening, it ended.

Sgt. John McLoughlin, PAPD: I thought I had died. I lost all sense. I had no sight. I had no smell. I had no hearing. Everything was just silent.

Al Kim, vice president of operations, TransCare Ambulance: I was burning. I remember being really hot, like head to toe, like, *This is bad, really bad — like hotter than a sauna or steam room.* My shirt was gone. It was all ripped and burned. I lost all my nostril hair. I lost a part of my eyebrows and all my eyelashes were gone too.

Elia Zedeño, financial analyst, Port Authority, North Tower, 73rd floor: I tripped over something, and I ended up on top of somebody, a police officer. He was screaming, "My eyes are burning!" and at the same time telling me, "Don't worry, everything is going to be fine." I think that is the mind of somebody who is trained like this. He was screaming — I am talking about *screaming* — and at the same time saying, "Well, don't worry, everything is going to be fine, we are getting out of here."

Capt. Sean Crowley, NYPD: I've never heard screaming like I did on that day. It was all men. It was unbelievable screaming. I'm thinking about how I'm probably going to die and about my kids.

Tracy Donahoo, transit officer, NYPD: People were screaming. I was screaming, "Shut up! Shut up! Shut up!" Everyone calmed down. I was like, "I'm a police officer, we're gonna get outta here!" I don't know how far my voice can carry in there, and I didn't know if we were really encapsulated in cement and would never get out.

Vanessa Lawrence: I remember at one point feeling amazingly calm. It always feels strange to say this, but I thought I couldn't breathe anymore, and I actually got really, really calm, and went, *Okay. It's fine. I can't breathe anymore and this is okay.* Then I got this feeling in my stomach that went, *No, you can do it. You can do it. Do it.* I got this boost again and it was, *Okay, I can fight this — I can.* That was one of the strangest feelings of them all, that calmness of going, *I give up,* but then that pound in my stomach.

I also then felt this arm beside me, and this voice. I clung hold of it, and this voice says, "We've got to wait till it settles." I remember turning and looking, and he'd got his coat and put it over us both and then I saw his badge and it was a fireman. I remember grabbing tight hold of him. The power of it — having somebody there beside me — helped me.

Tracy Donahoo: In the academy, they said, "If you think you're gonna die, you're going to die." So I'm not gonna die here. This is not my day, I'm not dying here.

Lt. Joseph Torrillo: I was buried under the South Tower. I can't breathe. I'm suffocating. It's darker than midnight. I could see nothing.

Det. Sgt. Joe Blozis, crime scene investigator, NYPD: After the building collapsed, there was a calmness that I'll never forget. When the dust cloud came, you heard nothing and you saw nothing.

Monsignor John Delendick, chaplain, FDNY: People I was standing with were all of a sudden dead. I looked one way, and they went another way and didn't make it out.

Tracy Donahoo: I was thinking of my family, and I was thinking of my annoying little puppy I had at home that was driving my mother crazy, and I was like, *She's gonna kill me, being stuck with this dog.*

Elia Zedeño: I was trying to breathe, and I was trying to spit out what I had in my mouth, but I couldn't, so I had to dig my hand in. I dug my hand into my mouth and pulled out a lot of stuff. I was going to be able to breathe, but the moment that I pulled the stuff out, more stuff came in.

Capt. Sean Crowley, NYPD: Picture taking a handful of flour and sticking it up your nose and in your mouth. That's what breathing was like.

Elia Zedeño: There were these desperate moments. I couldn't breathe. I kept digging, and digging, and digging, and digging, until my mouth, until the dirt started to settle a little bit, and I was able to get that first breath.

Heather Ordover, English teacher, HSLPS: I crouched next to a man with a green-striped Oxford cloth shirt. I helped him cut it with my Swiss Army knife scissors so he could put a piece over his nose and mouth. We shared water.

Ada Dolch, principal, HSLPS: Everyone kept saying you had to put water on tissues or on a piece of cloth, wash your face, or put something over your mouth so you don't breathe in that smoke.

Heather Ordover: I caught up to a police officer: "Do you know where we're going?" He said, "No, Staten Island Ferry?" "Have you been trained for this kind of thing?" Half-laugh. "Sort of."

Ada Dolch: I felt like I was choking. I got up, and I could take tiny little bits of swallow — I couldn't do a deep swallow because it hurt. A man said, "You have to take water and spit." I didn't have water, but I remember saying to him, "I'm the principal, I don't spit." You teach the kids that's not what you do. He said, "You need to take water and you need to gargle." He was standing by an old antique water fountain in the park. I took water. I spit. I cleaned my throat. I spit.

Rosmaris Fernandez, student, HSLPS: The air cleared out a little. I found a couple of my friends, and I felt less worried. I knew that I was not alone anymore. A teacher from the nearby High School of Economics and

Finance asked every student to follow him to the Brooklyn Bridge and so we did. I then lost him and kept on walking north on the FDR Drive.

William Jimeno, officer, PAPD: There was a lot of dust. I looked up, and about 30 feet above me I could see light coming in — apparently there was a hole there. I started feeling a lot of pain on my left side. I could see a big thick wall of concrete on me. I was trying to get my bearings, but I couldn't really see. That's when I heard Sergeant McLoughlin say, "Sound off! Where is everybody? Sound off!" Dominick Pezzulo was buried to my left in a push-up position. Dominick said, "Pezzulo!" I said, "Jimeno!" That's all we heard. For the next two minutes, I would yell, "Chris!" for Christopher Amoroso. And "A-Rod!," which was Antonio Rodrigues's nickname. "A-Rod! Chris! A-Rod! Chris!" That's when Dominick said, "Willy, they're in a better place."

INSIDE THE PEOC

"SIR, AUTHORITY TO ENGAGE?"

Underneath the North Lawn of the White House, the vice president and assembled aides attempted to comprehend the crisis from inside the Presidential Emergency Operations Center, a.k.a. the White House bunker, and tried to figure out how many more hijacked planes were in the air. They knew of at least one: United Flight 93.

Mary Matalin, aide to Vice President Dick Cheney: We saw [on TV] the building collapse.

Commander Anthony Barnes, deputy director, Presidential Contingency Programs, White House: There was a deafening silence, and a lot of gasping and "Oh my god" and that kind of thing.

Mary Matalin: Disbelief.

Commander Anthony Barnes: There are four or five very large, 55-inch television screens in the PEOC. We would put the different news stations — ABC, CBS, Fox, NBC — on those monitors. I remember Cheney being as flabbergasted as the rest of us were, sitting there watching on these monitors. Back in those days, a 55-inch TV monitor was a really big TV. It was almost bigger than life as the Towers collapsed.

Dick Cheney, vice president: In the years since, I've heard speculation that I'm a different man after 9/11. I wouldn't say that. But I'll freely admit that watching a coordinated, devastating attack on our country from an underground bunker at the White House can affect how you view your responsibilities.

Mary Matalin: We had to go right back to work.

Richard Clarke, counterterrorism adviser, White House: Many of us thought that we might not leave the White House alive.

Matthew Waxman, staff member, National Security Council, White House: One of the things we were all very conscious of down in the PEOC was that the White

313

House Situation Room was staffed with our close colleagues and friends who were staying in those spots despite a clear danger. The Situation Room, which is only half a floor below ground, was abuzz with activity. Some of the colleagues who continued to work in it were people who wouldn't normally be posted there, but they felt a responsibility to stay there to help manage the crisis. Especially early in the day, there was a palpable sense that close friends and colleagues might be in some significant danger.

Ian Rifield, special agent, U.S. Secret Service: There was a sense of frustration too, because we were sitting there. Everybody wanted to fight back. We're trained to go to the problem, and we were sitting there. There was a lot of tension in that regard. You wanted to do something to protect the complex and the Office of the President even better than we were, but we were doing the best we could with what we had.

Condoleezza Rice, national security adviser, White House: Norm Mineta, the transportation secretary, was tracking tail numbers of the aircraft on a yellow pad. He was calling out: "What happened to 671? What happened to 123?" He was trying to make sense of what was going on.

Nic Calio, director of legislative affairs, White House: Norm Mineta was sitting in front of these TV screens that had all these planes on them. It was pretty remarkable when you saw the number of planes in the air.

Condoleezza Rice: My first thought was, *Get a message out to the world that the United States of America has not been decapitated.* These pictures must have been terrifying. It must have seemed liked the United States of America was coming apart. My test was to keep my head about me and to make certain that people around the world didn't panic.

Nic Calio: The activity was so high and things were happening so quickly, at least for me, there wasn't any time to be afraid.

Matthew Waxman: There was this stark contrast between the chaotic information bombardment about what was happening around Washington, around the country — some of it accurate, some of it inaccurate — and the calm and careful deliberation of a lot of the senior decision makers.

Nic Calio: The vivid memory I have was we were in this cocoon — receiving and sending all this information, at the same time not knowing where our families were. It was probably midafternoon before we were able to try and contact our families. That was worrisome. I didn't know where my kids were. There was an overriding uncertainty about what was going on, what would actually happen, and what would have to follow.

Col. Bob Marr, commander, NEADS, Rome, New York: We were in foreign territory; we are used to protecting the shores, way out overseas. Our processes and procedures weren't designed for this.

Maj. Gen. Larry Arnold, commander of the 1st Air Force, NORAD, Tyndall Air Force Base, Florida: We can't see the aircraft. We don't know where it is because we don't have any radars pointing into the U.S. Anything in the United States was considered friendly by definition.

Lt. Heather "Lucky" Penney, F-16 pilot, D.C. Air National Guard: Our chain of command didn't go up to NORAD, didn't go up through the 1st Air Force, which oversaw operations in the United States. They had no method to be able to reach down — or even be able to know that the D.C. National Guard was there and available. There were no rules of engagement. I hadn't even thought about what that kind of mission might be like on American soil.

Commander Anthony Barnes: I was running liaison between the ops guys who had Pentagon officials on the phone and the conference room where the principals were. The Pentagon thought there was another hijacked airplane, and they were asking for permission to shoot down an identified hijacked commercial aircraft. I asked the vice president that question and he answered it in the affirmative. I asked again to be sure. "Sir, I am confirming that you have given permission?" For me, being a military member and an aviator — understanding the absolute depth of what that question was and what that answer was — I wanted to make sure that there was no mistake whatsoever about what was being asked. Without hesitation, in the affirmative, he said any confirmed hijacked airplane may be engaged and shot down.

Col. Matthew Klimow, executive assistant to the vice chair of the Joint Chiefs of Staff, Gen. Richard Myers, Pentagon: No one had ever contemplated the need to shoot down a civilian airliner.

Maj. Gen. Larry Arnold: I told Rick Findley in Colorado Springs [at NORAD's headquarters], "Rick, we have to have permission. We may have to shoot down this aircraft that is coming toward Washington, D.C. We need presidential authority."

Maj. Dan "Razin" Caine, F-16 pilot, D.C. Air National Guard: I handed our wing commander the phone to talk to the high levels of government to get the rules of engagement.

Dick Cheney: It had to be done. Once the plane became hijacked — even if it had a load of passengers on board who, obviously, weren't part of any hijacking attempt — having seen what had happened in New York and the Pentagon, you really didn't have any choice. It wasn't a close call.

Matthew Waxman: That really grabs you by the collar, when you hear the vice president giving the order to shoot down an unidentified aircraft flying toward the national capital. That stands out as one of the most frightening moments of the day, partly because it highlighted the sense of continuing danger. There was also the realization of the enormous dilemmas that faced decision makers at that moment with very little time and imperfect information.

Commander Anthony Barnes: I knew, without a doubt in my mind, that that was a historical precedent — that never before had we given permission to shoot down a commercial airliner. I got back on the phone — it was a general of some sort in the Pentagon — and on that secure line I was talking on, made sure that he understood that I had posed the question to the National Authority and the answer was in the affirmative. We made sure that we did not stutter or stumble because the emotion at that point was very, very high. Fortunately we didn't have to use that authority.

Josh Bolten, deputy chief of staff, White House: Vice President Cheney was very steady, very calm. He clearly had been through crises before and did not appear to be in shock like many of us.

Commander Anthony Barnes: The president was safer aboard Air Force One than trying to come home, and Mr. Cheney — without question — he was in charge. He was in charge of the space and we would bring him information.

Dick Cheney: As bad as the events of 9/11 were, some of us had practiced exercises for far more dangerous and difficult circumstances — an all-out Soviet nuclear attack on the United States. That helped — that training kicked in that morning.

Eric Edelman, principal deputy assistant to the vice president for national security affairs, White House: He was a calming influence on people because you'd sort of be embarrassed to, in front of him, betray any sense of, *Oh my God.*

Condoleezza Rice: There were times that day that it felt like an out-of-body experience. But you keep functioning, even though you don't really believe it's happening.

THE MILITARY RESPONDS
"WE'RE IN A LITTLE TROUBLE HERE"

With the order from Vice President Cheney, the military scrambled to find planes it could bring into the fight — even if that meant launching them unarmed, launching them on a kamikaze mission to crash their own fighters into hijacked airliners. It was an unbelievable and unprecedented mission, the weight of which was not lost on the pilots gathered to take it on. What was not yet widely known was that the United 93 passengers were planning, at the same time, to take the plane over themselves.

Col. Matthew Klimow, executive assistant to the vice chair of the Joint Chiefs of Staff, Gen. Richard Myers, Pentagon: It was a very painful discussion for all of us. We didn't want the burden of shooting down the airliner to be on the shoulders of a single fighter pilot, but we also didn't want to have that pilot go all the way up the chain of command to get permission to shoot. It was decided the pilots should do their best to try to wave the airplane off, and if it's clear the airplane is headed into a heavily populated area, the authority to shoot can be given to a regional commander.

Lt. Heather "Lucky" Penney, F-16 pilot, D.C. Air National Guard: This sounds counterintuitive, but when the magnitude of the situation hit me, I really lost all emotion. I was really much more focused on *What are the things I need to do to enable us to protect our capital? What are the things I need to do to facilitate us getting airborne?*

Brig. Gen. David Wherley, commander, D.C. Air National Guard: My translation of the rules to Sass [Lt. Col. Marc Sasseville, F-16 pilot] was, "You have weapons-free flight-lead control." I said, "Do you understand what I'm asking you to do?" They both [Sasseville and Lt. Heather "Lucky" Penney] said yes. I told them to be careful.

Lt. Col. Marc Sasseville, F-16 pilot, U.S. Air Force: As we're going out to the jets, Lucky and I had a quick conversation about what it is that we were going to do and how we were basically going to do the unthinkable if we had to.

Lt. Heather "Lucky" Penney: We would

be ramming the aircraft. We didn't have weapons on board to shoot the airplane down. Both Sass and I had 105 bullets, lead-nosed. As we were putting on our flight gear in the life support shop, Sass looked at me and said, "I'll ram the cockpit." I made the decision I would take the tail off the aircraft.

Lt. Col. Marc Sasseville: We didn't have a whole lot of options.

Lt. Heather "Lucky" Penney: I had never been trained to scramble the aircraft. It would typically take about 20 minutes to start the jets, get the avionics systems going, go through all the preflight checks to make sure the systems were operating properly, program the computers in the aircraft. That's not even including the time to look at the forms, do the walk-around of the airplane, and whatnot. We usually planned about half an hour to 40 minutes from the time you walked out the door to the time that you actually took off.

Col. George Degnon, vice commander, 113th Wing, Andrews Air Force Base, Prince George's County, Maryland: We did everything humanly possible to get the aircraft in the air.

Lt. Heather "Lucky" Penney: I just got my radios up and I was yelling at my crew chief, "Pull the chocks!" He pulled the chocks and I push my throttle. The crew chief was still running under the tail so that my gear would come up — there are safety pins that are all in the airplane — and so they were pulling all those safety pins as I was taxiing to go do an immediate takeoff. I didn't even have an inertia navigation unit. I didn't have any of that set up. It was lucky it was a clear, blue day because we didn't have all the avionics. They were not yet awake when we took off.

Lt. Col. Marc Sasseville: I was thinking, *Wow, we're in a little trouble here.*

Lt. Heather "Lucky" Penney: Sass and I fully expected to intercept Flight 93 and take it down.

Lt. Col. Marc Sasseville: I was going into this moral or ethical justification of the needs of the many versus the needs of the few.

Lt. Heather "Lucky" Penney: I genuinely believed that was going to be the last time I took off. If we did it right, this would be it.

Maj. Gen. Larry Arnold, commander of the 1st Air Force, NORAD, Tyndall Air Force Base, Florida: Bob Marr quotes me as saying that I told him that we would "take lives in the air to save lives on the ground."

Lt. Heather "Lucky" Penney: Seeing the Pentagon was surreal. It was totally surreal to see this billowing black smoke. We didn't get high. We were at about 3,000 feet. We never got above 3,000 feet, at least on that first sweep out.

Lt. Col. Marc Sasseville: There was all this smoke in my cockpit. It made me nauseous to be honest with you — not from an *Ugh, this stinks,* it was more from an *Oh my God, we've been hit on our own soil and we've been hit big.* I couldn't believe they had gotten through and they managed to pull off this attack.

Lt. Heather "Lucky" Penney: The real heroes are the passengers on Flight 93 who were willing to sacrifice themselves.

Lt. Col. Marc Sasseville: They made the decision we didn't have to make.

Lt. Heather "Lucky" Penney: I don't remember how many miles we got away from D.C., but we flew quite a bit down the Potomac. We said we need to go back over and fly over D.C. because we've clearly sanitized the area. When we returned to D.C., that was when things began to settle down.

THE FOURTH CRASH
"LET'S GET THEM"

A few minutes before 10:00 a.m., United Flight 93 passenger Edward Felt, a 41-year-old married father of two who was traveling as part of his job as a computer engineer for BEA Systems, called 911 from the plane and reached emergency dispatcher John Shaw in Westmoreland County, Pennsylvania. It was the first tip to Pennsylvania authorities that there was trouble in the skies overhead. This is an abridged transcript of their call.

Ed Felt: Hijacking in pro —

John Shaw: Excuse me? Hey somebody's reporting a —

Felt: Hijacking in progress.

Shaw: Sir, I'm losing you, where are you?

Felt: United Flight 93.

Shaw: Wait a minute, wait, United flight. United Flight 93.

Felt: Hijacking in progress!

327

Shaw: Okay, where are you? Where are you?

Felt: I'm in the bathroom, United Flight 93.

Shaw: Okay, where are you?

Felt: I don't know.

Shaw: Where are you?

Felt: I don't know where the plane is.

Shaw: Where did you take off?

Felt: Newark to San Francisco.

Shaw: I got it, okay, stay on the phone with me sir.

Felt: I'm trying to . . . [unintelligible] at the bathroom. I don't know what's going on.

Shaw: Hey somebody get the FAA, Newark to San Francisco and they got a hijacking in progress. Okay, yeah. Get somebody from the airport on the line. This is a hijacking in progress. Are you still there, sir?

Felt: Yes I am.

Shaw: What's your name, sir?

Felt: Edward Felt.

Shaw: How big of a plane, sir?

Felt: It's like a 757.

Shaw: This is a 757. Hey we need — It's a 757. Sir, sir?

Felt: Yes.

Shaw: Okay, how many people on the plane?

Felt: It was — it was pretty empty, maybe [unintelligible].

Shaw: Can you still hear me, sir, sir, sir can you still hear me? It's over [unintelligible]. There's a plane . . . said the plane's going down. It's over Mt. Pleasant Township somewhere. Sir? It's going down. You better make an announcement on [unintelligible]. It's over Mt. Pleasant somewhere. Hello?

Alice Ann Hoagland, mother of United Flight 93 passenger Mark Bingham: The uniqueness of Flight 93 is that it was in the air longer than the other flights. People on board were able to find out about the fate of the other three flights and mount an effort to thwart the hijackers, even if they weren't able to save their own lives.

Deena Burnett, wife of United Flight 93 passenger Tom Burnett: It was silent, and I could feel my heart racing. Tom said, "We're waiting until we're over a rural area. We're going to take back the airplane." I became very frightened and I begged, "No, no, Tom. Just sit down, be still, be quiet, and don't draw attention to yourself." He said, "No, Deena. If they're going to crash this plane, we're going to have to do something."

I asked, "What about the authorities?" He said, "We can't wait for the authorities. I don't know what they can do anyway. It's up to us." He said, "I think we can do it." Neither of us said anything for a few seconds. Then I said, "What do you want me to do? What can I do?" "Pray, Deena, just pray." "I am praying. I love you." Tom said, "Don't worry. We're going to do something," then he hung up. He never called back.

Lisa Jefferson, Verizon Airfone supervisor: As that plane took a dive, I could hear the commotion in the background. I heard the flight attendant screaming. People hollering out, "Oh, my God! Jesus, help us!" [Todd Beamer] asked me, if he didn't make it, would I please call his wife? I told him I would, but I asked him if he would like me to connect him to her right then. He said, no, he didn't want to upset her. She was expecting their third child in January, and he knew she was home alone. He gave me his home phone number.

Lyzbeth Glick, wife of United Flight 93 passenger Jeremy Glick: Jeremy said there were three other guys as big as him, and they were going to jump on the hijacker with the bomb and try to take back the plane. He asked if I thought that was a good idea. We debated a little bit. He said that they were going to take a vote, and asked what did I think he should do. I said, "You need to do it." He's a very strong man, and large — six feet, 220. He was a national judo champion, so he was really well equipped with self-defense. He was joking, "I have my butter knife from breakfast." Despite everything, he was able to be a little bit humorous. Then he said, "Okay, I'm going to put the phone down. I'll be right back. I love you."

Philip Bradshaw, husband of Sandra Bradshaw, flight attendant, United Flight 93: We talked about how much we loved each other and our children. Then she said: "Everyone is running to first class, I've got to go. Bye." Those were the last words I heard from her.

Lisa Jefferson: Todd turned to someone else and he said, "Are you ready?" I could hear them; they responded. He said, "Okay. Let's roll." That was the last thing I heard.

Transcript from the United Airlines Flight 93 cockpit voice recorder:

9:57 a.m.

Voice in Arabic: Is there something?

Voice in Arabic: A fight?

Voice in Arabic: Yeah?

Voice in Arabic: Let's go guys. Allah is greatest. Allah is greatest. Oh, guys. Allah is greatest.

Voice in Arabic: O Allah. O Allah. Oh the most Gracious.

[*Sounds of a struggle, grunting*]

Voice in English: Stay back.

Voice in English: In the cockpit! In the cockpit!

Voice in Arabic: They want to get in there. Hold, hold from the inside. Hold from the inside. Hold.

Voice in English: Hold the door.

Voice in English: Stop him.

Voice in English: Sit down. Sit down. Sit down.

Voice in Arabic: There are some guys. All those guys.

Voice in English: Let's get them.

Voice in English: Sit down.

Voice in Arabic: Trust in Allah and in him.

10:00 a.m.

Voice in Arabic: There is nothing.

Voice in Arabic: Is that it? Shall we finish it off?

Voice in Arabic: No. Not yet.

Voice in Arabic: When they all come, we finish it off.

Voice in Arabic: There is nothing.

Voice in English: I'm injured.

Voice in Arabic: O Allah. O Allah. O Gracious.

Voice in English: In the cockpit. If we don't, we'll die.

Voice in Arabic: Up, down. Up, down, in the cockpit. Up, down. Saeed, up, down.

Voice in English: Roll it.

Voice in Arabic: Allah is the greatest. Allah is the greatest.

Voice in Arabic: Is that it? I mean, shall we pull it down?

Voice in Arabic: Yes, put it in it, and pull it down.

Voice in Arabic: Cut off the oxygen. Cut off the oxygen. Cut off the oxygen. Cut off the oxygen.

Voice in Arabic: Up, down. Up, down.

Voice in Arabic: What?

Voice in Arabic: Up, down.

Voice in English: Shut them off. Shut them off.

Voice in English: Go, go, move, move.

Voice in English: Turn it up.

Voice in Arabic: Down, down.

Voice in Arabic: Pull it down. Pull it down.

Voice in English: Down. Push, push, push, push, push.

Voice in Arabic: Hey. Hey. Give it to me. Give it to me.

Voice in Arabic: Give it to me. Give it to me. Give it to me.

Voice in Arabic: Give it to me. Give it to me. Give it to me.

10:03 a.m.

Voice in Arabic: Allah is the greatest.

Voice in Arabic: Allah is the greatest.

Voice in Arabic: Allah is the greatest.

334

Voice in Arabic: Allah is the greatest.

Voice in Arabic: Allah is the greatest.

Voice in English: No!

Voice in Arabic: Allah is the greatest. Allah is the greatest.

Voice in Arabic: Allah is the greatest. Allah is the greatest.

Lyzbeth Glick, wife of United Flight 93 passenger Jeremy Glick: I didn't want to listen to what happened, so I gave the phone to my dad. It wasn't until a couple of days later that I found out what had transpired. My father told me later that he had heard a series of screams. Then there was a series of more screams, and then it sounded like a roller coaster. Then there was nothing.

As the passengers and crew aboard Flight 93 tried to wrest control of the plane from the hijackers, their decisions in the air would alter the lives of those who lived in the small towns in Somerset County, near Shanksville, Pennsylvania, who suddenly found themselves in the midst of the nation's still-unfolding tragedy. The crash sowed even further confusion among the military and air traffic controllers who were mustering the government to respond to an attack they still didn't understand.

Sgt. Patrick Madigan, commander, Somerset Station, Pennsylvania State Police: While we were watching, I said, "At least there's no terrorist targets in Somerset County." Shortly thereafter, we received a call [from Ed Felt] that a plane was over Somerset, and my first thought and reaction to that was, *What am I going to be able to do about it?*

Rick King, assistant chief, Shanksville Volunteer Fire Company: I called my sister, Jody [King Walsh]. Jody lives in Lambertsville, which is not very far. As I was talking to her, she said, "Rick, I hear a plane." She said, "Rick, it's loud. It sounds like a jet." I said, "Oh, my God!" I walked out onto my front porch, and I could hear the plane. I could hear the engine screaming.

Anita McBride Miller, resident, Stonycreek Township, Pennsylvania: Out of nowhere, this absolutely unbearable, horrific noise was going on outside. It was deafening. It shook the windows and rattled the rafters.

Douglas Miller, coal truck driver, James F. Barron Trucking: I happened to look up in the sky and there was this giant aircraft, coming straight down.

Tim Lensbouer, crane operator, Rollock Incorporated: I can't describe what it sounded like, almost like a missile type — and it came over us real fast and then it hit the ground. All of a sudden, all the lights went out. It went black and the whole building shook.

Douglas Miller: I remember getting on the CB [radio] and asking my buddy, "Did I see that?" He said, "Yeah." He said, "It didn't look good."

John Werth, air traffic controller, Cleveland Air Route Traffic Control Center: We never lost them from the radar until they took the steep descent into the crash. We observed the target all the way to the southeast of Pittsburgh, until 10:03 a.m.

Stacey Taylor Parham, air traffic control specialist, Cleveland Air Route Traffic Control Center: I vectored another nearby plane toward the incident site and asked if he would look for smoke.

Terry Yeazell, pilot, Falcon 20 corporate jet, airborne over Pennsylvania: Stacey asked if there was any activity off the right side of the airplane, like smoke or something like that. There were a lot of small white clouds around. After looking for a while, I saw a puff of black smoke, a black cloud floating. As we got closer, we could see basically a forest fire burning next to a tree line in a field of grass.

Yates Gladwell, pilot, Falcon 20 corporate jet, airborne over Pennsylvania: It was a big black hole and it was smoking.

Ben Sliney, national operations manager, FAA Command Center, Herndon, Virginia: The other plane reported the smoke plume. That drew a close to the day in reality, but we didn't know that yet — in our minds, the attacks were not over, and we continued to track the remaining eight or 10 or maybe even a dozen planes, monitor their progress, report on what they were doing. Until they were resolved, until their radios came back on, they landed, they did whatever they had to do.

Maj. Gen. Larry Arnold, commander of the 1st Air Force, NORAD, Tyndall Air Force Base, Florida: We did not know that was the last plane. The war was still on as far as we are concerned.

Lisa Jefferson, Verizon Airfone supervisor: I kept calling out Todd Beamer's name, hoping and praying either him or anyone would pick up that phone. Someone touched my shoulder and said, "Lisa, that was their plane" — the plane had just crashed in Pennsylvania — "you can release the line now." I kept calling and calling. I held that phone an additional 15 minutes, praying someone would pick up.

Lyzbeth Glick, wife of United Flight 93 passenger Jeremy Glick: My dad stayed on the line for over two hours, hoping beyond hope.

Deena Burnett, wife of United Flight 93 passenger Tom Burnett: I kept waiting. I held on to the telephone for almost three hours, waiting for him to call back to tell me he had landed the plane and everything was fine and he would be home later. I started thinking about what I could cook for dinner. I was thinking about sending the kids to school and who could come pick them up, because I didn't want to miss his phone call. So I just sat there.

FEAR AT THE PENTAGON

"THERE WAS NO PLACE FOR US TO RUN"

The first hour of rescue efforts at the Pentagon proved to be a frustrating stop-and-start, as fire responders noticed that the outer rings of the building — which bore the brunt of the plane's impact — were in danger of collapsing, and officials feared reports that more hijacked aircraft were inbound.

James Schwartz, assistant chief for operations, Arlington County Fire Department: There was this sense of the battlefield — of war, if you will. We were very clear that there may be more waves of the attack coming. At one point early on, [FBI Special Agent] Chris Combs said to me, "There are still eight more aircraft that are unaccounted for." We were waiting. *Is there going to be another airplane, like there was in New York, at the Pentagon?* This is an attack the likes of which we've never seen before.

Chris Combs, special agent, FBI, Pentagon: The FBI command center was relaying to me all of the other stories that were out there about other attacks happening. There were stories that the White House had been hit, that the State Department had been hit. One thing I remember hearing was "Hey, Cleveland has been hit as well." I remember thinking, *What's in Cleveland? Why are they hitting Cleveland?*

Thomas O'Connor, special agent, FBI, Pentagon: We were standing with a guy from the Metropolitan Washington Area Airports Authority, who had a radio, and he said, "Hey, you've got a plane that's off radar." He said, "It's a good distance out." I was like, "Okay." But he said, "They're calculating back" — at the speed it was going or should be going, and the direction — "how long it would take to get to Washington, D.C." It was more of an urgent matter than I had first thought it was.

Chris Combs: It was on track to D.C., and it was 20 minutes' flight time out. They said we had 20 minutes.

James Schwartz, assistant chief for operations, Arlington County Fire Department: I made a decision to evacuate the incident scene at the Pentagon.

John Jester, chief, Defense Protective Service, Pentagon: We were outside and heard the fire trucks blowing their horns. They said it was for recall, to come down off the building because of a report of a second plane inbound. They pulled the firemen off the building for a while.

Chris Combs: We looked around and decided the safest places were under the overpasses on the highways. We sent everyone there.

Capt. Charles Gibbs, Arlington County Fire Department: I refer to it as "Everybody out of the pool." On the heliport side, we went back to the other side of Washington Boulevard, which in reality probably wasn't far enough, but that's where we went.

James Schwartz: We picked up all the victims, we got everybody as much as we could off of the incident scene. We stood there getting radio transmissions from the Washington Field Office of the FBI counting down.

Chris Combs: It was pretty eerie — the Pentagon is absolutely in flames, and there are thousands of first responders and people from the Pentagon huddled underneath all of these overpasses, waiting.

Thomas O'Connor: The hard part of being under the bridge was that you knew the firefighters weren't in there fighting the fire — and every minute they weren't fighting the fire, it was getting further out of hand. They were really frustrated.

Capt. Charles Gibbs: That was probably 10, 15 minutes, just sitting there.

Thomas O'Connor: They were actually counting down the time.

James Schwartz: We were standing there looking out at the sky, looking to see if an airplane is going to pierce the clouds.

Chris Combs: We got to about five minutes past the deadline. People were getting a little antsy. Members of the command team were asking me, "Hey what's going on? Where's this plane?"

James Schwartz: We were waiting for a word from somebody.

Chris Combs: It was about 10 minutes after that they said it was a confirmed crash at Camp David, and we were good to go.*

* This report — of a crash near Camp David — was the garbled initial news of the crash of Flight 93,

James Schwartz: At that time I ordered everybody back to the incident scene.

Capt. Robert Gray, Technical Rescue, Station 4, Arlington County Fire Department: We walked up to the front of the building, and it was unbelievable. My thought was, *This feels so evil, that somebody has done this, and they did it with a loaded plane.* It was overwhelming. We basically started on the first floor and worked our way in. It was obvious on the first floor once we got all the way to where the plane had hit that there weren't any survivors.

---

whose Pennsylvania crash location was initially misplaced as being close to the presidential retreat in Thurmont, Maryland, along the Pennsylvania border.

THE FIRST CASUALTY

"OH MY GOD, IT'S FATHER MIKE"

One of the most memorable figures at the Trade Center was Father Mychal Judge, one of the FDNY's six chaplains, a gregarious, gay, recovering alcoholic Irishman, known throughout the city for ministering to firefighters, the homeless, and AIDS victims. He'd been an FDNY chaplain since 1992 and had responded to numerous emergencies, including the 1996 crash of TWA Flight 800, which exploded over Suffolk County, New York. On 9/11, he was one of the first to arrive at the World Trade Center and is believed to be the only priest who entered the Twin Towers that day.

Mychal Judge, chaplain, FDNY:
It's fantastic how I can sometimes begin a day and go through a day, but not realize that everything that happens — every single thing that happens — is somehow within the divine plan.

Friar Michael Duffy: Priests and firemen both enter people's lives at a point of crisis. They have similar outlooks on life — it's the need to help, to rescue. So you have Mike Judge wanting to do that in a spiritual way, and the firemen wanting to do it in a physical way. It was a natural match.

Malachy McCourt, actor: There's a very old postcard of a giant Jesus looking in the window of the Empire State Building in those long, long robes. That was Mike Judge in New York. He was everywhere over the city.

Friar Michael Duffy: On 9/11, one of our friars, Brian Carroll, was walking down Sixth Avenue and actually saw the airplane go overhead at a low altitude. Then he saw smoke coming from the Trade Towers. He ran into Mychal Judge's room and said, "Mychal, I think they're going to need you. I think the World Trade Tower is on fire." He jumped up, took off his habit, got his FDNY uniform on, and — I have to say this, in case you think he's perfect — he did take time to comb and spray his hair. He ran down the stairs and got in his car with some firemen and went to the World Trade Towers. One of the first people he met was the mayor, Mayor Giuliani.

Rudy Giuliani, mayor, New York City:
Father Judge was walking in the other direction. I was walking south, he was walking north. "Father Judge," I said, "please pray for us." He put a smile on his face and said, "I always do." I said, "Thanks." We didn't quite have a chance to do the whole joke — I used to say to him, "Pray for me." He would say, "I will." I'd say, "It's more effective if you pray 'cause you're in a lot better shape than I am with God." He would say, "Yeah, but it's better if you do it 'cause it's more unusual, and it will be more of a surprise to God."

For the better part of an hour, Father Judge was a constant, reassuring presence to emergency workers — praying aloud in the North Tower lobby and dashing outside at one point to administer last rites to a firefighter, Danny Suhr, hit and killed by a person falling from the burning tower.

Gregory Fried, executive chief surgeon, NYPD: I saw Mychal Judge, the fire chaplain, and I said, "Father, be careful." He said, "God bless," because he always said "God bless." Then he headed right and I went left.

Bill Spade, firefighter, Rescue 5, FDNY: I'd known him from other incidents, other things and weddings and all. I'd say, "Hey Father, how you doing, you remember me?"

347

He'd say, "Sure I remember you, you got that 20 I lent you?" He was there in the building, in the North Tower. He had his rosary at his side, in his right hand, and he was saying the rosary. He was white. Everything that he was seeing was really bothering him.

Christian Waugh, firefighter, Ladder 5, FDNY: You could see it in his face. He usually joked around. He was always saying hello to somebody. This time he was stone-faced.

Chief Joseph Pfeifer, Battalion 1, FDNY: He was in the lobby with us and I could tell he was praying.

Lt. Bill Cosgrove, NYPD: That's when the whole building shook. The lights went out. There was this giant vacuum sound. We thought it was our building [South Tower] that was collapsing. It wasn't. The pressure was sucking the windows out of Tower One. It was totally dark.

Wesley Wong, assistant special agent in charge, FBI: I took a couple of steps, and I tripped over what I thought is a piece of debris. I could barely make out the outline of a fireman's bunker coat. I say to some other firemen, "Hey, I think one of your guys is down." Two other firemen go to look in the darkness.

Lt. Bill Cosgrove: One of the firefighters put the light on him — and I remember him saying, "Oh my god, it's Father Mike."

Wesley Wong: We picked up Father Judge and we headed out.

Lt. Bill Cosgrove: I took an arm. Someone else took an arm. Two other guys took his ankles.

Wesley Wong: We brought Father Judge back in the orange chair that you see in the famous picture of him. That orange chair was sitting by its lonesome in the mezzanine level. Some of the firemen started working on him, trying to help his breathing. He was in real bad shape at that point.

John Maguire, finance associate, Goldman Sachs: I saw the firemen carrying a man I later discovered was Father Mychal Judge in a chair. I offered them a hand. It took five men because the ground was shifting on top of the debris, which made it difficult to walk.

Shannon Stapleton, photographer, Reuters: I noticed some rescue workers carrying this man in a chair. I knew it was a pretty intense image. They weren't too happy.

Lt. Bill Cosgrove: I remember looking up because one of the firemen was yelling at a photographer. He was telling him in no uncertain terms, "Get out of the way."

Christian Waugh: At the time, I thought photographing Father Judge that way was in very bad taste. I went after Shannon Stapleton, the photographer. I started screaming at him. I knew that thing was gonna be out on the internet in a half hour.

John Maguire: We carried him to a street corner and laid his body on the sidewalk. I pushed on his chest with a thought of starting CPR. No response. We folded his hands and covered his face with a jacket.

Jose Rodriguez, officer, NYPD: We knelt down. I grabbed Father Judge's hand. He was already dead. Lieutenant Cosgrove put his hand on Father Judge's head and we said an Our Father.

Friar Michael Duffy: The firemen took his body. Because they respected and loved him so much, they didn't want to leave it in the street. They quickly carried it into St. Peter's Church. They went up the center aisle, and they put the body in front of the altar. They covered it with a sheet. On the sheet, they placed his stole and his fire badge.

Monsignor John Delendick, chaplain, FDNY: They told me Mychal Judge's body was in St. Peter's Church. I went up there — I had to walk around a bit to do that — and they had him lying in state, almost, in front of the altar. I prayed a little bit.

Friar Michael Duffy: Mychal Judge's body was the first one released from Ground Zero. His death certificate has the number "1" on the top.

James Hanlon, former firefighter, FDNY: The first official casualty of the attack.

Craig Monahan, firefighter, Ladder 5, FDNY: I think he wouldn't have had it any other way. It was as if he took the lead — all those angels, right through heaven's gates. That's what it seemed like to us. If any of those guys were confused on the way up, he was there to ease the transition from this life to the next.

AROUND THE TOWERS
"NOBODY IS COMING TO GET US"

Inside the North Tower the remaining rescuers and building occupants realized they, too, faced immediate peril as they learned that the South Tower had collapsed.

Capt. Jay Jonas, Ladder 6, FDNY: The emergency power came up and the lights came on. I looked at [fellow firefighter] Billy Burke and I said, "What was that?" I said, "Billy, you go check the south windows, and I'll go check the north windows and we'll meet back here." I couldn't see anything when I went to my window. All I could see was white dust pressed against the glass. We met back at the stairway and I expected Billy to tell me that something happened with our building. With a straight face, he looked at me and says, "The South Tower's collapsed."

John Abruzzo, staff accountant, Port Authority, North Tower, 69th floor: When we got to the 20th [floor], I remember hearing a rumble. We knew it didn't sound good. We knew we had to get out of there and not stop for anything.

David Norman, officer, Emergency Service Unit, Truck 1, NYPD: Our colleague at the command post, Kenny Winkler, came over the radio and told us that the South Tower had collapsed. Now I know this sounds a little silly, but if you didn't see that footage on TV, and you were locked in a room that doesn't have any windows, when somebody tells you a 110-story building is gone, you want to say to them, "Are you sure?" We communicated some message like that to Kenny, like, "Are you sure?" I think I may have even said, "Calm down," to him, "relay that message again." He came back very boldly: "There's nothing left of the building! You need to get out of there! Your building is in imminent danger of collapse!"

Capt. Jay Jonas: My mind was exploding. I knew from all my studies that a high-rise building had never collapsed before. Now the sister one to the one I was in had collapsed. You start doing the math.

Sharon Miller, officer, PAPD: I said to the chief, "Hey, Chief. This building is coming down next." He goes, "We're going up a

354

couple more and then we're getting outta here."

Capt. Jay Jonas: I had this terrible feeling that, *Man, we're not going to make it out of here. We're on the 27th floor. We're in no-man's-land. It's going to be hard to get out of here.* In addition to that, I had this feeling, *Jeez, I wonder how many firemen died?* That was the linchpin that said, *All right. This is no longer a doable mission for us. It's time to get out of here.* I looked at my guys and said, "If that one can go, this one can go. It's time for us to get out of here." They were a little — not standoffish — but they were like, "You mean we've got to go downstairs now? We climbed all this way for nothing?" I says, "Come on. Let's go. It's time to get out of here." I told them to keep their tools with them, because the first thought might be, "Well, let's jettison everything and go." I says, "No, you keep everything." As it turns out, it was good that we did.

Det. David Brink, Emergency Service Unit, Truck 3, NYPD: I wanted to go. I had just survived the first collapse, and I was like, *All right. I really don't want to go through that again.* The South Tower was on fire, obviously, and in ruins on the ground. We saw a lot of civilians. I thought to myself: *Well, these* *are the people that we're here to help. We can't abandon them now.*

David Norman: We felt that we were no longer part of the solution. We were now part of the problem.

Lt. Gregg Hansson, Engine 24, FDNY: I remember turning to the lieutenant in Ladder 5, Mike Warchola, and telling him, "Just heard a Mayday to get out of the building. We're all leaving." None of us were really in a hurried state at that point because on the 35th floor everything was as calm as could be.

Sharon Miller: I had a bunch of firemen behind me. You could hear their radios crackling. "Holy this!" and "Holy that!" And "Two just came down — One's comin' down next. Mayday, Mayday!" When PAPD Chief [James] Romito heard "Mayday!" that's when he said, "All right, let's go. We gotta get outta here." We were at the 31st floor, 32nd floor, and we all turned around and started coming down.

John Abruzzo: We made it out to the West Street entrance. There was glass all over the place. They had to lift the chair physically off the ground to carry me out into the street. They put me down to rest. It took an hour and a half to get from the 69th floor down to street level. If it weren't for the evacuation chair and the 10 people who brought me down, I would not have made it.

Pasquale Buzzelli, engineer, Port Authority, North Tower, 64th floor: We were the only people on the 64th floor of the North Tower. It wasn't until we felt the building shake and vibrate that we started questioning, "Okay. Now this is getting more serious."

Louise Buzzelli, Riverdale, New Jersey, wife of Pasquale Buzzelli, Port Authority, North Tower, 64th floor: The second building to get hit started to crumble and come down. I kept thinking: *That building is just like his building.*

Pasquale Buzzelli: Steve and I looked at each other and he said, "What the fuck are we still doing here? Let's get the fuck out." We gathered up rags that we wet, flashlights, whatever we could find, not knowing what we'd encounter on the way down. We formed a line and got ready to leave. We took a head count: 16. I was in the front, not because I was leading or anything. It happened to be where I was standing. Then Pat said, "All right. Let's go."

Genelle Guzman, office assistant, Port Authority, North Tower, 64th floor: Finally we decided to go down the staircase. My friend Pasquale was leading the way. I held on to [my coworker] Rosa's hand. She was holding on to me. She was crying. I didn't cry for some reason. I was trying to comfort her.

Pasquale Buzzelli: We encountered some firemen sitting on the stairs. They were tired and sweaty with their gear. They said, "Keep going straight down. Keep moving." I don't think their radios were working. If they had known themselves that Tower Two had collapsed, they would have been going down the stairs with us too. Instead they were going up.

Louise Buzzelli: I'm praying that I hear the phone ring and it's him, and he's going to tell me that he's out and he's somewhere on his way across the river or somewhere away.

Genelle Guzman: Pasquale kept making a couple of stops to ask, "Are you guys OK?" We kept saying, "Yes, we're doing fine." We kept walking and walking and kept counting the staircases because they had the number written on the columns. I was trying to tell Rosa, "We're almost there." I was wearing high-heeled shoes, so she was telling me, "Do you want to take your shoes off?" I'm like, "No, I'll be all right. I'm doing OK." My feet were killing me going down the stairs, and I wanted to stop but didn't want to lose a minute.

AFTER THE COLLAPSE
"TOWER TWO IS GONE"

---

*Those who survived the collapse of the South
Tower emerged into an unrecognizable landscape. Lost and traumatized, some fled, while
others searched the wreckage for signs of hope.*

**Gregory Fried, executive chief surgeon,
NYPD:** I can't tell you how long I was down,
but then it stopped. I wasn't dead, but I was
really hurting a lot. I squirmed to my feet,
and I guess the rubble was about shoulder-
high in certain areas. My head was fairly well
out of it, but I felt my right buttock, my right
cheek. That was where all the pain really was.
It was swelling, so I knew I was bleeding. I
took my belt, wrapped it around, and started
heading to the Hudson.

**William Jimeno, officer, PAPD, buried
under the rubble of the South Tower:**
Sergeant McLoughlin said, "What's everybody's condition?" Dominick said, "I'm
trapped, I think I can shimmy out of here." I

360

told Sarge, "I'm in a lot of pain, my whole left side, I've got concrete on me, and I'm being crushed." At this point, Sergeant McLoughlin was more stuck. He was in a fetal position, about 15 feet back. I could hear him, but I couldn't see him. This hallway somehow collapsed and had separated us. He was very calm.

After about seven, eight minutes, Dominick shimmied himself up. We were in a very tight compartment, and I was lying on my back at a 45-degree angle. Sarge said, "Are you free?" Dominick said, "Sarge, I can go out this hole." The hole was about 30 feet up — it looked dangerous. Sergeant McLoughlin said, "No, if you leave, you'll never find us. You need to get Jimeno out, and you and Jimeno get me out." It went on for a couple minutes. We're human beings — and here you're presented with a situation where you can go out for help, go for freedom and come back, or you stay in — literally — a hellhole, with your team. Sergeant McLoughlin, myself, Dominick Pezzulo, Antonio Rodrigues, and Christopher were all fathers — we all had kids. There's no superheroes here — we're regular human beings. Dominick had a real tough decision.

In the end, he said, "I'm going to get Will out." He worked on me for about 15 minutes. At that point, he stopped. He said, "I can't

361

get you out." This was about 20, 30 minutes after the initial collapse.

Chief Joseph Pfeifer, Battalion 1, FDNY: I remember walking north on West Street, walking through the blackness of downtown. I realized my brother was gone, and hundreds of firefighters were gone. All I could think of was how much we really used to love working downtown, and all the times we used to talk on the phone, or at the house, or at parties about the job. I realized all that was gone.

Al Kim, vice president of operations, TransCare Ambulance: I looked around and there were firefighters' jackets everywhere. They were everywhere. I remember climbing over debris, and someone yelled, "There's someone alive here." Ran over. There was a guy who looked pretty messed up. We had no equipment. There was an ambulance burning, and all those vehicles I lined up, they were all on fire. Every last one of them. I went in one of those, grabbed some stuff. I grabbed the longboard, and whatever we did, we did. I don't remember doing any of it, but we did it.

Jean Potter, Bank of America, North Tower: I started walking in the gray dust. I was soaked because in the Concourse water had been pouring from the ceiling. People

362

Al Kim, center, helps a firefighter amid the rubble.

were yelling at me to cover my mouth, but I said, "Which way are the Towers? Are they behind me?" I didn't want to be walking toward them. I made my way to Chinatown and tried to use the phone. I wanted to get as far away from the Towers as possible.

Steven Bienkowski, Aviation Unit, NYPD: All of Lower Manhattan was covered in a giant white dust cloud. As we came around in our helicopter to the North Tower again, you could still see people falling and jumping, except it didn't look so violent anymore because you weren't watching them hit the ground. It almost looked peaceful because they were falling into a white cloud.

Andrew Kirtzman, reporter, NY1: My taxi headed toward Chambers Street near City Hall and the taxi driver slammed on the brakes. He said, "I'm not going any further. Get out of here." I fumbled for my money and this woman outside opened up the cab and climbed in next to me. She yelled, "Get me out of here!" I said, "Give me a second. I'm leaving." "You're leaving?" I said, "I'm a reporter. I've got to go cover the story." She looked incredulous. He dumped me out on the street, and I was alone on Chambers Street, which on a daytime on a weekday is normally packed. The street was covered with white soot. It was eerily quiet and it was incredibly disorienting.

Lila Speciner, paralegal, Port Authority, North Tower, 88th floor: It looked almost like a snow globe, only it was flying papers and dust from the falling building. We still didn't realize what had happened. We are soaking wet and I had debris in my hair, my ripped stockings, whatever. There were emergency people wandering around. "Are you hurt? Go here. If you're not hurt, walk north. Go away from this building. We don't know what's going to happen next. Walk away."

Frederick Terna, Holocaust survivor and Brooklyn resident: As ashes were falling, I was back in Auschwitz, with ashes coming down. In Auschwitz, I knew what the ashes were. Here, I assumed I knew what the ashes were — it was a building and human remains.

Det. Sgt. Joe Blozis, crime scene investigator, NYPD: Maybe I'm exaggerating, but it looked like maybe 18 inches of paper were covering the streets. Just tons and tons of paper from all those office buildings. The paper was catching on fire, which caused our emergency vehicles to catch on fire. We needed equipment before it was burnt up, so we were emptying out the trucks, taking the oxygen out, tools, ropes, and everything.

Dan Potter, firefighter, Ladder 10, FDNY: I started to see people coming out of wherever they took shelter. I rearranged myself, get myself focused again. I said, "That was the South Tower. I'm pretty sure it was the South Tower." Now I said, "I got to get to my wife."

Lila Speciner: As we got further and further away, there were some office buildings. People called us in and said, "Do you want to wash up? Our phones are working. Do you need to call family?" We got T-shirts from some company that had a picnic and had extra T-shirts. Everything we were wearing was soaking wet and dirty.

Lt. Joseph Torrillo, director of fire education safety, FDNY: All the screams around me were turning to cries, and the cries turned into whimpers, and the whimpers turned to silence. I didn't hear anybody else anymore.

Across New York Harbor, in New Jersey, a junior Coast Guard officer, Lt. Michael Day, put in motion a massive boatlift to help evacuate people from the tip of Lower Manhattan.

Lt. Michael Day, U.S. Coast Guard: We were all in the Command Center, riveted, because we had these large-screen TVs and CNN reports, and when the first tower collapsed we lost one of the means of communication with the small boats; our 41-foot utility boats were on their way over there. We lost the radar image after the first tower collapsed because of all of the debris. We got reports there were people congregating on the lower tip of Manhattan. That's when it really kicked in, when the first tower collapsed — the havoc.

Rick Schoenlank, president, United New Jersey Sandy Hook Pilots Benevolent Association: There was a call that was put out by the Coast Guard for all boats to render assistance to Lower Manhattan. Our boat — the 184-foot *New York* — got underway and went steaming full ahead up to the Battery.

We sent a number of launches that we had to go up and assist as well.

Lt. Michael Day: The marina was filled with firefighters, police officers, rescue workers, and they were jumping onto the boats that were there, all on the sides, and they were getting overloaded again. Firefighters were throwing off their gear and leaping onto the tugs as they were leaving. We probably had 25 to 30 firefighters in the water floundering because this building had come down.

Edward Aswad Jr., officer, NYPD: We came across the marina. We got on a boat, or we were trying to get on a boat. [My NYPD colleague] Sean keeps saying he needs water, and I'm rummaging through this boat — there was this silver cabinet, like a cooler, and I opened it and there was water and beer. We start getting bottles of water and we're pouring it all over our faces, our heads, taking our jackets off.

A few blocks from the World Trade Center, the city's leaders, who had been forced into make-shift command posts because New York's emergency management center in Seven World Trade Center had been damaged, found themselves on the run again following the collapse of the South Tower.

Rudy Giuliani, mayor, New York City: We walked out into the lobby of 100 Church Street, and within seconds, I had the feeling we had gone from bad to worse. What I saw outside on Church Street was a big cloud going through the street.

Sunny Mindel, communications director for the mayor of the City of New York, Rudy Giuliani: Everything was gray — a color world went monochromatic from all the soot and the ash. In this monochromatic world, the first bit of color came in the form of a guy named Tibor Kerekes, who was on the mayor's security detail. He came into the building and was completely gray except for the blood.

Rudy Giuliani: Tibor Kerekes was all beaten up, blood coming down his face, and looking like he was somewhat in shock. Now, he was a black belt karate, in the military — you don't get tougher than Tibor. To see him shook up, from pain, heightened just how bad this was.

Andrew Kirtzman, reporter, NY1: A police officer came up to me and said, "Get off this street." I said, "I'm sorry. I'm a journalist," as though this press pass were like a magic device. I said, "I've got to find Giuliani." He said, "Oh, Giuliani is right over there." Sure enough, about 10 feet away from me was Giuliani, surrounded with all of his aides: Bernie Kerik, the police commissioner, Tommy Von Essen, the fire commissioner, Tony Carbonetti, and a whole bunch of his aides. They emerged, and that's when I ran into them.

Rudy Giuliani: I said, "Okay, we're going out. We'll go up Church and we'll look for a new command center and we'll make the decision as we're walking along, but let's get out of this building." I grabbed Kirtzman's arm and said, "Come on, Andrew, you're coming with me."

Andrew Kirtzman: Relations between Giuliani and me had not been particularly warm. In the year preceding that moment I'd written a book about him called *Rudy Giuliani, Emperor of the City.* Giuliani vowed never to read it. When he waved me over, suddenly everything changed. He said, "We're going to walk north. We've got to get out of here." Because the Office of Emergency Management had been destroyed, City Hall was evacuated, One Police Plaza had lost contact with the world, there was no place for him to take command.

Rudy Giuliani: We started walking north.

369

People started following us, and we kept encouraging people to come with us.

Sunny Mindel: As we travel up Broadway, like a bunch of pied pipers, people are gathering with us.

Rudy Giuliani: As we were walking we were conferring, like, *Where should we put the command post?*

Andrew Kirtzman: It was pretty weird that here was the mayor and the entire leadership of the city, and they were as helpless as anyone walking down the street. As a citizen, it was pretty frightening that no one was in charge — or the person who is supposed to be in charge had no way of operating.

Sunny Mindel: I remember coming upon one older woman, who was seated in a park. She was drinking a Starbucks, she wasn't moving — she was sitting there drinking her coffee. I didn't want to frighten her, but I thought, *She needs to get outta here.* I went up to her, and I said, "Ma'am, you need to go north," and she says, "No, I'm fine here." I said, "You really have to get outta here." But she wasn't frightened. I think she maybe had that same reaction I had when I looked at the TV and went, "This is not my life, this is something I'm watching."

Having just survived the collapse of the South Tower, siblings John and Michele Cartier formulated a plan to escape the devastation of Lower Manhattan, even as they worried about their brother James, not knowing whether he too had escaped.

John Cartier, brother of James Cartier, electrician, who was working in the South Tower: We made it not that far and went into a deli. The deli owner was like, "Take everything. Take water. Take whatever you want."

Michele Cartier, Lehman Brothers, North Tower: At that point John had his water, I grabbed mine, and I remember grabbing one for my brother James, and throwing it into the briefcase I had. We started talking about John's motorcycle, and where it was, and how far away.

John Cartier: I walked back toward my bike. It was on the sidewalk, completely covered in soot. I was like, "I hope this damn thing starts. Please God, start." It fired right up. I pulled up, Michele got on the bike, and we slowly left. People were taking pictures of us, covered in this soot, leaving.

Michele Cartier: I'm in this blue skirt and on my brother's motorcycle. I was completely disoriented. I had no idea which way we were going.

John Cartier: We only had one goal: *Make it home.* She kept on asking me about James. I said, "He probably got out on the west side." That's what I thought.

Michele Cartier: Then he said, "Just pray. Just pray."

THE RESCUE AT SHANKSVILLE
"YOU WERE HOPING YOU WOULD FIND SOMETHING"

Just like their colleagues in New York and Washington, the first responders and officials around Shanksville were forced to improvise a response to a worst-case scenario.

James Clark, first assistant chief, Somerset Volunteer Fire Department: It was ten o'clock or so when our pagers tripped for a large aircraft down.

Alan Baumgardner, Somerset County 911 coordinator: It seemed like immediately every phone line in the center was lit up. Everybody grabbed for a phone and they were all the same call: *A plane has gone down out near Lambertsville.*

Rick King, assistant chief, Shanksville Volunteer Fire Company: I got into the station. I remember the dispatcher saying, "A plane down. Lambertsville Road, Lambertsville area." I asked who was dispatched with us, and they said, "Your station, Friedens and Stoystown." I knew County 911 thought it was a small plane, so I said, "County, I heard this plane crash. I'm convinced it was a commercial airliner." I said, "I want additional departments." I called for Central City, Somerset, Listie, Berlin, and I called for Somerset's Hazmat Unit. They started to dispatch those.

Sgt. Patrick Madigan, commander, Somerset Station, Pennsylvania State Police: We all packed up and headed to Shanksville.

Rick King: Keith Custer was sitting beside me in the officer's seat. Keith said, "I can't swallow. My mouth is dry." Mine was too. It sucked everything out of me. We've been in situations where we've been on terrible car accidents and things like that. This was different. I knew that somehow this was related to what was going on.

Keith Custer, firefighter, Shanksville Volunteer Fire Company: It was total silence in that truck the whole way out there. I don't think we said but five words to each other.

Rick King: We had a cell phone in the engine at the time, and I got on the cell phone, being afraid for what was happening to our country, and I called my wife and I said, "Go get our kids out of school. I don't know what's happening." I was thinking planes were now somehow going to be indiscriminately falling out of the sky. I said, "While you're there, you might want to tell the school to close early."

Kevin Huzsek, paramedic, Somerset Area Ambulance Association: We got a short ways down from our station on Route 30, looked over to the horizon, and saw a big large cloud of black smoke. We advised our dispatch center to dispatch every ambulance that had two or more ambulances in their station in Somerset and Cambria County.

The first to reach the crash scene in Shanksville were local neighbors who witnessed the crash, workers from a nearby salvage yard, and two coal truck drivers. Not long after, volunteer firefighters began to arrive. Then, within hours, state and federal officials — and scores of reporters — would descend on the former mine site en masse, setting up a temporary town that would exist for months as investigators sifted and searched through the wreckage. The crash site of Flight 93 perplexed many of those responding, as the soft earth of the former mine swallowed up the wreckage and buried much of the plane in the ground.

Douglas Miller, coal truck driver, James F. Barron Trucking: We turned in and then immediately made a right, which took us to the crash scene, within 30 yards. There was nobody else there at the time.

Robert "Bobby" Blair, truck driver, James F. Barron Trucking: The trees were on fire.

Douglas Miller: The heat — I assumed it was from the jet fuel — was so intense I had to remark to Bob, "Hey, we better back up," because I thought it would blister the paint on my hood. You could feel the heat through the windows.

Robert "Bobby" Blair: We had taken our fire extinguishers, and we knocked the fire out that was blowing across the field pretty quick. There was a large tire laying there right at the hole; it was still burning. We both tried to knock it out, but then as soon as you quit spraying, it started back up again.

Eric Peterson, resident, Stonycreek Township: When I got up there, there was actually still pieces of mail and stuff like that falling from the sky.

Douglas Miller: There wasn't anything to tell you that it was a plane when you first looked — it looked like maybe a truck delivering mail or maybe something carrying a lot of paperwork might have wrecked. There was paperwork — letters and envelopes — scattered everywhere.

Kevin Huzsek, paramedic, Somerset Area Ambulance Association: Shanksville Fire Department's engine was actually arriving at the same time that we were. We went back first, their engine followed, and I believe a unit from Stoystown Fire Department was right behind them.

Merle Flick, firefighter, Shanksville Volunteer Fire Company: It wasn't too much to see.

James Broderick, trooper, Pennsylvania State Police: I remember opening the car door and going to step out. I happened to look down and there was a piece of a human body — a bone or a joint. I knew no one could have survived that crash, seeing that small of a piece. I got back in the car. I knew that I had pulled too close. I backed up.

Ralph Blanset, fire chief, Stoystown Volunteer Fire Company: Trooper Broderick and I were standing next to the crater, and one of my firemen came up and said, "Are you in charge here?," which is protocol for fire companies. Rick King of the Shanksville Fire Department said, "I'm in charge." Before he got that out of his mouth, Trooper Broderick says, "I'm in charge. This is a crime scene." That settled everything real quick.

James Broderick: I knew that we had to secure the scene, keep people out, because people were starting to pick things up.

Rick King: People are coming to me and saying, "What do we do? What do you want us to do?" There wasn't anything to do.

Norbert Rosenbaum, firefighter, Stoystown Volunteer Fire Company: They said, "Go on to a search and rescue." When I saw the parts and everything, I said, "I don't think you're going to be rescuing nobody. It's too big a hole." I did see a lot of stuff that I'd seen before; I was in Vietnam. There was just parts of human pieces. That's all it was — pieces.

James Broderick: I remember the smell. Once you smell diesel fuel mixed with the human body, you'll never forget that smell.

Lt. Robert Weaver, Pennsylvania State Police: That was the first thing that hit me — the smell.

Michael Rosenbaum, firefighter, Stoystown Volunteer Fire Company: Something was smelling really sweet. I didn't know what it was, and I thought it was a flower or something that was in the woods. It had a sweet smell to it. I had asked my dad several times and he wouldn't tell me. Later that day, one of the other firemen told me what it was.

Sgt. Denise Miller, Indian Lake Police Department: I thought, *This is what hell must look like.* The ground was smoking and smoldering.

Keith Custer, firefighter, Shanksville Volunteer Fire Company: We did a little sweep around, and it was probably 10, 15 minutes before we realized there would be no survivors.

Cynthia Daniels, EMT, Somerset Area Ambulance Association: Kevin [Huzsek] radioed the Somerset manager, Jill Miller, and Jill told him that we might as well go back to the ambulance hall and regroup. There was really nothing we could do. There was nothing — no one to take care of.

Kevin Huzsek, paramedic, Somerset Area Ambulance Association: The conversation was very bleak.

Tim Lensbouer, crane operator, Rollock Incorporated: We hollered all the way down through the woods and there was nothing there, just the pine trees burning. We searched and searched. We ran and ran. There was nothing other than paper. One of us found a book bag, a little kid's book bag.

Cpl. Louis Veitz, collision reconstruction specialist, Pennsylvania State Police: We actually found money that was still intact. I can remember finding pocketbooks with family pictures in it, clothing, someone's shoe.

Sgt. Craig Bowman, Crime Investigation Unit, Pennsylvania State Police: An open Bible was laying there. Considering the condition of all the other debris, it was relatively unscathed.

T. Michael Lauffer, trooper, Pennsylvania State Police: I actually found a flight book from one of the flight attendants laying down there, down in the hemlocks. That's when I knew it was a United flight, because it had "United Airlines" printed on it. "Bradshaw" was the name in it.

James Broderick: I remember it was Flight Attendant Sandra Bradshaw. It had a picture of her and her family. I had taken that with me, because we started to take things back

380

and place them on the back of a fire truck. Things were starting to blow away or burn. We wanted to protect everything that we could that could be possible evidence or things that could possibly be returned to the family members.

Clyde Ware, assistant chief, Stoystown Volunteer Fire Company: You kept looking and hoping for the impossible that day.

Lt. Robert Weaver: We were talking and I said, "I can't believe this is a commercial plane." Within minutes, [FBI agent] Wells [Morrison] got a phone call and confirmed it was Flight 93. He said, "Yes, it's confirmed — this is Flight 93."

Keith Custer, firefighter, Shanksville Volunteer Fire Company: Then we put it all together: "Hey, this is the fourth plane."

Paula Pluta, resident, Stonycreek Township: I started thinking, *What in the world do they want with Shanksville, Pennsylvania?* There's nothing here!

Sgt. Denise Miller, Indian Lake Police Department: When I first got out there to the site, I was actually a little nervous. I wondered what the importance of the field was and what possibly the government had hidden under the ground there that they wanted. I couldn't figure out why the plane had come down here.

Wells Morrison, supervisory special agent, FBI: What became the priority now was to preserve the crash site and attempt to obtain anything of evidentiary value.

Not long after Flight 93 crashed, the first media arrived at the scene and began to confirm for the world that another attack had occurred, ending in a field near Shanksville.

Laurence Kesterson, staff photographer, *Philadelphia Inquirer:* All we had was "There's a plane that crashed in western Pennsylvania. Go!" My boss said, "Just go. Just get on the turnpike and go west. We'll call as we know more."

Peter M. "Mike" Drewecki, photographer, WPXI-TV, Pittsburgh: We were trying to pinpoint exactly where Shanksville was because I had never heard of it before.

David Mattingly, national correspondent, CNN: This was in the days before everyone had a GPS in their car, so I still had to get there the old-fashioned way: I had to stop and buy a map.

Cpl. Jeffrey Braid, Aviation Patrol Unit, Pennsylvania State Police: It was eerily quiet on the radios for the airplanes. The whole ride out to Shanksville, there was really no communication between airplanes and ground.

Tony James, investigator, FAA: I drove to the FAA's Hangar 6 in Washington, which is located at Ronald Reagan Airport, and I put my stuff on the airplane. It was myself, two NTSB [National Transportation Safety Board] people, and the two pilots. We were the only airplane in the air. We were talking to air traffic control and they said, "You're cleared direct. Go as fast and as high as you want to go."

Cpl. Jeffrey Braid: We were five miles out, and we still didn't see anything, so we started contacting the ground units and said, "Are these the right coordinates?" We still didn't see any smoke or debris. We got almost right on top of it, and then we started seeing the cars and stuff.

Tony James: We get up here and we could see the woods burning and we made a couple of low fly-bys, which got a lot of people's attention.

Braden Shober, firefighter, Shanksville Volunteer Fire Company: Keith Custer pointed up in the sky and said, "That's not supposed to be there." We looked and there was a large plane flying toward us. At this point we all know that there aren't supposed to be any planes in the sky because the FAA's put everybody on the ground. It was a little eerie. You started looking around. *Where are we going to hide?*

Keith Custer: What do you do to get away from a plane that's coming at you? Do you try to outrun it? It's coming at you so fast.

Capt. Frank Monaco, Pennsylvania State Police: There was a giant jet liner right over our heads. It was like a *Twilight Zone* episode — everybody was frozen in their tracks. Nobody was moving. Nobody was talking. Everybody was stunned. "Is it another one?"

Keith Custer: When it went by us, everybody kind of did a "Wow."

Peter M. "Mike" Drewecki, photographer, WPXI-TV, Pittsburgh: There was a gathering of workers standing in front of Highland Tank Company. Some were smoking cigarettes; some were standing around, scratching their heads. They knew why we were there, and they just pointed their thumbs over their shoulders and said, "Whatever it is you're looking for, it's up that way."

Jon Meyer, reporter, WNEP-TV (Scranton, Pennsylvania): The next thing I knew, I was right where the crater was. It was an overwhelming experience. The only way I knew it was a plane was the size — it was a big crater.

Peter M. "Mike" Drewecki: I was met by a photographer from the *Greensburg* [Pennsylvania] *Tribune-Review* by the name of Sean Stipp. It's strange — you're not looking at each other, but you're looking at the things you have to shoot. I remember saying, "Sean, this is the beginning of World War III."

David Mattingly, national correspondent, CNN: The first live report I did was over the telephone. I was explaining where I was — this bucolic setting, this pasture on the right, this cornfield on the left, these rolling hills around me, this blue sky above me. It seemed a highly, highly improbable location to be doing a story about what appeared to be some terrorist attack.

As word spread of the fourth crash, the families of victims aboard Flight 93 learned that their greatest fears had been realized.

Alice Ann Hoagland, mother of United Flight 93 passenger Mark Bingham: We heard the news that Flight 93 had crashed in Pennsylvania. They had the footage on television so fast, and it showed rescue workers already on the site with a big, gaping, smoldering hole. That's the way I found out Mark had been killed.

Deena Burnett, wife of United Flight 93 passenger Tom Burnett: I realized I had been running around the house all morning in my pajamas. I needed to get dressed. I went upstairs. I had the telephone with me. I put it on the ledge by the shower so that in the event I didn't hear it, I could see it ring. I never took my eyes off the telephone while I was showering. I got dressed and went downstairs. The policeman was standing at the bottom of the stairs, and I could tell by the look on his face that something was wrong. He said, "I think I have bad news for you." I remember turning toward the television and seeing that there had been another plane crash. I ran over to the TV and I asked, "Is that Tom's plane?" He said, "Yes, it's Flight 93." I felt my knees buckle.

Lyzbeth Glick, wife of United Flight 93 passenger Jeremy Glick: They told me that Jeremy's plane had gone down. The police were at my house, and somebody said there had been some survivors on the plane. I thought, *Okay, if there are survivors, he's going to be one of them because he's a survivor.* My minister came over and we sat there and prayed. I knew since there was no call, it wasn't good news. United probably called three hours after the plane went down. I said, "You don't even need to tell me, I know."

AT SCHOOL IN ARLINGTON, VIRGINIA

"THAT VERY SLOW, QUIET PANIC"

Since the attacks happened in the morning, teachers all around the East Coast were faced with a decision they had not been trained to make: how to talk to their students about the tragedies happening in New York and Washington, D.C. One of the schools that faced this dilemma most profoundly was in the Pentagon's hometown, just a few miles from the crash site. H-B Woodlawn School officials tried to calm their 600 students — many of whom had family members working at the Pentagon, the Capitol, the White House, or other government offices — as panicked parents began to arrive to take them home.

Ray Anderson, principal, H-B Woodlawn School, Arlington: At about nine o'clock, kids started coming into the office who had gotten off the bus. They were wearing Walkmans and listening to the radio, and they're talking about terrible things happening in New York City.

Frank Haltiwanger, assistant principal, H-B Woodlawn School: Sometime during the first period, the second tower was hit.

Ray Anderson: We had to adjust to this unbelievable thing. You had no frame of reference for it and quickly realized that this was going to be a real problem for students being in school. I got on the PA and I told everyone, told the teachers to turn off all the TVs. People didn't need to sit around all morning and watch these horrible events.

Theresa Flynn, librarian, H-B Woodlawn School: My phone rang, and it was my mother — she had heard an explosion at the Pentagon and ran out her front door. She said, "We're in trouble. You need to get home."

Frank Haltiwanger: When the Pentagon was hit, that changed everything — because we had a number of kids who have parents who work there.

Ray Anderson: The phone system quickly became inoperative, and cell phones became inoperative. Everybody was trying to use the phones at the same time.

Theresa Flynn: People stopped teaching. They didn't know what to do. About a third of our staff and students had family members who were at the Pentagon, who were working downtown. The news was not helpful. They started saying: "Car bomb at the State Department." "There's another plane in the air." "We don't know how many planes are in the air." "They're all heading toward D.C." Everybody was panicking, but it was that very slow, quiet panic.

Frank Haltiwanger: We were able to maintain reasonable order downstairs by keeping the kids in the classrooms. There were two or three students who either had parents at the Pentagon or parents who were in the air to New York who became hysterical and were running down the hall. I had some come into my office. I found another teacher who was a good counselor and had that teacher sit with them.

Ray Anderson: Parents started showing up at school, wanting their children.

Frank Haltiwanger: I'd say 50 or 70 parents came. Most of them came, checked on their child, and left.

Ray Anderson: I got on the PA, now it's probably about 10:15 — 10:30 at the latest — and said, without being any more specific, "We may need to do our tornado drill today."

I reminded people the tornado drill is not the fire drill — where we all go outside and get away from the building — the tornado drill is when we all go down to the basement and first-floor hallways.

Mary McBride, assistant principal, H-B Woodlawn School: Mercifully, those parents working at the Pentagon were all right. That was the most important piece of almost the whole day for us — because that didn't happen for one of our principals.

Ray Anderson: The husband of the principal at Hoffman Boston Elementary in Arlington was on the plane that hit the Pentagon — it flew right over her building. She had some notion that that might be the case, but she stayed at her post as principal of the school, doing what I was doing at my school until the day was over. Then, at the end of the day, she found out her notion was correct.

Theresa Flynn: We had in the library 100, 150 people standing there — we had a television at either end of the library. There's not a sound other than the news. The news anchors were beginning to spout theories about Osama bin Laden. A young boy — he was in ninth grade at the time — he turned to me and said, "Why did they do this to us?," which was a big question from the kids. I

said, "Well, they don't like us very much."
He said, "Why not?"

Aboard Air Force One, Somewhere over the Gulf of Mexico

"WE HAVE NO PLACE TO GO"

Whisked aboard Air Force One minutes after the Pentagon attack, President George W. Bush and his entourage tried to understand the carnage below — and figure out where they could go themselves. When President Bush and Vice President Cheney finally connected by phone they discussed the day's most momentous order: authorizing fighters to down hijacked aircraft. It remains unclear whether that conversation took place before Vice President Cheney issued his shoot-down order in the PEOC.

The custom Boeing 747 that served that day as Air Force One contained the president's private cabin and office — known as the "airborne Oval Office" — at the front of the plane on the main deck; from there, stairs led up to the flight deck and communications suite. Other cabins toward the rear of the aircraft on the main deck housed the White House Medical Unit, staff, guests, security, the press, and crew. Isolated far above the earth, their communication networks disrupted, the passengers and crew tried to figure out what had transpired on the ground, and existed in a time frame all their own.

Dave Wilkinson, assistant agent in charge, U.S. Secret Service: Once we heard a plane had crashed into the Pentagon, that's when we said, "We're not going back to Washington." It's all about that direction of interest. At the start, the threat's in New York. Then the plane hit the Pentagon, and it's about our seats of government.

Col. Mark Tillman, presidential pilot, Air Force One: The initial conversation was that we'd take him to an air force base, no less than an hour away from Washington. Maybe we'd try to get him to Camp David. That all changed when we heard there was a plane headed toward Camp David.* I made the takeoff, climbed out, probably 25,000 to 30,000 feet, and I gave it to the backup pilot. I had three pilots on board that day. I said to keep flying toward Washington.

Maj. Gen. Larry Arnold, commander of the 1st Air Force, NORAD, Tyndall Air Force Base, Florida: We were talking to the

* Initial reports of Flight 93 were garbled, claiming that Camp David, the presidential retreat along the Maryland-Pennsylvania border, had been targeted.

Secret Service and they were on again, off again about whether they wanted us to follow him. There was an AWACS [airborne surveillance] aircraft off the East Coast doing a training mission, so we diverted that aircraft toward Sarasota to pick up the president when he took off. They said, "Okay, we will follow the president. Where is he going?" We said, "We don't know."

Ari Fleischer, press secretary, White House: As we were flying out of Sarasota, we were able to get some TV reception. They broke for commercial. I couldn't believe it. A hair-loss commercial comes on. I remember thinking, *In the middle of all this, I'm watching this commercial for hair loss?*

Andy Card, chief of staff, White House: Blake Gottesman was my personal aide, but he was filling in that day as the president's aide. I said, "Blake, it's your job to make sure that people don't come up to the suite. No one comes up unless the president calls for them."

Karl Rove, senior adviser, White House: Andy [Card] and I were with the president. He got a call from Cheney. He said "Yes," then there was a pause as he listened. Then another "yes." You had an unreal sense of time that whole day. I don't know whether it was 10 seconds or two minutes. Then he said, "You have my authorization." Then he listened for a while longer. He closed off the conversation. He turned to us and said that he had just authorized the shoot-down of hijacked airliners.

Andy Card: As soon as he hung up the phone, he said, "I was an Air National Guard pilot — I'd be one of the people getting this order. I can't imagine getting this order."

Dave Wilkinson: Every kind of communication that day was challenged. Even the president talking to the Situation Room was challenged.

Master Sgt. Dana Lark, superintendent of communications, Air Force One: People were coming up to the communications deck with various requests. A Secret Service agent comes up and says, "The president wants to know the status of the first family." I have to tell him I don't have a way to find out. I can't fathom what that was like for the president.

Karl Rove: He was so even-handed. He was so naturally calm during the day.

Master Sgt. Dana Lark: We've got multiple systems — commercial and terrestrial systems

— and they're all jammed. I started to have tunnel vision: *What the hell is going on? Did someone sabotage our comms?* It wasn't until later I realized all the commercial systems were all saturated. It was all the same systems the airplane pilots were using at the same time, talking to their dispatchers.

Col. Mark Tillman: We started having to use the military satellites, which we would only use in time of war.

Andy Card: One of the president's first thoughts, from Sarasota to Barksdale [Air Force Base, Louisiana], was Vladimir Putin [president of Russia].

Ari Fleischer: Putin was fantastic that day. He was a different Vladimir Putin in 2001. America could have had no better ally on September 11th than Russia and Putin.

Gordon Johndroe, assistant press secretary, White House: Putin was important — all these military systems were put in place for nuclear alerts. If we went on alert, we needed Putin to know that we weren't readying an attack on Russia. He was great — he said immediately that Russia wouldn't respond.

Ari Fleischer: I'd never heard the word

"decapitation attack" before, but people like Andy, who had been there during the Cold War and had the training, knew what was going on. The Secret Service said to the president, "We don't think it's safe for you to return to Washington."

Andy Card: Then we hear that Flight 93's gone down. We're all wondering, *Did we do that?*

Col. Mark Tillman: All of us, we assumed we shot it down.

Dave Wilkinson: Hearing all of this, we're thinking that the further we're away from Washington, the safer we are.

Col. Mark Tillman: We get this report that there's a call saying, "Angel was next." No one really knows now where the comment came from — it got mistranslated or garbled between the White House, the Situation Room, the radio operators. "Angel" was our code name, but the fact that they knew about "Angel" — well, you had to be in the inner circle. That was a big deal to me. It was time to hunker down and get some good weaponry.

Maj. Scott "Hooter" Crogg, F-16 pilot, 111th Fighter Squadron, Houston: I had just gotten off alert at Ellington Field in Houston. Normally we pull 24-hour alerts, mostly for drug interdiction. I'd just gotten back into bed and was watching TV and saw the reports of a plane hitting the tower. When that second plane hit, it eliminated any doubt. I had to get back to work. It was very somber at the air base. We got these cryptic messages from Southeast Air Defense Sector. I asked maintenance to put live missiles on the fighters and arm up the guns. Two heat-seeking missiles and rounds from a 20mm gun isn't a lot to take on a hijacked plane, but it was the best we could do. We dispatched two fighters to go protect Air Force One.

Col. Mark Tillman: We put a cop at the base of the stairs [leading to the cockpit]. That was something we'd never done before.

Staff Sgt. William "Buzz" Buzinski, security, Air Force One: Will Chandler, the lead air force security officer, was summoned to the front, and he stayed up there, providing security at the cockpit stairs. That got us thinking: *Is there an insider threat?*

Staff Sgt. Paul Germain, airborne communications system operator, Air Force One: Colonel Tillman said at that point, "Let's go cruise around the Gulf for a little bit." This was our Pearl Harbor. You train for nuclear war, but then you get into something like this. All the money they pumped into us for training, that worked.

Dave Wilkinson: Colonel Tillman took us to a height where if an aircraft was coming toward us, we'd know it was no mistake. I was confident we were safer in the air than we were anywhere on the ground.

Col. Mark Tillman: I took us up to 45,000 feet. That's about as high as a 747 can go.

Ann Compton, reporter, ABC News: We were standing in the press cabin. A Secret Service agent was in the aisle, and he pointed at the monitor and said, "Look down there, Ann, we're at 45,000 feet and we have no place to go."

Condoleezza Rice, national security adviser, White House: I called the president, and he said, "I'm coming back." I said, "You stay where you are. You cannot come back here. Washington is under attack."

Karl Rove: There was acrimony. President Bush doesn't raise his voice. He doesn't pound the desk. But as we made it across the Florida peninsula, Andy Card and [presidential military aide] Tom Gould kept raising objections about returning to Washington. At one point, Cheney and Rumsfeld called and said the same thing.

Dave Wilkinson: He fought with us tooth and nail all day to go back to Washington. We basically refused to take him back. The way we look at it is that by federal law, the Secret Service has to protect the president. The wishes of that person that day are secondary to what the law expects of us. Theoretically, it's not his call. It's our call.

Eric Draper, presidential photographer: He was visibly frustrated and very angry. I was a few feet away, and it felt like he was looking through me. He turned away in anger.

Karl Rove: Gould came in and said, "Mr. President, we don't have a full fuel load. We've got too many extraneous people on board. We can't loiter over Washington if we need to." He suggested, "Let's get to a military base, drop off the unessential personnel, fill up with fuel, and reassess."

Sonya Ross, reporter, AP: We didn't know where we were going, but they must've been circling, because we kept watching the local feed of a Florida station going in and out. That was our tiny window into the outside world.

Ari Fleischer: We didn't have satellite TV on the plane. The news would frustratingly come in and go out. I was not aware of the punishing coverage that the president was receiving for not returning to Washington. The anchors were all asking, "Where's Bush?" They instantly criticized him.

Karen Hughes, communications director, White House: Since I was home, I saw quite a bit of TV coverage just like the American people were seeing it, and I realized that it looked like the American government was faltering. I was on the phone with my chief of staff at the White House when she was told to evacuate. I could actually see the Pentagon burning. But I knew that lots of government was functioning — planes were being grounded, emergency plans were being implemented. I thought someone should be telling the American people that, so I wanted to talk to the president. When I called the operator to try to reach Air Force One, the operator came back on the line and said, "Ma'am, we can't reach Air Force One." Mary Matalin had passed along that there was a threat against the plane. It was chilling. For a split second, I was so worried.

Sonya Ross: Ann Compton of ABC News and I were trying to come up with timelines — what time was it when Andy Card came in and whispered to the president. We were listening through headsets to the television, but we weren't really paying attention. Then I heard the reporter say, "The tower's collapsing." I looked at the TV and had a completely shocked reaction.

Eric Draper: We were in the president's office when the Towers fell. You knew that there'd be a loss of life in a catastrophic way. The room was really silent. Everyone peeled off one by one and the president stood there, alone, watching the cloud expand.

Andy Card: I asked the military aides, "Where are we going? I want options. I want a long runway, a secure place, good communications." They came back and said Barksdale Air Force Base. I said, "Don't tell anyone we're coming."

Dave Wilkinson: It was the perfect compromise — close and secure and we could let off a lot of passengers there. We needed somewhere that had armored vehicles.

Andy Card: I went into the president's cabin and told him, "We're going to Barksdale." He said, "No, we're going back to the White House." He was pretty hot with me. I kept saying, "I don't think you want to make that decision right now." He went back and forth.

403

It wasn't one conversation — it was five, six, seven conversations.

Col. Mark Tillman: We asked for fighter support. We heard, "You have fast movers at your seven o'clock." They were supersonic, F-16s from the president's guard unit. They led us into Barksdale.

Maj. Scott "Hooter" Crogg, F-16 pilot, 111th Fighter Squadron, Houston: The horn went off again at Ellington Field in Houston and F-16 pilot Shane Brotherton and I launched. We didn't even know what the mission was. We were told, "You need to intercept the Angel flight." We had no idea what that meant. We'd never heard Air Force One called that before.

Rep. Adam Putnam (R-Florida), aboard Air Force One: Rep. Dan Miller and I went up to the president's cabin and he gave us a briefing. He told us that "one way or another" all but a couple planes were accounted for — that was his phrase. "One way or another." He told us Air Force One was headed to Barksdale and was going to drop us off there. When we left the cabin, I turned to Dan and said, "Didn't you think that was an odd phrase?" He didn't notice it. I said, " 'One way or another,' that sounds like there's more to it than that." I said, "Do you think there's any way we shot them down?" We were left hanging.

Gordon Johndroe: I was sitting across the table from [CIA presidential briefer] Mike Morell in the staff cabin. I asked, "Mike, is something else going to happen?" He said, "Yes." That was a real gut punch.

Brian Montgomery, director of advance, White House: I asked Mike Morell who he thought this was. He said "UBL." No hesitation. *Who's UBL?* Those of us not up on the lingo of Langley, we had no idea.

Mike Morell, presidential briefer, Central Intelligence Agency: The president called me into his cabin. It was packed with people. The Democratic Front for the Liberation of Palestine had issued a claim of responsibility for the attack. The president asked me, "What do you know about these guys?" I explained that they had a long history of terrorism, but they didn't have the capability to do this. Guaranteed. As I was leaving, he said to me, "Michael, one more thing. Call [CIA Director] George Tenet and tell him that if he finds out anything about who did it, I want to be the first to know. Got that?"

Sonya Ross: I was nervous. I was thinking — it seems really morbid — but I was think-

405

ing, *What if they come after the president? We all turn into "and 12 others." No one knows your name if you go down with the president.* But Eric Washington, he was the CBS sound guy, he had his seat reclined, his feet up. He said, "What are you worried about? You're on the safest plane in the world."

Gordon Johndroe: Air Force One was the safest and most dangerous place in the world at the exact same time.

Karen Hughes: When I finally did reach Air Force One and spoke with the president, the first thing he said to me was "Don't you think I need to come back?" He was champing at the bit to come back. I told him, "Yes, as soon as you can." Everyone has different roles, and I wasn't thinking about the national security side — I was thinking about it from a PR perspective.

Andy Card: Mark Tillman said, "I don't care what he says. I'm in charge of the plane."

Dave Wilkinson: The president once told me that the biggest piece of advice he'd gotten from his mother when he became president was always to do what the Secret Service says. I reminded him of that several times that day. The president and I knew each other very well — we'd spent a lot of hours at his ranch — and tongue-in-cheek several times that day, I said, "Remember what your mother said."

Master Sgt. Dana Lark: There were so many people coming up to the upper deck, because we weren't picking up the phones downstairs. It got too crowded. Finally, someone came up and told everyone to get out. The only member of the staff who was up with us was [White House Staff Secretary] Harriet Miers — she was sitting at one of the CSO seats, with a legal pad taking down the historical record.

Andy Card: The president's wondering about his wife, his kids, his parents. Then he's wondering, *Is there another city? What's next?* We're all thinking, *We can't do anything about it. We're in a plane, eight miles high in the sky.*

Dave Wilkinson: We called Mark Rosenker [the director of the White House Military Office] up to the front of the plane and told him to get us on the phone with the commander at Barksdale. He gave us full assurance that the base would be locked down.

Andy Card: I was comforted to find Barksdale was already on alert. It was going to be secure. No random terrorist would have mapped that Barksdale was where the president was going to go.

Lt. Gen. Tom Keck, commander, Barksdale Air Force Base: We were already in a practice THREATCON Delta, the highest threat condition. I said lock her down for real. My deputy told me that at THREATCON Delta, general officers have to wear sidearms. I tried to refuse, but he insisted. So I was wearing my sidearm, which I never do. We got this radio request — Code Alpha — a high-priority incoming aircraft. It wanted 150,000 pounds of gas, 40 gallons of coffee, 70 box lunches, and 25 pounds of bananas. It wouldn't identify itself. It was clearly a big plane. It didn't take us long to figure out that the Code Alpha was Air Force One.

Ann Compton: As we were landing going into Barksdale, Ari came back to the press cabin and said, "This is off the record, but the president is being evacuated." I said, "You can't put that off the record. That's a historic and chilling fact. That has to be on the record."

Among Those Who Knew

"BIN LADEN COMES TO MIND"

While the country absorbed the news and horror of the terrorist attacks in Washington, New York, and Pennsylvania, TV anchors and reporters turned to experts who could explain the attacks — which to most Americans seemed to come out of nowhere. Few Americans knew the name Osama bin Laden. Midday on 9/11, Washington NBC-4 TV anchors brought into their studio a man who knew the background of the attacks.

Doreen Gentzler, anchor, NBC-4: We want to turn now to a guest who is joining us in the studio. It's Paul Bremer. I want to make sure I'm getting your name right because I'm just meeting you. You're a terrorism expert?

L. Paul Bremer III, former chair, 1999 National Commission on Terrorism: Counterterrorism, I hope.

Doreen Gentzler: And can you talk to us a little bit about who could . . . I mean there are a limited number of groups who could be responsible for something of this magnitude. Right?

Paul Bremer: Yes, this is a very well planned, very well coordinated attack, which suggests it's very well organized centrally. And there are only three or four candidates in the world really who could have conducted this attack.

Jim Vance, anchor, NBC-4: Bin Laden comes to mind right away, Mr. Bremer.

Paul Bremer: Indeed, he certainly does.

Since the mid-1990s, two squads of the FBI's Joint Terrorism Task Force in New York, known as I-49 and I-45, had been carefully tracking the rise of a terrorist group known as al-Qaeda. Even though his name was new to most Americans on September 11, the organization's leader, Osama bin Laden, had been on the FBI's radar for some time, having been added to its Ten Most Wanted list in June 1999 for his role in planning and financing the 1998 U.S.

410

embassy bombings in Kenya and Tanzania. In 1999, careful work by law enforcement intercepted an al-Qaeda plot to attack the United States during the Millennium celebrations, and in 2000, al-Qaeda terrorists attacked the USS Cole in Yemen, killing 17 U.S. sailors. The State Department's ambassador-at-large for counterterrorism, Michael Sheehan, spoke angrily to military officials in 2000, frustrated at the Clinton administration's lack of focus in combating the rise of bin Laden's terrorist group, presciently exclaiming, "Does al-Qaeda have to hit the Pentagon to get your attention?"

By 2001, FBI agents from I-45 and I-49 were chasing bin Laden's group around the world. That Tuesday morning found a team of agents still in Aden, Yemen, investigating the Cole bombing, and another team of agents in Scandinavia, where on Monday night, September 10, they'd raided a house hoping to catch one of the embassy bombers. In Washington on September 11, at 8:00 a.m. ET, FBI counterterrorism agents had briefed the new FBI director, Robert Mueller — who had started on September 4 — on the status of the al-Qaeda investigation and the Cole bombing.

The 9/11 attack on the World Trade Center hit just blocks from the FBI squad's offices at 290 Broadway, a few blocks from the FBI's main office at 26 Federal Plaza, and pulled many of those same agents who had long tracked bin

411

Laden out into the debris-filled streets, catching them in the Towers' collapse. Ironically, the attacks would ultimately kill veteran FBI agent John O'Neill, who had led the al-Qaeda task force and who had retired in August from the bureau to start a new job as the security director at the World Trade Center.

John Anticev, special agent, FBI Joint Terrorism Task Force: People on the ground get to see the future before everyone. I think NYPD detective Lou Napoli and I were the first people to write UBL into bureau files in the early 1990s. You knew this Afghan movement was more than fighting Russians. We just didn't know to call it al-Qaeda.

Robert "Bear" Bryant, deputy director, FBI, 1997–99: The first time I ever heard the name Osama bin Laden was from John O'Neill. John O'Neill was very much aware of who he was, who his group was. Al-Qaeda.

John Miller, correspondent, ABC News: In 1998, I sat with Osama bin Laden in a hut in Afghanistan as he told me he was declaring war on America: "We are sure of victory. Our battle with the Americans is larger than our battle with the Russians. We predict a black day for America and the end of the

United States." From the moment bin Laden declared war on America, one of his frustrations seemed to be that he couldn't get America to declare war back.

Jackie Maguire, special agent, FBI Joint Terrorism Task Force: The JTTF's very famous for the work it has done on the first World Trade Center bombing in 1993. It also sent people all over the world — the East Africa embassy bombing case was run out of New York. The USS *Cole* bombing was run out of New York.

Fran Townsend, director, Office of Intelligence Policy and Review, U.S. Justice Department: From his time down in the international terrorism section at headquarters in Washington, John O'Neill began to see the [World Trade Center bomber] Ramzi Yousef case. As things progressed, John completely threw himself into it. He read everything he could get his hands on about radical fundamentalism. He was already beginning to focus on it before the first World Trade Center, and think about it and look at the implications of it.

By the time the first bombing happens, from things he said to me, he already got in his mind this was a major and long-term problem for us that we were ill-equipped to deal with.

413

Steve Gaudin, special agent, FBI Joint Terrorism Task Force: It was hard to get people to pay attention. That spring, we'd put four of the embassy bombers on trial. I remember Puff Daddy was on trial in municipal court, and Johnnie Cochran was the lawyer. It was a circus. That's where all the cameras were. No one cared about what was going on at the federal courthouse.

Richard Clarke, counterterrorism adviser, White House: In June of 2001, the intelligence community issued a warning that a major al-Qaeda terrorist attack would take place in the next many weeks. They said they were unable to find out exactly where it might take place. They said they thought it might take place in Saudi Arabia. We asked, "Could it take place in the United States?" They said, "We can't rule that out."

Abby Perkins, special agent, FBI Joint Terrorism Task Force: There was lots of chatter over the summer of 2001. Things were happening, people were on standby. It was a heavy summer. We thought it'd be an international attack.

Adm. Edmund Giambastiani, senior military assistant, Office of the Secretary of Defense: We knew there was a higher threat level, but not where, when, or how.

Fran Townsend: John O'Neill was frustrated by the U.S.'s inability to really appreciate and get our arms around this threat in an effective way. He definitely thought we were vulnerable in the summer. He definitely felt that something was going to happen, something important was going to happen.

Jerry Hauer, New York director of emergency management, 1996–2000: The night of September 10th, he had said to me, "We're due, and we're due for something big."

Steve Bongardt, special agent, FBI Joint Terrorism Task Force: I remember reading that morning, on September 11, 2001, an intelligence report that bin Laden was re-opening Tora Bora, his compound in Afghanistan. I was wondering, *What the hell is he doing?*

George Tenet, director, CIA: The system was blinking red.

The 9/11 Commission: Time ran out.

Steve Gaudin: We were in the office at 290 Broadway when the first plane hit. It sounded like the air conditioners had kicked on, a low thump, but it was late in the season for the air-conditioning. We thought it was a civil aviation issue first. But we threw on our raid

415

jackets — maybe NYPD would need help on crowd control.

Wesley Wong, assistant special agent in charge, FBI New York: My thought was that firemen are going to come, and they're going to put the fire out. People are going to come down the stairwells. NTSB will come in. They'll do the accident investigation. There's really nothing for the bureau to do.

Jackie Maguire: We saw people who had obviously been hit by debris, who were bleeding. A few people sitting on the streets, a lot of people crying, emotional.

Abby Perkins: You didn't know how far it went; I can only see what's in front of me. But we knew we were at war.

Steve Bongardt: I stopped a firefighter and asked, "What can we do?" He said, "Just get people away from the building." He started to leave, then he turned back: "Give me your flashlight — we're going to need extras." I gave him my Maglite.

Fran Townsend: When the first plane hit, my first instinct was to call John, and I did. I didn't get through. As I was standing there on the phone, I saw the second plane, and of course by then, there's no doubt of what the

416

issue is. After the second plane went into the South Tower, he paged me to let me know he was OK. That was the last contact I had.

Jackie Maguire: As soon as the second plane hit, I think everyone knew what was going on.

Fred Stremmel, terrorism analyst, FBI: We knew it was terrorism, but we were in denial. It's like being told you have cancer. You want to deny it for as long as possible.

Jackie Maguire: Everyone knew right away this was most likely al-Qaeda.

Steve Bongardt: My immediate thought was, *This is why they're polishing up Tora Bora.*

Steve Gaudin: We said, "We gotta start collecting evidence." It was a combination of shock and autopilot.

Abby Perkins: Steve Gaudin found a piece of the plane.

John Anticev, special agent, FBI: When I got there, you saw people fleeing. It was like Godzilla. I said, "Fucking al-Qaeda."

Wesley Wong: I was down in the command center at the World Trade Center lobby, and

John O'Neill saw me and he came up to me. John always had his cell phone to his ear — no matter when you saw him, he was always on his cell phone. Just like that morning, the morning of 9/11, he had his cell phone. He saw me and said, "Wes. What can you tell me?"

He had just retired from the FBI and he was on his second day as director of security for the World Trade Center. I said to John, "You're no longer with the FBI. You don't have a clearance. I can't tell you what's going on." Even under times of stress and crisis, I can be a smart aleck. He said, "Wes, if you don't tell me, I'm going to wring your scrawny little neck." I told him what I knew, and he asked, "I've heard that the Pentagon has been hit?" I said, "We're hearing that. Let me confirm," and I called headquarters. They confirmed that the Pentagon had been hit.

I relayed this back to John. He said, "Well, I need to go check on my people in the South Tower." As he walked away I said to him, "Hey John. I owe you lunch. I missed your going-away lunch. When this is all over, let's have lunch." He said something that's music to every agent's ear. He said, "Wes, I'm on an expense account now — lunch will be on me."

John O'Neill was last seen in the stairwell of the 48th floor of the South Tower.

Jackie Maguire: We heard the rumble of the first tower starting to fall. We went running.

David Kelley, assistant U.S. attorney, Justice Department: I was with Barry Mawn [FBI assistant director in charge of the New York Field Office] and we took off running. Then we were completely buried. I couldn't breathe. It's a very fine powder — it was like being buried in a huge pile of Xerox toner. I knew I was a faster runner than Barry. I figured immediately he didn't make it.

Abby Perkins: We were hiding in a bank building. As the tower fell, I remembered how many victims in the embassy bombing in Nairobi had been hurt or killed by glass. I wanted to get away from the glass windows. I was thinking, *What does it feel like to be buried in concrete?* We thought we might be trapped there for a long time. My colleague Debbie Doran and I, we remembered Rosie, who had been rescued from the rubble in Nairobi but died of dehydration. Debbie's always organized, she's the planner of the group, and she was immediately trying to find trash cans we could fill with water.

Steve Gaudin: Then you're looking and there's no more tower.

David Kelley: Later, I called Mary Jo White, the U.S. attorney in Manhattan. I told her Barry Mawn was killed. She laughed and said, "I just talked to him — he told me *you* were dead."

Jackie Maguire: Leads were already coming in. People were already calling into the FBI with suspicious activity they had seen.

John Miller: John O'Neill had spent the better part of 10 years fighting terrorism and the better part of five trying to nail bin Laden. Now Osama bin Laden had struck the two buildings in his care. I called O'Neill's phone all that day, hoping, hoping for a miracle.

Steve Gaudin: We started walking north to 26th Street, to the garage where the FBI was setting up a command post. It was devastating. The day never really ended.

Escaping the Pentagon

"WE HAVE TO HAVE EVACS —
DO YOU COPY?"

The initial rescue efforts at the Pentagon were led primarily by the military and civilian Pentagon workers, coworkers who rushed into flames and smoke to find lost, missing, and injured colleagues and follow the military's dictum of "No person left behind." Nearly everyone who was rescued from the Pentagon was found in the first 30 minutes.

James Schwartz, assistant chief for operations, Arlington County Fire Department: All the credit that public safety, fire, EMS, and the police departments get for their efforts on 9/11, I think what gets lost is the truly heroic efforts of the civilian and uniformed personnel that work in the Pentagon. They were the ones who really got their comrades, got their workmates out.

Capt. Paul Larson, Arlington County Police Department: When I got there, there was probably a wall of two or three thousand military personnel coming out of the building, and as soon as they heard the screams for help, all of them immediately turned around and went right back into the building to help whoever needed help.

Capt. Charles Gibbs, Arlington County Fire Department: We were there probably within about 10 minutes. We met up with Chief Schwartz. He said, "Go up there" — he was pointing to the impact site, which is on the heliport side — "and see what's going on and let me know." I got my gear on, and me and firefighter Keith Young proceeded up there and Fort Myer Fire Department was on the scene.

James Schwartz: Among the responding units were the crash fire rescue vehicles at National Airport, which were positioned on the west lawn and at that point really were able to provide the greatest amount of extinguishment capability. There was a large fire.

John Jester, chief, Defense Protective Service, Pentagon: The smoke was so bad you couldn't see, and the heat was so bad. There was thousands of gallons of aviation fuel on fire in the hallways.

Steven Carter, assistant building manager, Pentagon: Visibility was maybe two feet. There was a definite feel of heat coming through the area, but the overwhelming thing hitting my senses was the dense acrid smoke.

Chris Combs, special agent, FBI, Pentagon: I can remember very vividly walking through the parking lot, feeling the immense heat from that fire. At first it confused me. I was like, *Wow, what is burning in there?* I did not know it was an airplane.

Steven Carter: Looking up into the second and third floors, I could see people in the windows banging to get attention or to get out, but the windows were not breaking. The back wall had blown off, and it had become the only escape for some people in that area.

There was a large contingent of Pentagon occupants dipping their shirts into the water that was accumulating and putting them over their faces and attempting to reenter the building to help get people out.

Staff Sgt. Christopher Braman, chef, U.S. Army: As soon as I came out the stairwell, I encountered a DPS officer carrying a lady struggling with a baby. I grabbed the baby from the officer's hands, together we ran for about 60 yards, and I placed the baby back in the woman's arms. The woman kept saying, "Where's my baby? Where's my baby?" I realized the woman was in shock because the baby was in her arms, and she had no idea. The officer instructed me, "Go get help, go get help."

Steven Carter: They were using the center courtyard to stage a triage area for injured people. They were putting them all around on the grass. There were medical teams that were bringing in equipment as much as possible, but there were very few supplies out there and a whole lot of people.

John Milton Brady Jr., safety technician investigator, Department of Defense: People were panicking. They didn't know which way to go. I stood there, using the flashlight as a beacon and calling to the people to come toward me and they started doing that.

Staff Sgt. Christopher Braman: I saw this ambulance pulling up. I got to a firefighter, and it was almost like he was oblivious to what I was telling him. He was downloading all his equipment as fast as he could. I kept telling him, "I have a baby, I need help. I have a lady and a baby." All of a sudden his eyes became fixated above me. They brought a woman from behind me who was burned from the back of her head to the back of the thighs. She was a dark-complected woman, but she was bright pink in color from the amount of burns that she received.

Lt. Michael Nesbitt, Defense Protective Service, Pentagon: I got a phone call and someone said he understood that we needed helicopters. I said that was correct. He said to tell them where to go, and they would have 40 birds in the air. I said that sounded good.

Lt. Col. Ted Anderson, legislative liaison officer, U.S. Army, Pentagon: I kicked open a fire exit door and screamed for people to follow me. I guess there were 50, maybe 100 people who followed me out that way. I saw a field of scattered debris — it was all gray and metallic. Everybody was moving to my right, and I turned to my left and ran toward the debris. There was nobody with me except Chris Braman.

Staff Sgt. Christopher Braman: At that point I met a lieutenant colonel, Ted Anderson. He's a leader in my eyes. He kept saying, "My general didn't die on my watch. My general didn't die on my watch." He had come out and he was delirious.

Lt. Col. Ted Anderson: I got as close to the building as I could, trying to find a door that we could get into. We found two women out on the ground next to the building. They had been thrown out by people who were rescuing folks inside. One woman was conscious. The other was unconscious. I picked up the conscious lady. She had a broken hip and was in horrible, horrible pain. Both had been terribly flash-burned. The fire was bearing down on us. The heat was horrendous. I told her it was going to hurt, and I picked her up and threw her on my back. She screamed in pain. I ran her about 400 yards to the other side of the helipad. Chris Braman carried the other lady. We laid them there and other people came up to render aid. Chris and I ran back.

Staff Sgt. Christopher Braman: There was an opening adjacent to the point of impact. We crawled through — the firemen went with us. You couldn't see anything. It was so dark that I was told they call it "country dark."

Lt. Col. Ted Anderson: Inside we screamed for people to come toward our voices. We couldn't see anything. The smoke was billowing, and it was hard to breathe. I got on the floor and I felt my way down the wall. I felt a body right in front of the door. It was a woman, extremely heavyset. She was conscious. She was bleeding from the ears and the mouth, and she was definitely in shock. She was pinned against a wall by a huge safe. It was a six-drawer safe that had fallen and was wedged up against her. We had to try to get her out. It seemed like forever, but we were finally able to pull her free. We had to drag her from the building.

Staff Sgt. Christopher Braman: It was so hot inside you could feel the heat. My face was burning. All I had was a T-shirt and an undershirt, that I ripped off and put over my face.

Lt. Col. Ted Anderson: Chris and I went back into the building and were trying to figure out what we were going to do. I noticed this bright flash that went by me. I thought it was the ceiling caving in. I heard Chris scream, "Help me." It was a person on fire, trying to get out of the building.

Staff Sgt. Christopher Braman: We jumped on top of that man, and we put him out as best we could.

Lt. Col. Ted Anderson: We picked him up immediately and carried him out. We got him as far away from the building as we could and gently laid him down. He was burned — horribly, horribly burned — from the top of his head all the way to the bottom of his feet. He had no color in his eyes. They were all white. I could see it was a civilian because he had a suit on. You could see that he had a white shirt on, but the whole front had been burned away. The back of his collar was still affixed, the belt to his pants was still affixed and melted into the side of his body. Everything else was charred black down the front.

Lt. Col. Rob Grunewald, information management officer, U.S. Army, Pentagon: The plane came into the building and went underneath our feet, literally, by a floor. A friend of mine down the table, Martha Cardin, yelled for help, and I told Martha, "I got you, Martha. I'll come get you." Where everybody went and how they get out of the room is very unique, because those are where decisions are made that are fatal, or cause injury, or cause mental fatigue, or great consternation. A bunch of my officemates that were in that meeting went in one direction and unfortunately didn't make it. The person that sat to my right, the person that sat to my left, apparently went out the door and took a right, and they went into the E-Ring, where they apparently perished. A decision to go in one direction or another was very important.

Maj. James Phillips, Defense Protective Service, Pentagon: If the plane had hit any other part of the building, there would have been a lot more devastation. Ironically, the part that was hit was the newly renovated wedge.

Philip Smith, branch chief, U.S. Army, Pentagon: It was truly a miracle that the plane hit the strongest part of the Pentagon — it had been completely renovated to all the new antiterrorism standards — and it was virtually unoccupied. In any other wedge of the Pentagon, there would have been 5,000 people, and the plane would have flown right through the middle of the building.

Lt. Col. Rob Grunewald: As we got out of the conference room, we were into the cubicle farm. It's the typical Dilbert office space, where you have tens and hundreds of cubicles in various different configurations: four desks here, six desks here, a corridor here, a hall here, a row here, an aisle here, 20 here, copier room, fax room, enclave over here. So now, on our hands and knees, in the dark, it was trying to keep yourself oriented, *Where do you go? Where is safe, and how do I get there?* The plane was burning on the floor below us. As we were crawling, the floor buckled, and there was flame coming up through there like a blowtorch.

Capt. Darrell Oliver, Quadrennial Defense Review Office, U.S. Army: We formed up on litter teams to assist in getting others out of the building. The flames had gotten too severe for us to go back in, and the firemen directed us to stay at the door.

They would bring individuals out, and we would get them to the triage area. One of the first individuals we got was severely burned on both arms. The firemen carried her to our litter and put her down. We had to position her on the stretcher, and in order to position her on a stretcher, we had to touch her. Her skin was as white as a piece of paper. As we touched her, her skin was coming off in our hands.

Lt. Col. Rob Grunewald: The smoke was beginning to get very thick, and was coming down further and further and further, and we were crawling on our hands and knees. You can't see where you're going, and because of the force of the blow, there were chairs thrown about, there were desks thrown about, file cabinets had fallen over, and copiers and faxes and walls. I pushed things out of the way. Martha was holding onto my belt, and we kept going.

I kept crawling through the corridor into the brand-new cafeteria, which wasn't even open yet, because we had just moved into the renovated space. At that point I realized that there was no more fire, there was no more smoke, and we were relatively safe. I got up. I gave Martha to some people. I said, "Martha, I'm going back inside to search for some more people." She advised against it, but I did it anyway, though I didn't get far. By that time, the smoke was down very, very close to the ground so you couldn't see. It was quite obvious that if I was to go back in that I would put myself in harm's way.

Sheila Denise Moody, accountant, Resource Services Office, Pentagon: I was in a state of shock. I was still seated at my desk with my hands on my lap, and I really hadn't moved other than from the force that pushed me back a little. Burning debris from the ceiling fell and landed on my hands. I shook my hands, I got up out of my chair, and I started to look around. Everything around me was on fire.

Louise Rogers, accountant, Resource Services Office, Pentagon: Everything went black. The only noise was the crackling of flames, and it was sheer devastation. I remember the grit from the soot in my teeth. I looked around, trying to figure out how to get out — fortunately, being at the fax machine, I was standing in front of a table, a worktable, that was in front of the window. Then I tried to figure out if I could get my feet out of the debris. I picked up one foot after the other and walked over to the table. The window had been blown out by the impact, and I climbed out.

Sheila Denise Moody: I was trapped in my

cubicle space with nowhere to go and no way to get out. There was another coworker who was seated in the cubicle behind me and she cried out, "What's going on? What's happening? Is anybody there?" I said, "I'm here, I'm here." She said, "Who is it?" I said, "It's me, it's Sheila." She said, "My skin is on fire. I feel like I'm burning." I told her, "I know it hurts, baby, but we've got to find a way to get out of here."

Louise Rogers: As I was walking out the window, the very first Pentagon police car came around the building. He saw me, stopped, and walked toward me, and told me to sit down in the back of the police car. I told him, "I saw someone else in the office that couldn't get out." She was alive — I didn't realize that not everyone was alive at that point — but she was having trouble. He came back with some help, some others, to get her out. She went into the intensive care ward, but she was one of the ones that didn't make it.

Sheila Denise Moody: I could see a window to the right of me. It was too far up. I was able to reach it with my hand and try to bang on it, but the glass was too thick. When I hit the window, I left a blood print of my hand on the window. I didn't even realize at the time that I was bleeding. I said, "God, I don't believe you brought me here for me to die like this." No sooner had I spoken those words than there was a voice I could hear through the smoke. "Is there anybody in here?" I called back to him, I said, "Yes! We're here!" He said, "I can't see you." I said, "I can't see you either, but we're here. Please keep coming."

With those last words, the smoke and the fumes started to take my breath away. I couldn't speak anymore, and I started to cough and choke. Coughing and choking, something ran through my mind and said, *Clap your hands.* I started to clap my hands together as hard and as loud as I could, hoping that he could follow the sound. I could hear a fire extinguisher.

Staff Sgt. Christopher Braman: There was a woman on her knees clapping her hands. She couldn't breathe. I reached for her, reached through the clouds.

Sheila Denise Moody: Just for a split second through the smoke, I could see the silhouette of a figure. I stepped over some debris, reached out through the smoke, and there was a hand reaching back, and he pulled me out.

Staff Sgt. Christopher Braman: Her hands were stuck up in this position, her face was covered full of ash. I was told later on that's a natural fetal position for burn victims. The colonel and I ran her to safety.

Sheila Denise Moody: When Sergeant Braman came to the smoke calling, "Is there anybody in there?," my voice was still the only voice that called back to him.

Staff Sgt. Christopher Braman: Colonel Anderson and I went into the building at least four times. The heat inside was so hot it felt like the sun kissing you.

Sheila Denise Moody: My rescuer is Sgt. Christopher Braman. In talking to him in the months since then, I found out that he actually came into the area that I was in on his third time into the building, trying to get in to see who he could help and save. Of all the people that he was able to pull out and able to help, I'm the only one who survived.

Lt. Col. Ted Anderson: We were getting ready to make entry again, and the firemen stopped us. Other firemen showed up and they physically restrained us and pulled us away from the building. I was completely and totally out of my mind at that point, reverting to full combat mode. So did Chris. He had been in the Ranger regiment. He fought in Mogadishu. As far as I was concerned, this was a combat situation.

Staff Sgt. Christopher Braman: We were so jacked up on adrenaline. Colonel Anderson kept getting into fights with different authority figures — firemen, military, it didn't matter who it was. There was no question that this was another battle zone.

Sheila Denise Moody: It was chaos. People were running in every direction and they were crying. They were screaming. I went to the line where they had people who were wounded. As I was walking in that direction, I heard someone call my name, "Sheila!" I looked up and it was Louise. She was sitting in the back of a police car.

Louise Rogers: There were more and more people coming out, and we kept moving farther and farther back out of the way until we were sitting back up against the guardrail at the highway.

Sheila Denise Moody: I think they ended up putting like three or four of us in the back of the ambulance and taking us to Arlington Hospital.

Louise Rogers: By that time I wasn't feeling too good. As soon as I got into the ambulance my hands started to hurt — there was a burning pain. I said to the medic, "Well, this is starting to hurt." Then I passed out. I don't remember much of anything for days after that.

Lt. Col. Ted Anderson: A three-star general showed up, along with a couple other generals, and I explained to them what was going on. This three-star general basically felt the same way I did, and he went to the on-site fire commander and said, "Look, I will take full responsibility. We need to make an attempt to go in and get our people out." He was overruled by the fire captain. I have since come to know that the fire captain was correct to do so. I am now certain that they saved my life and I'm certain they saved Chris's life as well. My whole outlook on the American firefighter changed that day. Those guys were the real heroes of the day for me. I have talked to firemen who later went into that area, and there was no way out. That last burned guy we brought out was the last person to come out of the building alive on the exterior side of the Pentagon.

Sheila Denise Moody: We lost 34 coworkers that day between the accounting division, which was the office that I was in, and the budget office, which was right across the hall.

That area sustained pretty much a direct hit from the airplane.

Dennis Smith, maintenance inspector, Pentagon Building Manager's Office: I had turnout gear, fire department self-contained breathing apparatus (SCBA). I had air for an hour. I was sweeping every room to see if anyone was still alive. As I made my way through the smoke and flames, there was water all over the floor, nine or 10 inches on the floor because the pipes had broken. Stairwells were like waterfalls. There were body parts floating around. I saw a foot, a torso, a lady hanging upside down from a chair. Someone's head sitting on a file cabinet, totally burned. I found people sitting at a conference table totally charred. I found a man standing with his arms up in defense, leaning against the wall. Apparently, he saw it coming. He was totally burned. I went floor to floor on the collapsed fourth corridor side and yelled to see if anybody was still alive. I didn't find anyone.

Capt. Robert Gray, Technical Rescue, Station 4, Arlington County Fire Department: Jet fuel was in everything. It was laying on the film on the surface of the water that we were walking through, so it made the gear smell.

Lt. Comm. David Tarantino, physician, U.S. Navy: The flames and the smoke were too intense by that time, and even the rescue crews couldn't really penetrate into the buildings. Not too many people were brought out after that.

Capt. Robert Gray: It was really remarkable because you'd be on the second or third floor and you'd find a room that was absolutely pristine. It's surrounded by complete destruction. The duct work down on the floors, the file cabinets completely ripped apart. And then one room just like this, where there's not even but a light layer of smoke on the wall. The flags, magazines sitting on the desk. It was how the gas mixed with the air and vented through the buildings under pressure, and then blew certain areas up and preserved others.

Capt. Charles Gibbs, Arlington County Fire Department: The military had their corps people with stretchers and all that, but there were no people.

In the minutes after the Pentagon attack, Secretary of Defense Donald Rumsfeld found himself torn between his official role — which called for him to lead the nation's response — and his human desire to examine the crash

438

scene and help the injured men and women under his command.

Aubrey Davis, officer, Protective Service Unit, Defense Protective Service, Pentagon: The secretary was walking fast, and we were walking fast with him. As we proceeded down that hallway, a colonel ran up with a cut on his forehead and said, "Sir, it's dangerous, don't go down there."

Gilbert Oldach, officer, Protective Service Unit, Defense Protective Service, Pentagon: We were in smoke and finally saw that light. The doors were open and the sun was coming in. You could see the light.

Donald Rumsfeld, secretary of defense: I saw the field out there sprayed with pieces of metal.

Aubrey Davis: I remember the secretary reaching down and picking up a piece of the plane with the name of the aircraft or something on it. He said, "This is American Airlines."

Donald Rumsfeld: Oh my Lord, the whole place was burning. People were being pulled out and stretchers were being carried to ambulances.

Aubrey Davis: The Communications Center kept asking where the secretary was, and I kept saying we had him. They couldn't hear.

Victoria "Torie" Clarke, assistant secretary of defense for public affairs: Several times in the next half hour or so people would ask where the secretary was. The answer was "out of the building." We took that to mean that he had been taken to a secure location. But he had gone out to the site.

Mary Matalin, aide to Vice President Dick Cheney, White House: There was a real concern in getting information about the casualties at the Defense Department. At first, we thought Secretary Rumsfeld had been hit, then we heard he was pulling bodies out of the rubble. We couldn't quite get a location on the secretary of defense.

Joe Wassel, communications officer, Office of the Secretary of Defense: There were people to our left sitting on the grass. They were starting to set some triage when we heard someone say, "Hey, I need some help."

Aubrey Davis: I recalled that Secretary Rumsfeld had been in the navy. He was like the captain going down with the ship — he

440

was going to make sure everything was OK before he went back.

Donald Rumsfeld: I tried to get some folks to help out and helped out a bit myself. I talked to some people about what had taken place.

Aubrey Davis: At one point someone ran up to the secretary asking for help. The secretary asked him what he needed, and Rumsfeld motioned to his communications guy, Joe Wassel. He said, "Tell him what you need." He said we need helicopters and such. We were still trying to get the secretary off the site of impact. We heard that the Park Police helicopter, Eagle One, was going to land to take him out of there. He said, "No, if they land they will use it to transport the injured."

Donald Rumsfeld: I decided I had done what I could, there were enough people there, and went inside.

Victoria "Torie" Clarke: The next thing we knew he had come in to the command center — dirty, sweaty, with his jacket over his shoulder.

Col. Matthew Klimow, executive assistant to the vice chair of the Joint Chiefs of Staff, Gen. Richard Myers, Pentagon: About 10:30, Secretary Rumsfeld joined us. He immediately asked for an update, especially on the rules of engagement. We explained the policy we had agreed with General [Ralph] Eberhart: we were going to try to persuade a potentially hijacked plane to land — but if it was headed to a large city, take it down. Everybody was calm and cool. Rumsfeld then confirmed with Vice President Cheney what the ROE was. It was around 10:30 that we received a report that there was an unknown aircraft about five miles out. It was a blip on the radar screen that had disappeared. We thought this was it. The plane was minutes, maybe even seconds away from hitting us.*

---

* This may have been more garbled communication about Flight 93, which government officials in Washington still didn't know had crashed in Pennsylvania.

442

In Between Collapses

The 29 minutes between the collapse of the South Tower and the collapse of the North Tower were filled with tension for those inside the remaining building — as well as for loved ones waiting for word on whether their family members could or would escape. Due to faulty communications, not all of the firefighters inside the North Tower received the order to evacuate, so even in the final minutes of the North Tower's life, some FDNY firefighters trudged upward toward the crash zone. Others, though, heard the warnings and simply refused to leave.

Thomas Von Essen, commissioner, FDNY: To understand all this, it is important to understand what it means to be a firefighter. Firefighters do not run away. They do not leave if they think they can stay.

Capt. Jay Jonas, Ladder 6, FDNY: The period of time between the two collapses was the scariest. The unknown was about to come

443

up and get you. It was like watching the old Frankenstein movies when you were a kid, and you had the spooky music playing in the background. Well, the spooky music was playing, because that monster was about to come up and get you. That was the most anxiety I had the whole day.

Joe Graziano, firefighter, Ladder 13, FDNY, North Tower stairs: They told us to evacuate Tower One. We ran into a fireman, Billy Kasey, from Engine 21. He was carrying a gentleman who was having heart problems, a big guy, and Billy was having trouble. I turned to my captain, Walter Hynes, and said, "Cap, I'm going to help this guy down."

Capt. Jay Jonas: Over the radio I did hear Chief [Pete] Hayden calling for an evacuation, for guys to get out. In particular, he engaged Paddy Brown. He called him by name: "Capt. Paddy Brown. Command Post to Ladder 3. Capt. Paddy Brown. Evacuate the building." Paddy got on the radio and he said, "I refuse the order. I'm on the 44th floor. I got too many burned people here. I'm not leaving them." Even in that high-anxiety situation, I thought, *Wow! That's unbelievable!* That was an incredible act of bravery.

444

David Norman, officer, Emergency Service Unit, Truck 1, NYPD: We started to move quickly down the stairs. We would inform everybody on the way down, other fire department units that were on these floors, "Listen, we've been told to evacuate. We're leaving." We ran into some Port Authority personnel who were in disbelief. They seemed to think that if they are 20, 30 stories below the affected fire floor, they're safe. They said, "I don't know why you guys are leaving. It's not that bad."

Joe Graziano: Billy and I coaxed the gentleman down. We said, "Look, we're not going to leave you. We'll get you out." We didn't think there was any urgency at all. The man's name was Ralph. That's all I remember about him. Ralph was a trooper. I remember passing other firemen in the stairwell. I passed all the guys from 2 Truck, and Capt. Freddy Ill, who I knew. The strap on my mask was falling down, and I said, "Freddy, do me a favor and fix my strap." He tugged it, and I kept on walking.

Bill Spade, firefighter, Rescue 5, FDNY: A police officer, John D'Allara, came over to me and we start talking. I certainly was never aware that the fire department was evacuating the buildings. People were filing by, walking through the block strewn with debris.

445

Then there was only a trickle of people coming by. Officer D'Allara said, "Maybe we should go back to the doorway and see how many are in that stairway." I said, "Yeah, I guess we should." We went back to the staircase and his boss was there, Sergeant [Sean] Curtin. As soon as we got to the staircase, he said, "I think we should leave now." It was only the eight of us in the staircase at this time. I said, "We go together, we stay together."

David Norman: When we got down to the bottom I realized the magnitude of everything. I thought, *There is no building. There is literally no building left.* I said to the rest of the team — and I think they saw the urgency in my face — I said, "Listen. We got to go and we got to go now. There's nothing left of that building." When you're told that and when you see it are two different things.

Capt. Jay Jonas: We were heading down the stairs and right around the 20th floor we ran into Josephine Harris. She was standing in the doorway. She was crying. She was one or two weeks shy of her 60th birthday. She had made it down from the 73rd floor — she was a bookkeeper for the Port Authority — with the help of somebody from her office. She told them to go ahead. She probably physically couldn't make another step.

Billy Butler, firefighter, Ladder 6, FDNY: When we came upon Josephine, somebody said to me, "Help with this woman."

Capt. Jay Jonas: Tommy Falco looked at me and said, "Hey, Cap, what do you want to do with her?" I looked at her, and it seems like an easy decision to make: "Of course we're going to help her." Every fiber in my being was screaming at me to get out of this building. That spooky music was playing. Looking back on it now, yeah, it was an easy decision to make. But it really wasn't, because not only was I endangering myself, I was responsible for five firemen and their families. That's not an easy decision to make. I looked at her and I couldn't say no. I said, "All right. Bring her with us." And we did.

Billy Butler: I started down with Josephine.

Capt. Jay Jonas: Now we're going very slow. What was once a normal gait going down the stairs, now it's only one step at a time. We were creating a logjam of people behind us. On a couple of occasions, we had to step aside to allow that logjam to clear, and then we would continue.

Billy Butler: Everybody was trying to push us along and it was a very slow process.

Following the two attacks and the first building's collapse, worried family members across the region began to hunt for their loved ones — some heading straight to the World Trade Center — even as the survivors fanned out into a city still unsure of what had transpired.

Dan Potter, firefighter, Ladder 10, FDNY: My focus was to try to get to [my wife], but as I was trying, there were a lot of firefighter duties I had to do also. When somebody said, "Check that escalator," I went and checked the escalator real quick. But there was always that ring in the back of my head: *I have to find out what she's doing.* Still, there were victims in the Deutsche Bank that I helped out. You had to do your job as a firefighter. You are dressed to represent New York City as a firefighter. Yes, I've got to take care of my wife, but I still have to be a firefighter.

John Napolitano, father of FDNY firefighter John Napolitano: When the South Tower came down I tried to get into the city from our house in the outer boroughs, but I couldn't. I said, "My son's very good at what he does. He's probably somewhere safe or has people somewhere." I didn't want to think the worst, obviously. I went to my daughter-in-law's house.

Dan Potter: I crossed Greenwich Street and went right into the Deutsche building. I walked into that building and there was a woman shuddering. I said, "Okay, go to the back of the building and you'll be okay." Five or six people came around the building, all bloody — all different faces, hands, and all covered in gray. They were walking like zombies. I said, "Just go to the back."

Jeannine Ali, controller, Morgan Stanley, South Tower: We walked up to the Seaport. There was a Pizzeria Uno — this is actually a very funny story — on the second floor of the Seaport. There were chairs and stuff outside. We put our stuff down on the chairs, and we went to go inside this Pizzeria Uno — it was locked. The bartender was leaning against the bar, watching the television with his back to us, cleaning a glass. We were pounding on the door, like "Let us in! Let us in!" He turned around and said, "We don't open till 11:30." I said, "Look at the TV! Let us in!" He kept saying, "We're not open yet. We don't open until 11:30."

Dan Potter: I saw a children's nursery, so I ran in there real quick to see if there were any kids in there. There was too much debris. I had to go back to Greenwich Street. I thought, *I'll go around, try to get to the com-*

449

mand post, get to the North Tower to save my wife.

John Napolitano: My daughter-in-law was at work when it happened. She worked for Computer Associates, and a lot of colleagues knew that her husband was a firefighter. They said, "You better take your kids and go home." When I got to the house, a lot of their friends were already there, and Anne was sitting there and their two little girls were playing. Elizabeth was going on six, and Emma was going on three.

Dan Potter: I came out of the Deutsche building and I ran into an old friend of mine who I hadn't seen in probably 17 years, a fire marshal, Mel Hazel. He didn't recognize me because I was covered in everything. What he did recognize was the 31 on my helmet, because he had worked there as a fireman. He said, "Hey, 31, you all right?" I realized who he was, and I said, "Mel Hazel. Mel it's me, it's Dan." He said, "Oh my God, I couldn't recognize you. Need a hand?" "I have got to find Jean. Jean's on the roof of the first tower. I'm convinced she's up there. Can you help me with that?"

Capt. Jay Jonas: On the way down I ran into Lt. Mike Warchola from Ladder 5, and this was to be his last day in the fire department. He was going to retire on September 12th. I knew Mike. We were firemen together. He and two of his firemen were working on a man in the stairway having chest pains. I looked at him. I said, "Mike, let's go! It's time to go!" He said, "That's okay, Jay, you have your civilian, we have ours. We'll be behind you."

We kept going and made it to the fourth floor and Josephine Harris fell to the floor. She was yelling at us to leave her, to leave her alone. We weren't going to leave her.

Billy Butler: The whole building started to rock.

Capt. Jay Jonas: The floor started having little wavelike ripples in it.

Billy Butler: Then everything went black.

THE SECOND COLLAPSE
"IT WAS LIKE A MUSHROOM CLOUD"

At 10:29 a.m., 102 minutes after it had been hit by American Airlines Flight 11, the North Tower collapsed, its level-by-level pancaking almost exactly the same as the South Tower's. Hundreds were caught inside the building, including many people trapped in or above the impact zone. Thousands more who had just evacuated, or were watching the events unfold, were caught in the vicinity around the World Trade Center.

Richard Eichen, consultant, Pass Consulting Group, North Tower, 90th floor: There was a ring of EMTs by the door — they started to come for me, and I said, "No, take her," because Lucy was now on my back again. I handed her off to an EMT. We were four steps on the sidewalk when someone behind me said, "Watch out!" I remember turning, like, *What the heck do you want now?* I saw he was looking up. I looked up. That was the building starting to collapse.

Joe Graziano, firefighter, Ladder 13, FDNY: Billy and I finally got Ralph to the lobby. As we got outside, Tower One came down. I could see the building come right at me. I still had no idea that the South Tower had already come down.

Bill Spade, firefighter, Rescue 5, FDNY: There was an overhang, I believe, at Six World Trade Center. So we were trying to get through that courtyard area. Things were still coming down from above. NYPD officer John D'Allara said, "I'll go first." We all followed him.

David Norman, officer, Emergency Service Unit, Truck 1, NYPD: We went, almost like you'd see in the war movies, in groups of two. Someone would run and get to a point safely, then that person would look and cover for you while you moved.

Bill Spade: We weren't out of the Trade Center 30 seconds, and I heard that noise again.

Pasquale Buzzelli, engineer, Port Authority, North Tower, 64th floor: I was probably on the 22nd floor when all of a sudden the building started to shake violently. There was a huge sound from above, this loud, loud noise. I must've dove down about five or six stairs and pushed myself right into the corner. I basically curled up in a fetal position, and I covered my head with my hands.

Genelle Guzman, office assistant, Port Authority, North Tower, 64th floor: The dust, the building, the walls just opened up.

Lt. Gregg Hansson, Engine 24, FDNY: It was a complete white-out in the courtyard. It reminded me of being in a blizzard. All of a sudden, there was this thunderous roar. My first thought was that it was another plane coming in, that's how loud it was. It felt like it was right on top of us. Then it went completely dark. To this day I don't know how it's possible we survived. The police officers behind us were killed in that collapse. I know Bill Spade and two of the police officers had taken the rear.

Stephen Blihar, officer, Emergency Service Unit, Truck 10, NYPD: I heard this sick cracking noise. I looked up and Tower One was curling over my head like a wave.

Dan Nigro, chief of operations, FDNY: The same sound, the same dust cloud. My brain and my body couldn't deal with it this time. I knew we lost hundreds of firefighters.

454

Juana Lomi, paramedic, New York Beekman Downtown Hospital: We ran to the corner. By the time we got to the subway steps, there were so many people trying to walk in there that we ended up being pushed all the way down. Everybody fell. It was like a ball of people falling on the steps.

James Luongo, inspector, NYPD: I was running and running and running. I came up to a fireman who was also running, a tall skinny guy. I looked over and I saw that it said "Chaplain" on the helmet. It was Fire Department Chaplain John Delendick, from St. Michael's Church in Brooklyn. I was running with him, and I said to him, "Are you a priest?" He said, "Yeah." I said, "Are you a Catholic priest?" He said, "Yeah." "How about absolution?"

Monsignor John Delendick, chaplain, FDNY: This police officer came up next to me, running with me, and said, "Father, can you hear my confession?" I told him, "This is an act of war, so I'm going to give everyone general absolution," which I did. General absolution in the Catholic Church is forgiving all at one time.

James Luongo: As you're running, you're looking over your shoulder — you could feel some of the shrapnel flying by. I saw a cop in

455

front of me fall. I figured he got hit with a piece of shrapnel. I reached down and picked him up by his gun belt, because he was going to get trampled. I said to him, "You all right? Where did you get hit?" He said, "No, I dropped my pen." It goes to show you how people's minds go — here he is running for his life and he bent down to pick up a pen that he dropped.

Bill Spade: I remember getting picked up and blown into the wall. I hit my face so hard, I thought I lost my eye. I said, "I'm not dying here." I found a window and rolled into it. Inside was an office. I put my head under the desk. Everything was coming down. I said goodbye to my wife and kids.

David Norman: I found a fire truck and I jumped underneath the rear axle. I was the only one, initially, underneath the fire truck, and then every inch of that fire truck was occupied by somebody doing the same thing. Debris started hitting the fire truck. I thought to myself, *Man! I'm going to get crushed by this fire truck. I ducked under here for cover, and now I'm going to get crushed by it.*

Pasquale Buzzelli: I heard people screaming. It was loud, like boulders, safes, whatever, a freight train type of noise. In that next split second, I felt the wall that I was laying next to give way and crack open.

Louise Buzzelli, Riverdale, New Jersey, wife of Pasquale Buzzelli, Port Authority, North Tower, 64th floor: The phone rang and it was one of Pasquale's aunts. As I was on the phone with her, I started to see his building change — something was changing about it. The smoke started to get blacker and bellow out more. I started to see the antenna move and then I knew: that's it — his building is now going.

Pasquale Buzzelli: I found myself freefalling. I felt this wind, abrasive wind. I stayed tucked into a fetal position. I saw flashes of light from impacts hitting my head — five or six. I was seeing those stars you see when you get hit in the head.

Louise Buzzelli: I spoke with him maybe 25 minutes before that, so I knew that there was no way that he made it down from the 64th floor with a whole crowd of people. I kept screaming, "No! No! No! No! No!" Every ounce of energy in my body drained out of me. I collapsed on the floor, screaming uncontrollably. Watching it come down and thinking, *Our baby will never get to know her father. She'll never get to meet him.*

I couldn't watch anymore. I went outside. I

457

don't know what was worse — being outside in the beautiful sunshine on a gorgeous day where there were September flowers and peacefulness and birds chirping or being inside with the horror, watching that. I couldn't fathom how I was in my garden and my husband — I watched him die, along with thousands of other people.

Lt. Col. Tim Duffy, F-15 pilot, Otis Air Force Base, Cape Cod, Massachusetts: We went over by Kennedy and turned a plane away that was over there. I was going to check out the North Tower and see how it was doing. I flew by. I was looking straight at it; I realized it was exploding right before my eyes. It was the sickest feeling I've ever had.

Frank Lombardi, chief engineer, Port Authority, North Tower: I saw the antenna of Tower One slowly starting to fall, as if a missile was going back into its silo.

Dan Potter, firefighter, Ladder 10, FDNY: A police officer came running down the street, and said, "North Tower's coming down now, any second now, any second." Just as he passed, we heard the same crumbling.

Jean Potter, Bank of America, North Tower: I was in Chinatown when I heard the North Tower collapse.

Dan Potter: It sounded like a freight train, like rumbling thunder. We laid in front of Deutsche Bank because we figured you couldn't outrun this field of stuff coming down. If it clocks you, you're out — you're done.

Andrew Kirtzman, reporter, NY1: There was this massive, massive boom, and a huge plume of smoke. As the building fell like a pancake, that smoke and soot and fire, it went north. It started to chase us, and we went running for our lives.

Lt. Terri Tobin, NYPD: People are screaming, "The second one's coming down. Get out of here." The best thing was to run toward the water, so I started to run. I took a hard hit to my back, and it knocked me from my feet right down to my knees. I turned around and saw the black cloud coming, approaching very quickly.

Rudy Giuliani, mayor, New York City: I feel somebody grab me and start running me, like you'd run an animal or a horse, like, "LET'S GO!" And we must have run about a third of a block. I didn't even know what was going on.

Andrew Kirtzman: Giuliani's bodyguard threw his arm around Giuliani and started running. We all bolted and we were being followed by this mushroom cloud.

Rudy Giuliani: He's running me, and I said, "STOP." We turned around and I could see this tremendous cloud coming up through the canyon. It really looked like a nuclear attack.

Tracy Donahoo, transit officer, NYPD: All of the sudden this black smoke came flying around the corner like a monster you would see in a movie. It whipped around and came up Broadway.

Richard Eichen, consultant, Pass Consulting Group, North Tower, 90th floor: I was running up Fulton Street, and the guy in front of me was walking, and I pushed him to the side. Another guy ran in front of me, and I swept him away. He stumbled, and I hope I didn't seal his fate doing that. I jumped over the hood of a car — which is hilarious if you know me — and continued.

Joe Esposito, chief of department, NYPD: We were pushing people into any open doorway, any building they could get into. You watched it roll toward you like a tidal wave.

Richard Eichen: The whole morning

seemed like one calamity — biblical-level calamity — after another. An hour before, I was eating a bagel, reading the newspaper, and worrying about my country club food — and now I'm in the middle of some biblical [devastation].

Charles Christophe, attorney, Broadway: We're totally covered with dust. It's unbelievable — like you're in a movie and science fiction. It's not reality. You don't know what's going on. I didn't have anything with me except my cell phone. I was trying to reach my wife, Kirsten, all the time.

Ian Oldaker, staff, Ellis Island: We got to South Street Seaport pretty quickly. We went to a bar, which was full. We got some juice and water. As we were watching it on CNN, we could actually see the Towers through this glass window. The TV was right in front of us, and we could see the Towers to our left. We could see the second one starting to fall. You saw the whole bar turn their heads to look through the window. As the second tower fell past the point where you couldn't see it anymore, everyone turned back to the TV and watched it fall all the way.

Monica O'Leary, former employee, Cantor Fitzgerald, North Tower: I was in my neighbor's apartment when our building fell.

I remember falling to the ground and screaming, "They didn't have enough time! They didn't have enough time to get out!" I laid on the ground screaming. I knew they were gone.

Robert De Niro, actor, New York City: I lived about nine blocks north of the World Trade Center. I had my big-screen television to my left, and I had the big picture window in front of me. When I saw the North Tower start to go down, I had to look at my television to confirm what I was seeing with my own eyes. It was unreal.

Roger Parrino, lieutenant commander of detectives, NYPD: I have no memory of any noise. I didn't hear anything landing near me. I could see shit landing near me, but I couldn't believe I wasn't being hit. I saw stuff hit. I saw a car flip. All of sudden I felt like I was covered in blankets. That's the only way to describe it. It was really super soft and basically very comfortable. I felt like it was 20 blankets. Then, in one split second, I began to suffocate.

David Norman: That's when also the wave of concrete dust — it was so thick — overwhelmed us. I couldn't breathe. It's almost as if you took the blown-in insulation — that powdery insulation — and you started trying to breathe through it and you couldn't.

Dan Potter: I remember swallowing the smoke and it was like those gray woolen socks. I felt like I could almost eat it.

Stanley Trojanowski, firefighter, Engine 238, FDNY: You're choking, trying to breathe, your eyes are full of debris, you can't see anything.

Richard Eichen: I realize my mouth is packed with this debris — the dust. I dug my mouth out with two fingers — putting them in and digging my mouth out. Then I realized I still couldn't breathe, so I stuck my finger down my throat and I was able to open a breathing passage.

Dan Potter: We don't know where we are. I scratched the street, and I could see the blacktop, and I said, "We're on the street, we're on the street!"

Gary Smiley, paramedic, FDNY: Every time I'd breathe in, it was as if my head was stuck in sand.

Bill Spade: I had to reach in my mouth to take clumps of stuff out. When I breathed it hurt. It seemed like I was inhaling glass. I looked around. There were only four of us left — me and three other firemen. We lost the police officer and all those in that alleyway.

Sharon Miller, officer, PAPD: I got separated from my partners somehow. I stopped and looked to see where everybody else was — the captain, chief, everybody. I couldn't find anybody. I don't know how far I ran; I ran until I saw Inspector [Lawrence] Fields and a police officer. They were standing around the corner. I ran over to them and told them who I couldn't find. They were looking at me like I was crazy. They said, "What are you talking about?" I said, "I went in the building with Chief [James] Romito, Captain [Kathy] Mazza, Lieutenant [Robert] Cirri, Richie Rodriguez, Jimmy Nelson, Jimmy Parham, Steve Huczko." I said, "I got separated from them." I never saw them again. They never found them. They were all killed.

TRAPPED IN THE RUINS

"I THOUGHT I WAS DEAD
UNTIL I STARTED TO COUGH"

By the time the second tower collapsed, more than 2,600 people would be dead in the rubble around the World Trade Center, including 343 New York City fire-fighters, 37 members of the PAPD, 23 members of the NYPD, and a dozen other government agents and first responders, as well as former FBI agent John O'Neill.

A lucky few would survive the collapse, either inside the Marriott Hotel or buried amid the wreckage of the North and South Towers.

Jeff Johnson, firefighter, Engine 74, FDNY: When we got into the banquet room, we were trying to find our way around and get our bearings. That's when the second collapse happened.

Frank Razzano, guest, Marriott Hotel: Jeff obviously knew what it was because he said, "Hit the ground." We got buried under more rubble.

465

Jeff Johnson: Same thing: complete black, couldn't breathe, stifling. You couldn't breathe. You couldn't open your eyes.

Frank Razzano: I remember saying to myself, "This can't be happening to me twice in one day. This is impossible." I'm thinking to myself, *You can't be lucky enough to survive it twice.* I started to pray.

Jeff Johnson: I was so mad. I said, "Don't let me go." I was praying. I didn't think I was going to make it.

Frank Razzano: Every breath you took you breathed in soot and ash. It was like drowning.

Jeff Johnson: I yelled, "Is everybody okay?" I heard, "I'm okay." "I'm okay." "I'm okay." But I didn't hear the fourth "I'm okay." I go, "Who's okay?" They yelled out their names, but none of them was Pat. I started screaming for Pat Carey now.

Frank Razzano: Jeff started to look for a way out. He was frantically looking around to figure out how we were going to get out of here, and found a very small opening in a wall on the West Street side of the building. He said, "This is our way out. We are going to climb down."

Jeff Johnson: We took the drapes, and we put it out of the hole so that we could back out. I went last, the civilians went first. They put their butts and their legs out first and crawled out. The first guy went out, then the next guy went, and then Frank went, and then I backed out.

Frank Razzano: I saw the banquet manager of the hotel. He went down the drapes and he made it. I figured, if he could do it, I could do it.

Jeff Johnson: They just left. I didn't know who Frank was until a year later. I still don't know the names of the other two. Those three guys disappeared, basically walked into the rubble.

Frank Razzano: I can't call it a street because it wasn't a street. There was nothing recognizable as a street — it was a debris field. The first thing I remember seeing, as I looked up, was that grill work from the World Trade Center stuck in the debris.

William Jimeno, officer, PAPD: Again, we had no idea that Building Two had come down at that point. We heard another explosion, *Boom!* Same as the first one. I remember Dominick [Pezzulo] backing up a little bit, and I said to him, "This is it. It's over." It sounded like a humongous locomotive coming at us. All I could think was, *I'm gonna die.* One of the things I've always done with my girls — Allison and Bianca — was I would make the sign-language sign for "I love you." I made the "I love you" sign — and I crossed them over my chest. I figured if I was going to die and they found me, they would at least tell my wife that I was crossed like that, so she would know I was thinking of her.

I could hear Sergeant McLoughlin yelling. Dominick gets sat down like a rag doll with a piece of concrete that came through this little void. I was getting hit more. I was yelling. Just like the first collapse, it seemed to take forever, but it happened quick.

The collapse also caught the firefighters coming down Stairwell B with their injured civilian, Josephine Harris, and a PAPD officer evacuating with them, David Lim.

Capt. Jay Jonas, Ladder 6, FDNY: All the air that was in the building was being compressed, creating tornado-like winds in the stairway. We kept getting battered by debris. It was like 30 people were punching you at the same time. It's industrial-strength dust. We covered up and waited for what we thought was going to be our demise. But for us, it didn't come.

Lt. Mickey Kross, Engine 16, FDNY: It was a tremendous roar. Then the wind — very, very fierce wind. It started lifting me up off the ground.

Capt. Jay Jonas: That scary feeling, that anxiety that I had between the two collapses? Once the collapse started, it went away. I felt very much at peace. Whatever was going to happen is — it's on its way.

Lt. Mickey Kross: I crouched down and got to the corner of the staircase by the railing, and I got as small as I could possibly get. I guess the best way to describe it is that I tried to crawl into my fire helmet.

Capt. Jay Jonas: Then, just before it got to us, it stopped.

Lt. Mickey Kross: Debris was hitting me, and it went dark. The next thing was total silence. Nothing. No wind, no noise, no light. Nothing.

Joe Esposito, chief of department, NYPD: I said to my sergeant, "We just lost a lot of people." I remember saying, "If we lost under a hundred, it'll be a miracle." It was a miracle. We lost 23, which is still an outrageous number, but that's a miracle.

William Jimeno, officer, PAPD: When everything was settled, I looked over to my right, and I could see Dominick. The concrete had crushed him. He said, "Willy, I'm dying." Sergeant McLoughlin was yelling, in a lot of pain. I was also in a lot of pain, but I was fighting, trying to talk to Dominick. I said, "Hold on, Dominick, hold on."

Those last couple of minutes, Dominick said to Sergeant McLoughlin, "Can I have a 3-8?," which is a break for a Port Authority Police officer. In the midst of pain, he was finding humor. Sergeant McLoughlin, even though he was yelling, said, "Yeah, you can take 3-8." Dominick said, "Willy, don't forget I died trying to save you guys." His last minutes, he struggled to take his firearm out of his holster. He pointed it up toward that hole in the rubble far over our heads. We had been yelling, "PAPD officers down!," hoping someone would hear us. He pointed his firearm up in the air, to that hole, and fired his gun as a last-ditch effort for someone to hear us. Then, he slumped over and died.

I was really, really lost, mentally. We had not only lost our first two officers — Christopher [Amoroso] and Antonio [Rodrigues] — but now I watched Dominick pass. It was very, very tough. I said, "Sarge. Dominick's gone." Sarge said, "Hold on. Hold on. I know." This went on for a while, trying to talk each other back and forth. I said, "Sarge, what do we do? What training do we have?" He said, "Will, this is beyond any training anybody has ever had."

Sgt. John McLoughlin, PAPD: Nobody trained for this.

Lt. Mickey Kross, Engine 16, FDNY: I was encapsulated in the debris. I couldn't move much, and I realized I didn't feel like I was injured. I got my wits about me. I said, "Okay. Let me see what I have, what equipment I have." I was feeling around. I still had a light. All the other equipment I was carrying was gone.

Billy Butler, firefighter, Ladder 6, FDNY: Immediately, you look at yourself to make sure all the fingers are there, the toes are there, and you wiggle them to make sure that nothing is broken. I was beat up, but I was okay. I was trying to extricate myself, and pick these large pieces of drywall off myself, when Josephine suddenly came up out of the dust, like the Blob coming out of the swamp. She scared the shit out of me.

Lt. Mickey Kross: I couldn't see clearly, and I thought I was blinded. I'm thinking, *Oh, Jesus, I'm trapped in the World Trade Center and now I'm blind — is this going to get any worse?* I was feeling my eyes, and I felt this crust. It was like a quarter inch of dirt encrusted, like concrete. I tried peeling it off, and it wasn't going. I was able to take my glove off, and I stuck my pinky in my mouth. I was trying to wet my finger and peel this crust off my eyes. Eventually, I got most of it off, and I opened my eyes and I was able to at least see this little tiny area I was in. I wasn't blind; I had my eyesight.

Capt. Jay Jonas: My first thoughts were: *Who do I still have? Who's still alive?* I gave out a roll call, and all my people answered. I didn't know Josephine's name yet. I called her "the woman" and said, "Do we still have the woman with us?" They said, "Yeah, she's still here."

Josephine Harris, bookkeeper, Port Authority, North Tower, 73rd floor: Somebody was watching over us that day. We had no broken bones. We have no scars.

Capt. Jay Jonas: In my mind, okay, things are looking good. *All right, let's dust ourselves off and get out of here.* It didn't quite happen that fast.

Genelle Guzman, office assistant, Port Authority, North Tower, 64th floor: When it finally stopped, there was total dead silence. I thought I was dreaming. I shut my eyes, hoping that when I opened them, it would be all a bad dream. I realized it was not. I couldn't move. I tried to get up. I was pinned. I was laying sideways, feet crisscrossed. I couldn't move. I couldn't see anything. The dust — everything — was in my mouth. It was complete dark. I realized that this was actually happening.

Pasquale Buzzelli, engineer, Port Authority, North Tower, 64th floor: I had some bumps on my head when I woke up. I was numb. I looked up, and I could see clear sky — a blue sky. For that one instant, I thought I was dead because I felt no pain. I thought I was dead until I started to cough. Then I started to feel pain in my leg, and that's when I realized, *Oh, my God! I can't believe I actually survived this. I'm alive.*

After the Collapse

"SUCH CALM AND PEACE"

The collapse of both towers carpeted Lower Manhattan with debris and dust; as survivors emerged from the clouds, they found a city tragically transformed and a once-familiar urban landscape rendered almost unrecognizable. Scores of first responders and civilians were buried in the debris and trapped in nearby buildings where they had sought refuge from the collapse.

James Luongo, inspector, NYPD: It was like that hush afterwards — I don't know what the explanation for it was — but there's that hush that comes over the city with a major snowfall.

David Norman, officer, Emergency Service Unit, Truck 1, NYPD: When you walk outside in a snowstorm and it's such calm and peace — that's what was moments later.

Sharon Miller, officer, PAPD: It was very

quiet, almost like cotton was all over the place, like marshmallows or something.

Richard Eichen, consultant, Pass Consulting Group, North Tower: The street, it was like being on a beach. Your feet would sink into it, and every time you took a step there was like more puffs of smoke. People — we were all the same color.

David Norman: We were literally caked. We were all gray. Although we had navy blue uniforms on, we were all white-ash gray with debris.

Al Kim, vice president of operations, TransCare Ambulance: We were like zombies for a few minutes or hours — I couldn't tell you.

Det. David Brink, Emergency Service Unit, Truck 3, NYPD: There were some vehicles that were on fire and the tires were exploding from the fire. I was like, "Where the hell's the fire department? Why aren't they putting these fires out?" Then I looked over. I saw one of the fire trucks on fire, and it sent me back to reality, "Oh, yeah. Now I know why."

Bill Spade, firefighter, Rescue 5, FDNY: This room seemed to be filled up right to the top with debris. We couldn't get out. I looked around. One of the firemen asked, "What are we going to do now?" One was a lieutenant there and he said, "We breathe the air off the floor. We clear away the stuff and we stay low and try to breathe the oxygen low." I said, "I ain't staying in here." One of the guys said, "We can call for help." I said, "Nobody's coming here and getting us."

Gary Smiley, paramedic, FDNY: I started crawling my way out of there, digging through the rocks and the debris. Just as I got out, a fireman who had also been lodged in the debris had gotten himself out. Both of us staggered around. I don't know how long we walked for.

Bill Spade: I tried banging the walls to make a hole in the wall, but we weren't getting anywhere with that. We were very tired and spent and beat up. We were in this room I figured around an hour. One of the younger firemen said, "I think I found a way out. At the end of the office building, top window left, there seems to be an opening." We walked along the wall — we had to feel our way around, it was a little dark — making our way over stuff, and sure enough there was a spot up there with a little light. We made our way up on top of the debris to get up in there and made it wider. We went to the edge of where we were, up about 35 feet in the air. I remember looking out. Everything was on fire.

Gary Smiley: People started calling out, "Is anybody out there?" We went toward their voices. It was a deli owner and his wife. They pulled us into their deli. About six or seven cops and some firemen were already in there, all variously injured and having a hard time breathing. They had taken a hose out of the kitchen to clean everybody off.

Jeff Johnson, firefighter, Engine 74, FDNY: I finally got out. I could see a couple of flashing lights, what we call Mars lights, the revolving lights on top of a fire truck or a police truck. I saw the yellow bumblebee stripes of a couple of coats, because they reflect instantly off any light. There was no street anymore.

Alan Reiss, director of the World Trade Center, Port Authority: It's quiet except for one thing — the PASS alarm.

Det. David Brink: The PASS alarm — it's a really shrill sound and that means that a firefighter is down and in trouble and he's motionless. All you heard were these PASS alarms going off, over and over again. You couldn't tell where they were coming from.

Al Kim: It was everywhere. That's all you heard. *Beep, beep, beep, beep, beep* sounds everywhere.

Alan Reiss: All you heard was a lot of them going off.

Jeff Johnson: I made my way toward a fire truck. It so happened that there was a chief there and a fireman from Rescue, Paul Hashagen, who I happen to know. Paul was saying, "Are you okay?" I said, "Yeah, are you all right? What's going on?" He said, "The Towers collapsed." I turned around and I looked and I saw the Towers were actually gone. I couldn't believe it.

I immediately went to the chief, and I started trying to get his attention. It was frustrating to me, because he wasn't listening to what I was saying. I was looking at him — man to man — looking right into his eyes, and saying, "Chief, I'm missing Ruben, I'm missing this guy, we don't know where that guy is, we were up on the 22nd floor." I'm giving him all the information I can think of, popping out of my head. My friend Paul said, "Jeff." I said, "What?" He said, "Jeff, turn around." I turned around and I realized there was no 22 — the Marriott was gone. The chief said to us, "Head for the water."

At the Waterfront

"ALL AVAILABLE BOATS"

For those at the tip of Lower Manhattan, the only viable evacuation route turned out to be the water. A makeshift, unorganized armada of more than 130 ferries, pleasure yachts, sightseeing vessels, Coast Guard and police vessels, fireboats, and tugboats gathered — many without being asked — at Battery Park and nearby piers. By the end of the day, they had collectively evacuated somewhere between 300,000 and 500,000 people from Manhattan — a maritime rescue larger than the World War II evacuation from Dunkirk.

Lt. Joseph Torrillo, director of fire education safety, FDNY: Two of the ambulance crews, they were digging and digging and they found me. They got me out from underneath the rubble. They put me on this long, stiff piece of plastic called a spine board and strapped my hands to my chest. They taped my neck onto the spine board — they thought I had a broken neck — and they ran with me to the marina in the back of the World Financial Center and they put me on the deck of a boat.

With that, there was a loud rumble and a roar and the people on the boat started screaming, "Oh, my God! Here comes the other building!" Everybody jumped off the boat. I was left all alone and was getting hit with the glass from the North Tower. Frantic, I bent my finger and the release belt opened and my hands were free, and I ripped the tape off of my neck. I rolled off the stretcher, and I jumped into the doorway, not knowing I ended up diving headfirst into the engine room of the boat. The North Tower was hitting the deck of the boat. The boat was rocking. I thought it was going to go under.

Peter Moog, officer, NYPD: I heard a lady yell, "Help, TARU!" She had read the shirt I had on which said "TARU" [Technical Assistance Response Unit] on the back. She was a lieutenant I knew, Terri Tobin, and she had a huge piece of concrete embedded in her head and two very large jagged pieces of glass in her back, both left and right of her spine. She was lying on the ground.

Lt. Terri Tobin, public information officer, NYPD: He was a real cutie. He said, "I think I should carry you down to the water." I responded, "Peter, that's okay, I saw EMS.

They wrapped my head." He said, "No, through your blouse — between your shoulder blades — there's a shard of glass sticking out of your back."

Peter Moog: I carried her down to the water. Another officer and I got her down on a boat by the North Cove Marina.

Lt. Terri Tobin: An NYPD harbor boat pulled up, and the captain — who I knew — hopped out and saw me. He said, "You need to go to a hospital." But I couldn't get on board with a shard of glass in my back because they were afraid that if the boat rocked, it would cause more damage. He called over two EMS workers, and as I held on to a railing, they put their feet up against the railing, and ripped this glass out of my back.

Peter Moog: There were one or two fireboats and some civilian boats that people were being loaded onto. One of our harbor boats pulled in, and I knew a guy on it, Keith Duvall. He said, "Grab a sledgehammer. We'll break into one of these yachts and take it." There were about a thousand people there, all waiting to get the hell off the island. Keith and I broke into a boat. I said, "Rich people always leave the keys in the boat." We ended up finding the keys and Keith got the boat started. I think he made about 10 trips back and forth to Jersey, taking about a hundred people a trip.

Jeff Johnson, firefighter, Engine 74, FDNY: I was heading toward the water, and I ended up coming out at the south end of the marina. There was a hose from the marina, and that was the first time I was able to flush my eyes. I ran into somebody else I knew, Det. Keith Duvall, who was on a boat. He was shuttling people back and forth to Jersey. All we basically said was, "Keith, are you okay?" "Yeah. Jeff, are you all right?" "Okay." Just friends, just checking.

Lt. Joseph Torrillo: Maybe about a half hour later, as I was losing consciousness, I heard banging on the deck of the boat and I heard voices, and I heard somebody say, "Start the engines. Start the engines." Somebody came down that long, steep flight of stairs to start the engines, and in the darkness, he stepped on my chest. I let out this loud scream. I scared the daylights out of him.

James Luongo, inspector, NYPD: We were down by the Hudson, and New York Waterways had pulled up and there was a line of people to evacuate. It was surreal because the people on the boat were saying, "Women and children. Women and children. Women and children."

Rick Thornton, ferry captain, *Henry Hudson,* New York Waterways: It was like being the last lifeboat on the *Titanic.*

Tom Sullivan, firefighter, Marine 1, FDNY: Mothers and nannies with infants in their arms were dropping their children down to us. At one point we had four or five of them wrapped in little blankets, and we put them in bunks down in the crew quarters. I put four babies in one bunk, like little peanuts lined up in a row.

Lt. Michael Day, U.S. Coast Guard: There was a small boat that was at the lower tip of Manhattan. I thought the boat was going to flip over because so many people were trying to get on.

Jack Ackerman, Sandy Hook harbor pilot: At any given time, Battery Park was ringed by 10 or 12 boats waiting for people.

Herb Jones, engineer, Mary Gellatly: We went back and forth all day long, carrying as many as our boat would hold. It was a lot of people — a lot of people.

Jacqui Gibbs, vice president, JPMorgan Chase: When we arrived at the pier, thousands of people were waiting in line — thousands. Yet you could hear a pin drop — that was the scariest part of it. We walked blocks and blocks trying to find the end of the line. The wait lasted three hours.

Rick Schoenlank, president, United New Jersey Sandy Hook Pilots Benevolent Association: They started hanging sheets over the bows of these tugs that said "New Jersey" or "Brooklyn." People were getting on. They were in bad shape, these people, and they needed to get off the island.

Lt. Michael Day: We decided to make the call on the radio. "All available boats, this is the United States Coast Guard aboard the Pilot boat, New York. Anyone available to help with the evacuation of Lower Manhattan, report to Governors Island." About 15, 20 minutes later, there were boats all across the horizon.

Rick Schoenlank: All these commercial boats, tugs, ferries, fishing boats, launches, dinner boats — everybody converging on the lower part of Manhattan to conduct the evacuation.

Capt. James Parese, Staten Island Ferry: Tugboats — I've never seen so many tugboats all at once.

Keturah Bostick, student, HSLPS: My classmates Chante, Luis, and I met up in a men's bathroom at the ferry. We stayed there until we saw Mr. Sparnroft and some other students going on the Staten Island Ferry.

Heather Ordover, English teacher, HSLPS: All I wanted to do was get off that island. I joked with a teacher I had never wanted to go to Staten Island so badly.

Keturah Bostick: From a pay phone close by I called my mother, crying, saying, "Mommy, I'm all right — don't worry about me. Some students are going to Staten Island, I'll call when I get there."

Heather Ordover: I looked at the water and saw another ferryboat. In my book Jersey was currently a helluva lot safer than crossing any bridge to Brooklyn. We rounded up whoever wanted to go with us and muscled over to the boat. All we had to do was yell, "We've got students," and the adults parted like the Red Sea.

Tim Seto, student, HSLPS: There were thousands and thousands of people on this little ferry. Everyone was standing, trying to make room for as many people as possible.

Keturah Bostick: As we rolled by the Statue of Liberty, I wondered if the statue was going to blow up. Was all of Manhattan going up in flames, and, if so, was my family okay?

Heather Ordover: We were underway — wearing life vests that the ferrymen kept saying we didn't need. That may have been the funniest thing I heard all day. Try telling someone who is fleeing a crumbling building that they don't need a life vest — what, like we're having a good-luck day?

Bert Szostak, equity broker, 100 Wall Street: A blue New York Waterway ferryboat was there, about half full, and we got on, not caring where it would take us. There were three passengers aboard of Arab descent who had backpacks, and people — average people, not police officers — demanded to know what was in them. The guys looked scared and opened their backpacks. Inside were just books.

Capt. James Parese, Staten Island Ferry: There was dust all over the boat. People were crying, people were covered with dust, and some people had no shoes. We had at least 6,000 people on the boat.

Lt. Michael Day: We had hundreds of people waiting to get over here and we had a captain — he said, "I don't have a crew." The ferry had 350 people on it. He said, "I need some help." There were some New Jersey state troopers, and I said, "Hey, would you mind helping this guy?" They said, "No problem, whatever we can do." I was like, *I hope nothing happens to this ferry.* I broke more rules that day than probably I've enforced in my whole Coast Guard career.

Paul Amico, dock builder, Amico Ironworks: If we had injured people on board — mostly firemen — we immediately released the ladder and sent that boat back to Jersey.

Lt. Joseph Torrillo: The boat skipped across the Hudson River, and I could hear a lot of commotion, people yelling on the deck to people on the shore of Jersey City. There were ambulances waiting there.

Joseph Lott, scheduled to attend the Risk Waters conference, had escaped the building after going to change his shirt to wear his new tie. He evacuated south toward Battery Park, where he ended up on one of the escaping boats.

Joseph Lott, sales representative, Compaq Computers: We sat on the ferry for maybe four or five minutes and then all of a sudden the ferry took off. Within two minutes, we were in bright sunshine. Beautiful day, Statue of Liberty was in front of us, the water was lapping against the ferry. I looked around, the ferry was completely packed: there were some injured people, most of us were covered in soot and ash and dust. We were all sitting there, and all I could think about was how much burnt asbestos was in my mouth at that point — it was very gritty. I said, "I've got to have something to drink." I went up to the little snack bar on the ferry, and there was nobody there. Inside were all these beers, sitting on ice. I grabbed a handful of beers, and I walked back to my colleagues, and I said, "Look what I found! Does anybody have an opener?" And so somebody produced an opener, and said, "I'll open if you give me one of those!" We all sat down, and we drank this beer, and I can't remember a beer that ever tasted that good.

Frank Razzano, guest, Marriott Hotel: As we were going across the river, I was looking back at the city, expecting to see the World Trade Center — expecting to see a tower with the top off. They weren't there. I said to the guy driving the boat, "Where is the World Trade Center?" He said, "Buddy, they're gone." I said, "Look, I was there when the tops of the buildings came down, but where's the rest of the building?" He said, "Buddy, it wasn't the tops of the buildings. They collapsed down to the foundations."

Michelle Goldman, labor attorney, One Battery Park Plaza: As we got off the boat in Jersey City, rescue workers formed a pathway for us. They helped people who had trouble walking. They gave us bottled water, food, and towels. It almost felt like reaching a finish line.

Across New York City, everyone seemed dazed in the wake of the collapses. Officials struggled to discover who had survived. Those who had been injured sought treatment amid the chaos.

Dan Nigro, chief of operations, FDNY: As you got back to the scene and saw what was left of it, it looked like war.

Monsignor John Delendick, chaplain, FDNY: Dan Nigro came walking down Chambers Street. He said, "Who's in charge? Do we know who's in charge?" I said, "Chief, I don't know. I think you are."

Dan Nigro: I was told the command center was now at Barclay and Broadway, at the tip of City Hall Park, and Deputy Chief [Tom] Haring from Division 6 was in charge. I felt that if that was the case, that meant everyone else had been killed — every other ranking member of the department.

Monsignor John Delendick: A lot of stuff at that moment was a blur. People started combing through the stuff, trying to find people.

Dan Nigro: I wanted to get back to the fire command post and see if the people I left at West Street survived. On the way there, I ran into someone I knew and he said, "Dan, Pete's gone. Pete's gone."

Sharon Miller, officer, PAPD: My husband had started driving home to New York from Florida. His daughter somehow got through to him, and said, "Dad, I saw Sharon. She's out of the building, she's all right. She's with two other officers." While we were running up West Street, she had seen me on TV. He didn't really believe her. Then another of his friends called him: "Ray, Sharon's fine. I saw her on TV. Ray, I have a 50-inch TV. I saw her." He was at a rest area. He sat down and he lit a cigar. Then he drove the rest of the way home.

Al Kim, vice president of operations, TransCare Ambulance: I started to see clean shirts. That was a big deal. The cavalry had arrived, if you will. I remember seeing people I knew with no dust, no burns — they were normal. It was a welcoming sight.

Richard Grasso, chairman and CEO, New York Stock Exchange: My colleague Howard turned to me with the phone in his hand and said, "It's the mayor." I took the phone, and he said to me, "How you doing?" I was numb — my only thought was to repeat his question and I said, "How you doing?" It sounded like the Budweiser commercial. "No, how you doing?" I finally said, "How am I doing? You're supposed to be dead." He said, "I'm not dead, I'm fine."

Det. David Brink, Emergency Service Unit, Truck 3, NYPD: We were walking up and we saw a church, St. Paul's. One of the doors was open so we all piled up inside, the five of us. I hid in the front by the altar and started praying. I fell to my knees and said, "Thank you, God, for letting me survive this," and I said, "Please give me the strength to go on and help other people that are there." I said, "I know we lost a lot of guys in there. God, please watch over them."

My eyes were crusted through with pieces of glass and dust and debris. I couldn't see. I found the holy water there — I was looking for any water — so I scooped my hands in the holy water. I was washing off my eyes, and my face was wet.

I needed something to wipe my face off with. My uniform was covered from head to toe in the dust. I went in by where the altar is, and they had the vestments and the other little cloths that were used for the rituals and ceremonies of the Catholic Church. I found the little one — it was a little white cloth that they would put over the chalice when they were doing the wine ceremony — and it had a little red cross stitched into it.

I dipped that in the holy water and started wiping my eyes off. I looked up, and the priest had come out. I said, "Oh, boy. I'm in trouble now." He says, "No, my son. That's what they're supposed to be used for. It's okay." I said, "Thank you, Father," and I dipped it again in the holy water. Then I put it around my neck, and tied it there because the cool water felt good on the back of my neck.

Richard Eichen, consultant, Pass Consulting Group, North Tower: I managed in a meandering way to get into Beekman Downtown Hospital. They had a ramp and stairs and I said, "I'm taking the ramp. I had it with stairs for today, thank you." They put me in an elevator, downstairs, to what must have been a cafeteria they set up as a triage center. A woman in scrubs came over and set me up. She opened up some water and poured it over me, over my front, trying to figure out how badly I was hurt. They led me to a seat in front of a doctor — a young woman — and she did maybe three or four big X stitches on my forehead, to close it up.

I heard what happened for the first time in the nurses station — they were playing the television. I was still not really comprehending it. I remember thinking, *Holy crap. I don't know who did this, but they knocked down our building. We're all in the street. This is a time to do something antipersonnel. Biological.* What do I know about this stuff? I put my shoes back on, no socks, put my pants back on — they were gray at this point. My shirt was in a bag — it was a hospital bag — and I was wearing the gown, and I walked out.

MIDMORNING
AT THE PENTAGON

"CAN YOU GET AIR SUPPORT?"

By late morning, officials realized few survivors would still be found inside the Pentagon. They labored to grasp the extent of the damage to the massive building, contain the still-spreading fires, and gather evidence of the attack. Meanwhile, evacuated Pentagon workers spread out across Arlington, beginning an anguished journey home as the initial shock of the attacks wore off. The morning's collective nervous anxiety that more attacks might be afoot wouldn't lift until the military arrived at the scene overhead.

Chris Combs, special agent, FBI, at the Pentagon: I grabbed a DPS guy — their SWAT team was there — and said I wanted the SWAT team. We had learned from studying with the Israelis that oftentimes after an attack the terrorists knew there would be a command post, and they would run a suicide bomber into the middle of it.

Stephen Holl, deputy chief, Arlington County Police Department: We put up a couple of our countersnipers on the Drug Enforcement Administration building on the other side of [Interstate] 395. That way they could overlook the entire south parking lot, where a lot of the relief efforts were set up.

Chris Combs: The other thing I requested right away was for the FBI to send our surveillance teams. If there was a truck bomb sitting somewhere else in Arlington or if there were four guys in a minivan with automatic weapons, we needed to find that before they hit us. We took our surveillance teams and had them drive around the Pentagon on the outskirts, looking for any other type of attack.

Scott Kocher, contractor, SAIC, Pentagon: This woman pulled up her car, turned on the radio. The announcer mentioned one of the Trade Centers had collapsed. Nobody could make much sense of that, because it seemed impossible. It wasn't till later that we fully understood what that had meant.

Stephen Holl: One of the detectives brought a small television set to the command post, set it up on the back of one of the SUV tailgates. I looked occasionally, but I couldn't watch it. What we had at the Pentagon was mind-numbing enough. I couldn't even imagine what was happening in New York City.

Mike Walter, senior correspondent, *USA Today Live:* There was a guy from the *Wall Street Journal.* I remember him coming up to me later in the day, and he said, "Both the towers have collapsed." I was like, "What?" He's like, "There's nothing left." He pointed to the Pentagon and said, "Look at that — this is the biggest story we'll ever cover in our lives." He said, "I'm not even sure it's going to end up on the front page tomorrow." That was pretty amazing. Obviously the Pentagon did end up on the front page, but I think it's always been a secondary story to what happened in New York.

Thomas O'Connor, special agent, FBI, at the Pentagon: We really didn't know that the other buildings in New York fell until late that first night. We were so engulfed in what we were doing.

James Schwartz, assistant chief for operations, Arlington County Fire Department: I did not know of the collapse of the World Trade Center until after ten o'clock that night.

Chris Combs: We were really working frantically to collect as much evidence on the outside of that building that we could.

Thomas O'Connor: The FBI evidence recovery was based out of the back of my bureau car for several hours until we got more people down there.

Jean O'Connor, special agent, FBI: We started doing line searches outside. You put individuals side by side, and you walk in one direction, and you are looking for evidence on the ground.

Chris Combs: We're trying to find any piece of an airplane, any personal effects. We're very conscious of any remains. There were pieces of aircraft in every direction hundreds of yards away. In fact they found pieces of the airplane in Arlington Cemetery, which was across a four-lane highway and another 200 yards of grass.

Jean O'Connor: The plane had actually hit one of the tall light poles as it was coming in, shearing the light part of the pole off, and it went through a cab's windshield and landed right next to the driver's leg. The cab driver, we called him one of the luckiest men that day. Had he been six inches in the other direction he wouldn't have fared so well. Tom actually handed the guy his cell phone and said, "Call your family and let them know that you're okay."

Chris Combs: Very early I knew we didn't have enough people on the scene. We had people in D.C., and more people in Northern Virginia in Tysons Corner who were sent to Dulles Airport because the hijacked plane left from Dulles. We had to have people there to grab evidence. I had two major sites in Virginia operating at the same time.

Jean O'Connor: Tom was talking to one of the other FBI team leaders, who had gone to our equipment warehouse. He said, "What do I need to bring?" Tom said, "Bring everything."

Lt. Jim Daly, Arlington County Police Department: I was at the command post — we were on the ramp from 395 down to Washington Boulevard — and I looked over to South George Street. If there was ever an image of Armageddon, that was it. All I saw were hundreds and hundreds of people walking with nowhere to go. These were civilians, they were military, but there was no one telling them where to go — a block of humanity going down George Street.

David Allbaugh, technical services, Pentagon Library: We walked up Army Navy

Drive, walked past the Navy Annex on Columbia Pike down under the overpass for Fort Myer, talked a little bit, trying to figure out what was happening.

Bruce Powers, director of readiness analysis, U.S. Navy, Pentagon: I knew there was a shopping center about a half-mile away. I knew there were public telephones that I could use. I arrived at the phone banks, and each one had 25 people standing behind it. I knew a phone in the garage, got there, phone was available, rang up my wife — busy — because people were calling her to say, "Is Bruce okay?" I called our daughter and asked her to let her mom know as quickly as possible that I was okay, and that I was starting to walk home.

Scott Kocher, contractor, SAIC, Pentagon: We decided we were going to go home. Our first stop, as we were going on Columbia Pike, was a hotel. We walked in, and there was a long line for all the phones. We walked for a ways down Columbia Pike.

Bruce Powers: I walked and walked and walked and after seven miles I finally got home.

Lt. Col. Ted Anderson, legislative liaison officer, U.S. Army, Pentagon: Along with a buddy of mine, we were trying to figure out how we were going to get home. Everything was inside, including my car keys. We started strolling off, two well-dressed guys who looked like they had fallen off the turnip truck and dragged through an onion field. We were caked in soot and blood. It was nasty-looking. We got on a Metro train headed toward Springfield, Virginia, and people looked at us in disbelief. Nobody spoke on the train. It was total silence. Everybody was in shock.

Robert Hunor, contractor, Radian, Inc., Pentagon: I felt guilty about it later, but you almost have a feeling of elation. You're not supposed to be happy — you realize the gravity of the situation, you realize that this is really bad. But there's a survivor's *Hey, I walked away from it* euphoria that hits you. *Wow! I'm still here. I survived!* My colleague and I both felt that way. I ended up staying with that coworker for the rest of the day. We ended up walking all the way back to Falls Church [about seven and a half miles]. They'd shut down the Metro. They'd shut down Route 66. They shut down all the bridges into Washington, D.C.

Jennifer Meyers, dispatcher, Arlington County Emergency Communications Center: All of us who worked that day can recall moments that will stay with us for the rest of our lives. Mine was a phone call from a man who spoke with extreme calmness — I believe he might have been in shock. He told me he knew his wife had been on the plane that went into the Pentagon, and he knew she was no longer alive. What he was requesting was for me to assist him in finding out who was sitting next to her. He wanted to know what her last words had been — he wanted to speak to the survivors. My heart sank. His voice is ingrained on me forever. What I was not allowed to release to the public yet was that they were almost certain there were no survivors on the plane.

Maj. James Phillips, Defense Protective Service, Pentagon: My wife was on my mind. She works in the building for the army. During the course of the day, I continued to try to contact her. From what I saw from the outside — I'll be honest with you — I thought she was gone. I didn't say anything to anybody until after four or five hours had passed. Around 2:45, I got a call from home. I thought it must be her, but it was my daughter, who was a freshman. She asked, "Did you hear from Mom?" I said, "No, baby, I haven't." About an hour later, I received a call — and it was her. You don't know how that made me feel.

Robert Hunor: I saw one of my coworker's wives — she was very pregnant, and she had an ashen look on her face. I didn't realize it at the time, but her husband was still missing. Out of the four people from my team who were missing, they managed to locate two that day, but her husband was never located. No remains were ever found.

Rep. Martin Frost (D-Texas), chair, House Democratic Caucus: At the time, my wife was the adjutant general of the army — she was a one-star general — and she'd been scheduled to be at a meeting with her boss in the Pentagon that morning. She was not able to go — she sent two of her staff. The point of impact of the plane at the Pentagon was her boss's office — a three-star general. He was killed, and my wife's two staff who were attending the meeting were killed. Had my wife gone to that meeting, she would have been killed. If events had gone slightly differently, I might've been killed, and my wife might have been killed on that day.

Chris Combs, special agent, FBI, at the Pentagon: A gentleman came up to me and said, "I have to get into the Pentagon." I said, "Sir, nobody is going in the Pentagon. It's a crime scene. We still have the fire throughout the building. Nobody's getting in." Then I noticed that there was somebody standing behind the guy who was talking to me, and he kept tapping his shoulder — his own shoulder — trying to tell me something. I looked at the guy that I was talking to, and he had four stars on his uniform. I quickly realized this was a four-star general from the army. He said, "I'm in charge of the national command center. I have to get in that building." I realized, "Yes, you do." We had to grab a group of Pentagon police and FBI agents to escort them in.

Lt. Jim Daly, Arlington County Police Department: A young lady came up to me, looking very distraught. She had left the office about four or five minutes prior to the plane hitting to deliver mail to another portion of the Pentagon. As she was walking down the corridor she felt the heat of the explosion. Everyone in her office had been killed.

Capt. Randall Harper, Defense Protective Service, Pentagon: I was looking at an officer I had worked with for a couple of years, and all of a sudden he breaks out crying. The sergeant said to me that he had seen some pretty traumatic things. I had to collect myself. You had a chaotic situation going on, but you still had to be concerned about people. It was that kind of day. In combat you expect it. You never expect anything like that in America.

John Milton Brady Jr., safety technician investigator, Department of Defense: A general who was in charge of the army personnel was trying to enter the building to save his people. He kept saying it was his staff in there and he wanted to get to them. He broke down and cried. He was a two-star.

James Schwartz, assistant chief for operations, Arlington County Fire Department: We transported 94 people to the hospital that morning. Only one of the 94 that we transported that morning subsequently succumbed to her injuries — meaning that if you got out of the Pentagon that morning either with assistance or on your own, you lived.

Continuing confusion and alerts about incoming planes that might be hijacked left Pentagon rescuers and first responders off-balance, unsure of whether they themselves were still a target and wishing for more security.

Capt. David Herbstreit, Arlington County Police Department: We were called away from the Pentagon proper two or three times because of incoming airplanes.

Capt. Charles Gibbs, Arlington County Fire Department: There was another "everybody-out-of-the-pool evacuation, unknown incoming plane." Everybody drops everything and pulls back. You watch. That was another 15- to 20-minute delay.

Thomas O'Connor, special agent, FBI, at the Pentagon: I got on the radio — and I know you're not supposed to swear on the radio — and called back to the desk and said, "Tell somebody to get some f'ing air support up here!" Like, who the heck am I to be calling for air support? It was literally 30 seconds later that a fighter jet flew over the Pentagon — had nothing to do with any of us FBI guys. It hit the sound barrier, went over, and there was a big boom when it went by. All the guys we're standing there with are like, "That's a pretty powerful guy." I'm like, "Yeah!"

Maj. Dean Eckmann, F-16 pilot, Langley Air Force Base: NEADS wanted to know the extent of the damage to the Pentagon. I flew by the Washington Monument, turned back, and flew low over the Pentagon. I told them the two outer rings have been damaged. Nobody indicated to me anything about an airplane hitting the Pentagon, and they asked me if I knew what had happened. I told them I guessed it was a big fuel tanker bomb because of the amount of the smoke and flames coming up.

Dennis Smith, maintenance inspector, Pentagon Building Manager's Office: I saw that F-16 up there fully loaded, and I was like "YES! It's all cool now."

Staff Sgt. Christopher Braman, chef, U.S. Army: I saw an American jet fighter, "Guys, I'm here, guys I'm here." It was the prettiest thing I've ever seen.

MIDMORNING AT THE CAPITOL
"NO ONE COMMUNICATED"

In and around Capitol Hill, aides, journalists, staff, and members of Congress wondered what would come next — and where they should go.

Rep. Mike Ferguson (R–New Jersey): I was walking past the Supreme Court. All of a sudden, there was a very loud boom. Looking back, it was a sonic boom from one of the military aircraft that had been scrambled over Washington. When that happened, I and everyone around me stopped, winced, and paused for about two or three seconds. Then everyone started to run.

Eve Butler-Gee, chief journal clerk, U.S. House of Representatives: We went about three-quarters of the way down the Mall and didn't know what to do. We were told we needed to be prepared to take cover. My colleague Gigi Kelaher and I were standing there looking at each other, thinking, *This is the Mall. There are no trees. Take cover?* We tend to make jokes when we're nervous, and we looked at this little reflecting pool that was part of the decoration of the Mall. It was about five feet by four feet in diameter, and we said, "Well, if worst comes to worst, we'll dive in here."

Brian Gaston, policy director for House Majority Leader Richard Armey (R-Texas): No one knew what to do.

Brian Gunderson, chief of staff for House Majority Leader Richard Armey (R-Texas): Communications on September 11th were a real problem. Back then, communications were somewhat primitive by today's standards. We had BlackBerrys. We had moved out of the Capitol so quickly that a lot of people were stuck — women were stuck without their purses, men didn't have their suit jackets, and a lot of people didn't have their cell phones and their BlackBerrys.

Tish Schwartz, chief clerk, House Judiciary Committee: BlackBerrys were working. Cell phones weren't.

Sen. Tom Daschle (D–South Dakota), Senate Majority Leader: The members were taken to the top floor of the Capitol Police building, which is very near the Capitol campus. They pulled the shades down, which

I always thought was an odd thing to do. Our most immediate concern was to try to connect with our families. The cell phones weren't working, so we all stood in this rather lengthy line — House and Senate, Republican and Democratic. I recall feeling almost like a refugee, standing in line waiting to get my turn to use the landline to call my wife.

Rep. Martin Frost (D-Texas), chair, House Democratic Caucus: I went back to my town house. I turned on the television and watched the news.

Sen. Tom Daschle: There was discussion of going to the secret location. Some suggested going to Andrews Air Force Base. Some suggested that maybe we shouldn't concentrate all the leadership in one location. There was a great difference of opinion. Ultimately, we decided to disperse. I went to the office of one of our consultants and stayed there for a while, watching developments on the TV screen.

WITH THE SECRETARY OF DEFENSE

"THERE'S NO WAY WE'RE LEAVING THE PENTAGON"

Once Donald Rumsfeld returned from the crash site to the Pentagon's National Military Command Center (NMCC) inside, the nation's military leaders — who still didn't know whether the attacks were over or whether a second wave might be in the offing — tried to understand what had transpired already, formulate a response, and take the action necessary to secure the country, even as the rescue and firefighting efforts continued outside their command post. Those inside the military's operations hub found themselves stymied by poor communications systems and, as the morning unfolded, fearing the smoke from the still-spreading fires inside the damaged portion of the building.

William Haynes, general counsel, Department of Defense: There were very poor communications. We didn't have secure video teleconference capability [in the NMCC] that we had upstairs. The secretary was on a regular handset with the vice president.

Victoria "Torie" Clarke, assistant secretary of defense for public affairs: Donald Rumsfeld was making phone calls to the White House. Condi Rice and the vice president were there, and he was on the phone to [CIA Director] George Tenet pretty quickly.

Col. Matthew Klimow, executive assistant to the vice chair of the Joint Chiefs of Staff, Gen. Richard Myers, Pentagon: At 10:40 a.m., we had a conference call with Vice President Cheney. The vice president said, "I understand we've taken a plane down." I'm sure he was referring to Flight 93. I remember Secretary Rumsfeld looking at General Myers — everybody was puzzled. Secretary Rumsfeld said, "We can't confirm that."

Joe Wassel, communications officer, Office of the Secretary of Defense: The White House initiated a phone call with Secretary Rumsfeld from Air Force One. I said, "This is a really bad connection, but this is a strange day." Normally, I wouldn't put the secretary on such a bad connection, but obviously that day we were going to do any comms we could get.

Adm. Edmund Giambastiani, senior military assistant, Office of the Secretary of Defense: We lost air-conditioning in the building soon afterward.

Donald Rumsfeld, secretary of defense: The building was burning and filling up with smoke. It was hard to see, your eyes were smarting, and it was hard on your throat.

William Haynes: There was a lot of smoke starting to infiltrate the NMCC.

Steven Carter, assistant building manager, Pentagon: We got calls from both the secretary's office and the Joint Staff offices and were constantly on the phone with the NMCC about conditions. Were we going to be able to hold, or would it get worse? Was the fire going toward them, and were we looking toward evacuation of the entire Pentagon?

Victoria "Torie" Clarke: Different people — Larry Di Rita, the deputy defense secretary, Steve, the vice chairman of the Joint Chiefs — said at different times they wanted to get the secretary out of the building. To my recollection, he never said no, [but] he kept working. He was constantly writing down notes on his yellow pieces of paper.

Col. Matthew Klimow: Deputy Secretary

of Defense Paul Wolfowitz had asked Secretary Rumsfeld, "Where do you want me to go? I could go to the PEOC" — the Presidential Emergency Operations Center in the White House — "or I could go to Site R." Site R is the top-secret, deep underground bunker — nuclear proof — outside the Beltway but within helicopter range. Secretary Rumsfeld told him to go to Site R and set up our headquarters there.

Donald Rumsfeld: I made the decision to stay here as long as I could.

Victoria "Torie" Clarke: The secretary would not leave, but the people who truly understand the procedures and the need for a functioning leadership said the deputy had to go off-site. One of the main reasons the secretary wanted to stay where he was at the Pentagon was he knew the communications were the single most important thing — with the White House, the CIA, FAA, the president — and they were working well. He felt a great deal of confidence with that.

Col. Matthew Klimow: Helicopters started arriving at the Pentagon. They picked up Deputy Secretary Wolfowitz and Mary Turner and our staff sergeant in charge of General Myers's office, and they all went out to Site R.

Dan Creedon, departure controller, TRACON, Reagan National Airport, Washington, D.C.: These Doomsday and Continuity of Government plans — different elements of the military and FAA practice every day to move the decision makers of Washington to a safe, undisclosed location. That all happened that day. It had been developed for years and modified as things went on. Now here were all of these helicopters and various other things coming into the area to pick people up and fly them to safe locations. Meanwhile the fighters were airborne and armed. We did not trust anybody. How we didn't accidentally shoot down one of the evacuation aircraft is a testament to the D.C. Air National Guard guys, the F-16 pilots, and the air traffic controllers who were calling the shots.

Lawrence Di Rita, special assistant to Secretary of Defense Rumsfeld: I went to Site R with the deputy. We started to make plans to be able to continue our operations somewhere else. I'm not sure that even then that I knew that a plane had hit our building. I knew that something had happened.

Col. Matthew Klimow: There were only six of us in the room. Secretary Rumsfeld, General Myers, the legal counsel Bill Haynes, the press spokeswoman for the secretary Torie Clarke, and Vice Adm. Ed Giambastiani, and then myself. I was in the corner taking notes. I had a terrible headache and couldn't focus. I really thought I was going to pass out. Vice Adm. Giambastiani kept talking to me — talking, and talking, and talking — and all I could think of was, *Would he please shut up and leave me alone? I don't feel well.*

Adm. Edmund Giambastiani: I'm a submariner, so I'm used to living in an enclosed environment. We measure the atmospheres all the time.

Col. Matthew Klimow: Finally the admiral started to shake me, and he said, "Colonel, Colonel, you don't understand — I'm a submariner. I know what's going on." He said, "There's no oxygen in this room. It's filling up with carbon dioxide." I said, "Well, we could move. I've been trying to get hold of the Navy Operations Center. I can't raise him, but the Army Operations Center is up and going." I didn't know at that time the Navy Operations Center was taken out, all hands dead. He said, "I want you to go find an air monitor and see how bad the air quality is."

To my surprise, around the corner comes Captain Donahue with an Arlington County fire captain and their air quality specialist. The air quality specialist said, "OK, here's

515

the story: in some of the corridors in the Pentagon, the air is filled with about 88 percent carbon dioxide. That's lethal." He said, "In the outer office here in the NMCC you're at 33 percent oxygen. In the SCIF [for the videoconference], you're at 16 percent oxygen, and you cannot survive at 13 percent. You need to leave." I remember interrupting Secretary Rumsfeld and General Myers, passing this information to them, and a dramatic discussion took place about whether to evacuate the Pentagon.

Victoria "Torie" Clarke: Rumsfeld looked up and realized that there were about 75 people in the immediate vicinity, and he said something to the effect that they could leave if they wanted to. Myers said, "Sir, they will not leave unless you do. They will go down with you." I remember writing notes, and in the margin I wrote, "Uh oh, this could be pretty serious." He went right back to his work.

Col. Matthew Klimow: General Myers expressed concern about all the troops that were still operating in the Pentagon and their health. He was thinking like a soldier. Secretary Rumsfeld was thinking more strategically. He said, "There's no way we're leaving the Pentagon." He said, "This is the symbol of America's military power. We can't leave."

AT BARKSDALE
AIR FORCE BASE

"WE ARE AT WAR!"

At around 11:45 a.m. ET, Air Force One landed at Barksdale Air Force Base, outside Shreveport, Louisiana, where only hours earlier the military had been practicing a Cold War exercise, code-named VIGILANT GUARDIAN, aimed at responding to the threat of a Russian attack by nuclear bombers. Barksdale's own fleet of B-52 bombers had been armed that morning with nuclear weapons, ready to fight an imaginary war. Instead, Air Force One brought with it a new kind of conflict.

Col. Mark Tillman, presidential pilot, Air Force One: Going into Barksdale, there's this plane that appears. The fighter jets were with us. I still remember the F-16s starting in on this guy — bearing, range, altitude, distance. You see the F-16 roll off — they ask, "Hey, who has shoot-down authority?" I say, "You do." That was a big moment. It turned out to be a crop duster, some civilian flyer who didn't get the word.

Gordon Johndroe, assistant press secretary, White House: You cannot hide a blue-and-white 747 that says "United States of America" across the top. You can't move it secretly through the daylight. Where does local TV go when there's a national emergency? They go out to their local military base. We're watching ourselves land on local television. The announcer's saying, "It appears Air Force One is landing." The pool is looking at me like, *We can't report this?*

Staff Sgt. William "Buzz" Buzinski, security, Air Force One: Barksdale was going through a nuclear surety inspection. They already had these cops in flak jackets and M-16s. They were all locked and loaded. As soon as we landed, they surrounded the aircraft.

Brian Montgomery, director of advance, White House: As soon as we landed, Mark Rosenker — director of the White House Military Office — and I went off the back stairs. There's this guy who looks like Gen. Buck Turgidson from *Dr. Strangelove* — big guy, all decked out in a bomber jacket. He was straight out of central casting. We said, "What do you need?" He said, "See those planes? Every one is loaded with nukes — tell me where you want 'em." We looked over and there were rows of B-52s, wingtip to wingtip. I joked, "Gosh, don't tell the president!"

Capt. Cindy Wright, presidential nurse, White House Medical Unit: I remember how different it was, landing at Barksdale. We'd gotten off the plane and we were at war.

Dave Wilkinson, assistant agent in charge, U.S. Secret Service: My biggest concern was the Humvees. Would they be there? When I saw the four or five Humvees pull up, I had a real sense of relief. One of the other agents raised the concern that the air force wanted to drive the president — the Secret Service are normally the only people who drive the president. I said, "That's the least of our concerns."

Col. Mark Tillman: We let the president out through the bottom stairs, because you want that low vantage point in case there's a sniper.

Ari Fleischer, press secretary, White House: Normally, there's a whole infrastructure that flies ahead of the president. All that was waiting for him in Barksdale was this up-armored Humvee with room for a standing gunner. The air force driver was nervous and driving as fast as could be.

Andy Card, chief of staff, White House: The guy was driving really fast, and in a Humvee the center of gravity isn't as low as you think. The president said, "Slow down, son, there are no terrorists on this base! You don't have to kill me now!"

Col. Mark Tillman: I went down to the tarmac to see about having the plane refueled. We could carry 14 hours of fuel. I wanted 14 hours of fuel. It turned out we'd happened to park over a hot refueling tank they used for bombers. This civilian is arguing with our crew, "The fuel pits are only authorized for use in time of war." This air force master sergeant — God bless him — overhears this and roars, "We are at war!" He whips out his knife and starts cutting open the cover. That defines to me what the day was like.

Lt. Gen. Tom Keck, commander, Barksdale Air Force Base: The president had landed already and I was on my way to meet him. He was on his way to the conference center. I gave a sharp salute, and his first words to me were, "I guess I put you on the map." He told me he needed a secure phone to call Governor [George] Pataki [of New York], so I took him to my office. As he started making calls, he stopped for a second: "Tell me where I am?" I said, "You're on the east side of the Red River in Bossier City, Barksdale Air Force Base, near Shreveport, Louisiana."

Brian Montgomery: Andy Card came out and said this was an opportunity to call loved ones, but don't tell them where we are.

Rep. Adam Putnam (R-Florida): When we got to Barksdale — keep in mind that we haven't really had good TV images — we were all overwhelmed with emotion, because we were all catching up to where everyone else had had a couple hours to process. I called my wife and said, "I'm safe. I can't tell you where I am." She said, "Oh, I thought you were in Barksdale? That's what I saw on TV."

Lt. Gen. Tom Keck: Andy Card and Karl Rove came into my office with him.

Karl Rove, senior adviser, White House: This was the first point where he gets fully briefed. All three strikes were over, so we knew the extent of the damage. His first instinct was to bring together the leaders of government, but everyone had dispersed. It's amazing how technology has changed. At the time, the only way to get everyone together was to go to Offutt Air Force Base [outside Omaha, Nebraska], the nearest facility that had multiple-site video teleconferencing. Now the president travels with a black Halliburton case that has a screen that can do it through any broadband outlet. It's amazing.

Col. Mark Tillman: I went into the base situation room. I told them I needed to get this guy underground. Where were all the places that I could do that? Offutt was the best choice.

Lt. Gen. Tom Keck: People forget how much confusion there was that day about what was actually going on. Intel officers were coming in all the time. One said that there was a high-speed object moving toward the president's Texas ranch. I saw him start thinking about who was at the ranch. It turned out to be a false report.

Maj. Scott "Hooter" Crogg, F-16 pilot, 111th Fighter Squadron, Houston: I was thinking, *I've done these Combat Air Patrols over southern Iraq for hundreds of hours, enforcing the no-fly zone, and now I'm doing it over the United States.* It was really strange. No one else was airborne.

Ellen Eckert, stenographer, White House: To wait for the president, they took us to the Officers' Club. I was basically the only person

522

on the trip who smoked cigarettes — or so I thought. While we're standing there, all of a sudden everyone's asking for a cigarette. "Wait, you don't smoke!" Everyone was so whipped up.

Lt. Gen. Tom Keck: Everyone was busy doing their own thing. The president was looking over the remarks he wanted to give the country. He asked the room, "I use the word 'resolve' twice in here — do I want to do that?" No one was answering him, so I said, "I think Americans probably want to hear that."

Brian Montgomery: We got with someone from the base and found this rec room or something like that with a bunch of memorabilia on the walls. Gordon and I started rearranging everything — got some flags, found a podium. We knew this was important. Everyone wanted to see the president.

Gordon Johndroe: Barksdale was a blur. It was really chaotic. No one really remembers the president's statement there. It was bad lighting, bad setting, but it was important to have him say something to the nation.

Sonya Ross, reporter, AP: I dictated a brief report to my colleague Sandra Sobieraj back in Washington, and then I left my phone on so she could hear the president's brief statement. He said, "Our military at home and around the world is on high alert status. We have taken the necessary security precautions to continue the functions of your government." He reiterated that it was a terrorist attack and urged people to be calm.

Ellen Eckert: I'd never seen the president look so stern. I was lying on the ground at the president's feet. We didn't know if the [TV news] feed was working, it was so iffy, so I was there lying down with my mic above my head in case no one else was recording his remarks.

Andy Card: We didn't want attention to where we were until we left. We videotaped the statement, so that it went out as we left.

Lt. Gen. Tom Keck: After the press conference, he came back to my office. He was sitting on my couch and watched the Towers fall on TV. He turned to me, because I was there, and said, "I don't know who this is, but we're gonna find out, and we're going to go after them, we're not going to slap them on the wrist." I said, "We're with you." I knew he meant every word.

Ari Fleischer: Andy Card made the decision to chop down the number of passengers.

We didn't know where we were going. Anybody nonessential had to be left behind and that included all the congressmen, which they weren't pleased with. Several White House staffers had to get off. Andy asked if we could take the press down to three. I thought five was the absolute minimum.

Rep. Adam Putnam: As we were waiting on board, supply trucks came up and started unloading food — tray after tray of meat, loaf after loaf of bread, hundreds of gallons of water. We realized they were equipping that plane to be in the air for days. It was really unnerving.

Gordon Johndroe: It was difficult telling half the press pool that they weren't coming with us. Their reaction was half-professional — *We're missing the story of our lifetimes* — and then their personal reaction — *You're leaving us in Louisiana and the airspace is shut down?*

Sonya Ross: They herded us out to a blue school bus. Gordon came on the bus. He read off who was going to come with them: AP reporter, AP photographer, TV camera, TV sound, and radio. Everyone else, he said, was going to be left behind. At that point, Judy Keen, the newspaper reporter from *USA To-*

day, and Jay Carney, the magazine pooler, they raised a stink. I scooped up my stuff and ran.

Karl Rove: As we're driving back out, the president said to me something like, "I know this is a dodge — they're trying to keep me away from Washington — but I'm going to let them have this one and go to Offutt, and then we're going home."

Lt. Gen. Tom Keck: As the president headed up the stairs, I said to him, "These troops are trained, ready, and they'll do whatever you want them to." He said to me, "I know." We traded salutes. He was on the ground an hour and 53 minutes.

Ellen Eckert: Ari told me I was off the plane. The press were not happy, but I was fine — I was thinking, *I'm safe here in Louisiana.* The plane fired up — it was loud, we were all standing nearby — and Gordon came to the back stairs and yelled, "Ellen, Ari says get on the plane! He's changed his mind!" That's not what I want to do. Then I thought, *I should be ashamed of myself. Everyone else is getting on that plane.* I was the last one on board.

Sonya Ross: As we left, they didn't know

how long we'd be gone. They told us that they'd arrange accommodations if we had to be gone a day or two. I told my bureau chief, "I don't know where we're going, and I don't know how long I'll be gone."

MIDDAY IN NEW YORK CITY
"HAVE YOU HEARD FROM MY DAD?"

Families and friends across the country tried to find out if their loved ones were among the day's victims; tens of thousands in New York were imagined missing, maybe presumed dead. Amid the morning's tragedy, three sisters tried to discover whether their dad, who worked at Windows on the World, was among those lost.

Joann Gomez, eighth grade, Junior High School 56: We were in class, and we heard this big explosion — our whole school shook.

Melissa Gomez, fourth grade, New York City: My principal had mentioned in the announcements the Twin Towers, that a plane hit.

Joann Gomez: My father, Jose Bienvenido Gomez, and my uncle, Enrique Gomez, were born in the Dominican Republic, Santiago. They came to the U.S. in the early 1980s and started working in the World Trade Center in 2000.

Joanna Gomez: Our dad was very excited to work at the World Trade Center. I remember when he told us — from our apartment, you were able to see the Twin Towers, so he would show us from our window, like, "Look! That's where I'm going to work!" He was a prep cook, so he was the one in charge of cutting the vegetables and the shrimps and so on. It was actually four brothers who worked there. Two of my other uncles also worked there — one was injured on 9/11 and the other one was in the Dominican Republic, so he wasn't there that day.

Joanna Gomez: I was only 13, so I only thought of the World Trade Center as the Twin Towers — not the World Trade Center. I asked my classmate if the World Trade Center is where the Twin Towers are. He was like, "Yeah, that's where it is." I started crying. Then they asked everyone to go to their homeroom class, and I met with my sister in the hallway.

Melissa Gomez: Then parents started coming.

Joanna Gomez: We were sent to the office, and we called our house, and they said that my cousin was going to pick us up from school. From school, we see the [South Tower] fall. I remember my cousin told me, "Don't worry. The tower where your father works is the one that has the big antennae and it's still up. There's still a chance. They'll get him through a helicopter or something."

Melissa Gomez: I was nine or 10 years old. I got home and I see everybody's crying, but I was confused. I don't know what's happened, because I don't know my father [worked in the Twin Towers] — I knew he used to work somewhere, but I didn't know it was there, specifically. I was still innocent.

Joanna Gomez: We were making calls and we were making pictures with signs, the age, the name. My mom didn't speak any English, so me and my sister had to go to the hospitals, talk to FBI agents. We had to do everything.

In Lower Manhattan, some of those caught in the collapse made their way out of the destruction, emerging from the clouds as dust-covered ghosts, fleeing across the Brooklyn Bridge on foot or making their way uptown into a New York City reeling from the disaster. Everyone was in a state of shock, desperate to tell their waiting families that they were alive. Strangers stepped up to aid the refugees as best they could.

David Kravette, bond broker, Cantor Fitzgerald, North Tower, 105th floor: I was walking, and I said, "I need to borrow a phone." I used this guy's phone. I talked to my wife a couple of seconds, and I lost the connection. The guy saw I was upset. He gives me a hug — a stranger. It's funny. This stranger gives me a hug and goes, "You'll be okay," and walks on. That was it.

Richard Eichen, consultant, Pass Consulting Group, North Tower, 90th floor: I walked out of the hospital. I met this woman, Pansy, who was walking out as well. We shared a Snapple. There was a guy at the hospital entrance, a security guard, saying, "Don't go out." I said, "No, I want to leave." He said, "All right, if you're going then — here," and he gave me a surgical mask. We walked across the Brooklyn Bridge, Pansy and I — she lived in Brooklyn, and my parents live in Queens. As I was walking across the bridge, I could feel the sun on my face. I remember taking the mask off, and it felt good to have the sun on my face. It's like, *All right, it's over.*

Somi Roy, resident, Lower Manhattan: It was like the scene from *The Ten Comman-*

dants, with Charlton Heston leading people across the Sinai Desert. There was a stream of people walking across the Brooklyn Bridge. Endless. Downstairs was another stream of people, all covered in dust, all with briefcases half-open, women with no shoes. They had to shut the FDR Drive, so it was eerily empty. The sound was different. Usually we have this constant roar in the background, of traffic.

Howard Lutnick, CEO, Cantor Fitzgerald, North Tower: We kept walking and wiping our faces and cleaning our mouths and our eyes. In the middle of the street. There were no cars. It was so strange, like the end of the world.

Betsy Gotbaum, candidate for New York City public advocate: People in our building were in shock, total shock. People didn't know what to do. We invited the elevator men in to come and watch because they didn't have a television.

David Kravette: I walked uptown to Howard Lutnick's apartment and we started meeting there, the few survivors. Howard Lutnick came up. He was covered in soot because he was down there when it collapsed. We started calling some of the spouses, and none of them had heard from their husbands or wives.

Jillian Volk, preschool teacher, Lower Manhattan: I thought my fiancé, Kevin, was out of the Trade Center. I truly thought he was going to walk into the school and get me. I waited at the school until maybe 10:30 or so. Most of the kids had gone by then, so I started walking north. I didn't know where to go.

Richard Eichen: This guy, Gary, was picking up his niece from Brooklyn Law School. He said, "Do you want a ride to your parents? Where do they live?" I said, "The Rockaways." I said, "I'm filthy." He goes, "Don't worry about it." He gave me a ride. We stopped off at his house to give me a drink of water, and they asked me, "Do you want to take a shower?" I said, "No, I really want to go to my parents' house." Then he drove me to Rockaway. My father had put out a flag in front of the house. I went inside and my sister said, "You want to take a shower?" I said, "Yeah."

Betsy Gotbaum: At one point, I went outside. It was a beautiful day, and I was terribly upset. We live right next to the park. It was completely silent. You couldn't hear anything. It was so eerie. I've never experienced anything like that in New York City in my entire life. The silence.

Even as people fled Lower Manhattan, thousands more firefighters, police, EMTs, paramedics, and first responders flooded in to what would become known as Ground Zero, both in hopes of rescuing survivors and also to take stock of the massive losses their own departments and colleagues had suffered in the collapses. Given the tight-knit, multigeneration traditions of the NYPD and FDNY, many of those responding had brothers, sisters, sons, daughters, fathers, mothers, or other relatives who had perished. They all confronted an apocalyptic landscape, full of fire, debris, and death.

Joe Finley, firefighter, Ladder 7, FDNY: I got in the car and drove in. The police had every entrance and exit closed. The only way you could get on the expressway was with your badge and your ID. There were hundreds of cars filled with cops and firemen streaming into the city.

Capt. Joe Downey, Squad Company 18, FDNY: I couldn't believe that the tower had fallen. I thought they were making a mistake. Until I got to the scene, I still couldn't understand that they all came down. I went to my dad's firehouse, Special Operations, on Roosevelt Island. We started regrouping there, and when a bunch of us got together, we came into Manhattan.

Paul McFadden, firefighter, Rescue 2, FDNY: They were saying tens of thousands of people were dead. It sounded like the whole New York City Fire Department had been killed.

Capt. Joe Downey: When I got to the firehouse, obviously, my first question was "Have you heard from my dad?" That was the first bad feeling I got — nobody had talked to him.

Joe Finley: At a rally point in Cunningham Park, Queens, hundreds of firemen waited for city buses to come in and pick them up. Nobody was saying anything to each other. We all looked out the window at the skyline of New York City, and the huge plume of smoke going miles up in the air.

Paul McFadden: There were cops on every corner, and you had to show your badge and then they waved you through. When I was in Rescue 2 earlier, Ray Downey had been the captain and now, on 9/11, he was the chief of all special operations, so I knew he'd be at the Towers. On our way there that day, I was saying, "Listen, when we get there we'll go right to the command post; we'll check in with Ray. He's going to be happy to see us and give us a job or an area or what have you to search."

Lt. Chuck Downey, FDNY: It was white all over the place. Dust almost looked like some type of snowstorm.

Jeff Johnson, firefighter, Engine 74, FDNY: The streets were six inches to a foot thick of this white-gray talcum powder–type of dust, and any time a fire truck or anything went by, it became impossible to breathe.

Joe Finley: We couldn't even hear our own footsteps. Nobody was talking. There was no sound, no cars. Downtown Manhattan in the middle of the day, and it was absolutely silent.

Capt. Joe Downey: I walked down West Street and the first gentleman I ran into was Chief Frank Carruthers. He was my dad's boss. I asked him, "Have you seen my father?" He put his head down and walked away. That's when I knew that he probably was gone.

Paul McFadden: When we got down to the World Trade Center site, the first two people I saw were Ray's two sons, Joe and Chuck. I went right up to them — because I thought this was a real good thing — and I said, "Joey, Chuckie, where's the command post? Where's your dad?" Joey looked at me and he said, "We're on our way home to my mother. My father's under the rubble." That was like getting kicked in the head by a horse. It was the last thing I expected to hear — that Ray was dead. That set the stage for the night.

Jeff Johnson: At the time, Building Seven was fully involved with fire. There was nobody trying to put that fire out. We were busy doing other things, obviously. It was pretty surreal to see that building on fire.

James Luongo, inspector, NYPD: At one point, there had to be 200 construction workers walking down West Street. I said, "Who's in charge?" They said, "Nobody's in charge. We're here to help." I'll never forget those men — big burly guys, coming down. So much of that day, so much of that day was just New Yorkers. People who can help people. A lot of credit goes to the fire department. A lot of credit goes to the police department and emergency response people. But that's what we get paid for. The amount of New Yorkers — just everyday New Yorkers — who stepped up to the plate that day was incredible.

Both Dan and Jean Potter emerged safely from the collapse of the World Trade Center, but with no sense of how to reunite with each other. Jean didn't know her firefighter husband was searching frantically for her.

Dan Potter, firefighter, Ladder 10, FDNY: There was fire in all the buildings around the Trade Center. All the paper that had come out of the Towers had carpeted nearby fire escapes. That paper and the fire escapes were all in flames, all the way down Greenwich. Fire all around us, cars on fire on the street — it's like a movie set. I said, "I've got to go find my wife."

Jean Potter, Bank of America, North Tower: This lovely gentleman asked me if I needed help. I said, "Do you have water and a phone?" I was in such a state. He invited me into his house — they had a brownstone in Chinatown — and I was in this fearful state. I said, "No, can I stay outside, please?" He brought a chair out and gave me a phone.

Dan Potter: I don't recall seeing any civilians. I do remember all the ambulances turned over, Ladder 113 burning. I walked past them quickly. I was focused on trying to find her, but there was nobody.

Jean Potter: All the while I was thinking Dan was studying in school, studying for the lieutenant's test. I was thinking, *He's in Staten Island. He's not home. He's not working. He's away, thank God.*

Dan Potter: My first plan is, "Okay, she'll be home. Then we'll worry about the next step." You try to put off the inevitable thought. I walked home, and I remember getting a bottle of water out of one of the juice places. The door was open, and no one was in there. I still owe the guy a dollar.

Jean Potter: In an emergency, Dan had always told me, go to a firehouse. I said, "I need to get to a firehouse." The guy helping me took me to the Chinatown firehouse.

Dan Potter: I walked to the apartment on Rector Place. The doorman, Arturo, was there. He said, "Can I help you, sir?" I said, "It's me — Dan." He didn't even recognize me at first. He said, "Are we safe here, fireman?" I said, "It's me, Dan — I live here. I'm looking for Jean. Did Jean come home?" He goes, "No, I haven't seen her." I said, "Okay." There were people in the lobby of our building. They thought I was a fireman coming to help them. Then they realized who I was. They were used to seeing me in slacks and penny loafers, never in gear covered in gray matter.

Jean Potter: This couple passed by the firehouse. She said, "My phone will work." I managed to call my mom. My mom heard my voice, and she started to cry. I said, "I'm OK." I said, "Dan's at school, so Dan's OK, so call June" — my mother-in-law — "and tell her that he's OK." I told her that because in my head, I still think he's in Staten Island taking the practice test.

Dan Potter: I went across the street, and that's when I sat on the bench. I had to collect my thoughts. *What am I going to do now?* I was sitting on the bench, getting a little upset. The guy clicked the picture. I told him, "It's not the time."

Matt Moyer, photographer: As I neared the marina I saw a solitary firefighter sitting on a bench. It was a quiet scene amid a very chaotic situation. His body language spoke of deep loss. When he finally heard the click of my shutter he lifted his head, looked toward me, raised his hand and slowly shook his head indicating, no more photos. I took my camera

from my eye and before I could speak he said, "I just lost my wife." His voice was full of heartache. All I could muster was "I'm so so sorry." He lowered his head and continued sitting on the bench.

Jean Potter: I felt I had to make myself useful, so I started answering the phone. Can you imagine? This woman covered in dust — I was in a state of shock. I said, "Give me the phone. I'll answer." Calls were starting to come in: "I'm so-and-so's dad, I'm so-and-so's wife." Then a few guys came in and told me, "OK, let's go in the back. We need to go back and relax."

Dan Potter: I went back inside the lobby. I said, "All my stuff is back in Ladder 10's compartments. I don't have keys to my apartment." I started to force my door to get inside the apartment. The door finally opened up, and the phone was ringing. The first call was one of Jean's aunts. I said, "Listen, I can't talk. I've got to go look for Jean." I hung up, and the next call was my dad. He's crying. He's very upset. I said, "Dad, I'm okay, but I can't find Jean." He goes, "I know where she is." I'm like, "Where is she?" He answered, "She's at the Chinatown firehouse." I said, "Oh my God. Thank you." I hang up the phone. I don't remember hitting any of the steps going down nine floors. I went back to the street and down and out. My truck is all covered in gray dust. I drove up through South Street and up to the Chinatown firehouse on Canal Street.

Jean Potter: I was sitting in the house, watching it on television.

Dan Potter: I walked into the firehouse and said, "You got a redhead in here somewhere?" Another firefighter, a real kid in the company, said, "Yeah, she's in the back room." I walked in, and that's when she saw me.

Jean Potter: He was in this bunker gear and coat. His eyes were blood red from the debris and the dust. I never thought he was down there. I expected him to pick me up in street clothes. Here he is, picking me up totally, totally covered, with blood-red eyes.

Dan Potter: We hugged. She's all covered in gray dust. We hugged and kissed. I said, "Okay, let's get you out of here. Where do you want to go?" She was very upset, shaking, and she said, "Let's go to my mom's house." It's an hour ride into Pennsylvania.

Jean Potter: Our life was like scrambled eggs. We were so grateful our lives were spared, but everything we knew that day changed. We were spared, but everything changed.

Herb Ouida, World Trade Centers Association, North Tower, and father of Todd Ouida, Cantor Fitzgerald, North Tower, 105th floor: I remember being on the street on Broadway, and people saying there's no more World Trade Center. I said, "What does that mean?" They said, "The buildings are gone." I absolutely could not believe it. When I got to my daughter's apartment I saw on the TV that the buildings had in fact collapsed like pancakes. I kept thinking: *Todd was on the 105th.* What stays with me and what will be with me until I die is the question: *What was it like for Todd? Did he know it was the end? Was he awake?*

Adrian Pierce, Wachovia Bank, North Tower: I went in the ladies' room of a nearby building. Everything was stuck to me. I rinsed my hair off, I rinsed my blouse off, and as I was coming out of the bathroom, there were two plastic bags. I wrapped one around my foot and I wrapped one around my head. Outside, two white guys were sitting on a bench, they had a traveling case, and I asked them: "Do you have a shirt I can put on?" One gave me the shirt off his back. I took my shirt off and I put his shirt on, and I wrapped my shirt around my foot. I was walking, and

544

I was crying. I found myself walking over the bridge.

Ian Oldaker, staff, Ellis Island: It was time to walk home. We started walking with this mass of humanity up the ramp to the Brooklyn Bridge. The scariest moment for me was seeing people screaming randomly. It would be quiet, quiet, quiet. Then someone would scream because they'd realize that they had lost their friend. One guy was standing next to me, walking, and he asked me where he was. I was like, "We're on the Brooklyn Bridge, man." He's in a suit. He asked me what happened. I said, "The World Trade Center collapsed."

We got across the Brooklyn Bridge into Cadman Plaza. We saw this line of buses. The bus driver was hollering at us, "I'm going south down Flatbush." We got on that bus and it was so quiet. Everyone was so entranced.

Adrian Pierce: When we got over the bridge, I sat on the curb. I said, "I can't go no more. I can't go no more." An ambulance stopped to pick me up and the driver said, "Miss, you need to come with me." I was crying. I said, "I don't want to go with you. I want to go home. I want to let my mother and my husband and my son know I'm okay."

Joe Massian, technology consultant, Port Authority, North Tower: I kept walking. It was shocking. Everybody was stopped on the sidewalks. People would look at me, put their hand to their mouth, and stand there crying. After a while I'm like, *Okay. What's going on? What don't I know about myself?* I passed a building that had a reflective glass, and I realized I was covered in material.

Jared Kotz, Risk Waters Group: Finally at about 11:00 a.m., I guess, maybe 11:30 or so — I'm not sure what time it was — I realized I hadn't eaten, and I realized my decision to forgo breakfast and run back to the office was another reason I had survived. If I had stayed there for breakfast, I wouldn't be alive. I was hungry, so I headed down to the street in search of a muffin or something to eat. I walked to the corner on Avenue A and people were evacuating southern Manhattan, coming from the World Trade Center area. Right at Tompkins Square Park, I saw a young man. He looked like he was in a state of shock. He was covered in dust from head to toe. The back of his knapsack, I remember, was the weirdest thing I could imagine. There must have been two or three inches of dust on top of his knapsack — this thick layer of dust — and he was also covered head to foot in a gray dust. I can't understand why I didn't stop to try to help the guy. I was in a daze of my own.

Robert Snyder, professor, Rutgers University, and collapse survivor: As I got further up into the East 50s, it was a strange scene. There were throngs of people headed north in the streets like me who looked like refugees out of movies about wars and catastrophes. Yet there was a lunchtime crowd watching us too. I saw this restaurant, and all the people who worked in the restaurant are sitting in the window looking at us walk by.

Constance Labetti, accountant, Aon Corporation, South Tower: We walked and walked and walked. We walked through pretty bad neighborhoods in Brooklyn, and people were out there with their hoses: "Do you want a sip of water from our hose?"

Vanessa Lawrence, artist, North Tower: It was strange walking past shops where people gathered around where there was TV screens or radios and I'd be like, "No! No! I can't!" I was looking forward, going straight ahead.

Bruno Dellinger, principal, Quint Amasis North America, North Tower: I kept walking on Broadway. There were groups of people, cars stopped, people watching. I kept redialing, redialing, redialing. It went through to my parents. When I spoke to my mom, I collapsed. It was too much. I couldn't articulate a word. I was crying — a big guy like me.

Joe Massian: I ended up getting to a stoplight where there was a box truck and a bunch of people sitting in the back. They were giving rides to people who wanted to head up north. The guy said, "Jump in and jump out when you want." I jumped in right around 14th Street, jumped out around 53rd, and headed over to Cushman & Wakefield, where my fiancée worked. When I got off the elevator and opened up the door — I remember the entire organization stood up in their cubicles and they started crying. I grabbed my fiancée. I said, "How did you know that I was okay?" She's like, "Your picture was on the internet. It was on MSNBC.com." It was also on the cover of Yahoo. It was on Reuters. It was on a bunch of different websites. I've learned a lot of people knew that I was out of the building.

Vanessa Lawrence: I managed to get ahold of my friend Amelia and she was like, "Come here, now!" I think she was near 28th Street. Amelia said when she saw me that I looked like a sculpture walking toward her. She said it was a really strange thing. I was completely covered. I showered and then I kept getting really itchy and sore. It took me three showers to really stop the prickly feeling I had on me and in my hair and everything.

John Napolitano, father of FDNY firefighter John Napolitano: I was in a car heading downtown with my brother-in-law. His cell phone rang, and he got very excited on the phone. He said, "Yes, yes, yes, yes, all right, all right." He said, "Turn around and go home." I looked at him and saw he had a lot of concern on his face. I said, "What's the matter?" He said, "Turn around and go home. You have to go home. Something happened. You have to go home." I did a quick U-turn.

Terri Langone, wife of FDNY firefighter Peter Langone: I went to get the girls at school. I definitely knew he was there. When I saw the building come down, I knew in my heart he was gone. I knew without a doubt. He was in the second tower to fall, Tower One. I found out about Peter's brother, Thomas Langone, later on that afternoon. He was a police officer with ESU Truck 10. He was in the other tower.

Michael McAvoy, associate director, Bear Stearns, Brooklyn: I decided to go to my brother's firehouse on 13th Street. From a few blocks away, I saw a ton of firemen, plus a ton of fire trucks. I had a little hope. The firemen were from firehouses all over the city. It was total pandemonium. I saw a fireman I know. He was covered in soot. I look him in the eye, I say, "Was my brother down there?" He says, "Yes." I say, "Any chance for survivors? You can tell me." He says, "Mike, I wish I had better news, but no. The place is the worst any of us have ever seen."

John Napolitano: I got to my house. I went upstairs and my wife was on the floor, kneeling, being held by her sister. She was saying, "My baby! My baby!" Over and over and over, "My baby! My baby!" I looked at my sister-in-law. She says, "We got a call. John's missing."

Paul McFadden, firefighter, Rescue 2, FDNY: I remember speaking to one fireman — it was probably by O'Hara's on Cedar Street — and he was telling me how his daughter worked on the 109th floor, and he was saying, "You don't think she made it, do you, Paul?" What do you say to a guy like that? I said, "We don't know. Let's keep our hopes up."

550

John Cartier, brother of James Cartier, electrician, who was working in the South Tower: We pulled up to my parents' house, and we were completely covered in the silky soot from head to toe, both of us. My parents came out and they were hugging my sister. Then I remember my mother asking about James. I looked at my father and said, "I couldn't get to him. I couldn't do it."

New York City's leadership found themselves refugees in their own city, unable to communicate, and tried to find a space to regroup and coordinate the rescue and response efforts.

Andrew Kirtzman, reporter, NY1: We kept walking, and Giuliani kept turning to me to say, "You've got to tell the public to stay out of here so our emergency vehicles can get through." He's like, "Please. Everyone south has got to get out of here. Go north. No one should come south." I said, "Well" — I've got my little StarTAC flip phone — "would you go on live with New York 1 and tell the city yourself?" I called New York 1 like 10 times, finally got through, and the control room was crazy busy. I said, "I've got Giuliani on the phone!" They were overwhelmed. I waited and waited. I don't know whether it was 30 seconds or three minutes. Suddenly the phone went dead. I was never able to get through to them. We were on our own.

Rudy Giuliani, mayor, New York City: A few police officers ran ahead and picked a hotel we could use as a command post.

Andrew Kirtzman: We were walking up Church Street. Giuliani's team decided at first to try the Tribeca Grand Hotel. The news had not hit them yet, and there were all these tourists. Tribeca Grand was this ridiculously trendy SoHo hotel, and there was this dissonance between this nomadic tribe covered with dust walking in, and all these trendy people wearing black, going about their day.

Rudy Giuliani: As we walked in, I looked at the fire commissioner and the police commissioner. They looked at me, and we walked right straight through and out. It was a totally glass building. We figured a glass building is not a good place to be.

Andrew Kirtzman: We kept walking up Church Street. There were crowds on the streets, on the sidewalks, and as they saw Giuliani they started cheering. One person was like, "Go, Giuliani!" We went a little further, and there was this young policewoman — she was trying to control this pandemonium as thousands of people were walking back and forth — and she made eye contact with us and Giuliani. She was scared to death. Giuliani rubbed her cheek as he walked by. It was fatherly. He tried to calm her down.

Now we're at the south end of Greenwich Village, and they decide to locate into a firehouse. There's a firehouse on the west side of Sixth Avenue. It was deserted because all firemen were at the Trade Center, and it was locked. The leadership of the city was gathered outside this firehouse door that we couldn't get into.

Bernie Kerik, commissioner, NYPD: We had to break in.

Rudy Giuliani: NYPD Det. John Huvaine had to knock open the door of the firehouse. He used a fire extinguisher to do it and we got in. That was the first time I was able to get on a hard line. The first thing I did was call Governor Pataki, because he had been trying to reach me. The governor said, "How are you? We were very worried about you. There were reports that you were missing." Then he said, "I've alerted the National Guard. Do you want them?"

In part I had not wanted the National Guard because I think the police department is so big and has expertise in an urban

553

environment that the National Guard doesn't have. I always resisted the National Guard. Immediately, I said, "Yes, I want the National Guard." I knew from the moment I saw the man jump that we were in over our heads. This was beyond the resources of the largest city in America. I needed all the help I could get. I said, "George, I need them."

Andrew Kirtzman: Giuliani, once he walked into that fire command office, he called New York 1 and gave them his message. New York 1 is a sister station of CNN, so they gave that to CNN and broadcast it to the world. I have to say, Giuliani was a flawed man, but he was the calmest one in the bunch. He never exhibited panic or fear. Someone once said that Giuliani was most hysterical when things were calm, and most calm when things were hysterical. This was the perfect example. The city, the world, was desperate for leadership. Bush was out of communication for hours. All they had was Giuliani, and he rose to the occasion.

Sunny Mindel, communications director for the mayor of the City of New York, Rudy Giuliani: I saw my colleague Beth Petrone. Her husband, Terry Hatten, was captain of Rescue 1. I asked her where Terry was, and she looked at me and said, "He's dead." I looked at her. I got angry with her, and I said, "No, Beth, you don't know that." Beth is possibly the most even-keeled person I know. She got agitated with me, and she said, "He's dead. I know he's dead. I know he was in there, and he's dead."

Andrew Kirtzman: It started then to sink in. I ran out of the firehouse. I was completely dehydrated, and I went into a deli across the street and got all the Gatorade I could. I asked that man whether I could use his phone. I called my parents. Suddenly it all hit me — it struck me how many people were losing their lives.

Det. Hector Santiago, NYPD: The boss [NYPD Commissioner Bernard Kerik] makes a command decision. "Okay, we're going to establish a command center. We're not going to let anybody know. I don't want it over the radio. We don't know what's happening." We confiscated a bunch of cars and motorcaded all the way up to the police academy, where we regrouped.

George Pataki, governor of New York: That afternoon, my team and Mayor Giuliani and the city's team sat down together to discuss what had happened and what we were going to do. There was enormous uncertainty as to whether there would be additional attacks. I made the decision that we could only have one response center — we couldn't have a city command center, a state command center, a FEMA national command center. We had to all be together.

Sunny Mindel: There was a facility at the police academy we converted into a press filing area, and we had to do a formal press conference that would be carried live. It suddenly occurred to me while we were in this facility, the city was still at risk. If we used the stage of the auditorium, our exact location would be very apparent to anybody watching TV. I looked at this room and said, "Everybody turn around. Sorry, we're gonna do this backwards."

George Pataki: I'll never forget one obviously homeless gentleman coming up and giving me a hug, and me telling him, "We'll get through this," and him saying, "Thank you, I'm sure we will."

MIDDAY IN WASHINGTON
"I LOVE YOU. AND I'M STAYING."

Underneath the White House, inside the bunker complex of the Presidential Emergency Operations Center, the vice president and aides struggled to comprehend what had transpired and to make sense of the casualty toll.

Commander Anthony Barnes, deputy director, Presidential Contingency Programs, White House: Things began to settle down — noonish, 1:00 p.m., we knew the last impact had already taken place by then. I knew from reporting that the airplane's impact point at the Pentagon was the Navy Operations Center. Being a navy guy myself, I can remember vividly imagining, *I've definitely got friends or shipmates that were in the impact point. I probably lost close friends.* As it turns out, I did.

Matthew Waxman, staff member, National Security Council, White House: I remember at one point somebody estimating out loud that something like 50,000 people had been killed as the Towers collapsed. There was a ton of information coming in — some of it accurate, some of it inaccurate.

Mary Matalin, aide to Vice President Dick Cheney: That was truly emotional, when we learned that Barbara Olson, a friend of all of us and the wife of the solicitor general, was on the plane that hit the Pentagon. The horror of seeing buildings collapse and seeing planes go into buildings, that didn't jibe with any experience anybody had had. But to isolate it to a person — terrified obviously — sitting on that plane, brought it home to everybody. That was a moment of real terror and emotion for all of us.

Matthew Waxman: The emphasis shifted from immediate crisis response to more deliberative discussion about what we did next. Basic questions like "Do we put the president on TV and what do we have him say?" but also starting to engage in planning for the days that would follow — organizing meetings to make sure the president could be best informed of what was going on, to lay out the necessary response options and things like that.

Also, a whole bunch of questions or issues that senior leaders had to deal with or answer, some of them big and some that seemed small. There were at least two foreign heads of state inside the United States who couldn't get home because air travel was shut down — Australia and Lithuania. There were questions like, "Hey, a foreign head of state is trying to exit the country. What do we do?"

Gary Walters, chief usher, White House: I received a call from Mrs. Bush's staff. Her assistant, Sarah Garrison, asked about the whereabouts of their personal maid and the dogs and the cat. She said, "I'm going to come back in with a Secret Service escort and get some clothes for Mrs. Bush. We don't know what's going to happen from here and we'd like to pick up the dogs and the cat." They went off to an undisclosed location.

As the fires continued to burn on the other side of the building, Pentagon leaders went to work to secure the country. Outside the command center, firefighters and operations personnel continued their efforts to save the Pentagon, while families waited for word of loved ones and the community rallied to help.

Col. Matthew Klimow, executive assistant to the vice chair of the Joint Chiefs of Staff, Gen. Richard Myers, Pentagon: I remember Secretary Rumsfeld, in command voice, said, "Okay everybody, what else can the enemy do?" He wanted us to think. That's Rumsfeld's way. He was always challenging his staff to think out of the box. Almost immediately General Myers piped up and said, "NBC," which means "nuclear-biological-chemical." That seemed like the most logical thing short of an airplane attack that the terrorists would probably try.

Adm. Edmund Giambastiani, senior military assistant, Office of the Secretary of Defense: At 11:47 a.m. there were only 200 aircraft still airborne across the United States. It was pretty amazing. At 12:18, there were 50 aircraft in the air.

Col. Matthew Klimow: The chief of the Pentagon police force, Chief John Jester, a civilian, came in to brief us. He said the lower-floor fires had not been contained at that time. It was just before 1:00. It was hard to know how many people were really in the building — some people were in meetings and they didn't know how many may be missing. General [Ralph] Eberhart reported that they were closing the massive doors about 1:30 at the NORAD bunker inside Cheyenne Mountain in Colorado Springs. That evoked this thought of the doomsday scenario. We didn't know what else could happen.

Joe Wassel, communications officer, Office of the Secretary of Defense: The secretary was very concerned about where Mrs. Rumsfeld was during all of this. Occasionally he would be in the middle of something and would ask, "Have we found Joyce yet?" Security found her at Bolling Air Force Base in a general's home sitting with the general's wife watching it all unfold on television.

Col. Matthew Klimow: My wife, Edie, had been coping in her own way with the situation. Finally Mary Turner, our secretary, got hold of her and said, "The general and Matt Klimow are OK." She drove to Williamsburg Middle School here in Arlington, Virginia, where our 12-year-old son was attending school. There were parents lined up outside. A teacher went to fetch my son, Daniel, and when Daniel came down the hall and saw his mother, the first words out of his mouth were, "Is Dad still alive?" She said, "Yeah."

Lt. Col. Rob Grunewald, information management officer, U.S. Army, Pentagon: Around noon, I say, "I'm going inside to call my wife," because cell phones weren't working. I go in and it's really eerie because there's nobody in the Pentagon. All the doors were locked. People were so security conscious that they locked all their doors and shut their doors. I could find no place to call my wife. Finally, I found an electrical closet and called my wife. She was all in a panic, and she said, "How are you?" I said, "I'm fine. I made it out." She says, "You sound terrible." At that point, I realized I had a terrible cough.

Staff Sgt. Christopher Braman, chef, U.S. Army: Seconds became minutes, minutes became hours. It was 1:47 in the afternoon. I shared a cell phone amongst 100 people — we couldn't get a call out. Whoever could get a signal, we used the phone. As it was my turn, I could taste the adrenaline in my mouth as I was shaking, and I could hear the fear in my wife's voice when she answered. I said, "I'm OK. I love you. And I'm staying."

Ileana Mayorga, management specialist, Volunteer Arlington: At 1:00 the phone started ringing, people who want to come and help. I put the names of all these people in an Excel sheet and what it is that they wanted to do. They wanted to help dig out the people at the Pentagon. They wanted to secure the area themselves. They wanted to enlist to go and fight. I had a man who called and he said, "I am 80 years old. I still fit in my pilot uniform from World War II. I can still see. I can still hear. I have kept up with

562

my training as a pilot. Tell whoever you can tell that I'm ready to report for duty." That broke my heart, this 80-year-old man saying that.

Chris Combs, special agent, FBI, at the Pentagon: By early that afternoon, unsolicited citizens were showing up with food and water. I can very distinctly remember being at the command center and all of a sudden every supermarket showed up with more food. All the vegetables, fruits — all kinds of fruits. I don't know if I was that hungry, but it was the best grapes I've ever had.

Ileana Mayorga: We had people from all over the United States calling. We had a company, a trucking business, and they had heard that they needed trucks to remove the debris. I was able to talk to one of the persons at the incident command, and they said, "Yes, we need trucks, but we need trucks that are new, because we need to preserve everything that we remove. Something that is old will be rusted, and so it is not going to help us." I called that lady. I said, "I'm sorry, yes, we need trucks, but they have to be new." The lady said, "At least I can purchase one. Tell them that I will purchase one that is new, so we can come and help."

Kyra Pulliam, dispatcher, Arlington County Police Department: We had one officer who stopped a pickup truck that had volunteer firefighters from Maryland, ready to go down and help.

Mike Walter, senior correspondent, *USA Today Live:* Later in the day, there was this kid, probably about 18 years old, showed up. He was trying to get past the police line. He had piercings and all this stuff, like, "Jeez, who's this guy?" He was getting very emotional, and he said to the police, "Please, I need to go, I need to give blood, I need to help these people."

Ileana Mayorga: It was completely amazing, the feeling of support, of unity. I felt so proud that my community, the Hispanic community, were calling. Suddenly the phones were ringing and saying, "This is the country that we chose to come to. Nobody will destroy our country." They would say, "I'm not legal in the United States. Do you think they will accept me to do volunteer work?"

Lt. Michael Nesbitt, Defense Protective Service, Pentagon: We have two phone closets — if we lost those phones, the Pentagon would be basically shut down. One individual, Al Tillis, the head of Verizon, had to walk home to Old Town, Alexandria [about five miles]. He rode his bike back here and kept the phone lines up. He didn't leave for five days.

to walk home to Old Town, Alexandria [about
five miles]. He rode his bike back here and
kept the phone lines up. He didn't leave for
three d...

AIRBORNE, SOMEWHERE OVER THE PLAINS

"I'D BET MY CHILDREN'S FUTURE"

Even hours after the attacks were over, the president's team still believed it was not safe for the president to return to Washington. Instead, they headed from Barksdale Air Force Base in Louisiana to Offutt Air Force Base, outside Omaha, Nebraska. During the Cold War, Offutt had been the home of the nation's nuclear forces, Strategic Air Command, and it had the military's best communications abilities outside of the Pentagon, as well as a secure underground bunker.

Lt. Gen. Tom Keck, commander, Barksdale Air Force Base: As he takes off, two F-16s pulled up on his wing. That made me think that we were finally getting our act together. Curtis Bedke, one of the other officers, told me later that as we watched them fly away, I said to him, "Do you feel like you're in a Tom Clancy novel?"

566

Maj. Scott "Hooter" Crogg, F-16 pilot, 111th Fighter Squadron, Houston: We started following Air Force One north. At some point, I was expecting them to turn east and head to Washington. The longer we're heading north, the more I realize something's still unsettled. *They still don't feel safe returning to Washington.* I asked for a tanker to come meet up, and after I hooked up, I asked him for every radio channel between here and Canada.

Ann Compton, reporter, ABC News: In each cabin on board Air Force One, three digital clocks stare out from the bulkhead — the LED numerals show the time in Washington, the time at the current location, and the time at the plane's destination. The three clocks read 1:36 p.m. Eastern Daylight Time, until the destination clock snapped to Central Time, 12:36 p.m. That was our only — stunning — confirmation that Air Force One was headed west, away from Washington.

Andy Card, chief of staff, White House: There were lots of tears. There were lots of quiet moments staring at a TV screen. No conversation. There were prayers. And the fear. It wasn't even a roller coaster, because we were just in the pits. "Oh my god, that's terrible." "And that's worse." "And that's even worse." All the time, we're being handed notes, taking telephone calls, giving orders.

Maj. Scott "Hooter" Crogg: It was an eerie silence on the radio. There's no one in the air. We're talking among ourselves, the fighter pilots on our radios. "I wonder if we're going to Canada?" A lot of "Man, this is fucked up." I'm also talking the guys through what happens if we have to shoot someone down. The world's watching, let's be by the book and let's do everything we can to protect the president. We know this would be a plum target, but we also figure no one would expect Air Force One right now to be flying north over Kansas.

Ari Fleischer, press secretary, White House: There was no live television. It put us in a very different spot than most Americans that day. People around the world were riveted to their television sets. We had it intermittently on Air Force One. We had it in Barksdale at the base commander's office. But there's no email on Air Force One back then. When you're in the air, you're cut off.

Eric Draper, presidential photographer: Everyone was starving for information. We couldn't hear anything unless the plane was flying over a major city.

Ellen Eckert, stenographer, White House: The plane is like *The Twilight Zone.* There's no one on board anymore. The staff cabin is empty, the guest cabin is empty. That's when it was really coming apart for me. I saw one of the agents was standing in the hallway, and I went up to him, "So this is the safest place to be? This is Air Force One, right?" He said, "We might as well have a big red X on the bottom of this plane. We're the only plane in the sky." That was scary. I went into the bathroom and used one of those Air Force One notepads to write a letter to my family — six siblings and two parents. *They're never going to see this, it's going to burn up in a fiery inferno.* One of the flight attendants opened the door and comforted me and gave me a washcloth to wipe. "We've got this. We're all together."

Maj. Scott "Hooter" Crogg: Fifteen minutes after we tanked up, we saw Air Force One start to descend. I did the math and figured out they were probably headed to Offutt. Well, now we had a full tank of gas. You can't land like that in a small plane, so we were doing afterburner 360s at 7,000 feet to burn off enough gas to land.

Mike Morell, presidential briefer, Central Intelligence Agency: On the way from Barksdale to Offutt, the president asked to see me alone — it was just me, him, and Andy Card. He asked me, "Michael, who did this?" I explained that I didn't have any actual intelligence, so what you're going to get is my best guess. He was really focused and said, "I understand, get on with it." I said that there were two countries capable of carrying out an attack like this, Iran and Iraq. But I believed both would have everything to lose and nothing to gain from the attack. When all was said and done, the trail would lead to Osama bin Laden. I told him, "I'd bet my children's future on that."

AFTERNOON IN SHANKSVILLE

"A LARGE, SMOLDERING HOLE
IN THE GROUND"

In Shanksville, rescuers quickly realized there was nothing to rescue. In their place, hundreds of state troopers and scores of investigators from the FBI, FAA, National Transportation Safety Board, and other agencies moved in to secure the scene of the attack and begin examining the wreckage. They knew they'd be there for a while.

Andrea Dammann, special agent, Evidence Response Team, FBI: That first day it was pretty much looking at the site, seeing what had happened, and trying to figure out what resources we needed to bring in.

Tony James, investigator, FAA: I recognized part of the landing gear and part of the engines. The FBI said, "Well, what we'd like to do is recover the cockpit." I said, "You'll never find the cockpit. You'll never find the people because they, they vaporize and go away because this airplane hit really hard."

Wells Morrison, supervisory special agent, FBI: We recovered a number of items of evidentiary, significant evidentiary value at our crash site. Unlike the World Trade Center and the Pentagon, we didn't have the tons and tons of debris on top of our aircraft, so we were able to recover things. We recovered items that we believe were used as weapons — small knives and things of that nature — from our crash site.

Sgt. Patrick Madigan, commander, Somerset Station, Pennsylvania State Police: This site was one of the richest, as far as evidence, of the planes that crashed on September 11th.

Wells Morrison: The first item — this is interesting — with all the utter devastation that occurred, the first significant item of evidentiary value was recovered by a state trooper standing post the evening of 9/11. It was the wallet of one of the hijackers, and it was intact, lying on the top of the ground. We also recovered what basically was a "to do" list from one of the hijackers. It was very productive.

Sgt. Denise Miller, Indian Lake Police Department: We watched for persons that were still trying to get into the area to get souvenirs. It was comical: we saw, as we were sitting in the field, a herd of sheep following something — the sheep were following people walking through the field to get to the site. We turned them back around.

T. Michael Lauffer, trooper, Pennsylvania State Police: We arrested a couple people that were coming in. Everyone wanted to see what was going on, I guess. They actually had mail from the flight, and they were carrying it out through the woods. We rounded them up. I remember it was a guy and a girl.

Braden Shober, firefighter, Shanksville Volunteer Fire Company: As things progressed there were remnants of little brush fires, spot fires that would flare up now and then. Because they didn't want all the equipment out and disturbing the scene, one would flare up and they'd have to send a crew of a couple guys in with Indian tanks that you wear on your back and spray water, take a rake, and knock these down.

Rick King, assistant chief, Shanksville Volunteer Fire Company: A good five, six hours afterwards — I hadn't been off the crash site that whole time, anywhere — we started to go out to the road. I saw satellite trucks everywhere.

Lt. Robert Weaver, Pennsylvania State Police: That first eight, 10 hours, went by like minutes. Before you knew it, we had a small city up there in an old mining company, and we had hundreds of people.

Tom Ridge, governor of Pennsylvania: I was enjoying a long weekend away from Harrisburg, Pennsylvania, in my home community of Erie, Pennsylvania. After word of the attacks, I had to immediately get to Shanksville. A couple of us, my staff and members of the state police detail, boarded an old army Chinook helicopter. As we were flying to Shanksville, there wasn't much conversation. I do remember that it was very silent, very solemn, everyone deep in their own thoughts. As we descended into the area, I expected to see what I had — and what Americans had unfortunately seen — during the coverage of commercial aviation accidents: a field littered with significant pieces of the airplane, the fuselage, the tail, the engine, the wings. I'll never forget my shock — my amazement — at seeing what was basically a large, smoldering hole in the ground.

Rick King: A big, two-winged Chinook helicopter came flying toward us, and then came over top the crash site. You could see, plain as day, a guy leaning out the window in a white shirt, and it was Governor Tom Ridge.

Sgt. Patrick Madigan: Governor Ridge flew in and landed at the site. He wanted a briefing, what was going on at that time, and I gave him what information I had, which was really limited at that time. I remember him making the statement that anything we needed to do our job, he'd make sure that was provided for us. I recall him being very, very concerned and very determined.

William Baker, 911 addressing specialist and deputy director, Emergency Management Agency, Somerset County: I remember Governor Ridge standing right across the table from me, and he said, "Obviously this is related to the other incidents."

Jere Longman, reporter, *New York Times*: They had a staging area in a cornfield where Governor Ridge had a press conference.

Rick Earle, reporter, WPXI-TV, Pittsburgh: Tom Ridge came in there and he stole a line from Lincoln's Gettysburg Address about people won't remember what we say here, but they'll never forget what these people did here.

Steve Aaron, deputy communications director for Governor Tom Ridge: The thing that most stands out to me that day was the flight home. You get back on the helicopter, and the rear of the helicopter is open, and so the whole way home is this beautiful sunset. It was a gorgeous day. We can't talk to each other because of the helicopter noise, so we're all sitting there with our thoughts.

AT MOUNT WEATHER

"THIS IS WHAT WE HAVE FOR THE NUCLEAR WINTER"

The day's attacks activated a system aimed at preserving the continuity of government of the United States, a classified system never before used. Within hours, helicopters from the air force's 1st Helicopter Squadron scooped up congressional leaders from the West Lawn of the Capitol and from Andrews Air Force Base and flew them to a mountain bunker originally built for the Cold War. Over the course of the day, other staff and personnel also flowed out to that "undisclosed location," later revealed to be Mount Weather, in Berryville, Virginia, 80 minutes west of Washington, while other officials were evacuated to Raven Rock, another massive mountain bunker intended to serve as the backup Pentagon and built in Waynesboro, Pennsylvania, near Camp David.

Rep. Dennis Hastert (R-Illinois), House Speaker: I was heading out to Andrews Air Force Base. I finally talked to the vice president. He was still in the White House. He said he brought all the planes down. After having a discussion with the vice president, he said, "You're going to an undisclosed location." Next thing, I was in a helicopter, flying over the south side of Washington. We flew over Reagan National Airport, and there's nothing moving on the tarmac. I looked out the other side of the helicopter and there were flames pouring out of the Pentagon building and blue-black smoke.

Sen. Tom Daschle (D-South Dakota), Senate Majority Leader: I was called and told that the decision had been made to evacuate to this undisclosed location. I could bring one staff person, Laura Petrou.

Laura Petrou, staff director for Senate Majority Leader Tom Daschle (D-South Dakota): We were told to report to the West Lawn of the Capitol. The helicopter was right there, with several armored vehicles around. I was already in the helicopter or about to get in, when somebody looked at me and said, "You have clearance, right?" I said, "No." They said, "Well, doesn't matter."

Brian Gunderson, chief of staff for House Majority Leader Richard Armey (R-Texas): We all piled into this helicopter, and the safety instructions were shouted at us over the helicopter's engine.

Laura Petrou: I remember thinking, *I have no idea where we're going or how long we're going to be there.*

Rep. Dennis Hastert: I ended up at an undisclosed location. Sen. Lott was there, as was Sen. Daschle and Dick Gephardt, the minority leader, other members of the leadership.

Brian Gunderson: We went deep in the countryside and then landed at the undisclosed location. We got out, and this gentleman walks up to the helicopter who I gather was the mayor of this facility. He said something very chipper, something along the lines of "Welcome to — ," and the name of this place. I remember being impressed that even though it's this guy's job to be ready for an event like this, he was, in fact, ready, and very calm about it. This day starts like any other, and next thing you know, he's got all these government officials descending on him in these Huey helicopters.

Laura Petrou: There's a web of people within the government who take over. They tell you what to do, and you do what they say.

Brian Gunderson: There were these guys standing in the landing zone wearing their gray urban combat uniforms, holding their M-16s.

Laura Petrou: They split our group up and put us in the cars. It was pretty odd driving into this underground place.

Sen. Tom Daschle: It's a very stark place. Rooms that are very nondescript — white walls, very basic chairs and tables.

Laura Petrou: It was very spartan. It was basically different shades of gray everywhere. We were taken through some tunnels and eventually into a room filled with cubicles, desks.

Steve Elmendorf, chief of staff for House Minority Leader Richard Gephardt (D-Missouri): There was a group of people there who had been staffing that location who had been waiting since the Cold War for somebody to show up.

John Feehery, press secretary to Speaker Dennis Hastert (R-Illinois): It was a sense of wonderment that "Oh, boy, so this is what we have for the nuclear winter."

Brian Gunderson: There were obviously preparations for us to stay for a long while if we had to. As we went through it, we crossed through one room that had a set of law books, a set of the U.S. Code, in case we had to do any legislating while we were there.

Sen. Tom Daschle: We were put on a speakerphone with the president — I think the president first, then the vice president second — to talk about circumstances. Basically, they recounted their own experiences, where they were, what they knew from intelligence briefings they had been given.

Brian Gunderson: They made some snacks available — I remember that there were a few bags of Cheetos or Doritos, and a few sodas that had been cracked open — and we all sat around and looked at the TV screen, and watched the tape of the Towers coming down. That's where we stayed for several hours.

Steve Elmendorf: While we were at the secure location, the main thing that struck me was our main source of information was CNN — still. We sat in a room — the top leaders of the House and the Senate together — and we watched CNN. Cheney called several times and briefed people, but I don't remember receiving any information that was any different from what I was watching on TV.

John Feehery: There was this sense of shock. There was also a sense of confusion. The members felt very nervous. The leadership on both sides — the House and Senate — were isolated from the rest of their members, and that's not where you want to be.

Laura Petrou: They didn't feel good about being separated from their colleagues and their families. Almost from the moment they got there, they wanted to go back.

Steve Elmendorf: One of the phone calls with Cheney, Don Nickles, who was the Senate Republican whip at the time, suggested that we ought to leave. He was agitated, asking, "Why are we all here? The situation is clear. We need to get back." Cheney was clearly annoyed by this, and his voice came out of the speakerphone in the middle of the table and said, "Don, we control the helicopters. We'll decide when you leave."

Brian Gunderson: I got calls from other leadership staff that were still at the Capitol Police headquarters, with other members of Congress. They basically were calling up saying, "Well, the mood's actually pretty ugly here."

John Feehery: One member of Congress told the Speaker that he thought he was a coward for not coming back. It was decided that we were going to have a press conference on the Capitol steps to show the American people that we were not going to let the terrorists win.

Brian Gunderson: At that point, all civilian air traffic had been grounded, so there were no nonmilitary aircraft flying over U.S. airspace. There was a feeling that the security situation had stabilized. That there was some confidence that there weren't going to be follow-on attacks, at least not immediately, and so that it was safe to go back. Eventually the decision was made that, yes, it's time. We can get back in the helicopters.

John Feehery: I called one of my assistants, Paige Ralston, who was back in the Capitol Police [building], and she helped organize this press conference on the Capitol steps. Trent Lott wanted it only to be the leadership involved. I made the call that we were going to have all the members there.

Rep. Dennis Hastert: We didn't know what was facing us but we knew that there was a lot of legislative things that we had to do. We got the word that the president was going to come back and land in Washington at 6:00. We figured we'd come in right behind the president.

AT GROUND ZERO

"WE'RE IN A SURVIVAL MODE"

As some semblance of organization came to the carnage at the World Trade Center — a suddenly hallowed space that in the days ahead would first be called "The Pile" and then "Ground Zero" — agony-filled rescuers worked determinedly to find survivors.

William Jimeno, officer, PAPD: Believe it or not, someone did find us. Probably within an hour after Dominick passing, someone came above the hole and said, "Who's down there?" I yelled, "Jimeno, PAPD!" I said, "We've got officers down." The voice left us. It was very, very frustrating, and I was very mad, and I said to Sarge, "How could they leave us?" Sergeant McLoughlin says, "We don't know what's happening up there, this person could be injured, this person could be delusional, you've got to keep focused." I said, "Sarge, I'm in a lot of pain. I'm in an extreme amount of pain." Sergeant McLoughlin said, "You gotta hold on."

584

Det. Steven Stefanakos, Emergency Service Unit, Truck 10, NYPD: They asked all members of the Emergency Service Unit who were there to mobilize — ironically — at the police memorial in Battery Park City. There's 10 Emergency Service squads throughout the city, we lined up in those 10 — one through 10 — right by the memorial. That's when we started to realize who was actually missing.

Sal Cassano, assistant chief, FDNY: I was taken to the hospital — a few broken ribs and some bumps and bruises — but I was cleared. I called for someone to take me back to headquarters and started to work in the Operational Center, handling phone calls, trying to put together a list of the people that were missing, the companies that were missing, and see where we were. We were trying to wrap our arms around this.

Dan Nigro, chief of operations, FDNY: We put out fires in the streets where all the cars were burning. We put out fires in some buildings as the day went on, but we realized we did not have enough water and time to put out Building Seven of the World Trade Center. I said, "After what happened, let's make a collapse zone around this building."

Scott Strauss, officer, Emergency Service Unit, Truck 1, NYPD: We came around the corner from City Hall Park, and we saw one of our Emergency Service vehicles on fire. It was like a movie. It's like, "No! This is Lower Manhattan — this doesn't happen in Lower Manhattan. It happens in the Middle East somewhere."

Lt. Michael Michelsen, Wilton (Connecticut) Fire Department: As they were pulling the trucks out of the wreckage that first day, starting to move things, you're looking at a fire truck — which most people view as incredibly strong and incredibly indestructible — these things were broken like little kids' toys. It was like they were made out of papier-mâché and then stepped on.

Scott Strauss: We were finding plenty of body parts, but we weren't finding anybody who was rescuable. We kept doing that all day long.

Dan Nigro: At that point, we were trying to find anybody, anybody we could rescue.

William Jimeno: We kept going back and forth, trying to keep each other going. I would yell at the sergeant if I heard him fading away; he would yell at me if I was fading away. All I could do was hope, and pray, and that's something we did. We prayed together, at one point. McLoughlin said, "I don't even know your first name." I said, "Will." He said, "Mine's John."

Still trapped inside the devastated but miraculously intact Stairwell B of the North Tower, a handful of surviving FDNY firefighters hoped their colleagues outside would find them.

Pasquale Buzzelli, engineer, Port Authority, North Tower: The firemen who were in Stairway B also, they were below me. They were like the second or third floor, I believe, and they were in more of a cocoon — part of the building that didn't collapse. I was on the 22nd floor, and I basically fell to what was the height of the rubble, which — if the building was still standing — it would have been the fourth floor. I basically fell 18 floors. I ended up maybe about 75 yards to the north. As it crumbled, the stair didn't stay exactly center.

I was on a pile of rubble, a little ledge, with my feet dangling from my knees down. I started calling out for people that I was with, to see if anyone was around me. I started calling out for help. I didn't see anyone for a while. An hour went by, and I was still calling out for help.

Lt. Mickey Kross, Engine 16, FDNY: I couldn't move too much, so I started pushing. Nothing was giving. I pushed over my head, and the debris started to move. I made a little hole for myself. I crawled out. I had a beam over me. I'm sitting on the beam and now I'm thinking: *What do I do now?* Now I'm in the staircase proper.

Capt. Jay Jonas, Ladder 6, FDNY: We got about half-a-landing down and the word came from downstairs: "We can't get out from down here." We're trying to figure out what happened. We're alive. We're coughing, gagging, we have very limited visibility. I can see walls of twisted steel around us. We're in a stairway that's intact but filled with debris. There are no lights.

Lt. Mickey Kross: I started hearing noises. I started hearing moaning, and guys were starting to communicate, yell out. These were the guys that I was trapped with. They were calling out, "Who's there? You guys all right?" I realized I wasn't alone. When you find out you're with other people, it makes you feel a lot better.

Capt. Jay Jonas: I got a Mayday message from Lt. Mike Warchola from Ladder 5, who we saw on the 12th floor, that he was trapped on the 12th floor in the B Stairway, and he's hurt badly. I was the highest one on the stairway so I started climbing the stairway, trying to move debris. He transmits a second

Mayday, and he's a little more distraught the second time. I'm trying to move the debris around, and I can't move it. It's too heavy. The third Mayday came in, and he was even more distraught than the previous time. I get on the radio and say, "I'm sorry, Mike. I can't help you." That was the last we heard of him. In reality, we found out later that the 12th floor didn't exist, that his "Mayday" was coming from the rubble.

Lt. Mickey Kross: I jumped onto the other staircase. Then I crawled up a few steps, and the other guys were there — Lt. Jim McQueen from 39 Engine, Chief Richie Picciotto, a couple of the other fellows. There were about six people under the landing.

Capt. Jay Jonas: We tried to get ourselves out and we couldn't figure out a way. I finally gave out my own Mayday message: "Mayday. Mayday, Mayday. This is the officer of Ladder Company 6. We're in the B Stairway and we're trapped." The first man to answer my Mayday was Deputy Chief Tom Haring, a friend. He said, "Okay. I got you recorded. Guys will be coming to get you."

Dan Nigro: When I heard the operation going on for Ladder 6 I thought, *They made a mistake.* I said, "You can't be rescuing anybody in the North Tower, the North

Tower is gone." I did not think it at all possible that anyone could be in that building and be alive.

Capt. Joe Downey, Squad Company 18, FDNY: When they located the guys in the stairwell, it was a mad rush trying to get those people out, to identify where they were.

Capt. Jay Jonas: We gave them — all these guys who came from all the firehouses in the outer boroughs — we gave them a focal point. This is, *Wow! The Six is trapped! Go get 'em!* That was the mission. One of the next people that came on the radio was Nick Visconti, a deputy chief. Nick came to my wedding. I said, "Wow! Nick's here! Nick's running my rescue!" He would ask me very strategic questions. He asked me about how I got into the building. I said, "We came in off of West Street. We walked through the glass doors. We made a right and a left and the B Stairway's your first left. You can't miss it."

I spoke to Nick a few days later, and he said when he asked me that he was surrounded by about 100 firemen who were ready to go. When I said, "We walked through the glass doors," there was a collective sigh because there wasn't a piece of glass intact for about 20 blocks.

Lt. Mickey Kross: We tried to force the door

off the stairway. They used the ax and the Halligan — it's like a pry bar — and they opened the door, but there was a wall of debris behind it.

Capt. Jay Jonas: I'm starting to get radio messages. One was from my neighbor, Cliff Stabner. "This is Rescue 3 to Ladder 6, Capt. Jay Jonas. This is Cliff. I'm coming to get you. Where are you?" I was very good friends with Cliff. He would get me choked up every time I would talk to him on the radio, because he would end every radio transmission by saying, "I'm coming for you, brother. I'm coming for you."

Lt. Mickey Kross: Now I figured at least they knew where we were. I didn't realize that everything was gone; it was a big pile of debris.

Capt. Jay Jonas: Another person that got on the radio was Bill Blanche, a chief over here in the First Battalion. I had worked with him — he was the only one that gave me a little glimpse into how bad it was going to be. He says, "This is going to take a real long time. It's really bad out here." I had come to the realization that we might be here for a few days.

Lt. Mickey Kross: They started searching

for us maybe an hour, two hours, three hours. I really lost track of the time.

Capt. Jay Jonas: We also had a chief that was below us, below the guys from Engine 39, named Richard Prunty. He was beyond the point that there was a huge area of debris. Every time I gave our location, he would get on the radio and say, "Don't forget about Battalion 2." "Yes, we have Battalion 2."

Lt. Mickey Kross: He was about 20 feet below us and he was trapped up to his chest in debris, and he was losing consciousness. I remember we were talking to him on the radio and telling him to hang in there. The last thing he said was, "Tell my wife and kids I love them," and that was it.

Capt. Jay Jonas: At one point during our entrapment after the collapse, we had an explosion that shook the area. One of my firemen from Ladder 6, Tommy Falco, looked up at me. He says, "Hey, Cap. What do we do now?" I looked at him and I says, "I don't know. I'm making this up as I go along."

The two sons of Ray Downey, FDNY's head of special operations, both firefighters, searched carefully for their father, reconstructing his movements amid the chaos following the twin collapses.

Lt. Chuck Downey, FDNY: There were so many guys looking to help out, but there was so much to cover. Voids all over the place. Everybody was crawling, whatever you could move to lift up. It's a tremendous amount of square area to cover.

Capt. Joe Downey, Squad Company 18, FDNY: Right from the start, we were trying to locate our father. Our agenda was to find out where he was and where he could possibly have survived. Right from the beginning, we were asking questions. He survived the first building, and he went back in.

Lt. Chuck Downey: There were quite a few people that saw him at the command post, saw him across West Street.

Capt. Joe Downey: As it was clearing — before it even cleared — they said he was the first one back out on the radio trying to get everybody out of the North Tower.

Lt. Chuck Downey: He turned people away. As he came out, he was, a couple of eyewitness reports said, all white — brushing stuff off his face, radioing people to get out of the

North Tower and directing others to head north on West Street.

Capt. Joe Downey: We know where he was when the second building came down. He was helping this gentleman coming out of the Marriott. Two of our firefighters were trapped in the Marriott when the first building came down, in the hotel lobby. They were working their way out. He saw the guys coming out. Him and Chief Stack — Larry Stack — stayed there with a heavyset gentleman that they couldn't move. It was the two chiefs and this civilian. I feel he knew he wasn't going to come out, and he made that conscious decision on doing what he had to do. He probably couldn't have lived with himself — the type of person that he is — if he did go away from the building when his guys were still in the building. He could have easily walked to West Street like everybody else. He couldn't leave that gentleman, and he couldn't leave his companies up in the North Tower.

Lt. Chuck Downey: He made a statement to FDNY Capt. Al Fuentes right when the South Tower came down: "There were a lot of good men in that building."

Capt. Joe Downey: I think it was almost a hundred guys from just his Special Operations Command that died. Special Operations Command includes the five rescue companies, seven squad companies, the Hazmat Unit. The only one of his companies that didn't get there was Squad 270. Every other company that was there was wiped out.

Pasquale Buzzelli, engineer, Port Authority, North Tower: There were some firemen searching the rubble. They were actually looking for those firemen with Josephine Harris, trapped in the stairwell, but they stumbled across me. When I saw the first fireman — I believe it was Mike Morabito — I said, "Hey! Help! I'm up here!" He said, "What do you need?" I was taken aback. I said, "I'm stuck. I can't get down." He's like, "Oh, all right. We'll get to you in a minute."

I'm like, "Okay." He said, "You need a rope or something?" I said, "Whatever you need me to do, just tell me." He looked at me again. He said, "Who are you with?" Because I had a blue shirt on, black pants, he thought I was another fireman, searching the rubble that got stuck. I was like, "I was in the building. It collapsed." I said, "I'm stuck here. I can't get down." He said, "Holy shit, guys! We got a survivor!" He got on the radio and then he goes, "Hold on! We'll get to you!"

Louise Buzzelli, Riverdale, New Jersey, and wife of Pasquale Buzzelli, Port Authority, North Tower: People started coming over to the house and the phone kept ringing and ringing and ringing. I didn't want to talk to anyone unless it was him on the other end.

Pasquale Buzzelli: I was about 15 feet up on the edge of a cliff. For a while they were looking up at me, like, *I don't know how we're going to get him down from there.* Jimmy Kiesling, who was part of their Special Ops and trained for that, luckily he was with them. He carried a bunch of ropes with him. I saw him make his way around me. He climbed around and up this mountain of debris, found his way, climbed down to me, and jumped in right behind me. He goes, "All right, big guy. We're going to get you down."

Louise Buzzelli: By the time Pasquale's mom and my father came — they lived in Jersey City — it was about 1:30 in the afternoon. The worst thing for me was to see her walk through the door and see me with this big belly. She screamed and fell apart. She grabbed on to me, and she was saying, "My son!" She said, "This baby's got to have a father! This baby's got to have a father!"

Pasquale Buzzelli: He was tugging on stuff

and looking at things. He finally found this pipe — it might have been the standpipe that used to run through the stairs — all mangled. He did a couple of loops with the rope, and he goes, "Throw yourself off the ledge, and I'll lower you down." I fell a couple of feet, then the rope got taut, and it grabbed me. I remember spinning a little bit. Little by little, he lowered me down.

Capt. Jay Jonas: It was soon after I spoke to Billy Blanche, about him saying "It's really bad out here," that a ray of light hit the stairway. It was a beam of light, like a pencil coming down. I could see a little sliver of blue sky. I looked down at the guys: "Guys, there used to be 106 floors over our heads and now I can see sunshine." I says, "This may not be as bad as we thought it was."

Lt. Mickey Kross: It was clearly sunlight. It was all dirty and full of debris. It looked like pepper was floating around in it, but it was sunlight! I'm amazed. A 106-story building above us and I'm looking up at the sun!

Capt. Jay Jonas: Things started to pick up. We had a little bit better visibility. We could look around. We could see all the areas where we would possibly get out. We thought that we may have been buried under mounds of debris, maybe several stories high. Now we realized we are on the top of the mountain. We found an area where we could breach a wall and we did. We could see outside.

Lt. Mickey Kross: We decided to go one at a time and try to climb out. We climbed up, got to the opening, and we started squeezing our way out.

Capt. Jay Jonas: We looked out initially, and we could see there's all kinds of buildings on fire. We could see smoke. We could see twisted rubble all around. At this time, firefighter Rich Picciotto wanted out of the stairway. I said, "Wait." Every decision that I was making was on the side of safety. I says, "Look. We've lived to this point. Let's be careful here before we do anything." We waited a little while longer, and then we could see a fireman in the distance. "It's all right. Now we can go." We had our lifesaving rope with us. It's a 150-foot-long rope in a bag. We rigged it up so we could lower Rich Picciotto out. He made contact with the fireman we saw in the distance, who was a fireman from Ladder 43. We start sending people out.

Lt. Mickey Kross: Just at that point, a couple of firefighters from the outside had made it to that opening and they helped us come out. They set up a rope because there was nothing to hold on to — it wasn't like you were coming out on a flat surface. You were coming out on twisted beams, and we were high, maybe about 20 feet in the air.

Capt. Jay Jonas: I knew we had people below us. I didn't know who they were. It wasn't until they came up that I knew who they were. That's when I saw Mickey Kross. I said, "Oh, I didn't realize it was you." Mickey came out, and Bobby Bacon from Engine 39. The rest of the guys from Engine 39, it took them a bit longer to get out. We still had Josephine Harris with us. I told one of the rescuers about Lieutenant Warchola in Ladder 5. I said, "They're on the 12th floor." He looked at me like this. I said, "Why the look?" He said, "You'll find out." There was no 12th floor.

Lt. Mickey Kross: I got to a point where I was looking down the pile, and I saw firefighters coming up. I knew they were fresh troops — they weren't covered in the dust. I had a bloody nose, and I was totally encased in this dust. I must have been some sight. I saw the guys coming up — it turned out to be guys from my firehouse. I saw my captain, and he said, "Mickey, you're alive?" They all thought I was dead.

Capt. Jay Jonas: Going across the rubble field we crossed between the North Tower and the smaller buildings. The New York office for the Secret Service, they had their ammunition depot inside the World Trade Center. Munitions started going off as we were crossing, and it almost sounded like a war zone. In addition to everything else that was going on, we could hear bullets going off. We're thinking, *This is bad.*

Scott Strauss, officer, Emergency Service Unit, Truck 1, NYPD: While we we're digging into one of these crevices, we heard gunfire. Not all of us had radios, so we weren't sure what was going on. We heard fighter jets flying overhead. Now everybody had the luxury — and I know it's not the best word to use — but they had the luxury of watching this on TV. We were in it. They had news commentators guessing or trying to explain what's happening. We were in the middle of this, and we were hearing gunfire. We were thinking whoever attacked us is now in a ground fight — they're coming in and they're going to shoot the place up and kill many more people.

William Jimeno, officer, PAPD: As the evening progressed, we heard more gunfire, and we didn't know what it was. Now today we know the ammunition was blowing off. I said, "Sarge, we must be in an ongoing gun battle with the terrorists."

Capt. Jay Jonas: They were getting ready to whisk me away to an ambulance, and I says, "Wait a minute — where's the command post?" They said, "Forget about the command post. We got to take care of you." I said, "No, you don't understand. There had to be hundreds of people looking for us." I said, "If somebody gets hurt now, I don't know if I can live with that."

The command post was a fire department pumper that was still hooked up to a hydrant. Chief [Pete] Hayden was on top, along with Chief [James] DiDomenico. They were standing on top of the pumper, so they could look out across the debris field. There had to be a couple hundred firemen surrounding the pumper. It was really quite a sight to see. I finally got Chief Hayden's attention, and I gave him a salute, and I started crying. He looked down, and he started crying too. He said, "Jay, it's good to see you." I says, "It's good to be here."

Lt. Mickey Kross: There was a table out there on West Street, and a chief sitting at it — like a picnic table. That was the command post for that area — that's all they had. I walked up to him and he said to me, "Give me your riding list." Your riding list is what you carry with everybody's name that's working. When you start every tour, you fill it out with a pen and a piece of carbon paper. It's very old-fashioned. You put your name, you put the company name, the date, the tour, battalion, division, officer, and underneath is the chauffeur — that was Ronnie Sifu that day — and who was working: Tim Marmion, Paul Lee, and Pete Fallucca. The original, it's clipped onto the engine, and the carbon goes in your pocket.

I gave it to him, and he looked at it. He said, "I have your name on the list." They had me listed as "missing, presumed dead." I said, "No, I'm here. Take my name off that list." They had a list like over 400 names. At this point, I remember looking at my watch, and it was 10 after 2:00 p.m.

Capt. Jay Jonas: I had one guy I know, Jimmy Riches, come up to me. He sat next to me at the ambulance. He said, "Jay, I was listening to your radio transmissions. That was unbelievable." He said, "Did you see Engine 4 in your travels?" I'm thinking to myself, *Jeez. Where's he going with this Engine 4?* I said, "No, I didn't see Engine 4." He said, "Oh." He says, "My son was working today." It hit me. I understood the question. Then I came to the realization: *Oh, my God! I wonder how many sons are working today?*

Pasquale Buzzelli: I stood up and right away I felt this, this lightning bolt, the shock

602

go through me. I had broken my foot. The firefighter said, "We have a ways to go. Can you make it?" I'm like, "Yeah. I want out of here." We started climbing and walking. There was one fireman in front of me, one behind me. They tied a rope off, and they each held one [end] in case I fell. I made it probably halfway, maybe three-quarters of the way. The pain in my foot from walking on it, I was sweating — I must have turned pale — so I said, "Guys," I said, "I need a breather. I need to sit for a couple of minutes."

They looked at me. They said, "We'll handle it from here. You relax. We got it." They got on their radios, and they formed a huge line of firemen over the debris. They brought a plastic gurney over, and they strapped me into it, and they basically dragged me over the rubble out to the west side, where they placed me in an ambulance.

When they put me in the ambulance, the paramedic — first thing — said, "All right, so what hurts?" I was like, "Before we get to that, I need a phone." I said, "My wife is home. She's seven-and-a-half-months pregnant. She knows I didn't get out of the building." I called my house, and my wife actually answered the phone.

Louise Buzzelli: It was about 3:30 that afternoon, and I happened to walk by the phone — because at that point, everybody else was answering the phone and saying, "No, she hasn't heard from him. We haven't heard anything. We'll call if anything happens." I walked by the kitchen, the phone was there, and I picked it up. I heard his voice on the other end.

Pasquale Buzzelli: I said, "Louise, it's me, Pasquale." She gasped, "Oh, my God, Pasquale! Pasquale! Oh, my God! You're okay!" I heard this huge uproar in the house.

Louise Buzzelli: He said, "I'm in an ambulance right now." He said, "I'm borrowing one of the emergency workers' cell phones to call you. I lost my phone, and I'm on the way down to Saint Vincent's Hospital. They're going to treat me down there." I was like, "Are you okay? What happened? Are you all right?"

Pasquale Buzzelli: I said, "I don't know how, but I'm alive. I wanted to tell you."

Louise Buzzelli: I couldn't believe the day that had happened from 8:30 in the morning until 3:30 that afternoon — a total 180. To know that he was alive, that I still had him and that my daughter and my future children would have a father, it was a blessing. Nothing else really mattered.

As the afternoon hours passed and rescue efforts solidified above ground, Will Jimeno and the other Port Authority officers trapped under the South Tower lost hope that they'd be found, as did Genelle Guzman, buried not far from where her coworker Pasquale Buzzelli had been rescued.

Genelle Guzman, office assistant, Port Authority, North Tower: I heard the Motorolas — the walkie-talkies — going off and you could hear movements, probably trucks. I could hear noises, but didn't hear anybody's voice. Nobody calling out. I called out a couple of times. I called out for help. I was getting breathless and I was going to shut my eyes and hope not to get up.

William Jimeno, officer, PAPD: Things were looking very bleak. I wanted to go to sleep, and not wake up. I remember being able to take out of my left pocket a card and my pen. My pen wasn't working really good — because of the debris — but I was able to etch into the card, *Allison I love you.* I put it back in there, hoping that they would find it if they found my body, because at this point I didn't think we were getting out of there.

Genelle Guzman: I was preparing myself to die. I thought about my mom and my family. I said, "I'm still breathing, I'm alive, and I need to do something." I need to pray. I said to myself, "God, do me a favor — if I have to die under the rubble, let my family find my body so we can have a burial." Then I asked for another favor from the Lord, I said, "If I have to die, at least let them get me out of here and see my daughter for one more time. If I make it to the hospital, I'll at least see my daughter for one more time." I'd shut my eyes again, wake up, and realize I was still stuck in this building. I said, "God, do me one more favor. I don't want to die. I want to live. I want to be able to see my daughter and my family." I asked God for a miracle. I asked him to save me. I kept begging the Lord for a second chance. I kept begging him.

At the Hospitals
"WAITING FOR THE INJURED"

Hospitals across New York City readied them-selves for massive casualties within minutes of the first attack, figuring that the large-scale destruction would surely result in thousands or even tens of thousands of injuries. Even farther away, up and down the East Coast, hospitals in cities like Boston prepared to receive overflow injuries and trauma cases. Throughout the day, injured office workers, Manhattan residents, and first responders did seek treatment, but the ar-riving patients only ever amounted to a trickle, not a flood. Doctors and nurses were left with the sinking realization that no patients meant no survivors.

Michael McAvoy, associate director, Bear Stearns, Brooklyn: I spent the rest of the day at the hospitals, at the firehouse, or at my friend's apartment in Greenwich Vil-lage. I looked over lists of people who were taken to various hospitals. No John McAvoy, my brother, no James Ladley, my friend who worked for Cantor Fitzgerald. You look at the list and try to will a name onto it.

Tracy Donahoo, transit officer, NYPD: I ended up, at some point, walking from my command to Saint Vincent's Hospital, 'cause they wanted me to get checked out 'cause I had blood coming out of my ears. I was a mess. When I got to Saint Vincent's, it was very creepy 'cause there was no one there. I expected so many people to be there, and I'd be waiting a long time to see a doctor. The doctors were very nonchalant when they saw me. They were waiting for the real bodies to come, the real people, and there was nobody there to come.

Harry Waizer, tax counsel, Cantor Fitzgerald, North Tower: I remember arriving at the hospital. I remember somebody asking me a few questions and I asked them to call Karen, my wife, and I gave them her phone number. I remember somebody saying, "We're going to have to intubate you." I said, "Do what you have to do." That's the very last thing I remember. I don't remember anything for about seven weeks.

Francine Kelly, registered nurse and nurse manager, Saint Vincent's Catholic Medical Center: I think we saw 350 to 450 patients within the first eight hours of 9/11.

We saw tremendous volumes of patients. We saw in those first couple hours some people who worked in the World Trade Center. We saw burns, shrapnel wounds, crush injuries, people in hypertensive crisis. Then as the day continued, then, we started to see rescue workers come in who were injured in their line of duty. Midafternoon, three or four o'clock, we were working nonstop. Then what happened, unfortunately, is all of a sudden things slowed down. That was very, very difficult for us, because you kept wanting to hear that ambulance siren.

Joe Esposito, chief of department, NYPD: They were waiting for the injured, and they never came.

David Norman, officer, Emergency Service Unit, Truck 1, NYPD: I had a scratched cornea. I was bleeding. I had burns on my legs. They brought us to Saint Vincent's Hospital. They cut all our clothes off. We're standing there pretty much naked out on Seventh Avenue, and then they gave us hospital gowns and brought us inside and triaged us at that point. They flushed my eye and some other stuff, and were able to remove some of the debris that was scratching my cornea. And then I got a patch.

Michael McAvoy: I walked back to Saint

Vincent's Hospital on Seventh Avenue. Maybe I should give blood? At the hospital, there were stretchers and gurneys and tons of nurses and doctors, but no new arriving patients.

John Cahill, senior policy adviser to Governor Pataki: We spent that day marshaling state resources for the response. We lined up so many doctors and blood donations, and the reality was, at the end of the day, very little of that was needed.

THE 9/11 GENERATION

"MOM, IS AMERICA GOING TO SURVIVE THIS?"

As the attacks that Tuesday morning unfolded and news spread across the country, it left the nation's children bewildered and confused — and imprinted on all of them, at all ages, lasting memories.

Babies

Sheryl Meyer, parent, Tulsa, Oklahoma: My son was going to turn one month old on the 12th. I had planned to take him out for his first walk in the stroller — it was very hot still in Oklahoma — and I woke up to a voice mail from my brother, who simply said, "Turn on the TV." I sat in shock all morning and, eventually, decided to go out on the walk anyway. I remember such a surreal feeling every time a plane would fly over, as many rerouted flights did until air traffic was suspended. I also remember looking at my son and thinking how one day, he would know about these horrific events. I wish he didn't have to know such evil exists.

611

Age 2

Jenna Greene, parent, Maryland: I was running late, driving my two-year-old son to daycare a block from the White House. We listened to little kid songs like "Wheels on the Bus" during the entire drive — I had no idea what was happening, except I heard a lot of sirens. The director of the daycare met us at the front door, looking frantic. "Go home," she said. "Turn around right now and go home. It's not safe here." I listened to WTOP radio on the drive back, and my son cried and cried — in part because we weren't listening to "Wheels on the Bus," but also because even he could tell something very bad had happened.

Age 3

Beau Garner, Michigan: My only memory is my mom standing in front of the TV watching the news. I don't remember seeing the Towers fall or seeing President Bush address the nation. The only thing I remember is how it affected my mother. The significance of the moment was somehow passed on to me regardless of my lack of comprehension; 9/11 was not just an early memory for me, it's my earliest memory. Just a flash.

Age 5 / Kindergarten

Lachlan Francis, Vermont: 9/11 is the first memory of my life. I remember a clearly distraught Mrs. Blanchard telling us that we would be going home early for the day. My daycare provider picked me and other students up in her minivan and brought us back to her house. This was the only day of daycare that we were ever allowed to watch television. My daycare provider watched the film of planes crashing into the Towers on loop as she frantically tried to call her daughter, who lived in Manhattan. The other students and I, clueless to the seriousness and tragedy of what we were watching, nonetheless sat transfixed in front of the couch, watching the video of planes crashing into the Twin Towers over and over and over again.

Blake Richardson, Connecticut: My mom said as soon as she saw on the news that the first plane crashed, she drove to school to pick up my siblings and me. Later, she explained to me that a plane crashed into the World Trade Center, and I had absolutely no idea what that meant. The next morning, I sat down in a circle on the rug with my kindergarten class, and we all talked about what happened. I remember being confused because my mom said "the World Trade Center" and my teacher said "the Twin Towers," and I thought they were two separate buildings. I didn't know about the other planes until maybe a year or so later. Now, I can't imagine how terrifying that must've been for my teacher — to have to explain something so horrific to a room full of five-year-olds.

Jing Qu, Illinois: My mom worked at one of the high-rise buildings closest to the Sears Tower in Chicago. The school got the students home early, but I did not know why at the time. I remember my mom was home earlier than usual, too. She gave me a bath and asked me, "Do you know what happened?" She then told me that there was a horrible accident at the World Trade Center in New York City, a place we had visited a few months before. Terrorism and patriotism were not yet ideas that I understood. My mother, along with all the other workers in the tallest buildings in Chicago, were asked to evacuate.

Age 6 / First Grade

Kelly Yeo, California: The sky was gray as my babysitter woke me up and told me, "You're not going to school today. There's going to be a war. Bad men have bombed New York City."

Rikki Miller, Michigan: I was in Mrs. Smith's first-grade class. We had a guest reader in the class reading *Nate the Great*. Mrs. Smith got a call. Slowly, students were called out of class. By the end of the day, only a few of us were left — my sister, a second-grader, and myself among them. When we got home, [my mom] told us about a terrible attack that took many lives. My mom didn't want us to be scared of school, so she wasn't going to pull us out.

Alma M., California: All the adults seemed weird. They were all on edge and something was wrong, everything was so quiet.

Age 7 / Second Grade
Robert Korn, Florida: Kids started leaving school early, picked up by their parents starting around 10:00 a.m. My mom picked me and my best friend up from our school. My mom was crying. She and my dad had both grown up on Long Island, and they lived in Manhattan together for over a decade before moving to Florida. When we got home, my dad made a couple sandwiches for my friend and me. He was a wreck. One of his friends from high school was a firefighter in New York City. He later found out that his friend died in one of the Towers, Thomas Joseph Kuveikis. I sat outside my house on the back patio with my friend; we ate our peanut butter and jelly sandwiches, and we watched the news. We sat there for at least three hours before my mom came back outside and turned the TV to the only network not show-

ing the news, Cartoon Network. I knew that what was happening was not normal.

Tania Cohen, New York: There were Black Hawk helicopters flying over the house into the city. My grandma went into the kitchen and made a big batch of pancakes.

Hiba Elaasar, Louisiana: I was a pretty shy and quiet child, but I had made my first friend on my own. After that day, my friend came over and said, "We can't be friends anymore, Hiba. My mom said until this is over, we can't be friends anymore."

Age 8 / Third Grade
Denise Sciasci, Pennsylvania: My teacher walked me up the steps with tears in her eyes, clenching my hand as if I was her own child. I wondered how something so bad could happen on such a beautiful, warm, and sunny day.

Alexa Cerf, Washington, D.C.: I was the new kid in school, so when the teacher said, "You might not know what the Pentagon is, but it's a building that's very important to us," I thought she meant important to our school. That a plane had hit a building on campus. I was too embarrassed to ask which building was the Pentagon, but I tried to look out the window for a plane that had crashed.

Rebekkah Portlock, Alabama: That was the first time I realized that truly awful things could happen to people who didn't deserve them.

Jessica Sweeney, New Jersey: "Is your mom OK?" I stared at my blond-haired best friend Alex as the rest of our third-grade class gazed at the TV. Alex's big blue eyes looked right past me as she said, "I don't know. She had a meeting there this morning." I put my hand on her shoulder. Alex's name stumbled from the loudspeaker, asking her to come to the office. I gave her my package of Dunkaroos — the one my mom had packed me for snack time — before my teacher took Alex downstairs. A few minutes later, Alex ran back into our classroom and hugged me, crying. She told me, "Her meeting in New York got canceled when she was on her way this morning. She turned around before she even crossed the bridge."

Manar Hussein, New Jersey: The banner on the screen appeared, with the words in the lines of "suspected al-Qaeda, an Islamic terrorist group, hijackers . . ." as the news anchor tried to explain that we were under attack. The words were foreign to these third-graders, but the word "Islamic" they knew very well — it was the word I had used to introduce myself in these early days of school.

A couple students started to look at me, riddling me with hard questioning stares. I couldn't help but feel ashamed and apologetic for something that had nothing to do with me.

Age 9 / Fourth Grade
Matthew Jellock, Pennsylvania: Toward the end of the day, the school called on the public address system to inform us about what had happened. We were asked to stand up for a moment of silence as the song "God Bless the USA" played on the PA radio. I saw the magnitude of what happened when I got home and watched the television. It was a very somber experience and I was feeling like *Why? Why did this happen?*

Selena Gomez, Texas: Everyone was distraught.

Age 10 / Fifth Grade
Karen Zhou, California: I was a figure skater and practiced on the 5:00 a.m. [PT] session that morning. I don't actually remember what I did during that hour-long session, but I do know that, at the end of it, I was happy. I bounded into the cafeteria, trying to get my mom's attention, gleefully peppering her with questions about whether or not she saw me practice. I expected her to be all smiles; instead, her face was a sheet of white,

618

as were all the faces of every other parent that was there.

Elizabeth Estrada, Texas: I didn't know what the Twin Towers were or where they were located. I sat on top of one of the desks and cried. My four-year-old sister, along with her teacher, was later brought into the classroom to watch the news. I remember deliberately sitting behind her so that she couldn't see me cry. I knew that even if she couldn't fully comprehend what was going on, she would still be scared because of all the chaos. September 11th, 2001, was the first time I ever doubted the safety of my country.

Kristin Camille Chez, Florida: I couldn't understand why anyone would want to hurt so many people. They couldn't possibly have known them all, what reason did they have?

Nick Waldo, Alaska: My mom told me that some planes had crashed, and being in rural Alaska, I thought a small plane had gone down because of bad weather. I was confused as to why it was a big deal. I said, "Oh, did we know anyone on them?"

Age 11 / Sixth Grade
Dana Meredith, Kansas: It was the tradition in my elementary school that the sixth-grade class take a three-day, two-night trip to

an outdoor learning center. My class took that trip from September 10 to 12, 2001. I spent September 11, 2001, having fun with my friends. Canoeing in the morning, hiking and exploring an old cemetery in the afternoon, playing soccer and watching *Apollo 13* in the evening. Very little was out of place, other than the looped contrails in the sky of planes forced to turn around — I still have a photo, taken on a disposable Kodak camera — and our principal canceling plans to join us because of "disciplinary problems" with a student, a white lie, I realized later. Our teachers sat us down the next day, before we left for home, to explain what had happened, although I could not conceive of the magnitude of the previous day's events, nor did I even know what the World Trade Center was.

Age 12 / Seventh Grade

Jose Godinez, California: The events unfolded well before I got up for the second Tuesday of seventh grade. The teacher turned on the news coverage. I was glued to the screen, fascinated by the new terms I was learning. "Terrorism" had not entered my lexicon before that day. My understanding of the Middle East, until that day, was limited to Ancient Egypt.

Irene C. Garcia, California: When my siblings got ready for school, I usually occupied my time with morning cartoons. I remember flipping through the channels and being annoyed that what seemed like every single station was broadcasting the same program. As a child I just wanted to watch my cartoons. I kept flipping the channels until I decided to watch what was going on. I remember smoke coming out of a building and the broadcaster stating what a sad and tragic thing occurred in New York.

Michael, Pennsylvania: I was looking up the World Trade Center in the encyclopedia that was in the classroom.

Dan Shuman, Minnesota: Mostly I remember the feeling that went unspoken — or maybe couldn't be put to words even by adults — that something horrible and incomprehensible had happened that had already changed things forever. At home, after school, I remember my dad telling me about when JFK was killed, when he was eight. He told me that America had gotten through that, and that it would get through this too.

Age 13 / Eighth Grade
Emily Bouck, Florida: My dad is a commercial airline pilot. He was working. All middle and high schoolers were herded into the gymnasium. I was hysterical on the bleachers. My Bible teacher pulled me out of

621

the crowd and took me to the principal's office: "Do you know where your dad is?" I didn't. My dad was one of the last planes in the sky — having to turn back to Fort Lauderdale midroute, inbound to a New York–area airport. He was able to answer by the time I called. I'm still thankful for those few moments he was able to tell me he was safe, and for the teacher who looked out for me.

Kat Cosgrove, New Hampshire: I didn't really understand the severity of it — a couple buildings a few states away had been hit by planes. I'm not sure I had ever said the word "terrorism" before. Once I got home I turned on the TV to try to figure out what was going on. I remember scrolling through more than 100 channels, seeing the same images of the Twin Towers falling, over and over. I counted 31 TV channels all airing live coverage of 9/11. When I saw that MTV and VH1 were also airing it, that's when I realized how big a deal it was and started to get scared. It was suddenly not an adult problem, but something that I was supposed to be paying attention to too.

Age 14 / Ninth Grade
Kathryn Mastandrea, Connecticut: I remember walking into my social studies classroom and my teacher had written, " 'Religion is outraged when outrage is done

in its name' — Gandhi." I couldn't process that it was an act of terrorism, I kept thinking that it was a series of terrible mistakes. Some of our teachers kept the news on, others attempted with the lessons of the day. At lunch, no one talked, and there was a line that stretched down the hallway to the two pay phones at the front of the school. As a bedroom community to New York, nearly everyone had at least one parent who worked in the city. My dad didn't work in Manhattan, but traveled each week for work. I remember waiting in the line, my stomach in knots, waiting to get in touch with my mom to hear that my dad was okay.

Sean B., Alabama: I was trying something new that year, going for a new look, a new identity. I was learning to skateboard and in a punk rock band. A guy by the name of Steven sat in front of me. He was a tenth-grader, but for one reason or another he's in my ninth-grade science class. Steven was the kind of guy I want to be — the character I was trying to become. Seconds after the television was turned on, before I have time to fully process what I was watching, I leaned forward and whispered to Steven, "Anarchy." He laughed, and I instantly feel dirty. The guilt only grew as we continued watching the news. One of the greatest tragedies in our country's history, and the first word out of my mouth was a joke.

Age 15 / Tenth Grade
Lourdes V. Baker, California: It was the first time I completely understood that nothing is simple, some things never make sense, and sometimes horrible things happen for no reason at all. It was the end of my childhood.

Bill Kuchman, New York: Something that stands out to me the most in my own memory of 9/11 was the juxtaposition between the surreal nature of the day and the monotony of the routines that I still followed. After spending the day at school, constantly trying to catch a glimpse of any new bit of information about the terror attacks, I still went to my high school job at my town's public library that evening. I was scheduled to work that day, and I never thought of breaking from that routine. I went to work and numbly made it through the four-hour shift I was working as a sophomore.

I can't remember how I found out that my local newspaper, the *Rochester Democrat & Chronicle,* had published an afternoon extra edition to cover 9/11, but by the time my dad picked me up from the library, I knew that I wanted a copy. After a weird Burger King dinner, my dad and I drove around, going from gas station to gas station in a futile at-

624

tempt to find a copy of that extra edition. By this point in the night, the extra editions of the newspaper were long gone, but the quiet quest around town to find one is burned into my 9/11 memories.

Age 16 / Eleventh Grade

Jon Kay, California: At around seven in the morning, the tone on KFI AM 640 changed drastically. Bill Handel read off the news ticker as if aliens had been spotted directly above Wilshire Boulevard. Picking up my carpool, suddenly 16 didn't feel so old.

Tahlia Hein, New Jersey: September 11th was also picture day in my high school. If you were lucky enough to have a last name like Anderson or Charles, you probably made it through the gymnasium queue before 9:00 a.m. Your smile looks genuine. If you were a Daniels or an Elton, you probably picked up on the fact that Something Had Happened — gossip spreads like wildfire in any high school — but hadn't yet gone back to a classroom with a television. If you're a Gore or a Hein, like me, you were screwed. You had to watch the whole terrible thing unfold before your eyes, and then you had to sit to have your picture taken for the yearbook. The command to "Smile!" sounded like the worst insult.

Age 17 / Twelfth Grade

Joanne Fischetti, Staten Island: We were told we should leave school and go immediately home. I remember walking to the park with my best friend and talking about whether things will be the same again and whether we'd be able to have a prom, be able to go to college, go to war, or what would happen next for America. It's amazing how easy it was to lose that feeling of safety.

College

Michael Szwaja, University of Illinois, Urbana-Champaign: I tried to focus on rehashing the reading I had done the night before for my ethics in journalism quiz. As I walked in the door and quickly took my seat, I realized the quiz wasn't going to happen. The professor had both TVs in each corner of the classroom tuned to two different channels, each reporting on that World Trade Center crash. "Just keep watching," our professor said. "Today's lesson just changed."

Mallory Carra, New York University: A long line of people waited for an actual pay phone while trying to use their cell phones. The internet on all of the NYU library computers was painfully slow. After 10 minutes of pressing "refresh," I read a three-lined AP story to my friend Jia aloud. "Two planes have crashed into World Trade Center." It took me a second to even realize what those words even meant. In this pre-Twitter world, I finally summed up my feelings in my Live-Journal at 9:14 a.m., "omg i am so scared."

Daphne Leigh, Ripon College, Wisconsin: I called my friend Andy over in the freshman boys' dorm. He very sleepily answered. In the calmest voice possible, I told him to turn on the TV and call me back. As we watched, it happened again [a plane flew into the second tower]. Almost immediately my phone rang. It was Andy, calling to tell me he saw it, and that he was "signing up." I was stunned, at first not even knowing what he meant. He kept talking, telling me that he had to call his mom, and that he'd stay and finish freshman year, but he was signing up because that's what you do. Andy did sign up. He joined the National Guard that year.

Natasha Wright, George Washington University, D.C.: I will never forget how surreal it was returning to the dorm and turning the TVs on. Finding out the Pentagon had been hit. Watching residents of the Watergate across the street from us be evacuated as we were on lockdown and couldn't leave. The panic began to spread; students on my floor cried together. Some residents packed bags to walk across the bridge and out of the city. Most of us sat in shock. I cried — a lot. We barely knew one another and we were instantly bonded.

Daphne Leigh: I contacted friends from home via our only means at the time, AOL Instant Messenger, as we were scattered around the country. We all shared the same fears.

Ernie Smith, Michigan State University: It was my first real time living away from home — I had only moved in two weeks prior. When those two towers were hit — there it was: my first real memory of being on my own.

Michael Szwaja: That was the first moment since I arrived at college where I felt like I needed my mom and dad, and they weren't there.

Courtney Kirkpatrick, University of Texas: Suddenly being out in the world felt exhausting.

At Offutt Air Force Base

"WE DIDN'T KNOW
WHO WAS FRIEND OR FOE"

At 2:50 p.m. ET (1:50 p.m. local time), Air Force One landed at Offutt Air Force Base, outside Omaha, Nebraska.

Adm. Richard Mies, commander, U.S. Strategic Command (STRATCOM), Offutt Air Force Base: We didn't know that he was coming to Offutt until about 15 minutes before. There wasn't much communication with Air Force One at all. There wasn't going to be any pomp and circumstance. I had my driver and a Secret Service agent, and the three of us went out to the runway to greet Air Force One in my plain Chrysler.

Sgt. Chad Heithoff, Maintenance Unit, Offutt Air Force Base: They announced a ramp freeze — meaning no one could move on the ground — and the next thing I knew there were security forces everywhere, full flak jackets, M-16s. We could see Air Force

One coming in, with two fighters escorting it. It was chilling and scary.

Staff Sgt. William "Buzz" Buzinski, security, Air Force One: Landing at Offutt was probably the one funny moment of the day. I'm a big guy — 6-foot-4, 270 — but Will Chandler's also a huge guy, he's 6-3, 250. We always said he's got hands the size of a TV screen. Well, we were the first two off the plane. The rear stairs are always down first; you get off and guide the front stairs in. When we got off, underneath the jet were five or six maintainers, who were trying to plug the plane into ground power. No one told us they'd be there — all we saw were this group of five guys. Chandler yelled: "Clear the area!" He just let out this bellow. Well, it was like cats scattering — they dropped radios, dropped the cable. They were panicked — there's this big guy coming at them. It was hysterical. I laughed.

Richard Balfour, security, Air Force One: We didn't know who was friend or foe, even on the bases. We kept everybody at arm's length, away from the aircraft.

Dave Wilkinson, assistant agent in charge, U.S. Secret Service: By the time we got to STRATCOM, there were like 15 to 20 planes still unaccounted for nationwide.

People will say it was only six, but there were a lot more than that. For everything we knew, they were all hijacked. But even as we landed, they started to kick them off quickly.

Adm. Richard Mies: I decided to bring the president down into the command center via the fire escape entrance. That was the most expedient option. I'd never used it before. It was there for emergencies. I had them open it from the inside.

Brian Montgomery, director of advance, White House: There were a lot of airmen in battle gear lining the route to the bunker. We pulled up to this five-story office building, and instead of walking in the front door, the admiral said, "No, we're going in there." We headed into this concrete building, just a door. We went down and down and down, pretty far underground.

Ellen Eckert, stenographer, White House: When he went into the bunker, wow. That's still a scene in the movie in my head all these years later. Clearly the only way to go was down. We stood outside, waiting. We smoked a million cigarettes, all my new chain-smoking friends.

Eric Draper, presidential photographer: I finally had a chance to call my wife. I said,

"Honey, I'm going to be home a little late tonight." I could hear her laugh through the phone, even as she was crying. She said, "I saw you with the president, so I knew you were OK."

Adm. Richard Mies: We went directly into the command center. That really caught [the president's] attention. All these soldiers, they're all in battle dress. CNN was prominently displayed — a lot of footage of the two towers. We had four to six TV screens, all energized. I sat him down where I normally sit, and walked him through what he was seeing, so he had an awareness.

Andy Card, chief of staff, White House: It was right out of a TV movie set — all these flat-screen TVs, all these military people, you could hear the fog of war, all these communications from the FAA and the military. But it was tough for the military folks — they all wanted to stand and show respect to the commander in chief, but you could tell they wanted to sit and do their jobs. Everyone was schizophrenic, half-sitting and half-standing, everyone was moving around. After a few minutes, the president turned to me, "I want to get out of here — I'm making it hard for these people to do their job."

Maj. Scott "Hooter" Crogg, F-16 pilot, 111th Fighter Squadron, Houston: All the rules that fighter pilots spend their lives living by were now out the window. When we landed at Offutt we got more gas and picked up maps for the rest of the country. There were always maps and approaches for the country in base operations, but all the maps always said, "Do not remove from base operations." We took all of them and stuffed them in our bag.

Colonel Tillman walked into base operations and we finally started to get some information. The president was actually an alumn[us] of our unit in Houston, and Colonel Tillman told us, "He feels comfortable with you guys and wants you to continue with us." We told him we'd sit back about five miles — you don't get that close to something that valuable, for all sorts of reasons — but if something happened, we can eat up that range real quick.

Adm. Richard Mies: The VTC [video teleconference] was the three of us, the operator, and his military aide. There was no real audience. We listened as everyone reported in. Richard Clarke of the National Security Council, Transportation Secretary Norm Mineta, Deputy Secretary of State Richard Armitage, National Security Adviser Condi Rice, CIA Director George Tenet.

Most of the initial conversation in the VTC was focused on who did this. There was a lot of speculation. It was too early to make definitive. Then we were talking about: How do we restore some sense of normalcy quickly, both for New York and for the country? And then how does the president get back to Washington?

Col. Matthew Klimow, executive assistant to the vice chair of the Joint Chiefs of Staff, Gen. Richard Myers, Pentagon: At 3:15, there was a teleconference with President Bush. The president was firm and in control and I felt inspired. I remember very well his exact words as he started the teleconference. He said, "I want everybody who's listening to this SVT" — which means secure video teleconference — "[to know] that no faceless thugs are going to hold this country at bay."

Norman Mineta, secretary of transportation: He said, "We're going to find out who did this. We're going to seek them out. And we're going to destroy them."

Col. Matthew Klimow: Someone spoke up, and I don't know who, and they used profanity. President Bush said, "Look, first thing: get the facts straight. Second: clean up your language. And my reaction was just what yours was." Everybody chuckled.

Josh Bolten, deputy chief of staff, White House: The whole tenor of the presidency changed immediately at that moment.

Mike Morell, presidential briefer, Central Intelligence Agency: When Tenet explained that he had evidence pointing to al-Qaeda, the president turned around and looked at me — his look clearly said, *What the fuck happened here? You were supposed to tell me first.* I tried to explain with my look that I was sorry — I didn't know how my message had gotten lost. I went to a nearby office and called Tenet's assistant, angry. I felt like I'd let the president down.

Andy Card: We all suspected that it was al-Qaeda. I'd thought that since the classroom door. It wasn't that dramatic of a moment actually. Think of what would've happened if he'd told us that it was Russia, China, or another nation-state? Or an American splinter group?

Maj. Gen. Larry Arnold, commander of the 1st Air Force, NORAD, Tyndall Air Force Base, Florida: We had just about everybody on the ground, but we were concerned about one aircraft. It was a USAir flight that had taken off from Madrid and was going to JFK. It was the last aircraft that had been called "potentially hijacked." The phone rang from Bob Marr and he said, "We just got word from USAir that that airplane turned around." I picked up the phone from my executive officer and I heard the president again talking to the secretary of defense. I interrupted and said, "Mr. President, the last airplane has landed. Everything is down that we can see." He did not question it. It was just, "I am going back to Washington."

Julie Ziegenhorn, public affairs officer, Offutt Air Force Base: We were working at our desks and all of a sudden, there was the president striding down the hallway. He walked right out the front door, waving to us. He shouted, "Thanks for all you're doing!"

Gordon Johndroe, assistant press secretary, White House: We were there with the press pool and our Secret Service agent said, "Oh my gosh, we've got to go right now. The president's leaving." Ann Compton was on with Peter Jennings. I didn't want to panic her or the nation by making it seem like we were leaving abruptly, but we needed to leave. I mouthed, "We have to go." She was on the radio and she said, "I'm told we're leaving. I don't know where we're going." Peter Jennings said, "Godspeed, Annie."

Col. Mark Tillman, presidential pilot, Air Force One: We thought he was going to be there for a while. I was in base operations and someone came in and said, "I think the president's headed back to the plane." I said, "Nah." He said, "No, I'm pretty sure I just saw him drive by." I started to race back to the plane. He'd already gotten there. He's waiting at the top of the stairs and told me, "Tillman, we got to get back home. Let's get back home."

Maj. Scott Crogg: No one told us that Air Force One was leaving, so we were like, *Oh shit, are they starting up?* We're racing to get our planes in the air, but it takes some time. We met the minimum safety requirements and hit the air. A 747 configured like that — gosh, that's a fast airplane. We didn't want to go supersonic, it'd burn up too much fuel, so we talked to them, and we had to reel them in.

With the president's orders and mind-set clear — but the president himself still hours away from Washington — aides back at the White House moved ahead with briefing the press about the state of the nation's response.

Nic Calio, director of legislative affairs, White House: We had a long discussion about what we should be doing, whether we should all be going out and be seen publicly. We decided to do a briefing. There was a discussion — Mary Matalin was there, Scooter Libby — about whether we should go out in force and say, "Here's the White House staff. We're out. It's safe." Our intent was to send a reassuring message. In the end, we just sent Karen Hughes.

Karen Hughes, communications director, White House: The Secret Service thought the White House press room was still not safe, so they took me, surrounded by agents with their weapons drawn, to the nearby FBI headquarters. I remember feeling vulnerable; we didn't know who the enemy was or where they might be lurking. My colleague Mary Matalin, counselor to Vice President Cheney, came with me; I remember being grateful to have a friend by my side. I read from a prepared statement I had typed myself. The text was faded and barely legible in places; the printer in the emergency center had been low on ink. "I'm Karen Hughes, counselor to President Bush, and I'm here to update you on the activities of the federal government in response to this morning's attacks on our country. . . ."

AFTERNOON IN AMERICA

"PROFOUND QUIET"

As the morning of September 11th passed, a stunned, wounded nation found itself enveloped in quiet — businesses and schools closed, traffic thinned, the normal air traffic overhead fell silent. Many Americans, both ordinary civilians and government officials, were glued to the television, soaking in the news, overcome with emotion.

Gabriella Daya-Dominguez, resident, Chatham, New Jersey: My husband worked in the South Tower, and I was about seven months pregnant. I tried to call my husband. I was rather frantic. I tried to call and call, I couldn't reach him. There was no answer. I spent several hours just pacing my floor. He finally did make his way back on the ferry, and our son's classmate's father gave him a ride home. He pulled up in a car I didn't know. I ran out to greet him, and I was amazed because his shirt was white. By this time, clothes were all sooty and stuff because the Towers had already collapsed. I remember my first thought was *His shirt is clean!* and then I ran into his arms crying.

Susannah Herrada, resident, Arlington, Virginia: My son was born that day in Arlington Hospital at 1:40 in the afternoon. The first plane hit, and then the second, and then the Pentagon, and then my doctor said I needed a C-section. For the longest time I wondered if he gave me the C-section because they were expecting so many injured from the Pentagon, and they needed to get my delivery over with. I said, "Look, the TV has got to go off. You guys have to focus on me" — my doctor and my husband are watching TV — so the TV got turned off. It was a hard time to have a baby. You're supposed to be so happy and you're not. Every mother has to struggle with that, but then the thought: *What world is this?* We weren't sure what was going to happen next.

Linda Carpenter, kindergarten teacher, Philadelphia: Although the sky was still the same beautiful blue that promised a perfect day on my drive to work, the sky now seemed eerily empty. Quiet, but not peaceful. I kept an eye on the sky on that drive home, fearful of the outdoors.

Wilson Surratt, executive producer, WPIX-TV, New York: A melancholy silence crept in. For the next few hours, we worked in a low hum of conversation and deep breaths. We struggled to hold it together.

Thomas Rodgers, attorney, Cambria County, Pennsylvania: I remember looking up in the sky to see if I could see any plane. It seemed like everything was so still and quiet when you did that because there was nothing, no noise. We get used to the noise of the planes going over us. All at once, you noticed the silence.

Theresa Flynn, librarian, H-B Woodlawn School, Arlington, Virginia: The profound, profound quiet.

Spc. Ben Bell, sentinel, Tomb of the Unknown Soldier, U.S. Army: The thing I remember was the flight pattern in D.C. It comes over the Potomac from the east and drops into Reagan. It's a loud part of Tomb guarding. You always heard the planes coming in — it's the only thing that disrupts the sanctity of the Tomb sometimes when you're out there. That silence, there were no people, there was nothing going on. The eerie silence. To hear that during the middle of the day, that was really eerie, not to have any sound, like the dead of night.

Preston Stone, resident, North Dakota: I lived about two miles from the Fargo airport, and the silence from grounded planes was striking and haunting.

Nate Jones, freshman, Wheaton College, Illinois: I was 1,500 miles away from all of this and I didn't feel safe. I remember looking at the sky in the afternoon and seeing no contrails, no jets anywhere. It was blue and empty and silent. I still can't look at blue sky the same way.

Charity C. Tran, student, University of Southern California, Los Angeles: I remember the silence of the sky, the deceptive peace of a clear blue sky, empty of its white specks of flying planes.

Anne Marie Reidy Borenstein, Maryland: The world seemed to have stopped. It was almost as if everyone was holding their breath, waiting for what would happen next.

Theresa Flynn: You don't know how quiet a place can be. There was nothing on 395, there was nothing on George Mason Drive. The one thing that was interesting is that every single house in the whole block — by the time the sun set, the people were home — and there was that blue light coming out of their windows with every single person watching TV.

Deena Burnett, wife of United Flight 93 passenger Tom Burnett: All I wanted to do was go to church. I knew my children were fine. The principal called to let me know the kids were okay and they did not know about the airplane yet. Several parents were picking up their children from school that day, but I decided to let mine stay — being there was better than being at home and seeing me fall apart. I needed some time to decide how to handle the emotions. So I went to church.

SEARCHING

"THERE'S SO MUCH LUCK INVOLVED"

Family members, coworkers, colleagues fretted and feared the losses at the World Trade Center as the day's staggering toll mounted. Survivors, for their part, realized how big a role happenstance played in who emerged from the morning's carnage. The search for the missing proceeded desperately, both at hospitals and at the acres of destruction that would come to be known as Ground Zero.

Mika Brzezinski, correspondent, CBS News: There was a "worst moment" for me. We brought in a security guard from the World Financial Center. As he was waiting to go on air, the guard told me he had seen a WABC-TV van crushed in the collapse. My husband [at the time], Jim Hoffer, worked for WABC. I began to get a little panicked that I had possibly lost my husband. I remember being two people — one person doing her story, the other totally numb, wondering, *Where the hell is my husband? What am I go-*

ing to do if I lose him? Right after my report, the producer got in my ear and said, "Mika, your husband's fine." I cried. I felt so lucky.

John Napolitano, father of FDNY firefighter John P. Napolitano: I thought, *I've got to call my friend Lenny Crisci. I have to tell him what's going on.* His brother, John Crisci, a lieutenant in Hazmat, was like an uncle to my son. I called Lenny's house and his wife, Millie, answered the phone. She was crying. I said, "Millie, is John missing?" She said, "Yes." I said, "So's my son."

Lenny and I went to a Brooklyn precinct, and they bent every rule in the book to get us over the bridge. We went and parked near Rescue 1 downtown. We saw guys from Hazmat. Lenny and I went up to them and asked about John Crisci, if they knew anything about Rescue 2 and the guys. They said, "No, nothing, nothing, nothing."

Susan Baer, general manager, Newark International Airport: One of the things that someone started doing early on was keeping a list of everyone we'd heard from, which made people feel better, on a blackboard in the conference room. Everybody could see it. So if someone said, "I heard from so-and-so! She didn't go to work today, or she was out at LaGuardia today," we'd write that name down. That day was fraught with that very raw emotion about who survived and who hadn't.

Sunny Mindel, communications director for the mayor of the City of New York, Rudy Giuliani: At some point, we announced where the victims' families should go: the Armory. The Armory was turned into the victim focal point, where they should gather. We headed over there as well. There were lines around the block. People clamoring for information. It was a warm day, people were out on the street. They were hot, they were frightened, they were heartbroken.

Kimberly Archie, resident, California: My brother was a pilot for United at the time. He normally flew Flights 92 and 93. His wife had surgery on September 10th, so he was not the copilot that day, but I will never forget seeing the news, and how I froze for what felt like hours in shock thinking my brother was on that plane. Even when I realized he couldn't be, it was so hard after that to not feel for the families of the victims as if it were us.

Linda Krouner, senior vice president, Fiduciary Trust, South Tower: Your survival was such a big degree of luck. There are so many points of luck that make you realize how random life is. People say, "Oh, you were so smart to leave." Who knows? The way it turned out, I was smart to leave, but I would have been smarter taking the elevator. There's so much luck involved in this, in who lived and who died.

Mark DeMarco, officer, Emergency Service Unit, Truck 1, NYPD: *Why did we get out?* In the beginning I had this guilty feeling. If I had made a right instead of a left, if I had been five minutes or two minutes slower, if I had gone to a different team. There were so many variables. Everybody who was there says the same thing: it was luck, nothing more than luck.

Stephen Blihar, officer, Emergency Service Unit, Truck 10, NYPD: It was a day of lefts and rights.

Norma Hardy, officer, PATH Command, PAPD: As it got later into the night, then you realized that a lot of our guys were still missing or unaccounted for. We started talking amongst ourselves — the Port Authority police — *Where did you last see this one? Who went this way? Who went that way?* We started to realize that they were in a lot of trouble.

Det. David Brink, Emergency Service Unit, Truck 3, NYPD: Out of the Emergency Service response from the NYPD that morning, 50 percent were lost. We lost 14 of the 23 guys.

Bill Spade, firefighter, Rescue 5, FDNY: My brother-in-law, who was in Rescue 5, called me up, and he said, "Bill, everybody's missing." I said, "What do you mean 'everybody'?" I named every guy I had breakfast with that morning. I kept naming names — Mike and this guy and that guy — he said, "No, Bill. They're all missing." Then my wife called me later that evening also. She said, "Did you get the bad news?" I said, "Yeah, everybody's missing." She said, "No, your uncle was on Flight 93." I remember I said, "All right." I said, "Give me all the bad news now you want. This is the worst day of my life."

At 5:20 p.m., the 48-story building known as Seven World Trade Center, which had been burning furiously after being struck by the wreckage and debris from the adjacent Twin Towers, collapsed into itself. Overwhelmed by its losses, the magnitude of the day's tragedy, and the lack of water pressure in Lower Manhattan following the Twin Towers' collapse, the New York Fire Department had decided to let the building burn.

Jeff Johnson, firefighter, Engine 74, FDNY: My eyes were really in bad shape. I had taken a piece of cardboard and cut a slit in it, so I could put it over my eyes to cut down on the amount of light. We got to Stuyvesant High School and they had a triage center set up inside. They gave me water and flushed out my eyes. I got up to go back out onto West Street, and as I was stepping down the stairs out to exit the high school, people were running again. I couldn't figure out what the heck was going on. A huge plume of smoke came up West Street. Building Seven had collapsed.

Det. David Brink, Emergency Service Unit, Truck 3, NYPD: I couldn't believe it. I was like, "You've got to be kidding me! How many more buildings are going to fall?"

Dan Nigro, chief of operations, FDNY: It would have been the largest collapse in the history of firefighting of a high-rise building if it had not been for WTC 1 and 2. We had another 48-story building came down in a matter of seconds, but thankfully, not one additional person was injured when that building came down.

William Jimeno, officer, PAPD: We heard a huge explosion, which sounded like the same thing that happened the first two times, but it was further away. We believe this was Building Seven coming down.

Scott Strauss, officer, Emergency Service Unit, Truck 1, NYPD: Building Seven comes down about 5:30, and they take the organized rescue effort off the pile. "Hey, guys! We're getting off. The buildings are coming down everywhere. Let's get off the pile. Let's regroup." It wasn't a "pile" until days later. We called it the Trade Center, and then the terminology evolved into "The Pile," and then it became "Ground Zero."

Jeff Johnson: At that point, I lost it. I broke down. A friend of mine, Eddie Callahan, saw me — he said he thought I was dead. There were a couple of these Chevy Suburbans, chief cars. Eddie had one, and he goes, "We're getting you out of here." They put a bunch of guys, as many guys as they could fit, into the rig that had been pretty beaten up. It was funny. We tried putting the air-conditioning on to cool us off — it was blowing so much dust we couldn't see to drive. We had to open the windows to let the dust out. He brought me back to my firehouse.

At Ground Zero, an impromptu bucket brigade had begun work, trying to sift through the acres of burning wreckage in hopes of finding survivors and recovering the dead. The fires at

Ground Zero would burn for another 99 days, until they were finally extinguished for good on December 19.

Paul McFadden, firefighter, Rescue 2, FDNY: The rubble, the field was so large that you're saying, "Where could you actually start?"

Omar Olayan, officer, NYPD: Once you got to the top of the rubble pile, there was all this smoke and the buildings on the side were on fire. At some point, you would get smoke inhalation and your eyes were burning out of your head and you couldn't do it anymore. So you would go over to One Liberty, the building, they would nebulize you a little bit, wash your eyes out a little, and then you'd get back on the line and do it again. They had little paper masks, but at some point we took them off because they would get black in about two minutes and it was worthless.

John Napolitano, father of FDNY firefighter John P. Napolitano: When we came onto West Street and saw the debris field, I didn't even know that was a street. It was steel all over the place, and smoke rising, and it was chaos. It was a movie set that some deranged director thought of. It was the most horrific thing that I ever saw in my life. *Where* *do we start? Where do we begin?* I saw the lines of rescue workers moving debris a bucket at a time. Lenny went over to the wall, and he started to write, "John Crisci, call home," on the ash. I was getting so overwhelmed, saying to myself, "I want to believe my son's here. I want to believe he's alive, but it don't look good." I walked over to the wall and with my finger I wrote a big message in the ash. I wrote, "Rescue 2, John Napolitano, I'm here and I love you. Dad."

Denise McFadden, wife of FDNY firefighter Paul McFadden: Paul called, and he was up on the pile. I didn't understand what he was saying because he was naming name after name that we knew, then saying, "Dead." I said, "Stop it. What are you doing?" I said, "Is this some sick joke?" He couldn't stop. He kept rattling off name and "dead." He couldn't say anything else.

Capt. Jay Jonas, Ladder 6, FDNY: I'm sitting at the ambulance, still with Tommy Falco, and he looks at me and he says, "Hey, Cap." He says, "How many guys do you think we lost here today?" I look out across the field and I says, "Oh, man! I don't know — maybe a couple hundred." I caught myself when I said it. I said, "What the heck did I say — a couple hundred?" Prior to that day our biggest life-loss fire we had was 12, and I'm saying a couple hundred. As it turns out I was off by almost a half. The numbers are staggering.

John Napolitano: At one point I joined the bucket brigade and I was moving the dirt. They would give me the buckets. I remember somebody saying, "This is a piece of the plane. You got to give it to a Fed." The guy pointed at me, because I was in civilian clothes, and I had dress pants on. They gave me this piece of metal — thin metal — and I was holding it. I walked off the mound, and I looked at a guy and he does look like a Fed. I went up to him and I said, "Listen. They said, 'Give this to a Fed.' " I said, "They gave it to me, but I'm an ex-cop, not a Fed." I said, "Are you a Fed?" He nodded his head, and he stood there watching everybody and everything, and he took it.

Paul McFadden: When everything settled, I lost 46 friends. They were either my friends or they were sons of my friends.

Capt. Jay Jonas: From the time we walked into that building till the time we got out late that afternoon, the world changed. By the time I saw sunlight again, the world was completely different. When we were trapped we couldn't fathom what it looked like outside. It was beyond our wildest imagination, how bad it truly was.

For much of the morning, President Bush, his staff, and members of the press accompanying him were still in the air, trying to find a secure place to land. At 2:50 p.m., they were finally able to deplane at Offutt Air Force Base, outside Omaha, Nebraska.

Still unsure of whether the attacks were over, officials took every action to protect the president, stationing Secret Service outside the Offutt bunker.

By midafternoon, President Bush was finally able to speak via secure videoconference with key advisors and national leaders.

As the dust cloud around the collapse site began to dissipate, the damage done to Lower Manhattan became clear, and striking.

In the wake of the attack, New York City's tunnels, bridges, and highways were all sealed off.

Maritime evacuations continued throughout the day, shuttling the injured and survivors to Brooklyn and New Jersey.

From the moment the alarm sounded after the first plane hit, to the aftermath of the Towers' fall, off-duty firefighters, police, and responders rushed to Ground Zero to help in rescue efforts. Many would spend the following days on the pile searching for friends and survivors.

The fallen facade of the World Trade Center near Church and Liberty Streets.

At 4:36 p.m., Air Force One departed Offutt to take the president home to Washington, D.C. The plane was escorted by F-16s.

Back at the
White House,
President Bush
met with staff
and advisors
to determine
that the active
attacks on the
United States
were over, and
made plans
to address the
nation later
that evening.

Around 7 p.m., lawmakers gathered back at the Capitol, singing a spontaneous rendition of "God Bless America."

Firefighters worked through the night to contain the blazing rooftop fire at the Pentagon.

After the president's address, Vice President Cheney and his wife, Lynne, left Washington to spend the night at Camp David.

By September 12th, armed fighters like this Vermont Air National Guard F-16 were patrolling the skies over major American cities.

The recovery efforts at what ultimately came to be known as Ground Zero proceeded in a ghostly landscape.

Detective David Brink worked the rescue and recovery effort at Ground Zero for months following the attacks.

FEMA veterinarians also contributed to recovery efforts by managing rescue dogs.

In the days and weeks after September 11, posters calling for information about missing loved ones wallpapered New York City storefronts, subway stations, and telephone poles.

Wedge 1 of the Pentagon in the aftermath of the attacks.

The helmet that protected FDNY Lt. Mickey Kross as the North Tower fell on top of him.

PAPD officer Sharon Miller's cap was recovered from the rubble at Ground Zero during clean-up efforts.

Citizen responder Welles Crowther wore one of his red bandanas as he rescued fellow coworkers in the South Tower.

Responders and members of the military unfurl a garrison flag over the facade of the Pentagon on September 12.

The Pentagon Memorial, comprised of 184 benches—one for each victim—opened in 2008.

The Tower of Voices memorial at the Flight 93 National Memorial, dedicated in 2018.

The Tribute in Light over the National September 11 Memorial, dedicated on the tenth anniversary of the attack.

9/11 AT SEA

"HOW DRASTICALLY THE WORLD HAD CHANGED"

Far from America's shores on September 11th, the aircraft carrier USS Enterprise *(CVN-65) was beginning its return voyage from an April deployment to the Persian Gulf. But as TV broadcasts brought word of the attacks at home, the ship changed course.*

Capt. James "Sandy" Winnefeld Jr., commander, USS *Enterprise:* There had been a lot of noise on the intelligence nets over the summer — some terrorist plot going on out there. We didn't know what it was, but we thought it could very easily be targeting our high-profile ship. We took exceptional precautions on our Suez Canal transit, from the Mediterranean into the Red Sea, because we were just worried. Obviously nothing happened, so we entered the Persian Gulf and spent three months there supporting operations in Iraq — this was enforcing the no-fly zone in Iraq, OPERATION SOUTHERN WATCH. We had just finished an extremely successful strike against an Iraqi surface-to-air missile battery, and we were finished with the operational part of our deployment and had exited the Arabian Gulf, on our way to a port visit in South Africa on the way home.

On the afternoon of 9/11 — the morning back on the East Coast — I was in my sea cabin reading and got a phone call from my safety officer to turn on the TV. He said, "There's something going on in New York." It was only a minute or so after I turned the TV on that I watched the airplane hit the second tower. Right there, it seemed pretty clear to me that we weren't going home. We weren't going anywhere because there was a good chance this attack originated from somewhere in Afghanistan. We knew all about al-Qaeda.

It was hard to describe the feeling of the Pentagon being hit — wondering if any of my friends were a victim of that attack, wondering exactly how bad the damage was, because it was hard to tell from the TV, and then this feeling that they struck right at the center of who the military is, who we are, what we believe, how we try to defend our country. Watching those two World Trade Center towers come down, that was probably the most shocking thing I've ever seen. That was like, *Oh my God, the world has changed.* Everybody on board was really angry, really shocked.

But we knew we would probably be part of the answer. Over the course of the afternoon, we had a number of meetings. Ultimately the decision was mutually made that we would turn north toward Afghanistan. Our goal was to be off the coast by the very next morning, ready to conduct strike operations if we were asked to do so. When I announced the change of course, I told the crew something like, "I know none of you are disappointed our port visit to South Africa has been canceled. We're out here on the front lines, and there's every possibility that sooner rather than later we'll be asked to answer for this heinous act that's been committed against our country."

You can imagine how helpless we felt at sea watching this all unfold on TV. Everybody was worried about what the terrorists were going to do next. It was the first time in my life that I felt safer at sea than my family was at home.

Weeks later, the USS Enterprise *would launch the first U.S. airstrikes on Afghanistan.*

Word of the attacks continued to spread throughout that Tuesday, finally reaching the U.S. Navy's fast-attack submarine USS Norfolk *(SSN-714) at dinnertime, when the stealthy submarine came to the surface to collect the day's news.*

Matt Dooley, crewman, USS *Norfolk:* We were at sea the week of September 11, 2001, for routine operations and training. When we left Norfolk Naval Station in Norfolk, Virginia, there were fishing boats and pleasure craft in the bay, and it seemed like a quiet day to be on the water. We cleared our communications broadcast early that morning and submerged for our daily tasking. When a submarine is underwater, it is out of communication with the outside world and therefore is required to clear communications broadcasts every 12 hours or so.

When we cleared our broadcast the evening of September 11th, we quickly learned how drastically the world had changed in the 12 hours since our morning broadcast. A sailor that worked in our communications room interrupted our captain as he was eating dinner and told him he was needed in the communications room. Moments later, the captain addressed the crew and read the initial reports over the ship's intercom system. I remember his first words and they still echo in my ears: "The United States has been attacked." We thought this had to be some type of government or military exercise. It all sounded like something from a movie. Since we couldn't see images of the news, we only had the images playing in our heads.

We stayed at periscope depth — just below the surface of the water where our antennas could come up and download communications — for the next few days to get information as it became available. None of us knew what we might be asked to do. It was about a week before we were allowed to come home and we got to see the images of the attacks for the first time. For a week, we only had text on paper and each of us in the submarine hoped it wasn't real. Finally seeing the footage for the first time is a feeling none of us can forget.

AFTERNOON AT THE PENTAGON
"WE STILL CONTINUE TO FIGHT THIS WAR"

By late afternoon, the scene at the Pentagon had settled down; across northern Virginia and Washington, injured personnel sought treatment, rescuers and firefighters settled in for a long siege at the crash site.

Capt. Gary Tobias, Arlington County Fire Department: They took a load of us on a bus down to the Pentagon to start relieving the people there who had been there all day.

Chuck Cake, firefighter and EMT, Arlington County Fire Department: Long about 4:30, the call came through that anybody that hadn't been to the Pentagon yet, "Get on the bus, you're going, it's your turn." I was sent to the interior. We were deployed to the C Ring to look for survivors, and to take care of spot fires. There was wreckage everywhere, and little spot fires all over the place, except there were bodies thrown in with it, too. There were still many, many victims in the building, most of them uniformed. That particular office must have been air force, because I saw a lot of air force uniforms. A lot of the people were burnt beyond recognition. But somehow or other the insignias all survived, and on some of the uniforms, you could still see the patchwork and stuff. We went and got body bags and sheets to put over people, even if for no other reason than to make us feel better.

Philip Smith, branch chief, U.S. Army, Pentagon: One arm is scarred up to about my shirt sleeve, and all of that turns black. While I was at the hospital, they trimmed all the dead skin off. My face was like one big scab.

Lt. Col. Rob Grunewald, information management officer, U.S. Army, Pentagon: It was getting later in the day, and I was becoming sick. I'm coughing up all kinds of black phlegm and stuff. An air force lieutenant colonel comes up and says, "Come on. Let me help you. We'll get you over to the medical tent." They asked, "What hospital do you want to go to?" I go into an ambulance. I am the only one on the highway. The highways were shut down. The siren was going. I was looking out, and I was the only game in town.

Philip Smith: One of my coworkers, a lady by the name of Martha Cardin, was also released. We weren't able to reach anybody by cell phone. All of the communications were down. I walk out of the hospital — and Arlington Hospital is a big hospital. The door that I walk out of, I run into one of my neighbors from a prior assignment, a friend, who had driven to Arlington Hospital to come and find me. I literally bump into him at the door. It was Maj. Rex Harrison. I said, "Rex! What are you doing here?" He said, "Well, I came to pick you up." I said, "Well, that's great! Thank you so much. Can we take Martha home?"

Lt. Col. Rob Grunewald: I got a Purple Heart for my injuries, and I got a Soldier's Medal for my actions that day. There were only maybe 11 or 13 people that got both medals. The Soldier's Medal is the highest medal you can get for bravery not in a combat environment. Somebody obviously thought I did something good — probably Martha.

Louise Rogers, accountant, Resource Services Office, Pentagon: I was at Washington Hospital Center in the Intensive Care Unit. It wasn't until about three or four o'clock in the afternoon that day that I woke up. I have some vague, nightmarish understanding that something happened. I was so out of it, I don't know what was real and what wasn't real. I remembered hearing my husband's voice for the first time, and having the thought, *Well, I don't have to fight to try to stay awake or be conscious right now. He's here, I can let him take care of everything.* And, *Go back to sleep.* So that's what I did.

By day's end, the military had rallied an impressive air armada to America's skies — hundreds of planes, flying over most major U.S. cities. Inside the Pentagon, the leaders sorted through the day's toll and what the next day would bring.

Victoria "Torie" Clarke, assistant secretary of defense for public affairs: Senators John Warner and Carl Levin came down to the building in late afternoon. They sat in one of the smaller workstations in the command center, and the secretary took a call from the president and put them on the phone. They were clearly struck by what had happened and came down simply to show their support. They went out with the secretary to tour the site in the late afternoon.

Lawrence Di Rita, special assistant to Secretary of Defense Rumsfeld: One of the things that stood out in my mind is the regularity that we got back to so quickly —

how quickly we were able to snap back into place and get back to work. The secretary was very clear that he wanted people back to work the next day.

Col. Matthew Klimow, executive assistant to the vice chair of the Joint Chiefs of Staff, Gen. Richard Myers, Pentagon: At 1725 hours — 5:25 — Secretary Rumsfeld said, "I want the chain of command to notify everybody that tomorrow, 12 September, is a normal workday at the Pentagon. I want everybody here reporting for work," which was, at the time, a pretty startling announcement.

Donald Rumsfeld, secretary of defense: I hadn't talked to anybody when I said that — it was more attitude. My impression was that the smoke and problems had declined and that there were undoubtedly significant portions of the building that could be occupied safely, and so I decided. I thought it would be a good thing for the Pentagon not to be shut down.

Adm. Edmund Giambastiani, senior military assistant, Office of the Secretary of Defense: We thought of having a press conference here in the building. We wanted to send the right message to the rest of the country and do a press conference in this building that night. At 6:00 p.m. we did it, even though it was still smoky in the passageways.

Victoria "Torie" Clarke: The building was still filled with smoke, and quite a few people thought the briefing should be held off-site. I was not the only one, but I was probably the most vocal advocate for briefing here in the building. We had to show that the building was up and operating, and it was important for people to see their secretary of defense and the leadership here. We also decided it was a good idea to have Senator Warner and Chairman Levin with him.

Adm. Edmund Giambastiani: The secretary was magnificent. Carl Levin and John Warner came over to show support. They were up on the podium with him. I think that set the tone for America that first evening.

Airborne, En Route to Andrews Air Force Base

"I'D NEVER HEARD OF AL-QAEDA BEFORE"

Air Force One left Offutt Air Force Base at 4:36 p.m. ET, en route to Andrews Air Force Base, outside Washington, D.C. The president, finally, was coming home.

Col. Mark Tillman, presidential pilot, Air Force One: I'm doing .94 Mach. We went as fast as we could across the United States. F-16s were coming out of D.C. to meet us, everyone was joining up with us. We had F-15s with us too.

Mike Morell, presidential briefer, Central Intelligence Agency: On the flight to Andrews, I finally got this packet full of all the intelligence the CIA had. It included the talking points that George Tenet had used to brief the president, but there was still a lot he hadn't been able to say. I shared all those details with the president. The second half of the packet was a set of intelligence passed to us by a European ally explaining that it had detected signs that al-Qaeda was planning a second wave. When I was showing that to the president, I could tell from his reaction, it struck him: *Gosh, this could happen again. This isn't over.*

Eric Draper, presidential photographer: I asked Andy Card at one point, "Who did this?" "Al-Qaeda." I'd never heard of al-Qaeda before.

Andy Card, chief of staff, White House: By the time we're coming from STRAT-COM, it was a skeleton crew aboard. The closer we got to Washington, the more the president wandered.

Brian Montgomery, director of advance, White House: I found the president at the front of the staff cabin at one point. I said, "We're going to hit 'em hard, right, when this is all over?" He said, "Yes, yes, we are." I knew that look in his eyes. He was mad.

Ellen Eckert, stenographer, White House: The president came back to the press cabin. I asked him if he was doing okay, and he said yes. I asked, "Have you spoken to Mrs. Bush?" He said, "Yes, she's fine." He patted me on the back, twice. Then Doug Mills, the AP photographer, said, "Keep your spirits up." The president said, "We won't let a thug bring this country down."

Sonya Ross, reporter, AP: I was typing away in the press cabin, working on my notes, when the president came in, and I don't think he saw me at first. I started typing that quote down, and he heard me typing and turned to me: "Hey, off the record!" He didn't say anything else.

Ellen Eckert: He gave Sonya the stink eye.

Gordon Johndroe, assistant press secretary, White House: He was trying to be a very calm and comforting presence to everyone.

Eric Draper: Everyone was trying to take it all in. I took this picture of Cindy Wright, a White House nurse, rubbing the president's back. At another moment, the president had his arm around Harriet Miers as they walked down the plane.

Capt. Cindy Wright, nurse, White House Medical Unit: What's funny about that picture is I don't really remember being compassionate or ministering to him — I do remember that he came in to check on me and the team. It was amazing to me that he was walking through the plane checking on

us. It was still fairly new in the administration, so we knew each other from talking and being at the ranch, but that was the first time we hugged — I'm a big hugger, and he is too.

Ann Compton, reporter, ABC News: We were finally able to say on the record — I called my bureau and told them — that the president was heading back to Washington and would address the nation from the Oval Office.

Col. Dr. Richard Tubb, presidential physician: The thing at that moment I was most worried about was a biologic attack. In the unlikely but high-risk scenario, I thought there was little harm to be prophylaxing the staff with antibiotics. I gave everyone on the plane a week of Cipro. I hoped by the time they ran out, we'd have figured out the fog of war and know whether we needed to continue measures.

Brian Montgomery: I noticed that Dr. Tubb was walking and talking to each person. He'd lean over and whisper to each person, pat them on the shoulder, and he'd hand over a little envelope, like what the military uses to put pills in. He got to me and said, "Monty" — that was my nickname — "how do you feel?" I said, "Other than the obvious, physically, I feel fine." "You don't feel disoriented?" "Nope." Then he said, "Have you ever heard of Cipro? We don't know what might've been in that school, so we're being careful." I asked him, "What's it used for?" He told me, "In case it's anthrax."

Mike Morell: It was about an hour from touching down, pretty late in the day — a lot of people were asleep, and the lights on Air Force One were turned down — the president came back into the staff compartment. I was the only one awake. One of the things that struck me: he transformed right before my eyes from a president who was struggling a bit with the direction of his administration on September 10th to a wartime president, just in a matter of hours. I could already see this new confidence and power in him.

670

Gordon Johndroe: I don't really remember eating, but the stewards put out some sandwiches and chips. The air force bills you for your meals aboard Air Force One, through the White House Military Office. I remember a couple days later getting a bill for $9.18. The bill said for meals on September 11th between Sarasota–Barksdale, Barksdale–Offutt, Offutt–Washington.

Mike Morell: The president's mil aide, Tom Gould, was looking out the window on the left side of the plane. He motioned me over: "Look." There was a fighter jet on the wingtip. In the distance, you could see the still-burning Pentagon. Throughout the day, all this is happening and you don't really have the chance to feel the emotion. But that got me. Tears filled my eyes for the first time that day.

Andy Card: We kneeled on the benches to look outside, you could see the fighter jets coming up pretty close to Air Force One. You just don't see that on Air Force One.

Karl Rove, senior adviser, White House: I realized this was no ceremonial escort — this was the last line of defense in case there was a MANPAD [surface-to-air missile] on the approach to Washington. They were go-

671

ing to put themselves between Air Force One and whatever the threat was.

Col. Dr. Richard Tubb: As we were coming in on final approach, Dan Bartlett came into my office and said, "Thanks, I took all those pills. Anything else I need?" I said, "What?! Absolutely not! That was supposed to be a week's worth!" I'm flipping through the *Physician's Desk Reference,* that huge book, trying to figure out what the toxic level of Cipro is.

Brian Montgomery: Dan was real worried for a moment. After all that happened that day, Dan was going to die from Cipro poisoning.

Col. Dr. Richard Tubb: I looked into it and told him, "Listen, you're going to be fine. You might want to take an antacid."

Col. Mark Tillman: As we're landing, I was thinking, *All I've got to do is get him on the ground, then I can hand him off to the Marines.* I was watching the fighters scream by underneath, doing suppression, trying to figure out if there was anything waiting for us. The landing itself, after everything, was entirely normal.

672

Maj. Scott "Hooter" Crogg, F-16 pilot, 111th Fighter Squadron, Houston: We had landed right behind Air Force One, and so we saluted as [the president's helicopter] Marine One took off. We knew the president was heading to the White House.

Ari Fleischer, press secretary, White House: There are several different routes that Marine One can take back — we took the most scenic, directly over the Capitol, down the Mall, at the Washington Monument, you bank right.

Andy Card: We only flew at tree-top level, zigzagging, to make it harder for a missile to hit us. We were really low to the water on the Potomac.

Ari Fleischer: Out of the front left of the chopper, the president had a clear view of the Pentagon. The president said to nobody and everybody, "The mightiest building in the world is on fire. This is the face of war in the 21st century."

EVENING IN WASHINGTON

"A SPONTANEOUS SONG"

With the president en route to Washington, scheduled to arrive around 6:00 p.m. ET, the congressional leadership hidden at Mount Weather began to make their way back as well. In the early-fall darkness, about 150 representatives and senators gathered at the Capitol around 7:45 p.m.

John Feehery, press secretary to Speaker Dennis Hastert (R-Illinois): We took a helicopter ride back from the secure location. Beautiful Virginia sunset, beautiful day, and seeing the flames still leaping up from the Pentagon. It was really quite a sight and quite emotional.

Sen. Tom Daschle (D–South Dakota), Senate Majority Leader: Yet with that soft September light was chaos all around. Smoke still billowing from the Pentagon. Fire trucks below, jets above, tanks and all kinds of security — just an amazing transformation of what started as one of the most tranquil and beautiful days of the year that morning.

Brian Gunderson, chief of staff for House Majority Leader Richard Armey (R-Texas): You knew something was very wrong with the world that day. We passed over some office buildings in northern Virginia that had dump trucks parked at the entrance to their parking lots to prevent possible car bomb attacks.

Steve Elmendorf, chief of staff for House Minority Leader Richard Gephardt (D-Missouri): It was very surreal to fly in in helicopters, see the smoke coming out of the Pentagon, land on the Capitol grounds with a heightened level of security. At that time, it was very rare to see the Capitol Police with a machine gun or a shotgun or anything remotely like that. We landed and there were all sorts of people with automatic weapons and SWAT gear surrounding us, surrounding the helicopters.

John Feehery: It had really become a fortress.

Rep. Martin Frost (D-Texas), chair, House Democratic Caucus: At some point, there was a report on television that members were going to come back and meet at a certain time, so I did along with everybody else.

Rep. Dennis Hastert (R-Illinois), House Speaker: We walked across the East Front of the Capitol and there were probably 200 — maybe 175 or 225 — members of Congress on the front stairs of the Capitol. *Wow, it's pretty amazing.* Members of the House, members of the Senate, Democrats, Republicans.

Sen. Tom Daschle: I don't recall seeing a smile the entire evening. It was facial expressions that were somber — very, very grave.

Eve Butler-Gee, chief journal clerk, U.S. House of Representatives: By then, of course, we had learned about Flight 93. It was very bittersweet because our sense was that that plane was headed for the Capitol building. Had it not been for those people, it could have been much, much worse. They gave their lives to save ours.

Rep. Dennis Hastert: Daschle came up and spoke for a couple 20 seconds or so. I got up and basically said, "Look this country will be okay, we're going to stand up, we'll be back to work tomorrow, we'll do the people's work and get this country going again. And we'll find out who did this and protect our country."

Sen. Tom Daschle: After the two speeches, there was a moment of silence that wasn't scheduled. Nobody really wanted to leave. People started holding hands. Somebody started to sing.

Rep. Dennis Hastert: As I turned back to go back to the place I was standing, somebody broke out in the crowd of members of Congress in "God Bless America."

John Feehery: I think it was [Rep.] Jennifer Blackburn Dunn who started breaking out in "God Bless America."

Sen. Tom Daschle: It didn't take long before everybody began singing along. It was probably the most beautiful part of the entire experience, totally unplanned, totally spontaneous. But probably more powerful than whatever the Speaker and I said.

Rep. Dennis Hastert: I remember the chills going down my spine. I remember thinking, *This country will be okay. We'll stand shoulder to shoulder.*

Eve Butler-Gee: I cried. That was the moment when I really lost it, watching that happen. The feeling was, no matter what happens, nobody's going to defeat us, either psychologically or in actual fact.

Celine Haga, staff, U.S. House of Representatives: In the hours and days and weeks later, when it was replayed on TV, it felt trite and corny, but in that moment, that night, it felt like we were clinging to something, like a lifeline.

Rep. Martin Frost: Then we dispersed.

Marine One arrived at the White House shortly after 7:00 p.m., landing on the South Lawn.

Alberto Gonzales, White House counsel: The rest of the afternoon, I just ran between the underground bunker, the Situation Room, and my office on the second floor of the West Wing, making sure that all of the legal issues were being evaluated as policymakers were making decisions. Finally at about 7:30, I stood outside the Oval Office with Karen Hughes, the communications director, and we watched as Marine One landed on the South Lawn. We greeted the president as he returned home. We followed him into the Oval Office and then back into his private dining room. There, with Ari Fleischer, the press secretary, Andy Card, the chief of staff, Condi Rice, the national security adviser, Karen and I and the president, we talked about what happened that morning. We talked about what were we going do in response to the attacks, and we talked about what the president was going to say in his address to the nation that night.

Nic Calio, director of legislative affairs, White House: I stuck my head in at one point and said, "How are you doing, sir?" The president said, "I'm ready, and you need to be ready too." He was calm, the look in his eye was intense, and then when he talked to the senior staff, he said, "We all have to be ready. We are at war. We have to let the American people know that we're going to protect them. In a month from now, we're all going to want to go back to baseball and football and not think about this, but it's going to be our job to make sure that we're always thinking about it."

Condoleezza Rice, national security adviser, White House: By that night, the president was in the mood to start handing out assignments. He really was determined that Don Rumsfeld was going to be doing his work to make sure the military was ready.

Commander Anthony Barnes, deputy director, Presidential Contingency Programs, White House: Karen Hughes banged out that statement on her knees because there weren't any other chairs in there next to a computer. She kneeled down beside a computer and banged out that statement in about 20 minutes. When the president got back, he edited it for a couple of minutes, and then it was to the Oval Office for the television cameras.

Josh Bolten, deputy chief of staff, White House: I was nervous for the president because I knew how important this was to the feeling in America that day.

In the Oval Office
"WE GO FORWARD TO DEFEND FREEDOM"

8:30 P.M.

Good evening.

Today, our fellow citizens, our way of life, our very freedom came under attack in a series of deliberate and deadly terrorist acts.

The victims were in airplanes or in their offices — secretaries, businessmen and women, military and federal workers. Moms and dads. Friends and neighbors.

Thousands of lives were suddenly ended by evil, despicable acts of terror.

The pictures of airplanes flying into buildings, fires burning, huge structures collapsing, have filled us with disbelief, terrible sadness, and a quiet, unyielding anger.

These acts of mass murder were intended to frighten our nation into chaos and retreat. But they have failed. Our country is strong. A great people has been moved to defend a great nation.

Terrorist attacks can shake the foundations of our biggest buildings, but they cannot touch the foundation of America. These acts shatter steel, but they cannot dent the steel of American resolve.

America was targeted for attack because we're the brightest beacon for freedom and opportunity in the world. And no one will keep that light from shining.

Today, our nation saw evil, the very worst of human nature, and we responded with the best of America, with the daring of our rescue workers, with the caring for strangers and neighbors who came to give blood and help in any way they could.

Immediately following the first attack, I implemented our government's emergency response plans. Our military is powerful, and it's prepared. Our emergency teams are working in New York City and Washington, D.C., to help with local rescue efforts.

Our first priority is to get help to those who have been injured and to take every precaution to protect our citizens at home and around the world from further attacks.

The functions of our government continue without interruption. Federal agencies in Washington which had to be evacuated today are reopening for essential personnel tonight and will be open for business tomorrow.

Our financial institutions remain strong, and the American economy will be open for business as well.

The search is under way for those who are behind these evil acts. I've directed the full resources for our intelligence and law enforcement communities to find those responsible and bring them to justice. We will make no distinction between the terrorists who committed these acts and those who harbor them.

I appreciate so very much the members of Congress who have joined me in strongly condemning these attacks. And on behalf of the American people, I thank the many world leaders who have called to offer their condolences and assistance.

America and our friends and allies join with all those who want peace and security in the world and we stand together to win the war against terrorism.

Tonight I ask for your prayers for all those who grieve, for the children whose worlds have been shattered, for all whose sense of safety and security has been threatened. And I pray they will be comforted by a power greater than any of us, spoken through the ages in Psalm 23: "Even though I walk through the valley of the shadow of death, I fear no evil, for You are with me."

This is a day when all Americans from every walk of life unite in our resolve for justice and peace. America has stood down enemies before, and we will do so this time.

None of us will ever forget this day, yet we go forward to defend freedom and all that is good and just in our world.

Thank you. Good night, and God bless America.

■ ■ ■ ■

After the president's Oval Office address, Vice President Cheney boarded a helicopter to fly to an undisclosed location for the night — a site that later would be revealed as Camp David. Cheney slept that night in the president's own cabin, known as Aspen, a violation of normal protocol made necessary because Aspen connected directly to the presidential retreat's own escape bunker.

Dick Cheney, vice president: As we lifted off and headed up the Potomac, you could look out and see the Pentagon, see that black hole where it'd been hit. A lot of lights on the building, smoke rising from the Pentagon. It helped bring home the impact of what had happened, that we had in fact been attacked.

Lewis "Scooter" Libby, chief of staff to Vice President Dick Cheney: I recall watching the vice president, who was staring out the window at the Pentagon, and wondering what he may be thinking about, the responsibilities he would have in the future. A pretty sobering moment.

David Addington, counsel to the vice president: The headquarters of the U.S. military was still smoking, and we were flying

685

over on our way to hide the vice president. *My God, we're evacuating the vice president from Washington, D.C., because we've been attacked.*

Dick Cheney: I remember sitting in the living room there [in the Aspen cabin], turning on the television, watching the reruns. I suppose that was the moment — as much as any — that it really hit home what the country had been through that day.

THE EVENING OF 9/11
"I SPENT THE EVENING JUST CRYING"

Families across the country struggled to understand what the attacks meant for their loved ones, while those directly affected continued to scatter and make their way home — sometimes without knowing how their own families had been affected.

Charles Christophe, attorney, Broadway: I tried to reach Penn Station and from Penn Station eventually to get the train to go to Maplewood [New Jersey]. Everything was closed. We had to wait hours. I think late afternoon, finally, they let the first train go. I was not able to catch the first one, but I did get the second one. People were looking at me, because I was totally covered with dust in my hair, my suit — everything.

Bruno Dellinger, principal, Quint Amasis North America, North Tower: When I arrived home, on my apartment door there was a Post-It from one of my interns who left a funny note: "If you're alive, I'm still alive."

Rosemary Dillard, Washington, D.C., base manager, American Airlines, and wife of Flight 77 passenger Eddie Dillard: I had to drive by the Pentagon. I wanted to stop, they wouldn't let you. I got home, went in the house, and I smoked four cigarettes. I figured if I smoked in the house, it would bring my husband back because he didn't smoke in the house. Then I had to call his brothers. I had to call my friends, the rest of his family, and my sister. My neighbors started coming over right away, because the flight attendants lived in the area. They came and brought me dinner. After that, it's kind of a blur. Life changed.

Linda Krouner, senior vice president, Fiduciary Trust, South Tower: I didn't really know what happened yet. I certainly knew we lost people. When I was at my sister's house in New York City, there was a fellow, he got my number. He knew I was in the building that morning and he said, "I'm so-and-so. Did you see my son? Did you pass him on the staircase?" This young fellow died; it was terrible. It was really one of these calls that you want to say, "I wish I saw him. I wish I could tell you something." I couldn't tell him anything.

Adrian Pierce, Wachovia Bank, North Tower: Cathleen — she sat behind me — we don't know where she was. Carlos, we don't know where he was in the building. Toyena, she got killed also. Jeffrey got killed. Antoinette was holding a guy — his name was Tom — she was holding his hand as we were coming out the building, and he let her hand go, and the building came down on her. We lost five people from Wachovia. I also lost 150 friends from Euro Brokers on the 88th floor. One friend in particular, Adam, he came out, he called his parents, and he said, "I'm okay." But he went back in the building, and he never came back out.

Charles Christophe: I was worrying about my wife, Kirsten [a vice president of risk services for Aon Corporation on the 104th floor of the South Tower]. I was worrying about our daughter, Gretchen, because we didn't have close relatives to pick her up from the daycare. I was hoping maybe, maybe Kirsten was able to get on the first train or on this train and I will meet her there or meet her at home.

Robert Small, office manager, Morgan Stanley, South Tower: I was home before I normally would have been home. I still thought we were supposed to have our Pop Warner football team pictures taken that

689

night. I still thought we were going to do that. I got a phone call from the league guy: "We're not taking pictures tonight." I said, "Okay," because it still hadn't hit me how dramatic and big the day was. It was still "my day," as opposed to what it meant to everybody else. Within the next day or two, you started realizing how many people it affected.

Deena Burnett, wife of United Flight 93 passenger Tom Burnett: I spent the evening just crying and being with friends, having neighbors come in and out, and having family call me on my cell phone to offer their condolences.

Rosemary Dillard: I was still calling his cell phone, and he had a pager — I was still paging it every so often.

Charles Christophe: I got to Maplewood — we usually parked our car by the train station, but I didn't have a key — so I had to walk to the daycare. I took my daughter from the daycare, and I asked about my wife. Only my daughter was there. All other kids were taken by their parents, and one or two people from the staff. She was a baby — 11 months old — and she didn't understand. She recognized my face, and obviously was happy to see me. One of the employees of the daycare drove me to my home. I didn't have a key. I had to break the window on the back door in the kitchen to enter. I immediately took care of my daughter — I had to feed her and change her and put her in the bath, because it was already six, seven o'clock. And then I was just sitting by the phone waiting for a call.

Jillian Volk, preschool teacher, Lower Manhattan: We spent the whole night going from hospital to hospital, checking the admittance lists. Then at seven o'clock that night, we got a phone call from Bellevue Hospital, saying [my fiancé] Kevin was admitted there. His dad got there before we did, and he found out it wasn't the right Kevin Williams. It was somebody else. We had been on this whole high, screaming. I searched the city for three days.

John Napolitano, father of FDNY firefighter John P. Napolitano: It was late, and the kids wouldn't go to sleep because my son, whenever he worked nights, he would always call and talk to them, and tell them a story over the phone. Then he would end with "Hugs and kisses," and they'd go to bed. They weren't going to bed because their father didn't call.

Charles Christophe: I was waiting for Kirsten's call. But nobody called.

Fernando Ferrer, candidate for New York City mayor: I organized a prayer vigil on the Grand Concourse at Love Gospel Assembly. What else could you do? That place was packed. We then made the rounds of firehouses. We saw guys come back covered in white dust. People had already set up — oh, I get emotional just talking about it — had set up shrines and brought flowers and stuff and lit candles. It was really something.

Perry Weden, Los Angeles: I had been dating someone for six months and was unsure where the relationship was heading. This normally very calm and collected man was anxious and shaken, distraught over the lives already lost and fearful that L.A. was in the crosshairs. We went to the Santa Monica Pier, a relative ghost town for a warm September day, an attempt to be defiant in the face of fear. He made a comment I would never forget, something about how if the world was going to end today, he was glad to have spent it with me.

Richard Kolko, special agent, FBI: I started the day in the Atlanta FBI field office assigned to the Joint Terrorism Task Force. By midday, I was driving to Washington, D.C. A New York agent who was stuck in Atlanta jumped in the car with me. The roads were deserted. It was nighttime, and we were somewhere in North Carolina heading north on I-95, well above the speed limit. Suddenly, the rearview mirror lit up with a North Carolina trooper right behind me. I pulled over. The trooper approached my window cautiously. He got to the window and clearly, carefully, and professionally checked us out. He asked if we knew how fast we were going and what was the rush. I identified myself as an FBI agent and said we were headed to D.C. He took one step back from the window, pointed north on I-95, and said, "Go get 'em."

Lt. Joseph Torrillo, director of fire education safety, FDNY: Eight hours later, I woke up and I didn't know where I was. I realized I was on the eighth floor of the hospital, in a room, but I didn't immediately know because I couldn't see. I'm like, *I don't know if I'm dead or alive.* That night, they found my car behind the firehouse. I was declared dead that night.

Lt. Mickey Kross, Engine 16, FDNY: The day had passed. I don't even know what I did. I know I walked around. I talked to some people. We did a little search. In fact, we found a police officer on West Street. He was dead. He was buried. We helped out where we could and the day passed.

I hitched a ride with one of the fire engines that was going north. I think there was about

40 of us hanging off this fire engine. They dropped me off on Third Avenue and 29th Street and I walked down the block. I walked into the firehouse and I remember my girlfriend, Christine, was there. A number of the wives were there and some of the firemen were there. That's when I found out that Ladder 7 was missing — that's our company that's quartered with us: 16 and 7. Everybody from 7 was missing. They all died.

Chris Mullin, firefighter, Ladder 1, FDNY: It was a depressed, dismal, miserable mood. Hundreds of firefighters, thousands of civilians are gone as quickly as you blow out a match. Gone.

Capt. Jay Jonas, Ladder 6, FDNY: I ended up walking from the World Trade Center to the firehouse on Canal Street. It was pretty quiet. I'm walking with all my gear on. I must have looked like Pig Pen from the Charlie Brown cartoon with this big cloud of dust following me. A bunch of Chinese people from the community start following me, and somebody broke off and came and talked to me. He says, "Are you okay?" I said, "Yeah. If I keep walking I'm okay." I says, "If I stop, I'm not going to want to start up again." Then they followed me to make sure I got to the firehouse.

Tracy Donahoo, transit officer, NYPD:
When I went home that night, I went home
to my mother and sat in the backyard — it
was another beautiful day. I was sitting in the
backyard, saying to my mother, "I don't know
if I can do this. I don't know if I wanna stay
on this job." I got up the next day and went
to work. I went back the day after that, and
the day after that, and I said, "I'll take it day
after day and see how I feel." Over time, I
was okay.

Pasquale Buzzelli, engineer, Port Authority, North Tower, 64th floor: I was
basically in a stretcher at Saint Vincent's and
they were moving me from room to room,
taking X-rays and things. My friend Phil
showed up. They gave me some clothes to
wear, because they had to rip the clothes off
of me that I had on. It was Disney or Mickey
Mouse, something that didn't fit. I put that
on.

There was a police officer there with a van
and he said, "Where do you want to go?" We
gave him the address, our other friend's
house. When I got to my friend's apartment,
it was the first time I was actually able to
watch it on television. I couldn't believe that
I actually survived.

Got in the car. We headed north and went
across the Tappan Zee Bridge and I was home
at eight o'clock that night. I pulled up at

home with all my family and friends there. It was nice. It was nice to be home — to see my mother and father, my wife, Louise.

Louise Buzzelli, wife of Pasquale Buzzelli, Port Authority, North Tower: I remember the first thing when we finally got him inside the house, my mother-in-law — she's from Italy — her first thing was, "You must be hungry!" She said, "Sit down! I want to make you a nice sandwich."

As the evacuation of people from Lower Manhattan slowed, the boats that had been busy all day shuttling people out of New York reversed their journey for a new mission: shuttling relief supplies and rescuers to Lower Manhattan.

Lt. Michael Day, U.S. Coast Guard: We started getting calls that supplies were coming into Jersey and all the bridges were shut down into Manhattan. They said, "Hey, can we get someone to pick up some supplies?" I asked if anyone would mind going over to New Jersey and picking up some supplies, and I was inundated. "Sure, I'll do it." "I'll do it." "I'll do it."

Firefighters would come up and say, "We're going to need water. We don't have any water." We'd call over to someone from New Jersey. We established a dialogue with the Office of Emergency Management over there. People were going to store shelves and buying water. It was coming over. There was a lot of stuff coming over — a lot of ice, a lot of restaurants were sending meals. It was very disorganized as far as what was coming. As we started meeting those needs, we started getting more and more requests. "We need acetylene for steel. We need oxygen. We need wrenches." We started making requests and things started coming. It was busy throughout that night.

At Ground Zero, firefighters and rescue personnel continued to swarm over the wreckage, looking for survivors. These efforts remained haphazard, filled by an army of volunteers, many of whom had no official rescue duties. Indeed, it was two U.S. Marines, Jason Thomas and Dave Karnes, who had traveled to the site on their own volition, who made the evening's sole incredible discovery.

Scott Strauss, officer, Emergency Service Unit, Truck 1, NYPD: We're all itching to get back in there and find civilians, find our friends, find somebody. Sgt. Timothy Adrat grabbed a bunch of us and we started searching — because they wouldn't allow us back onto the pile yet — we started searching the south side, the buildings on the south side of Liberty that were damaged by the collapses, but not completely collapsed. The pile of debris was massive.

Det. Steven Stefanakos, Emergency Service Unit, Truck 10, NYPD: We went to work trying to get to any voids that we could, trying to, from that moment, start any type of rescue and recovery that we could. It was pretty well established as nightfall started.

William Jimeno, officer, PAPD: It was around 8:00 that night when I heard two voices in the distance. I heard, "United States Marine Corps, can anybody hear us?" I couldn't believe it that I heard voices again. I started yelling as loud as I could. "PAPD officers down! PAPD officers down!" They kept saying, "Keep yelling, we hear you!" They made their way over, and I could hear three individuals. They said, "Who's down there?" I said, "Port Authority Police, Officer Jimeno, my sergeant's down. We have men down here. We have men who have died," and they said, "Hold on, buddy."

Scott Strauss: A firefighter comes over to us. He says, "Hey, I got a couple of guys that are hurt on the other side." So we started running over in that direction. We're climbing over this twisted steel — some were very, very hot — jumping from one to the other.

We're slipping on the dust. It was a very treacherous trek. Through the dust and through the smoke, I saw a guy waving a flashlight, I went over to him. I said, "What do you got?" He goes, "You got two guys, two cops down in this hole." So I look, and there's this hole a little bit bigger than the size of a manhole. I dropped down into it, about six to eight feet. It was like a very, very tiny closet. Paddy McGee, an Emergency Service police officer with me, also jumped in the hole, as did this civilian, Chuck Sereika, a former paramedic.

William Jimeno: Truck 1 came up. They hooked up with another civilian named Chuck Sereika, a paramedic.

Paddy McGee, officer, Emergency Service Unit, Truck 1, NYPD: The race was on.

Scott Strauss: We came down on an angle about 20 to 30 feet, crawling headfirst around I-beams, through these tiny crevices, pulling ourselves through. We got down to this little open area, and we turned left and we came upon Dominick [Pezzulo]. About 10 feet back was Will Jimeno. The only thing we could see of Will was his head, his right arm, and part of his right side. The rest of it — it looks like he was poured out of a dump truck.

699

William Jimeno: He said, "What's your name?" and I said "Jimeno." He goes, "Scott Strauss NYPD ESU Truck 1." I said, "Jimeno, Bus Terminal. Port Authority Police," and he said, "Listen, you got to hold on — you can't give up now."

Scott Strauss: I crawled in, and I had to crawl in on my side, and with my hands above my head. I was crawling in, pulling myself in, and I was literally using my hands to scratch away at the rubble. As I free up some debris I'm pushing it down along my chest to get it back out to Paddy and Chuck, and they took it and were throwing it down the elevator shaft, digging their way out.

William Jimeno: They could barely move in there. All I could see was their bald heads.

Scott Strauss: We were dry heaving. We were choking on the smoke. The firemen were yelling from up above us, "Get out of there." Will says, "You're not leaving me, are you?" I go, "No. We're not leaving you, Will." Did I want to go? You better believe I wanted to get out of there, but I couldn't. It had nothing to do with any macho stuff. It had to do with self-preservation. I don't think I could have left him, gone home to my kids, and known I left him there to die. So the three of us — Chuck, Paddy, and I — stayed.

William Jimeno: For the next three hours they worked on me, and it was very, very painful. They were able to free my right leg, and then it took a long time for them to try to get me from under this wall.

Scott Strauss: Chuck, Paddy, and I, we were exhausted. We were incredibly tired. We were in a bad way, in a bad environment.

William Jimeno: I remember saying, "I have a partner, he's here," and they thought it was Dominick. Sergeant McLoughlin kept quiet back there. I think what happened was that when they first started on me, I yelled once really hard — when they touched my leg, it was really painful. I saw that Scott backed away. I remember thinking to myself, *You need to shut up and eat the pain,* and that's what I did. I think Sergeant McLoughlin heard that as not to disrupt these guys — the best thing to do is to try to get us out of here faster.

Scott Strauss: All the time Will is talking about his partner. We don't know — the only person that's talking to us in this hole is Will. Dominick Pezzulo's dead. Will's talking about his partner: "You've got to get to my partner first. You got to get him out." I'm like, *He* *doesn't know he's dead,* thinking "he" is Dominick.

William Jimeno: It was a nightmare that night.

Scott Strauss: He's like, "Hurry up! Hurry! You've got to get to him. He's going to die if you don't get to him." I said, "Will, we got to do our job. We got to get you out, and then we'll get him out." We're scratching away, scratching away, and then we hear Sergeant McLoughlin's voice, and he goes, "Hey, how are you guys doing?" I'm like, "Who's that?" Will's like, "That's my partner," like, *You idiots. What do you think I've been talking about?* So we're like, "We thought *he* was your partner." He said, "No, that's Dominick. He's dead." I'm like, *Oh, my God!* Now we have another rescue that we have to do.

Det. Steven Stefanakos, Emergency Service Unit, Truck 10, NYPD: The two rescue sites started for the two Port Authority police officers that were trapped. Truck 1 guys, from their team, were working on that extrication. The rest of us walked around to any particular area where you might find a void that you could crawl into. Every single building in a perfect square around the Trade Center was completely demolished or damaged. The buildings were on fire still. You looked up and you said, "At any given time any one of these buildings could fall."

Scott Strauss: Will's screaming in pain and Sergeant McLoughlin is fading in and out this whole time. We're talking to McLoughlin and Paddy McGee — can't get any more Irish than him, he was born on St. Patrick's Day, he's in the police department pipe band — and John McLoughlin, another Irishman, and Paddy's like, "Hey, Irish eyes, are you still with us?" Sometimes he would answer, sometimes he wouldn't. When he didn't answer, Will would get worked up. "John, Sarge, come on, Sarge, hold on, Sarge!" Then you'd hear him in a groggy voice say, "I'm here. I'm here."

William Jimeno: They were able to put me on a gurney, and I remember telling the Sarge, "Hold on, Sarge."

Scott Strauss: We get him onto the Stokes basket and we send him out — up topside.

William Jimeno: As they started pulling me out on the gurney, up this hole, I remember looking around, and I said, "Where is everything?" Because I could see the moon, and I could see smoke, but I couldn't see the buildings. That's when a firefighter said, "It's all

703

gone, kid." That's the first time I cried that evening.

Omar Olayan, officer, NYPD: We heard people, some excitement — coming up the line was a basket with a body in it, one of the Port Authority officers they rescued. We pulled him out. It was exciting — a great moment. All day you've been there and there was nothing.

Scott Strauss: I crawl back down this hole. I'm physically shot. It's now like 11:00 at night, 11:30 at night. "John, I can't do any more. They're sending a fresh team in. You'll be fine. These guys are going to get you out." He's like, "Thanks, Scott. I appreciate it. I'll see you up top." I said, "Absolutely." Another emergency cop, Steve Clifford, comes in the hole — and I don't know why I said this to him — but I stopped him and I go, "Steve, personal friend. Make sure you get him out."

William Jimeno: My sergeant came out the next day, at 7:00 a.m.

Scott Strauss: The rescue workers, cops, firemen from all over the place — all of Nassau County, Connecticut, New Jersey, everywhere — Con Ed workers, construction workers are lining this path and they're help-

PAPD Sgt. John McLoughlin is rescued from Ground Zero.

ing me get down, helping the three of us get down.

William Jimeno: I remember as we got to the hospital, I'm thinking there's going to be thousands of people in there. That's the second time I cried. As they pulled me off the ambulance, I see these doctors standing around and nurses. I said, "Where is everybody?" They're like, "You're it." They're telling me there's nobody else.

THE DAY ENDS
"I WONDERED, 'DID THEY GET OUT?' "

As night descended on a country transformed and the calendar flipped from 9/11 to 9/12, lawmakers, first responders, government officials, and stricken families tried to make sense of the day they'd just experienced. Fear and uncertainty permeated everything, and across the country many faced a sleepless night. In Washington, the fires at the Pentagon illuminated the night sky, an ominous sign of a nation newly at war.

Jackie Maguire, special agent, FBI Joint Terrorism Task Force, New York: That night we started to relocate and put our command center up in an automobile and maintenance garage. It was well organized. It was amazing — they emptied all the cars out and the technical people set up the phone lines. Within the next day or two, we had a full-blown, fully operational command post. We identified the hijackers pretty quickly. Then they made the case squad. They made what was known as the PENTTBOM team. The FBI's code name for terrorism cases usually end with -bom; b-o-m. The first Trade Center was TRADEBOM, the East Africa Embassy cases were KENBOM for Kenya, and TAN-BOM for Tanzania, so they formed the PENTTBOM team.

Keith Custer, firefighter, Shanksville Volunteer Fire Company: Later on that night in Shanksville, we got called back for numerous brush fires. You couldn't put the fire out because the ground was so saturated with jet fuel. You'd put out as much as you could, and then it would burn underground for a while, and then it would spring up somewhere else.

Laurence Kesterson, staff photographer, *Philadelphia Inquirer*: I felt so removed from everything else. They kept talking on the news about something happening in Shanksville or western Pennsylvania. No one was getting the name right the first day. Clearly everybody was focused on New York. In the evening, I stayed at a Holiday Inn in Johnstown. I watched the TV — they were all reporting from New York. We were so fearful as to what was going to happen. I really wanted to get home to my family.

Peter M. "Mike" Drewecki, photographer, WPXI-TV, Pittsburgh: I think I slept an hour. I turned on CNN, and I remember there was a doctor who was outside the Trade Centers when they went down. CNN was running the videos of people actually jumping out of the windows, and after what I saw, I couldn't sleep. Who could? It was to the point where you were so agitated, you were so strung out on what you went through that sleep wasn't an option.

Bruno Dellinger, principal, Quint Amasis North America, North Tower: When I got home, the first thing I did was take my suit off, and — don't ask me why, I think it may be unconsciously because I thought there might be some human remains in those ashes — I collected them, put them into a small box. I was never able to ever wear that suit again, or the tie, or the shoes. For some reason I was inspired to collect that dust and keep it, and I still have it in a small box with the only thing that's left of my office: a set of keys.

Brian Pearl, resident, Greenpoint, Brooklyn: That night, a bunch of our friends got together at Enid's, a popular bar in the neighborhood. It felt good to be amongst friends if for no other reason than to remind me that I wasn't the only person who had no idea what to think, feel, or do.

Richard Grasso, chairman and CEO, New York Stock Exchange: I was having dinner on the Upper East Side at the only restaurant that was open. What sticks in my mind was on Second Avenue and 75th Street were these enormous dump trucks that were heading south. You knew where they were going. I got back in my truck about 10:30, and I'll never forget it — the city was so empty.

Rick Schoenlank, president, United New Jersey Sandy Hook Pilots Benevolent Association: Probably around 11:00 or 12:00, myself and seven or eight other pilots decided to go and see it for ourselves. We got off the boat, and we walked through the dust — like six inches of dust — that was covering everything. There were bulldozers slapping chains on the wrecks of firetrucks, police cars, ambulances, just dragging them down the street. You couldn't even tell what they were anymore.

There were searchlights centered on the pile. There were hundreds of people crawling all over it. Looking around on the perimeter of the whole site, it looked like a giant animal had taken a giant claw and taken swipes out of all the buildings. There were chunks of the buildings missing. All the windows were broken. Drapes and papers were flying around in the air. Fire and flame was coming out of some of the windows. It was a scene of total destruction.

Lt. Michael Day, U.S. Coast Guard: I walked into Ground Zero and I could remember there were body parts everywhere. I remember thinking, *This is a war.* I looked down and saw a foot in a shoe. I was fixating on it for a few minutes. It was like a siege, looking around and seeing National Guard guys with M-16s going through the streets of Manhattan. All the power was out around the area, and a lot of other buildings were on fire, and there was this eerie gray-like snow everywhere.

Rick Schoenlank: I was standing there, and I noticed after a while there was a very tall guy standing right next to me and with a full particle mask on. I looked at him once, and I looked at him twice, and I said, "Governor, is that you?" It was Governor Pataki — just happened to be standing right there.

Chuck Cake, firefighter and EMT, Arlington County Fire Department: Around 1:00 a.m., the fire was still burning on the Pentagon roof — you could see it glowing — it was decided to suspend operations until morning, and then try again.

Sgt. Anthony Lisi, Emergency Service Unit, Truck 6, NYPD: By the end of the night we were exhausted. It was about two, three o'clock in the morning, and our vehicle that we had driven had been destroyed. NYPD boats picked us up to take us back to Truck 6, which is in Bay Ridge. As we were driving up with the boat, there was cars waiting for us with their lights on, a guy standing by each vehicle. It was amazing. They knew what we went through, and they were waiting for us to take us back to the truck, take us home.

Jared Kotz, Risk Waters Group: In the middle of the night, or maybe three or four o'clock in the morning, I was awakened by a loud clap of thunder followed by a brief rainstorm. At that moment I realized it wasn't a dream, that I certainly had lived through an incredible day. First thing, my thoughts turned to my colleagues and I wondered, *Did they get out?* I didn't know.

Sunny Mindel, communications director for the mayor of the City of New York, Rudy Giuliani: I came home at three in the morning, four in the morning, to shower. I got into my apartment and stood at the threshold and thought, *What do I do with my clothes? I don't know what's on my clothes.* I got a plastic bag to put my clothes in.

I had to go back to work obviously very shortly after — all I wanted to do was shower, lay down for a few minutes. I fell asleep, and as I did I felt like the buildings were in my nose — there was all this cement — and I woke up screaming having a nightmare, hearing the sounds in this dream.

Tom Brokaw, anchor, NBC News: I got home at 2:00 a.m., sat down, and was staring out the window. I had a big stiff drink of scotch. I was curiously contained and controlled. I was doing this out-of-body examination and asking myself, *Why am I not melting down?* I had a second drink. I went to sleep. I slept for four hours. I felt rested. Then a phone call came — a very close friend of mine died of congestive heart failure the night before. It released something in me. For half an hour, all the emotion I'd bottled up came out. I sobbed.

Mike Walter, senior correspondent, *USA Today Live:* The last interview I did on 9/11 was with a colleague of mine — Lance, the photographer who was shooting for me that day. He said, "Let me turn the camera on you as a friend, talk to you about what we saw." We did the interview and he said, "Is there anything else you want to say?" My response was, "I'm so thankful this day is over." Lance started laughing. He's like, "Mike, this isn't over, this will never be over for you. There will always be the six-month anniversary, the one-year anniversary, the five-year anniversary, the 10-year anniversary. You'll be talking about this for the rest of your life."

Beverly Eckert, wife of Sean Rooney, VP of risk management, Aon Corporation, South Tower, 98th floor: We met when we were only 16, at a high school dance. When he died, we were 50. I remember how I didn't want that day to end, terrible as it was. I didn't want to go to sleep because as long as I was awake, it was still a day that I shared with Sean. He kissed me goodbye before leaving for work. I could still say that was just a little while ago. That was only this morning.

EPILOGUE

As September 12th began, the entire nation tried to make sense of the previous day's attacks and the tragic losses. At the Pentagon, the fires from 9/11 had flared up and again threatened the building. All told, thousands of Pentagon workers had been displaced and more than two million square feet of office space — the equivalent of the entire Empire State Building — had been damaged.

Lt. Col. Ted Anderson, legislative liaison officer, U.S. Army, Pentagon: I slept for a couple of hours, woke up, and thought it was all a bad dream. I popped on the news and, of course, I couldn't get away from the story. This was about two in the morning and I decided to get up and go to work. I put on my battle dress uniform, my fatigues, and my boots.

I got in a car and drove, and as soon as I turned onto 395, I could see the orange glow

in the distance. I remember very distinctly —
at about 3:10 in the morning — parking my
car, seeing this building on fire, and people
going into work. Ten thousand people showed
up to work at the Pentagon that morning. It
made me extremely proud.

**Lt. Comm. David Tarantino, physician,
U.S. Navy:** We all went back to work the next
day in a building that was still burning to
start planning our nation's response.

**William Haynes, general counsel, De-
partment of Defense:** I remember driving
in at 5:00 or 6:00 the next morning, seeing a
soldier on a street corner in downtown D.C.,
and thinking, *This is something.*

**Mike Walter, senior correspondent, *USA
Today Live:*** Washington, D.C., is such a
beautiful, magnificent city, and here were all
these people with weapons — the National
Guard's out there in their vehicles. It seemed
like you were in a banana republic.

**Adm. Edmund Giambastiani, senior
military assistant, Office of the Secretary
of Defense:** We started planning on the 12th
of September. We knew we would get into
some kind of global war on terrorism. At that
time, the casualty estimates coming in from
New York City were that we had lost 6,000

people in the World Trade Center — more than we had lost anywhere at any time in the history of this country on any one day.

Robert Hunor, contractor, Radian, Inc., Pentagon: It was about 10:00 a.m., and they were towing cars away from South Parking. There wasn't a lot — maybe 60 of them. None of them had moved since the previous day. It dawned on me that this guy was parking next to me yesterday, and he was never going to get in that car again. He was never going to drive home.

Scott Kocher, contractor, SAIC, Pentagon: The corridors smelled horrible, especially the upper levels. It wasn't too bad once we got back down into the basement. The Army Operations Center, where I worked, ironically was in danger of flooding, because they were pouring so much water onto the fire.

Chuck Cake, firefighter and EMT, Arlington County Fire Department: I remember working on the roof all day — tactic after tactic after tactic. It was a poured cement building, but it's got a wooden sheathed roof on top, and the fire was under the roof. You'd do a trench cut to put it here, then turn around, and it had gotten under you while you were doing the trench cut. We chased it for half the day, and finally, we got it at about 2:30 in the afternoon.

Across the country, those whose lives had intersected with the attacks experienced a wide mix of emotions as they came to understand the full impact — both personal and global — of what had occurred.

Lyzbeth Glick, wife of United Flight 93 passenger Jeremy Glick: The morning after Jeremy had died, I remember looking down at our daughter, Emerson — she was sleeping — and just crying because she would never know her father. I thought she would only know a sad mom. We had trouble having her — took us two and a half years — and then to have everything taken away. We had dreams for our family. Then something just kind of clicked in my head, and I said, "You know, I have a choice. I'm not going to ruin her life. I'm not going to ruin my own life."

The ticket agent at Washington Dulles Airport who had checked in the 9/11 hijackers there and made sure they made it safely aboard American Airlines Flight 77 arrived at work the following day, oblivious to his role.

Vaughn Allex, ticket agent, Washington Dulles International Airport, Virginia: I didn't know what I had done. I came to work and people wouldn't look at me in the eye. They handed me the manifest for the flight. I stared at it for a second, then I looked up, and said, "I did it." I had checked in a family — it was a retiree and his wife. I had time to talk to them. There was a student group — I checked in a lot of those kids, parents, teachers. They were all gone. Once it became known, people didn't talk to me.

For Susannah Herrada, whose baby, Dillon, had been born in Arlington on 9/11, amid the chaos and the injured from the Pentagon, the happiness of her own time in the hospital contrasted with the experience of everyone around her.

Susannah Herrada, resident, Arlington, Virginia: Neighbors kept on coming by — and some of them I didn't know well enough to have them see me half-naked trying to nurse a baby and in pain. They said, "Oh, we wanted to see something good." It's wonderful how this birth was able to be a blessing to so many people, but to me, it was like, *Get these people out of here.* One neighbor came by when the nurse was trying to get me out of bed and, oh my gosh, I was sobbing. The neighbors were so excited to see Dillon and to have something great happen.

Mary Dettloff, communications staff, Michigan legislature: My partner and I made an effort to patronize our favorite Middle Eastern restaurant a day after the attack because we feared people would retaliate against it. They had put a sign on their front door saying how sorry they were about the terrorist attack and that they didn't support it. I remember thinking how sad that they felt the need to do that.

Gabriella Daya-Dominguez, resident, Chatham, New Jersey: My father is Arabic. I remember feeling a sense of dread that week. I couldn't eat at all. Food tasted like paper. It was hard to put something in my mouth. I felt that there was going to be a backlash against Arabs. I remember being terrified.

Stacey Taylor Parham, air traffic control specialist, Cleveland Air Route Traffic Control Center: I remember sitting outside with my kids and how quiet it was. You don't realize how many airplanes you hear and see. They're such a part of the landscape. Sitting outside — the weather was beautiful for those next few days too — looking up in the sky, not seeing any airplanes at all. It was so quiet.

Susannah Herrada: At night, I would sit there and Dillon would wake up, and as I'd feed him I'd listen to the sound of the jets circling and protecting the airspace. I would lay awake and listen to that sound of the fighter planes overhead.

In New York, at what workers and rescuers called "The Pile," teams searched for the dead and the living, and bucket brigades began sorting and clearing debris, a process that would ultimately encompass 1.8 million tons of wreckage and stretch until May 30, 2002. Early on the second day, rescuers stumbled upon Pasquale Buzzelli's coworker, Genelle Guzman.

Paul Somin, firefighter, Rescue 2, FDNY: That morning we came back and we were under the command of a Lt. Larry Gray, a really senior veteran of the New York City Fire Department — someone we would call a salty guy. We went back down to the site. The decision was made: we were going to go where Jay Jonas, his guys, and Mickey Kross survived. We said, "Maybe somebody else survived there."

Genelle Guzman, office assistant, Port Authority, North Tower, 64th floor: Everybody in my family was in mourning already. They were up all night. They didn't even entertain the thought that I had made it after the collapse. They went through a moment of thinking I was dead and they were not going to see me again. And, as the Bible says, sadness comes at night, but joy comes in the morning. That's what happened to my family. They were sad at night, and the joy waited until the morning.

Paul Somin: We started climbing up. It was a crazy climb. Everything was on fire, the steel was all hot. We got to about the 15th floor of the building, where we knew that Jonas and those guys survived, and we started to search. First, we found a couple of firemen dead. We did not take the time at that point to try to extricate them because we were looking for people who were alive. There was an elevator shaft up there and at that point I started yelling in the elevator shaft, and I heard someone answer me back. I yelled again. I realized that we found somebody.

Genelle Guzman: They came up to that area on the heap of rubble because they saw a reflector jacket there, thinking it could be one of theirs. That's when I called out, because I heard them.

Paul Somin: We got everybody quiet. We tried to pinpoint her voice. Billy Esposito and I climbed down two more floors and realized her voice was getting fainter. We couldn't hear it anymore. We started to climb up and up and up. Suddenly I could hear her a lot better. She said, "Don't leave me! Don't leave me!" I assured her, "I'm not going to leave you." At that point, I said, "Tell me your name." She said, "My name is Genelle." We were literally standing on top of her, but we couldn't find her. I said to her, "Can you stick your hand or anything out?" Out of the rubble came her hand. Immediately I grabbed it — now we had her. Everyone was fired up. This was what we were waiting for. Everybody was exhilarated.

Genelle Guzman: Someone grabbed my hand, they called me by my name, and said, "Genelle, I got you. My name is Paul." The person had my hand, and I knew I was not dreaming.

Paul Somin: I basically held her hand. We started talking back and forth. The guys went underneath her, they went over the top of her. It took about 45 minutes, and they got her out.

Genelle Guzman: I got into the ambulance with a guy, and he said, "We're going to take you to the hospital now, OK? You're going to be fine." I made it to the hospital. I asked the nurse, "Am I going to go home now?" She said, "Oh no, honey, you're going to be here for a while." Then someone said, "Do you know how long you've been there?" I said, "I don't." They said, "You've been buried for 27 hours." She said, "Do you know that you were the last survivor that they pulled out?"

Paul Somin: Away she went. In our minds we're thinking, *Now we're going to start finding other people.* We started to climb out onto the pile, and we started finding more dead firemen. As it would turn out, she was the last survivor of the World Trade Center.

Genelle Guzman: I was praying for 27 hours. Being the last survivor — it was a huge thing. I felt totally different. When I came out of that rubble, I felt a total conviction. From there I knew that the Holy Spirit was working in me and had changed my life. Since that day, I've been serving the Lord. After I came out of the hospital in November, I went to the Brooklyn Tabernacle Church. I got baptized. I got married to my boyfriend. I've been living the Christian life since. I had two kids after that marriage and the Lord has been good to me.

Paul Somin: I guess it was a miracle — you think about that site that she was found, it is a miracle. It's a miracle that we climbed up there.

For the families and friends of those who were lost, 9/12 began an often long, always heartsick search for word of the missing. By Wednesday's end, the official death toll at the World Trade Center would stand at 82, but officials warned, "The death toll from the nation's deadliest terrorism attack is expected to rise considerably." Not knowing the true number, New York City asked the federal government for 5,000 body bags.

Herb Ouida, World Trade Centers Association, North Tower, 77th floor, and father of Todd Ouida, Cantor Fitzgerald, North Tower, 105th floor: We took his picture, I went to the hospitals. It was so terrible, all of us putting up pictures. None of us could accept the scope of the tragedy. The next day my wife said to me, "There's no hope." I said, "You're wrong." We went to a meeting of all the Cantor families. I remember Howard [Lutnick], the head of Cantor, telling us there was no hope. People were so angry at him for saying that. He was telling us the truth. We waited. We prayed. Eventually, we accepted it.

Heather Ordover, English teacher, HSLPS: The hardest was the next day. The rumors had been flying that my principal's sister was at Cantor Fitzgerald, on the 105th floor. She was missing, presumed dead. But all the children were home and accounted for.

John Napolitano, father of FDNY fire-fighter John P. Napolitano: We went back to the site every day. I knew a lot of the firemen down there — they had all grown up with my son — so we had no problem getting in. He was never found. Every day I'd go home and wish I could tell my wife something good. Never happened. I had no good news for them.

Lt. Joseph Torrillo, director of fire education safety, FDNY: Firefighters from the Jersey City Fire Department came to the Jersey City Trauma Center, where I was, and they actually took me back to Brooklyn, to my house. When they got me home, they gave me a list of all the missing firefighters. I was reading the list, and I couldn't believe it. Timmy Stackpole — I was with him when the building came down, but he went to the left, I went to the right. Timmy is gone.

Dan Potter, firefighter, Ladder 10, FDNY: At the end of the day, 60 friends of mine were killed. So were three very, very close friends — Mike Warchola, Vinny Giammona, and Brian Hickey.

Sal Cassano, assistant chief, FDNY: We lost 343 members. That was 4,400 years of combined experience. We had to rebuild the department from the ground up. We lost our chief of department. We lost our first deputy fire commissioner. We lost two of our most knowledgeable staff chiefs, dozens and dozens of officers. So how do we rebuild? We had promotions. The next day, I was the chief of operations. Other people were promoted to lieutenant much more quickly than they would have been — captain, battalion chief, deputy chief. We had to rebuild the department really from the ground up.

Constance Labetti, accountant, Aon Corporation, South Tower, 99th floor: I had assumed that my boss, Ron Fazio, had gone down ahead of me, being that he was the one that opened the door and hollered to people to hurry. By eight o'clock in the morning, the phone started ringing. It was my boss Ron's son, and I immediately started to tell him how much of a hero I thought his dad was, and he was amazing, and he got us all to the staircase. And he said, "Connie, Connie. Where did you see my dad last?" I said, "He didn't come home?" His son said, "No, Dad hasn't come home." I felt doom at that moment.

Aon lost almost 200 employees. The last that was heard of Ron was that he was out of the building. He lent somebody his cell phone as the Tower came down. So they think that he might have been hit by the falling debris. He's the reason I'm here. There's no question about it. There's absolutely no question that most of us survived that day because of him.

Lisa Lefler, employee, Aon Corporation, South Tower, 103rd Floor: I called the 800 number posted on the news to advise that I was OK and so were [my coworkers] Hon, Frank, and Karen. Aon already had information posted on the website and someone started a message board on Yahoo for employees. As more people logged on, you started to know more people were OK or not. There were people posting messages at all hours. I guess no one else could sleep, either.

That night, we received a very strange phone call at around 11:30, which I answered. The caller expressed surprise and relief to hear it was me. He said his name was Boyd Harden and he was a rescue worker working at Ground Zero and that he had found my briefcase. I was stunned. So was he when he asked where I dropped it and I told him I hadn't dropped it, it was at my desk on 103. For proof that it was mine, he called the number on my résumé, which was in the side pocket.

Philip Smith, branch chief, U.S. Army, Pentagon: On that day, in our division, we had 20 people. We had seven killed and three injured. We suffered about a 50 percent loss rate in one day.

Gabriella Daya-Dominguez, resident, Chatham, New Jersey: There were 11 people in our town that died. It's a commuter train town. The sad part was the cars left in the train parking lot that were never reclaimed.

Charles Christophe, attorney, Broadway: The next day I brought Gretchen to the daycare, went into the city, and started looking for Kirsten, from hospital to hospital, because there was no centralized information where you could see the victims. I had to wait in line. The first hospital — every hospital — they gave me a list of various hospitals where she might be, and I was checking. For almost two weeks, every day, that was my routine.

Michael Lomonaco, executive chef, Windows on the World, North Tower, 106th floor: It took days and days to compile the list of the missing — they weren't gone, they were unaccounted for. Someone had to have gotten down those stairs. They were going to pull people out of the rubble — like in devastating earthquakes how people get pulled out five days later. I believed that until the end of the week, until Sunday or Monday. We lost 72 people that worked at WOW.

Joe Asher, Cantor Fitzgerald, North Tower: I remember the day of the death certificates. People needed them to begin taking care of their spouse's estate. The city set up a system where a death certificate could be obtained with an affidavit from the next of kin and an affidavit from the employer. The employer's affidavit said essentially: name, Social Security number, date of birth, etc., worked for Cantor Fitzgerald at One World Trade Center and to the best of our knowledge was in the building on September 11. We did individual affidavits. The stack was a foot high. Each was two pages. Stephen [Merkel] our general counsel, sits down to start signing, and for each one, he would look at it, and if he knew the person, he would say something about the person. This went on for hours. It was just awful.

Dr. Charles Hirsch, chief medical examiner, City of New York: We were ready to start receiving the dead on 9/11. It went pretty much as we had planned. The only major difference from the standpoint of our agency is that in spite of all the planning, we had never conceived of a situation in which hundreds or thousands of people would be fragmented. We had no specific contingency plan for a mass disaster in which DNA would be the major source of identification.

Donna Pearce, resident, Manhattan: The city was plastered with missing persons flyers. No one wanted to be alone.

Katie Couric, anchor, *The Today Show*, NBC News: The most emotionally searing time was the days following, with all the signs and the Xeroxed pictures affixed to the chainlink fences. There was so much desperation to find people.

On Capitol Hill, legislators and staff began to plan the nation's response and recovery efforts, even as they now realized their own offices might be a future terrorist target.

Sen. Tom Daschle (D–South Dakota), Senate Majority Leader: I look back on September 12th as, in some ways, the best and the worst of our country. The best part was how resilient our country can be in the tragedies of this magnitude. The worst had to do with the vulnerability and loss of so many lives and the knowledge that there was agony and so much pain.

Brian Gunderson, chief of staff for House Majority Leader Richard Armey (R-Texas): As we came back to work to the Capitol on the morning of the 12th, there were a lot of changes. There were new security barriers that were thrown up, there were military Humvees with .50-caliber machine guns on top, with soldiers manning them. At a glance, it looked like there'd been a coup.

Tish Schwartz, chief clerk, House Judiciary Committee: It was really somber. The staff, everybody had a story. Everybody had a friend who was affected by the attack, somebody who knew somebody that died either in New York or the Pentagon.

Brian Gunderson: During that week, there were occasional new security alarms. There was one moment — think it was that first week — where the Capitol had to be evacuated again. It happened by surprise, no warning. All of a sudden the alarms went off, people had to get out. It was a very jittery environment.

Steve Elmendorf, chief of staff for House Minority Leader Richard Gephardt (D-Missouri): This had never been a place you had come to work before that you had to worry.

Mary Beth Cahill, chief of staff for Sen. Edward Kennedy (D-Massachusetts): When I first came to Washington, you could walk up to the Capitol, to every monument. You could walk in to talk to your representative, without having your bag searched. Now, we take for granted the way in which life has changed — and changed necessarily. It was a different world.

In Pennsylvania on Wednesday, September 12, investigators began sifting through the wreckage of Flight 93, looking for clues in the case that the FBI would call PENTTBOM, for "Pentagon/Twin Towers Bombing Investigation." For weeks afterward, the quiet town of Shanksville was the center of a 24/7 operation, broadcast live by hundreds of media outlets from across the globe.

Patrick McGlennon, special agent, FBI: The 12th was the actual first operational day, when the full-scale investigation began. Things started to move in the direction of bringing in our Evidence Response Teams, overflying the area, mapping it out, determining how large the scene actually was, and how many people we were going to need in there to effectively search it, document what was being found, and coordinate the overall effort. All the same sorts of things that you would do at any crime scene.

Cpl. Martin Knezovich, Special Emergency Response Team, Pennsylvania State Police: I was back out at seven the next morning. We were given specific areas to search these areas for any type of debris, parts from the plane, or anything that we could find dealing with the crash.

Sgt. Patrick Madigan, commander, Somerset Station, Pennsylvania State Police: There were several impromptu memorials that sprung up [in the days ahead]. One was at the media area. PennDOT [Pennsylvania Department of Transportation] erected two large flagpoles, and we put the state flag and the national flag there. A number of people left some mementos there. At the overlook, there was another memorial type of thing. There were hay bales there, and family members left a lot of personal mementos.

Lt. Robert Weaver, Pennsylvania State Police: Everywhere you looked, there were flags.

Thursday
On September 13th, the engine of America's economy began to chug back to life, and air traffic controllers — under strict security — began restarting air travel.

Gerald Earwood, pilot, Midwest Express, Flight 7: I was captain of the first aircraft to leave New York. I had to perform an inspection around the aircraft, a bomb inspection with local law enforcement and the FBI observing everything I did. I would open up a panel, read the checklist, look into the hole, step back, and three more people would do the exact same thing. It probably took about 30 minutes to do something that usually takes five or 10 minutes.

We loaded everyone up. We started to push back. The ground controller called and said, "We hate to tell you this, but there has been a bomb threat against your aircraft. You need to evacuate." So, I picked up the PA and said, "You aren't going to believe this, but we have a bomb threat and we have to evacuate." Everyone calmly evacuated the aircraft and walked out onto the runway. At that moment, one of our military aircraft flew over, and that got our attention.

When we got back on the aircraft and we were taxiing out, our friends from the military made another pass as we were leaving. I told my first officer, "I hope the military knows we are coming." I remember the missiles stuck on the bottom of the wings. I called and asked the tower, "Confirm with us that the military knows that we're about to be airborne here." He came back and said, "Yeah, they know you are coming." They sent us right over the World Trade Center. It was moving.

Jared Kotz, Risk Waters Group: On Thursday, I did get back to my office [in Lower Manhattan], and I remember these empty desks. The telephones ringing all day long — people were calling, hoping and hoping against hope — or maybe they wanted to hear their daughter or their loved one's voice and that was the only way they could hear it, to listen to the phone message. I never picked up the phones. I didn't know what to tell people.

Monika Bravo, artist, North Tower, 91st floor: I tried to get in touch with everybody who was part of our Studio Scape program on the 91st Floor of the North Tower — the other 15 fellow artists and the curators. I remember saying, "Why don't we try to meet in two days or three days so we can comfort each other?" The whole world was going crazy and everybody was coming to terms with what's going on. This first meeting happened Thursday. At one point in this meeting, I remembered I had the tape: "Oh my god, I saved the tape that I made of the storm on 9/10." I had learned with practice that to process very deep emotions, you have to transform them into something — that's why I'm an artist — so I decided to transform the tape into something and give it to everybody.

It's a very, very eerie video. I don't want to say it's premonitory, but if you see it from that perspective it's like, "Wow." I actually named the video "September 10 2001 Uno nunca muere la víspera." It is a saying in Spanish. *It's impossible for you to die on the eve of your death.* You only die when you have to die. You're never close to death. You die or you're alive.

Friday
September 14th saw more steps back to normalcy. President Bush journeyed to New York City, to Ground Zero, where he stood atop the wreckage and spoke to rescuers using a bullhorn.

Dan Bartlett, deputy communications director, White House: The real change in the president, in my opinion, didn't actually happen until that Friday, when he traveled to New York. The situation on Tuesday, you really didn't have time to reflect. In New York, the range of emotions that he went through — standing on the rubble, the bullhorn moment — but just as important, when he sat there in that room in private and met with those people who were still trying to learn the whereabouts of their loved ones, and hugging them.

Robert Beckwith, retired firefighter, FDNY: We kept working, and all of a sudden we heard the president was coming. I saw a couple of guys put their shovels down, and go out to the street. So I went out to the street. I see this pumper that we found — it was 76 Engine — and nobody was standing on it, so I jumped up. Right across the street was the command post. It was a tent with microphones all set up in front of it.

The president came right in front of me, and put his arm up. I grabbed his arm, I pulled him up — he's only got a little spot, 12 inch by 12 inch — and I turned him around. I said, "You okay, Mr. President?" and he said, "Yeah." Then he put his arm around my shoulder, and there he was with the megaphone, and he was talking, and talking to our right side. The guys on the other side, on the left side, were yelling, "U.S.A.! U.S.A.!" Then they stopped, and they said, "We can't hear you!" He turned and said, "Well, I can hear you. The whole world hears you, and when we find these people who knocked these buildings down, they'll hear all of us soon." Everybody melted.

Lt. Col. Rob Grunewald, information management officer, U.S. Army, Pentagon: Friday, to me, was mental anguish. Our office was having a muster formation at the AMC movie theater nearby. We were going to get together and the senior leaders of the army were going to come talk to us. Everyone who was physically capable was going to go. To see all the wounded and injured people, it was horrible — people with their arms bandaged, people on crutches, people in wheelchairs, people with burns to their scalps. A friend of mine, Ann Parham, the army librarian, just had her head wrapped up, bandaged on her ears that had burned. It was a terrible, terrible thing to see.

We got into the movie theater and what was left of the leadership — because the plane came in and took out the senior leaders of [the army personnel office, known as "G-1"], including General Maude. His wife, Teri Maude, got up and gave a speech. It was remarkable. We were all blabbering and blubbering idiots, and she was strong as strong could be.

That was why that day was the hardest, because not only were you seeing all these badly burned and broken bodies, but every few minutes you would hear of another person who was unaccounted for, another person who was confirmed deceased, another person who was in the hospital, badly burned. It was very, very difficult to get your hands around what was going on and the magnitude of this.

Linda Krouner, senior vice president, Fiduciary Trust, South Tower: That Friday was my birthday. There's a woman from my firm — Carmen Rivera — who was my trust officer on many accounts, and so I spoke to her a lot. She had a young family, and she was one of these beautiful younger women. She had the most engaging smile. My daughter wanted to give me a birthday present by locating Carmen Rivera and telling me that she was alive. She looked through different websites with her friends, but they searched and searched and they didn't find her.

Ali Millard, whose stepfather, Port Authority executive director Neil Levin, was killed in the attack: The Friday after September 11, there was a candlelight vigil, and a bunch of friends of mine were sitting on the sidewalk. My friend Lani said, "Ali, don't think of it as you losing a person; think of it as you gaining an angel." I don't really believe in angels or the afterlife, but the way I interpreted what Lani said was that people are only put on earth for a certain amount of time, and you're lucky to get to know them for as long as you do.

Saturday
Lisa Jefferson, Verizon Airfone supervisor: I was concerned because [United Flight 93 passenger Todd Beamer] wanted me to call his wife and relay the information to her. I didn't know how to call her and how would I tell her this, being a stranger. It didn't

sound right by me to call her and say, "Hello, Lisa. This is Lisa. I spoke to your husband." I talked to the FBI and they told me not to mention anything, not to contact her until they finished their investigation. I told them I wouldn't. All the while, I was thinking, *How would I contact her? What would I say?*

The FBI got back in touch with me on Friday and told me that I could call her. We contacted the United Airlines crisis team member who was in contact with Lisa Beamer and told him that when she was ready to talk, she could call me at home or at work.

We faxed the letter over to United on Friday evening. My phone rang at about 10:00 a.m. Saturday morning. It was Lisa. She said, "I understand you spoke to my husband." I totally froze. I didn't expect her to call. I wasn't thinking about it at that time. I said, "Yes," and I said, "Are you ready to talk?" She said, "Yes." We sat and we talked. I told her everything her husband told me to tell her.

Lisa Beamer, wife of United Flight 93 passenger Todd Beamer: As much as obviously 9/11 was traumatic for people like myself, for someone like Lisa, it was also a life-changing event. We keep in touch periodically to catch up and see how we're doing. We probably will continue to do that. The first couple of days after 9/11, not knowing the facts around what happened on that flight, not knowing what Todd's role was, was difficult. Having all that concrete information from Lisa, as well as Todd's final message to us was a great encouragement.

Mary Dettloff, communications staff, Michigan legislature: I remember my partner and I watched nothing but CNN for days until I couldn't take it anymore. I finally broke away on a Saturday and went for a walk in a nature area near Jackson, Michigan. I remember a plane flew overhead while I was out there and I just stopped and watched it. I did that for a long time after 9/11 — watched the planes fly over our house.

Adm. James Loy, commandant, U.S. Coast Guard: Maybe the fourth or fifth day, it dawned on me that the church at the end of Wall Street, Trinity Church, was within spitting distance of the Tower site and was part of the rest of the city that was deluged in debris. I sat in my office for a second and said, "Alexander Hamilton is buried in that cemetery." He's considered the founder of the modern-day Coast Guard because he established its predecessor, the Revenue Cutter Service. I couldn't stand the notion that he and his headstone were probably inundated with debris.

I called Master Chief Vince Patton into the office and I said, "Vince, I need you to get some senior enlisted folks from the captain of the Port of New York's office. I know they're up to their ass in alligators right now, but we've got to go fix that." He got a senior chief in New York on the phone. They went and began the cleanup of the entire Trinity Church yard. The word got out to the Trade Center site, and people, after finishing their unbelievably difficult work for a 12-hour cycle, came over and joined with these Coast Guard people to finish the job. I was damned if I could go to sleep that night without doing something about it.

Sunday

Tracy Donahoo, transit officer, NYPD: The mayor had said for people to resume their lives, start shopping, and support New York City. The Sunday after, I remember working on Fulton Street again. People were coming down, and they said, "Oh, I wanna go shopping at Century 21 [department store]." I would say, "There is no Century 21 right now." They said, "Oh, but the mayor said we can go shopping." "There's no Century 21 at this point. There's no Brooks Brothers, there's nothing at that area. He means go to 34th Street, shop there, and have a nice lunch."

On Sunday, September 16th, President Bush spoke to the press after a weekend war council meeting at Camp David. He noted the resiliency of the American spirit and that the New York Stock Exchange would reopen Monday after its first prolonged closure since the Great Depression.

George W. Bush, president: The markets open tomorrow, people go back to work, and we'll show the world.

The Coming Weeks
For nearly two weeks, the rescue effort at Ground Zero continued around the clock as firefighters, police officers, rescue workers, other first responders, and skilled tradesmen hunted for signs of the missing. Finally, on September 24, Mayor Giuliani announced there was no further hope of survivors.

Capt. Joe Downey, Squad Company 18, FDNY, and son of Ray Downey, FDNY head of special operations: Chuck [Downey, my brother] and I, we didn't leave the site for the first five or six days. We stayed there. We slept on the floors, we slept wherever we could find a bunk. We wanted to be there, in case we did find him.

743

Lt. Mickey Kross, Engine 16, FDNY: September 15th or something like that was my first night here. When I saw the site, it was at night, I saw the red glow, the smoke, and it was pouring rain. It felt like I was going into hell. I said, "Oh, jeez, maybe I made a big mistake coming here." After a few hours, it was a job again. We were looking for people, and I was back to work. From that point, I got better. I came back to reality.

Det. David Brink, Emergency Service Unit, Truck 3, NYPD: We would go down there with either steel rakes, we'd go down with shovels. We had plastic, five-gallon buckets that we were using to remove some of the debris. We'd also have little shovels and hand picks because oftentimes the only body fragments that we'd find were very, very small.

Lt. Mickey Kross: It was very long hours. It was cold. It was very demanding. When we first got here there was no setup for food or shelter. They didn't even have coffee. We were out in the rain all night, soaking wet. Eventually, they got it together and became better and better. The Red Cross came. They opened up the big tent and they had cots, and St. Paul's Church opened up and they had food.

744

Joe Esposito, chief of department, NYPD: If you were on the outside, you were wearing a heavy coat. If you were handling the bucket brigade, we circulated people closer and closer. As you got closer and closer and closer to this pit that you were taking pails out full of debris, it got warmer and warmer. When you were ultimately the first guy in there, you were in your T-shirt because it was on fire. It was like you were in an oven.

Sgt. Joe Alagna, aide to the chief, NYPD: You didn't even realize how dangerous it was. They would dig down and there'd be a void and you could see the beams glowing. They were still on fire and we were standing on top of it. It was tedious, hard work, and nobody complained.

Lt. Mickey Kross: They became my new family, the people that worked there: the firefighters, the police officers, the volunteers.

Det. David Brink: The fire department would take a sector. The NYPD Emergency Service Unit would take another sector, along with Port Authority and the corrections emergency service units. We also had the construction trades that were down here — heavy equipment operators, the operating engineers, the steel guys. I was very thankful

745

for those guys because they had the heavy equipment that could help us do our jobs.

Norma Hardy, officer, PATH Command, PAPD: It always seemed dark, even when it was daytime. You did whatever had to be done when you got there. Even though there were hundreds and hundreds of people, machines, people talking, and rescue dogs — it still seemed very quiet and very still a lot of nights that we were out there.

Bill Spade, firefighter, Rescue 5, FDNY: Then the funerals started. You would go to a wake for either one or two days, and then the funeral. Everybody had a job, whether you were a pallbearer, gave a eulogy, or just stood in formation outside the church. It was very draining. With my injuries I could hardly stand, but I stood for every one out of respect.

On days when I wasn't going for guys in my firehouse, I was going for other firemen, whoever was on Staten Island being buried, go to their wake or funeral. I tried to do even two-a-days sometimes. That became my life — besides seeing the doctors on the other days — for three months. I remember looking over the list of the 343 firemen and realizing that I knew 85 of them by first name.

Kenneth Escoffery, firefighter, Ladder 20, FDNY: It was a wake one day, a funeral the next day. Every week. Just for the 14 guys that responded from my house, that was more than enough. I would say that the average fireman probably went to 25, 30 funerals, not even counting the wakes. It got to the point where a lot of guys got burnt out. After a month or two, you had to shut down.

Tracy Claus, wife of Cantor Fitzgerald survivor Matt Claus: There were days we went to four [funerals] and could have gone to six. Matt didn't sleep for a long while, so I didn't sleep. I had a two-and-a-half-year-old at the time. From the chaos that was in our house, my daughter started to stutter. She started having nightmares. She said Daddy works in buildings that fall down.

Anthony R. Whitaker, WTC commander, PAPD, North Tower lobby: Four days a week, I used to stand in front of Banana Republic at the World Trade Center, probably for half an hour, between 8:30 a.m. and 9:00 a.m. I greeted people every morning, four days a week, for 28 months — thousands of people. One thing that really bothers me is that I don't know what happened to all those many faces that I used to wave at. In the *Daily News,* they ran spreads of photographs. One of the things that hurt me was that I recognized almost 80 percent of those people.

Thomas Von Essen, commissioner, FDNY: The emptiness from the losses that day has never left me, not for a moment.

Similar rescue and recovery efforts continued at the Pentagon. The fire and collapse so damaged the impact zone that it took expert urban search-and-rescue teams days of extensive, painstaking work to shore up the area before interior searches could resume. The Arlington County Fire Department didn't turn over control of the site to the FBI until September 21, and the FBI spent more than a week searching and securing the scene before returning it to the military's control on October 2.

Thomas O'Connor, special agent, FBI: We didn't actually get into the building for several days. Chief [James] Schwartz and the firefighters were in charge of the entire event. The firefighting going on inside the building went on for a lot longer than people realize. The urban search-and-rescue teams were the ones that were shoring up the building to a point where we could go in and then we would do recoveries.

Jean O'Connor, special agent, FBI: The first time I went in, I literally had a rope tied around my waist so I would be able to find my way back out of the building because the debris piles were so high and there was no pattern necessarily, no logical pattern.

James Schwartz, assistant chief for operations, Arlington County Fire Department: The arrangement was that you reported for duty at our training academy, and we bused you to the incident scene. Then at the end of your work period, you were taken back to the training academy. What we didn't account for was — in a similar vein to New York — people didn't want to go home. People would go back to the training academy, get dropped off by the bus, get in their personal vehicle, and drive back to the Pentagon. They'd get right back in and go right back to work.

Staff Sgt. Robert Walker, special agent, Office of Special Investigations, U.S. Air Force: That first week, we were there 14-, 16-hour days, long enough to go home, strip off the jeans and stuff we had, grab a couple hours' sleep, and come back.

Thomas O'Connor: We were pretty new to our neighborhood there, maybe a year or so. It was amazing, people were bringing food over. At first we said, "We don't really need anything." But when you have three hours to get home, shower, wash your clothes, get to sleep, get back up, get dressed, go, then when somebody brings over a sleeve of hamburgers, it made a huge difference. Somebody took our dog for almost the whole month that we were there. Kids were coming by, walking the dog, small things like that that really made a difference.

Staff Sgt. Robert Walker: The debris and such was loaded into these long dumpsters and then taken to the North Parking Lot, which we called the Rubble Pit, the Rubble Pile. The trucks would come and they would spread out this debris. They had cadaver dogs go over them, and if there were any remains in the rubble, they would photograph it, tag it, identify it — evidence — and have it taken over to the makeshift morgue that we had set up at the Pentagon. From there, we led some teams to go through the pile. We were actually separating — was it equipment like telephones, computer systems, was it personal items, personal equipment, was it classified information, personal books? Was it airplane parts? It was very labor intensive.

Lt. Jim Daly, Arlington County Police Department: I remember going home, and my wife coming up and asking me how things were. I said, "Well, I found a femur bone and found a bunch of other personal belongings." I remember my son coming up because I had put him to bed — he was five, and he heard the word "bones," and he said, "Daddy, are there bones in that plane?" I said, "There were chickens, chicken bones in that plane." He looked at me with a real quizzical look and he asked, "There were chickens on that plane?"

John F. Irby, director, Federal Facilities Division, Real Estate and Facilities Directorate, Washington Headquarters Services, Pentagon: It took a month before we got back to what we could call reasonably normal. That was more redefining normal than getting back to normal.

Philip Smith, branch chief, U.S. Army, Pentagon: For a long time in the Pentagon, the smells of the fire were there to remind you of what had occurred.

Sheila Denise Moody, accountant, Resource Services Office, Pentagon: It's still to this day — and will forever be — a miracle to me that I'm still alive. I was in the hospital up until October 4th. I had skin grafts on my hands, but the rest of my body pretty much healed fairly well. I still have pretty severe burns, scars on my arms and on my back. But amazingly enough, my face healed pretty well.

In Pennsylvania, investigators worked tirelessly, often feeling that their efforts were overlooked by the nation.

David Zacur, special agent, FBI: For the next three weeks at that crash site, they brought in excavators. They started to dig it out.

Tony James, investigator, FAA: We found the cockpit voice recorder and the flight data recorder somewhere around 25 or 27 feet. We stopped digging, I think, at 32 feet. We never did find what the FBI was actually looking for: the cockpit. That had disintegrated.

Andrea Dammann, special agent, Evidence Response Team, FBI: We'd leave the site and watch the news at night, and you'd see all these photos from all the other sites. Our colleagues would ask, "Well, how come we're not getting attention?" It's like, "Because we're not at a place they can see us all the time." But we were the ones who are actually recovering things important to the investigation. People were a little hurt by the fact that we weren't getting the same attention, because we didn't have the great loss of life that you had in the World Trade Center or the Pentagon.

Even as the U.S. launched a war in Afghan-istan aimed at destroying al-Qaeda, the terror group responsible for the attack, in October 2001 the victims, coworkers, and family mem-bers affected by the attack tried to bring a sense of normalcy back to their lives, though returning to "normal" often required a redefinition of "nor-mal."

Rosemary Dillard, Washington, D.C., base manager, American Airlines, and wife of Flight 77 passenger Eddie Dillard: Eddie loved history, and when I was offered the job here in Washington, he was so excited because of the history, the things we were go-ing to get to see, the changing of the leaves. We moved here in February 2001. He didn't get to see the changing of the leaves.

Harry Waizer, tax counsel, Cantor Fitz-gerald, North Tower, 104th floor, was burned over 35 percent of his body: It was many weeks before they were confident that I would survive. I woke up slowly. I found out about 9/11 by asking questions. The first thing I asked was, "What happened that day?" My wife, Karen, told me that a plane flew into the World Trade Center. I asked, "Was it terrorists?" She said, "Yes." I asked, "How many died?" and she said, "Five thousand," which was the number they thought at the time. I then started going through names, and I think that was almost as hard for her as it was for me.

Monica O'Leary, former employee, Cantor Fitzgerald, North Tower: Dave Kravette called and I didn't know he was alive. He said, "When are you coming back? We want you back." I was like, "I don't know when I can come back." He said, "Well, as soon as you're ready to come back, you've got a space here." Oddly enough, because I was laid off in the afternoon on September 10th, and because the Human Resources Department all died, I was never taken off the payroll. I went back to work again — it's not like they had to rehire me. I was never gone.

Stephen Larabee, Cantor Fitzgerald, L.A. office, whose son, Christopher, died in Cantor's New York office: It was hard coming back. There are a lot of ghosts there.

Charles Christophe, attorney, Broadway: Gretchen was, at that time, 11 months old. She didn't speak very much. Her behavior changed, because I was the only one picking her up, taking care of her, feeding her. Usually Kirsten took care of her in the evening — bathing her, feeding her, putting her in the bath. She stopped talking. It was quiet

754

most of the time. She had this sense that her mom was not there.

For a couple of weeks, after an exhausting search, I could not find her. I called Kirsten's family, and we decided to have a memorial service even though we didn't have a body. We had the memorial service at the end of September. It was September 30th. Over 400 people came — family members, friends, neighbors, Kirsten's college friends — so many people came the church could not accommodate everyone. It was very sad. You have only a portrait and flowers. We did the memorial service, and a week or two thereafter, two policemen came to my house and told me that they found the body. I was a single father, taking care of my daughter. I missed Kirsten very much.

Months
As part of a series of new air transportation security laws passed after the attacks, the U.S. government established the September 11th Victim Compensation Fund, to help families who lost loved ones in the attacks. Washington lawyer Ken Feinberg was appointed in November to oversee the process and mediate how much each victim's family would receive. As Feinberg said later, "I underestimated the emotion of this at the beginning." He worked for 33 months, pro bono, *to distribute over $7 billion*

from the U.S. Treasury; the average family received $1.8 million.

Kenneth Feinberg, special master, September 11th Victim Compensation Fund: I stated over and over again publicly on television and the radio, anybody who voluntarily wants to come and see me privately, I will see them. I remember [my first meeting] like it was yesterday. A 24-year-old woman came to see me, sobbing. "Mr. Feinberg, my husband died in the World Trade Center. He was a fireman, and he left me with our two children, six and four. Now, I've applied to the Fund, and you have calculated that I'm going to get $2.8 million tax-free. I want it in 30 days." I said, "Why do you need the money in 30 days?" She said, "Why 30 days? I have terminal cancer. I have 10 weeks to live. My husband was gonna survive me and take care of our two children. Now they're gonna be orphans. I have got to get this money while I still have my faculties. I've gotta set up a trust. I've gotta find a guardian. We never anticipated this." I ran down to the Treasury, we accelerated the processing of her claim, we got her the money, and eight weeks later she died. You think you're ready for anything and you're not.

Richard Grasso, chairman and CEO, New York Stock Exchange: For the balance of that year, no one rang either the opening or closing bell other than a first responder that we would get from Ground Zero — a firefighter or police officer, an EMS person, a Port Authority Police officer, visiting firemen from around the country, visiting police officers, the iron workers — all of the tradespeople who were there — were welcomed, not to ring that bell as a symbol of what was going on, but to ring that bell again, reiterating the message of America rising. It was always an extraordinary moment because whether it was an opening bell or a closing bell, whichever of the uniformed services or the trades, would first come and walk across the trading floor and they'd get a hero's welcome.

Lt. Joseph Torrillo, director of fire education safety, FDNY: The action figure Billy Blazes became the biggest-selling toy of the year. Because of September 11th, it became a collector's item.

Dan Potter, firefighter, Ladder 10, FDNY: We moved out of Battery Park in December of 2001, because you could hear the equipment working and the recovery process going on. It was very debilitating for Jean. She was very, very upset. It was heartwrenching to see broken buildings. People with devastated lives. People that lived around us had perished. You see the steel down the street. It was a very hard time.

Det. David Brink, Emergency Service Unit, Truck 3, NYPD: There was one evening — it was a cold December evening, probably around 6:30 at night — and nobody had gotten down there yet. They were getting their assignments. We were standing there, and my partner for the day had to go and use the facilities. I was standing down there, and I felt like I was the only living soul in the entire Trade Center site, out of all the acreage there. There wasn't a sound at all. All the equipment had come to a stop. There was nobody talking. It seemed like there was nobody down there except myself, but I was there with all these people's souls. There were almost 3,000 people waiting to be found, saying, "Please, come and find me."

Vanessa Lawrence, artist, North Tower, 91st floor: Afterwards I went through mixed feelings. I got to the point that I had to leave New York. I couldn't actually handle it anymore. There were too many things freaking me out — sounds, smells, anything.

Pasquale Buzzelli, engineer, Port Authority, North Tower, 64th floor: I was almost in this trance — watching, hearing the news, waiting by the phone to hear if they

758

found someone. I would lay there on the couch, eating and watching TV. I started to grow a little bit angry, thinking every day, *Wow, there are people out there that basically tried to kill me and they succeeded in killing my friends.*

My daughter was born on November 18th, and that was a relief at the time. It was a break. But time went on, and I started to distance myself somehow. I remember not being able to sleep at night, getting nightmares. You would fight this battle inside of you and you say: "Hey, asshole, you're alive, you should be happy." Then you are happy for a second and you say to yourself: "Hey, asshole, you're happy and someone else is dead — you're happy you're alive, what does that say about you?" Then you don't feel happy.

Louise Buzzelli, wife of Pasquale Buzzelli, Port Authority, North Tower, 64th floor: There was no escaping it. You'd say, "My God! He's so lucky. Look what he survived." But he didn't feel like he was lucky. He felt guilty. He felt like: "I don't want people to look at me and think: *You're so lucky, you're the luckiest man in the world, what are you going to do now? God has a plan for you.*" For years, he couldn't figure out what that plan was. He said, "I don't know what

759

the plan is, but I'm going to be the best husband, father, dad, son that I can be. That's how I'm going to live my life."

Frank Razzano, guest, Marriott Hotel: In the weeks afterwards, I tried to find out who the fireman was who had gotten me out of the building. About nine months later, my nephew called me up and said, "Uncle Frank, I was on my way into work, reading the *New York Post,* and there is a story in there about a fireman who won the Liberty Medal for saving the lives of three middle-aged men. It sounds like your story." It identified the fireman as Jeff Johnson. I wrote Jeff a letter asking, "Are you the fireman who got me out?" Three days later, his wife, Roe, called my wife, Stephanie, and gave her the telephone number at the ladder company. I called and made contact with Jeff.

The first words out of his mouth were, "I'm very sorry for that article that appeared in the *Post.*" I said, "What are you sorry about?" He said, "It made me sound like I was James Bond." I said, "Jeff, you have to understand something: to me, you're a hero. You got me out of that building. I would still be on the third-floor landing, scratching my head, figuring out what to do, how to get out."

Years
The trauma, drama, and tragedy of 9/11 forever affected those it touched, altering the course of the country, launching the United States into two wars that continue to this day. The children of those who first invaded Afghanistan in October 2001 are now eligible to serve and be deployed to continue fighting the same war more than 17 years later.

The significance of the date of September 11th, 9/11, was seared into the nation's collective memory, altering the way those affected looked at the calendar and even clocks. Even those for whom the date was meant to bear happy memories — like Susannah Herrada, whose son was born in Arlington amid the injured from the Pentagon — found themselves haunted. Choosing what and how to remember the day remains a complicated challenge, as does charting a life forward day to day, especially for those who suffered from ongoing health challenges related to either the attacks themselves or the cleanup work after. The death toll of 9/11 has continued to steadily rise.

Rosemary Dillard, Washington, D.C., base manager, American Airlines, and wife of Flight 77 passenger Eddie Dillard: I grieved while other people became afraid. I still think that we all walk on eggshells. I don't think that the young people who will be [reading] this will know the same freedom I knew growing up.

Susannah Herrada, resident, Arlington, Virginia, whose son was born on 9/11: The only other thing that we did for his first birthday is that we had all the neighbors over, and we said we want to celebrate the heroes of the day. We had a moment of silence during the party, and we said let's remember everybody. Every year on his birthday we take some time.

Jeh Johnson, U.S. secretary of homeland security, 2013–17: My birthday is 9/11. I haven't celebrated on that day since 2001. The memory from 2001 overwhelms the birthday.

Mary Matalin, aide to Vice President Dick Cheney: One of the strange things that didn't occur to me until the first anniversary was how much I didn't know was going on. I did not have the perspective seeing what the American public was seeing. When I watched the coverage on the first anniversary, I couldn't stop crying. I was shocked. We weren't watching TV. We weren't watching people jumping out of buildings. We didn't see all the chaos that the American people were seeing. It frightens me to the core to think what America must have been feeling watching that. We weren't exposed to it.

James Schwartz, assistant chief for operations, Arlington County Fire Department: I actually assumed the position of president of the PTA the following year, when the one-year anniversary was about to take place. There were a lot of parents in the school that wanted to let the anniversary go by. They didn't want to acknowledge it — "It was so horrifying, it will only traumatize the children, they don't need to see these images or be reminded of this." I said, "This is a learning opportunity. There is no escaping this." We did what I thought was a very meaningful event that honored the losses, reflected on the impact to the nation, and hopefully taught the kids something about what it means to be an American and what it means to serve others.

Ultimately, the toll of 9/11 has manifested itself in ways far beyond the initial casualty list. In New York, 9/11-related ailments bedevil the first responders who spent days, weeks, and months cleaning up the wreckage at Ground Zero. All told, more than 7,000 firefighters and EMTs in New York were treated for 9/11-related injuries. New York estimates that 20 percent of those first responders also suffer from PTSD.

The toll was great at the Pentagon as well:

nearly 10 percent of the Arlington County Fire Department resigned due to post-traumatic stress. First responders, including FBI agents, also struggled with physical illnesses linked to 9/11.

Philip Smith, branch chief, U.S. Army, Pentagon: We were all required to take classes at the Pentagon health clinic that were called "Get Your Life Back." To this day, when people go through trauma, I recommend that they get mental health care. You may not think that you need care, but what you'll learn is that if you don't deal with the stress, the mental stress, professionally, within five years it will manifest itself in a physical ailment.

Capt. Mike Smith, Arlington County Fire Department: 9/11 tore through the department like a bowling ball.

Dr. David Prezant, chief medical officer, FDNY: Due to the physical nature of their jobs, these illnesses have had a tremendous impact on our membership and their families. Since 9/11/01, over 2,100 FDNY responders have been awarded service-connected disability due to WTC-related illnesses — mostly respiratory or cancer. The death toll continues to grow. In the years that followed,

203 of the first responders we have been monitoring died, and over half of them have had their deaths attributed to WTC-related illnesses.

Bill Spade, firefighter, Rescue 5, FDNY: My lungs aren't too good. My wife took me to the hospital in January 2003. I was in the hospital again for three days. Basically the doctor said I have World Trade Center lungs. Then I realized it was time — March of 2003, I retired. Everything since 9/11, I count it as one more day on Earth than I ever thought I would have.

Lt. Mickey Kross, Engine 16, FDNY: I just got together with the survivors; the other night we had our annual dinner — we called it the "Survivors of Stairway B Annual Dinner."

Philip Smith: I truly believe it was a miracle of 9/11 that I survived. So I stayed on active duty in the army as long as I could. Statutorily, my limit was 30 years. I was able to do almost an extra year as a retiree recall. Today, I work in the same workspace in the Pentagon as a civilian, because every day that I serve, I support my soldiers that were killed, and the terrorists don't win. That means an awful lot to me.

Sharon Miller, officer, PAPD: I could never understand why I got out. How come I got out and all these guys who had kids and kids on the way didn't? I remember they had a benefit — I think it was a hockey game or a basketball game afterwards — I had my uniform on, I had "Police Academy" on the collar, and this guy said to me, "Did you know my dad?" I said, "Well, who's your dad?" He said, "Steve Huczko." I said, "Oh, yes — I did." I said, "I was with your dad on 9/11. The last time I saw him, he was helping a lady who was having trouble breathing. He was really good. He was doing his job." "Oh, wow. That's good!" Maybe that's why I got out, so I could tell these kids what their dads were doing, where they were, and how they were helping everybody.

Capt. Robert Gray, Technical Rescue, Station 4, Arlington County Fire Department: We still have some people who are really, really hung up on the fact that the Pentagon is in Arlington, yet every time it's referred to, they say "Washington, D.C." It's important to make sure people know that the Pentagon sits in Arlington, it's important to make sure that everybody knows about how Arlington as a community responded, how the region responded. I made a decision in 2002 that I wasn't going to let the whole fact that the memorial board at the Pentagon says

"Pentagon" and "Washington, D.C." under it bother me. Because I find myself even today, when relatives come in, you know what I ask them? "When are you coming to Washington?" And they're staying at my house.

Mahlon Fuller, Pittsburgh Watch supervisor, FAA: I go back to the Shanksville site on 9/11 every year. In 2003, I was sitting on one of the benches — there was a woman beside me. I could tell from the ribbon she was wearing she had lost somebody in the crash. I said, "Did you lose someone?" She said, "Yes." All I could say was "I'm so sorry." She said, "Did you?" I told her that I was a supervisor in the Pittsburgh control tower, and I still can't get over this. She said, "How are you?" She asked me that. How am I? What an amazing thing.

Theresa Flynn, librarian, H-B Woodlawn School, Arlington, Virginia: Years after, I talk to friends and relatives, and it always comes up. It always comes up. These are people who have been places with tornadoes and with hurricanes. I'll talk to my Florida relatives and we don't talk about Hurricane Wilma, but we talk about 9/11. I remember talking to one out-of-town person and I said, "I think the people in the D.C. area had a hard time getting over this. It's almost as if the entire city went into a kind of post-traumatic stress." She said, "Well, you're never going to get over it."

Vaughn Allex, ticket agent, Washington Dulles International Airport, Virginia: I had this wild thing in my mind that everything that happened on September 11th was my fault, personally. That I could have changed it. I felt there was no place for me in the world. There were all these support groups, and I didn't belong there because how do I sit in a room with people that are mourning and crying and they're like, "What's your role in this whole thing?" "Well, I checked in a couple of the hijackers and made sure they got on the flight." I might go weeks or months and everything would go along fine, then there would be something that would trigger it — like checking in somebody who said, "My husband got killed on September 11th." What I heard was, "You killed my husband on September 11th." You don't really move past it.

Capt. Jay Jonas, Ladder 6, FDNY: I got a phone call in about 2006 from somebody from headquarters. He said, "Is this Chief Jonas?" I said, "Yes." He said, "Are you working tonight? We have something we have to give to you." I said, "Can't you send it through the internal messengers?" He said, "No, this is something that has to be hand-delivered." A captain came to the firehouse, and he has this bag and it was sealed and everything, and it was my face piece, the plastic face piece from my helmet. When you're issued a face piece, they etch your name into it. It was pulled off the debris field and put in this bag. It wasn't cleaned or anything. When I opened up the bag and it had the smell of the World Trade Center. It was like, *Oh, that's it!* And closed it back up again.

Robert Small, office manager, Morgan Stanley, South Tower, 72nd floor: For the first six anniversaries after 9/11, I was still employed with Morgan Stanley. Basically, the world would stop, and we would get together in the conference rooms and watch the ceremonies. I knew a New York fireman who had found a shard of glass from the site, and he gave it to me. I knew a construction worker who was helping clean up — he was a mechanic for the bulldozers — and he had a piece of rock that had got wedged in one of the rotation devices, so he kept it and said, "Here, you have it." I used to bring in my two little pieces on 9/11 and say, "This is part of it." We would watch it as a group together. Over the years, fewer people would come to watch.

Then one year I wanted to be home, and I watched it all on television. I found out that

MSNBC does a rebroadcast of the *Today Show* from that morning as it happened. I finally got to watch what everybody else got to watch, hearing what people thought was going on, what had hit the first tower, and then hearing them describe the jumpers, and hearing them describe the aftermath. I was like, "Wow!" I could see how hard it was for people on the outside.

In January 2011, the firefighters of Ladder 6 served as the pallbearers at the funeral of Josephine Harris, who had died at 69, nearly 10 years after all of them had been trapped together in Stairwell B. The survivors called Harris their guardian angel, believing that had they not stopped to rescue her, they would have been killed in the collapse. The interior of her coffin was custom-embroidered with the image of a firefighter walking hand in hand with an angel.

Sal Cassano, now commissioner, FDNY: On a day that will always be recalled for its inconceivable devastation and unimaginable loss, the story of Josephine and the firefighters of Ladder 6 was nothing short of miraculous.

Jay Jonas, now a deputy chief, FDNY: You cannot say that something that happened to you is a miracle, but if she was not there for us to save, we probably would not have made it.

Peter DeLuca, owner, Greenwich Village Funeral Home: The six firefighters made the request that they be the ones who carried her in and out of church.

Jay Jonas: It was an honor to do this for her. We feel very happy that she is in God's hands.

Even as Harris was being laid to rest, the U.S. intelligence community was zeroing in on the man who launched the 9/11 plot. For nearly a decade, the CIA and U.S. government had continued to hunt for Osama bin Laden. Finally, they located a compound in Pakistan occupied by a mysterious, tall figure who never ventured outside the high walls that surrounded the building.

Senior Chief Petty Officer Rob O'Neill, SEAL Team Six, U.S. Navy: We had a few weeks to prepare for the mission targeting Osama bin Laden. I was certain he was there, in Abbottabad, because of how the CIA analysts had explained how they found him. I was convinced and the other guys were convinced that he was there too.

We also were pretty sure that we weren't going to come back from the mission — we had this new stealth technology, but no one

771

really knew if it worked. We didn't know how good the air defenses for Pakistan were. We knew that we were invading, and that they could shoot us down and be justified. We also thought we might simply run out of gas in the helicopters and end up on foot in a really, really bad part of the world. We thought if anyone's going to blow himself up and his entire family and martyr everybody, it's going to be bin Laden. He wasn't going to let us get him.

We went in there thinking this was a one-way mission. We had our last meals with our families and our kids — I know I did — and then hand-wrote letters to our families. We had to find people and say, "Hey, here's an envelope. If you don't see me tomorrow, you'll know what this is, and there are directions inside, but if you do see me tomorrow, give these back to me."

People were saying to each other on the mission, "If we know we're going to die, why are we going to go?" Then we talked about the people who jumped out of the Towers on a Tuesday morning. They didn't want to, they didn't know what was happening — all they knew was that it was 2500 degrees Fahrenheit and the better alternative than whatever hell was going on inside, in Windows on the World or at Cantor Fitzgerald, was to jump. They were not supposed to be in the fight. We all joined to be in the fight, and that's why we were going. We had that conversation about how the first ones to fight al-Qaeda were the passengers on Flight 93 that crashed in Shanksville, Pennsylvania. God knows how many lives they saved, but they killed themselves for the Western world. We had these conversations every night. That was why we went.

The terrorist leader behind the 9/11 plot was killed on May 2, 2011, as U.S. Navy SEALs raided the compound where he'd been hiding in Abbottabad, Pakistan. So that his gravesite would never become a shrine, the navy buried his body at sea.

Barack Obama, president of the United States, May 2, 2011: Good evening. Tonight, I can report to the American people and to the world, the United States has conducted an operation that killed Osama bin Laden, the leader of al-Qaeda, and a terrorist who's responsible for the murder of thousands of innocent men, women, and children.

It was nearly 10 years ago that a bright September day was darkened by the worst attack on the American people in our history. The images of 9/11 are seared into our national memory — hijacked planes cutting through a cloudless September sky; the Twin Towers collapsing to the ground; black smoke billowing up from the Pentagon; the wreckage of Flight 93 in Shanksville, Pennsylvania, where the actions of heroic citizens saved even more heartbreak and destruction.

And yet we know that the worst images are those that were unseen to the world. The empty seat at the dinner table. Children who were forced to grow up without their mother or their father. Parents who would never know the feeling of their child's embrace. Nearly 3,000 citizens taken from us, leaving a gaping hole in our hearts. . . .

Today, at my direction, the United States launched a targeted operation against that compound in Abbottabad, Pakistan. A small team of Americans carried out the operation with extraordinary courage and capa-

774

bility. No Americans were harmed. They took care to avoid civilian casualties. After a firefight, they killed Osama bin Laden and took custody of his body. . . .

The American people did not choose this fight. It came to our shores, and started with the senseless slaughter of our citizens. After nearly 10 years of service, struggle, and sacrifice, we know well the costs of war. . . .

Yet as a country, we will never tolerate our security being threatened, nor stand idly by when our people have been killed. We will be relentless in defense of our citizens and our friends and allies. We will be true to the values that make us who we are. And on nights like this one, we can say to those families who have lost loved ones to al-Qaeda's terror: Justice has been done.

Mike Morell, deputy director, CIA: In 2011, the very first telephone call that President Obama made after we were sure we'd killed Osama bin Laden was to President

Bush. President Obama knew that I'd been with him on 9/11, and so he asked me to fly down to Dallas after the raid to brief President Bush personally. I went down about two weeks later and walked President Bush through every aspect of the raid. I thought I could see in his face some sense of closure.

Sharon Miller, officer, PAPD: I look at the clock, and every time I look at the clock, it seems to be 9:11. I'm like, "Oh, 9:11, again." It just happens, something so simple like that.

Linda Krouner, senior vice president, Fiduciary Trust, South Tower: The sky in September can be particularly beautiful. When you look at a sky like it was on 9/11, you see it's that same clear, blue sky. The light is very different than the light in the summer. I said, "It's such a 9/11 sky."

Bruno Dellinger, principal, Quint Amasis North America, North Tower: If there is a beautiful day, I compare it to the morning of 9/11.

Philip Smith, branch chief, U.S. Army, Pentagon: I actually kept my uniform. I've kept it in this bag since 9/11. You can see the stains on my shirt. That's the jet fuel from where the tank exploded and the debris in it.

Army uniforms are surprisingly resilient because I was literally on fire from my head to my toe. This walked through the fires of the Pentagon and made its way out. I put it away and put it on the shelf. The army goes rolling along, and you keep moving.

Andrew Kirtzman, reporter, NY1: Life went on. The World Trade Center attacks were a horrendous catastrophe, but it's the nature of life that the next day people get up to go to work, government officials do their jobs, controversies erupt, and life goes on. Life went on after Pearl Harbor. It's the nature of life.

Rosemary Dillard, Washington, D.C., base manager, American Airlines, and wife of Flight 77 passenger Eddie Dillard: I never called it an anniversary, because when I think of an anniversary, I think of a happy time. I think of an observance, a time mark.

Richard Eichen, consultant, Pass Consulting Group, North Tower, 90th floor: I go down to the ceremony each year, and I go down to the ceremony for the guy who died between my legs. It sounds odd, but if it was just me and what happened to me that day, I don't know if I'd come down. I survived. My story is ongoing.

Sheila Denise Moody, accountant, Resource Services Office, Pentagon: I don't think there's a day that goes by that I haven't thought about the events of September 11th.

Dan Nigro, chief of operations, FDNY: We survive, we do our daily things, but you're always a part of 9/11.

ACKNOWLEDGEMENTS

The journey that grew into this book began in August 2016, a month before the fifteenth anniversary of the attacks, when I had the serendipity to sit at a Hoover Institution dinner in California next to Eryn Tillman. Two nights later, she introduced me to her husband, a.k.a. Colonel Mark Tillman, who loved my idea of reconstructing President Bush's travels on September 11th and opened up the door to his crew on Air Force One so that I could write about being aboard the most famous plane in the world on one of its most historic flights. My friends Gordon Johndroe and Ann Compton helped reconstruct who was onboard the president's plane on 9/11, Andy Card helped me track down numerous Bush alumni, and Lt. Col. Martin O'Donnell and Maj. Matt Miller helped me explore Offutt Air Force Base, and later, Barksdale.

I'd like to thank my talented one-time colleagues at *POLITICO Magazine* — Steve Heuser, Elizabeth Ralph, and Bill Duryea — for editing and publishing the original article on which this book is based, "We're the Only Plane in the Sky," and to Steve, especially, for plucking the Ellen Eckert quote to become its title. From there, I want to give an extra special thanks to *POLITICO*'s owner, Robert Allbritton; its editor, John Harris; and its counsel, Kathy Hanna, for all believing in me and this project and letting it grow into this larger, expansive history. I am grateful for your hard work, creativity, and friendship in helping me share this with readers.

This project — even more than most books, which are never as solitary an exercise as many realize — has a literal cast of thousands to thank and acknowledge. Altogether, this book, while mine, stands as the collective product of seventeen years of work by scores of oral historians, journalists, scholars, and officials who collected the stories of 9/11 — many of whose names I know, others whose names I don't. I'm grateful to all of them, named and unnamed here.

The National September 11 Memorial and Museum in New York was a deep supporter of this project throughout the two years it took to come to fruition. On my first day at the museum, Jess Chen led me through it and its heart-wrenching collection and exhibits; I will never forget turning around for the first time and seeing the crushed Ladder 3, nor standing in the galleries to listen to the victims' 911 calls and voicemails. Alice Greenwald, Amy Weinstein, and Jan Ramirez generously shared with me their knowledge and their archives, helping too to track down stray facts, voices, and make available every research request we could muster. Amy and Jan have built an unparalleled archival monument in their collection, an enduring gift for generations ahead. Amanda Granek helped nail down research details, and I'm grateful as well to Anthony Gardner, Alexandra Drakakis, Stephanie Schmeling, Bethany Romanoski, and Michael Chui, as well as my friends Allison Blais and Joe Daniels.

Moreover, this work would not exist without the hard work over the years of those who helped transcribe, edit, and publish the 9/11 Museum's oral history collection, including Anna Altman, Meredith Davidson, Jazmine da Costa, Luisa Diez, Anna Duensing, Jessica Evans, Katelyn Gamba, Elizabeth Gorski, Donna Kaz, Hillary Kirkham, Josh Levine, Wenonah Nelson, Kathryn O'Donnell, Molly Sloan, and Katrina Waizer, among others.

At the 9/11 Tribute Museum, I'm deeply grateful to then-curator Meri Lobel and her colleague, Connor Gaudet, who together built and assembled their oral history collection, and CEO Jennifer Adams Webb, who saw the value of this project and supported it too, as well as the interns, volunteers, and others who worked on their collection. Even after she left the Tribute Museum, Meri helped edit drafts, correcting everything from street names to titles, and providing a thorough copyedit.

At the Arlington County Public Library oral history project, their team included Heather Crocetto, Judith Knudsen, Joe B. Johnson, Diane Gates, and Bonnie Baldwin. At the Pentagon, the historians and interviewers involved in their effort to capture the building's story included Nancy Berlage, Rebecca Cameron, Alfred Goldberg, Richard Hunt, Diane Putney, Stuart Rochester, Roger Trask, and Rebecca Welch. I'm thankful too for the work and help of Todd Harvey at the Library of Congress and Kathleen Johnson in the historian's office of the House of Representatives.

At the Flight 93 National Memorial in Pennsylvania, I'm grateful to Brynn Bender, Barbara Black, Donna Glessner, and Kathie Shaffer, as well as their team of interns and volunteers who helped gather the stories of how their community was affected by the attack.

Moreover, while many of the above institutions had the good sense to capture the stories of 9/11 as soon as possible, their limited resources meant that many had never been transcribed, so Donna and Kathie spent months working with me to help transcribe dozens of oral histories that had been recorded but never put to paper. Donna read an early draft of the book deeply, providing pages and pages of thoughts, helping ensure the accuracy of the Flight 93 section, and suggesting additions to ensure the full sweep of the day was captured.

Beyond the archives dedicated to these stories, I would be remiss not to recognize the massive contribution of other journalists and 9/11 historians who have researched this hallowed ground before me, above and beyond the formal citations and footnotes.

In the months immediately following the attacks, the husband-and-wife team of Mitchell Fink and Lois Mathias captured a wealth of important stories in their book, *Never Forget,* some of which exist nowhere else. Jim Dwyer and Kevin Flynn's *102 Minutes: The Unforgettable Story of the Fight to Survive Inside the Twin Towers* remains too an invaluable guide to the New York attacks, as *Firefight: Inside the Battle to Save the Pentagon on 9/11,* by Patrick Creed and Rick Newman, does to the Pentagon's. In the air, Jere Longman's *Among the Heroes: United Flight 93 and the Passengers and Crew Who Fought Back* and Lynn Spencer's *Touching History: The Untold Story of the Drama That Unfolded in the Skies Over America on 9/11* both are critical guides to what transpired overhead, as are two fascinating aviation symposiums Spencer organized at the University of Texas — Dallas (both of which are archived by C-SPAN at www.c-span.org/video/?295417-1/). Jessica DuLong's book, *Dust to Deliverance: Untold Stories from the Maritime Evacuation on September 11th,* mixes fascinating NYC maritime history with wrenching stories of the water evacuation from Lower Manhattan, as does Mike Magee's *All Available Boats: The Evacuation of Manhattan Island on September 11, 2001.* Two other books, *Covering Catastrophe: Broadcast Journalists Report September 11,* compiled by Allison Gilbert, Phil Hirshkorn, Melinda Murphy, Mitchell Stephens, and Robyn Walensky, as well as *Running Toward Danger: Stories Behind the Breaking News of 9/11,* compiled by two of my friends, Cathy Trost and Alicia Shepard, helped fill in how journalists responded to the unprecedented story.

A talented team of *Washington Post* reporters, several of whom I've had the chance to know and all of whom I respect as writers — Monica Hesse, Caitlin Gibson, Jessica Contrera, and Karen Heller — collected numerous stories of children on 9/11, which I've supplemented with my own to create the section here on being a child and at college that tragic day. The team at the *Los Angeles Times* collected dozens of stories on their Tumblr blog in 2011, which proved an invaluable time capsule in the depths of the internet.

My then-agent, Will Lippincott, and lawyer, Jaime Wolf, both helped make this story a reality, as did my new literary agent, Howard Yoon, and my talented team at UTA: Andrew Lear, Katrina Escuedero, and Howie Sanders, before his departure. My assistant, Vanessa Sauter, enthusiastically sorted through mounds of footnotes, names, and tracked down increasingly obscure queries to translate the project from a draft to a manuscript to a book.

Jonathan Glickman and Adam Rosenberg at MGM instantly connected with this story. Liz Hannah was my partner for two days retracing Air Force One's travels on 9/11, walking the corridors and tarmac that President Bush traversed at Barksdale and Offutt, an experience that underscored in a way that words could never capture the fright and fear that would have been evident that day even from the sites of the attacks themselves.

I owe the single deepest debt of this book to Jenny Pachucki, a talented oral historian who has devoted much of her career to understanding 9/11 and whose fingerprints are on almost every single page of this book. I was lucky enough to snap Jenny up from the National September 11th Museum, where she'd actually collected many of these stories herself, working with Amy and others, and knew many of the voices in the preceding pages personally. For two years, Jenny was my guide through 9/11, helping me understand its nuances, the stories that needed to be captured, the voices, families, facts, legends, myths, and fictions that surround the day. She worked full-time for a nearly a year just gathering, reading, and sorting the oral histories collected in the preceding pages, as well as many more that ultimately didn't make it into the book. Jenny was my intellectual partner on the project at every step. I am indubitably indebted to her in ways big and small for her parrying of hundreds of my questions — by phone, email, and text — at all hours and days of the week, her travel up and down the East Coast to access archives large and small, and her work organizing more than 10,000 pages of research through countless memos and spreadsheets, as well as her work tracking down numerous photos. This book would literally not exist without her help and the decade of hard work and knowledge she brought to the project. Jenny, I never could have navigated this without you, and I'm thankful for your ongoing, lasting friendship. I hope I've done your life's work proud.

As I've been writing this book, I've said it was surely the most interesting and challenging puzzle I'll ever tackle. Assembling the myriad pieces and voices from that day into the portrait here was unquestionably the hardest and most emotional writing endeavor I've ever undertaken. This was my second book painstakingly edited by Jofie Ferrari-Adler and Julianna Haubner; I hope never to write another book without them. As long as the book is now, the first draft started at literally twice the length, and Jenny, Jofie, and Julianna worked for months to shape, organize, and narrow it across ultimately seven drafts, some of which Julianna devotedly diagrammed like Carrie Mathison pursuing a new plot. The four of us had deep, thoughtful, and challenging conversations about the level of editing we could do to the voices herein. We tried at every turn to balance personal style and authenticity with recognizing that spoken speech is often arduous to translate into written speech and ensuring that we captured people saying what they meant to say as they recalled high-stress, traumatic experiences. Jonathan Evans and Judith Hoover did yeoman's work helping to scrub the manuscript in copyediting. Ultimately, of course, all the editorial decisions (and remaining mistakes) are mine alone.

More broadly, there's a long list of people who have been critical to me being who and where I am today. Among them: Charlotte Stocek, Mary Creeden, Mike Baginski, Rome Aja, Kerrin McCadden, and Charlie Phillips;

John Rosenberg, Richard Mederos, Brian Delay, Peter J. Gomes, Stephen Shoemaker, and Jennifer Axsom; Kit Seeyle, Pat Leahy, Rusty Grieff, Tim Seldes, Jesseca Salky, Paul Elie, Tom Friedman, Jack Limpert, Geoff Shandler, Susan Glasser, and, not least of all, Cousin Connie, to whom I owe a debt that I strive to repay each day. My parents, Chris and Nancy Price Graff, have encouraged me to write since an early age, instilling in me a love of history and research and an intellectual curiosity that benefits me daily, and my sister, Lindsay, has always been my biggest fan — and I hers.

At home, I had the good-natured help of Sam Hubachek, the second-best addition to our family of the last year. My wife, Katherine, provided bottomless support and listened — as all writers' spouses are doomed to do — as I talked in wonder about this project and worked obsessively on it at odd hours during a particularly busy and transformative time. Thank you, KB.

Most of all, though, I'm grateful to each and every survivor and participant of 9/11 who shared their stories with me, other historians or journalists, or simply wrote down their memories for posterity — including those featured here, those whose stories I didn't have the opportunity to include, and those whose stories I've never even heard. There are millions of memories of that day, each unique, trying, and historic in its own way. I was surprised and heartened by the collective willingness to share and relive that trauma. Everyone I sought to interview over two years jumped to participate, even as a stranger contacted them out of the blue and asked them to discuss, in depth and at length, the worst day of their lives. Even reading the stories recorded by others often felt at times overwhelmingly heartrending and intimate. I cannot fathom the pain, physical or emotional, many of you experienced that day and after. I cried almost every single day as I compiled the first draft of this book and read or listened as you all recounted living through America's most dread-filled day. Together, your strength is a testament and inspiration to the resiliency of the human spirit, and I'm appreciative of your desire to help ensure that future generations understand what happened on September 11th. We must never forget.

— Garrett M. Graff
Burlington, VT
May 2019

SOURCES

The bulk of the 500 or so voices in this book are pulled from large-scale oral history projects conducted by a variety of museums, universities, and institutions that had the foresight to capture the contemporaneous memories of 9/11 survivors and participants for history.

The vast majority of the sources for this book are pulled from the oral history projects housed at seven institutions: The National September 11 Memorial & Museum (New York City), the 9/11 Tribute Museum (New York City), the Arlington County Public Library Oral History Project (Virginia), C-SPAN (Washington, D.C.), the Historical Office of the Office of the Secretary of Defense (The Pentagon, Virginia), the Flight 93 National Memorial (Shanksville, Pennsylvania), and the U.S. House of Representatives Historian's Office (Washington, D.C.), as well as interviews and stories collected by myself.

The primary sources for these oral histories are listed below, arranged alphabetically and by archival repository. Some of the collections are available online, in which case the web address is noted; otherwise, the oral histories are housed at and accessible through the institution's curator or historian's office itself.

Other, more limited or atypical sources — including books, magazines, and videos — are noted in specific endnotes below. In some cases, like Arlington County Assistant Fire Chief James Schwartz or FBI Special Agent Chris Combs, the same person contributed multiple oral histories to multiple institutions. In that case, the primary source responsible for the majority of that individual's quotations is listed below and any exceptions pulled from other oral histories are then specifically noted in the endnotes that follow.

National September 11 Memorial & Museum (New York City)
Joe Alagna
Jeannine Ali
Susan Baer
David Brink
Pasquale Buzzelli
Louise Buzzelli
Michele Cartier
John Cartier
Charles Christophe

Chris Combs
Monsignor John Delendick
Bruno Dellinger
Ada Dolch
Tracy Donahoo
Richard Eichen
Joe Esposito
Fernando Ferrer
Barbara Fiorillo
Joann Gomez
Joanna Gomez
Melissa Gomez
Betsy Gotbaum
Robert Gray
Rob Grunewald
Stephen Holl
William Jimeno
Jeff Johnson
Jay Jonas
Francine Kelly
Al Kim
Matthew Klimow
Jared Kotz
Mickey Kross
Linda Krouner
Constance LaBetti
Stephen Larabee
Vanessa Lawrence
Catherine Leuthold
Juana Lomi
Frank Loprano
Joseph Lott

Jackie Maguire
Joe Massian
Ileana Mayorga
Mike McGovern
Sharon Miller
Melinda Murphy
John Napolitano
David Norman
Jean O'Connor
Thomas O'Connor
Monica O'Leary
Ian Oldaker
Edna Ortiz
Jackie Pinto
Jean Potter
Dan Potter
Frank Razzano
James Schwartz
Robert Small
Philip Smith
Bill Spade
Scott Strauss
Joseph Torrillo
Harry Waizer
Robert Walker
Mike Walter
Judith Wein
Wesley Wong
Peter Zalewski

9/11 Tribute Museum (New York City)

Richard Balfour
John Cahill
Michael Cardozo
Sal Cassano
Chuck Downey
Joe Downey
Rudy Giuliani
Richard Grasso
Gregg Hansson
Norma Hardy
Charles Hirsch
Robert Hunor
Jan Khan
Andrew Kirtzman
David Kravette
Anthony Lisi
Frank Lombardi
James Luongo
Denise McFadden
Paul McFadden
Genelle McMillan
Sunny Mindel
Dan Nigro
Omar Olayan
Herb Ouida
George Pataki
Adrian Pierce
Bruce Powers
Alan Reiss
Ian Rifield
Rick Schoenlank

Colin Scoggins
Paul Somin
Lila Speciner
Steven Stefanakos
Elia Zedeno

Arlington County Public Library Oral History Project (Virginia)

Available online at https://libraryarchives.arling tonva.us/index.php/Detail/objects/195

David Allbaugh
Ray Anderson
Chuck Cake
Jim Daly
Gabriella Daya-Dominguez
Theresa Flynn
Charles Gibbs
Frank Haltiwanger
David Herbstreit
Susannah Herrada
Scott Kocher
Paul Larson
Mary McBride
Robert Medairos
Jennifer Meyers
Kyra Pulliam
Gary Tobias

U.S. Coast Guard Oral History Program (Washington, D.C.)
Michael Day
James Loy

Columbia University September 11, 2001, Oral History Project (New York)
Collection details available at https://library .columbia.edu/locations/ccoh/digital/9-11.html

Michael Lomonaco
Frederick Terna

C-SPAN (Washington, D.C.)
C-SPAN's 9/11 oral history videos are available at https://www.c-span.org/search/?searchtype =Videos&sort=Newest&seriesid[]=45

Mary Beth Cahill: https://www.c-span.org/ video/?300521-1/
Tom Daschle: https://www.c-span.org/video/ ?300751-1/
Dennis Hastert: https://www.c-span.org/ video/?300449-1/
John Jester: https://www.c-span.org/video/ ?301012-1/
Mary Matalin: https://www.c-span.org/video/ ?300727-1/
Gary Walters: https://www.c-span.org/video/ ?300426-1/

Flight 93 National Memorial (Shanksville, Pennsylvania)

Steve Aaron
Larry Arnold
William Baker
Alan Baumgardner
Robert "Bobby" Blair
Ralph Blanset
Craig Bowman
Jeffrey Braid
James Broderick
James Clark
Keith Custer
Andrea Dammann
Cynthia Daniels
Peter M. "Mike" Drewecki
Joyce Dunn
Rick Earle
Merle Flick
Mahlon Fuller
Yates Gladwell
Kevin Huzsek
Tony James
Lisa Jefferson
George "Bill" Keaton
Laurence Kesterson
Rick King
Martin Knezovich
T. Michael Lauffer
Tim Lensbouer
Jere Longman
Kristie Luedke

Patrick Madigan
David Mattingly
Patrick McGlennon
Jon Meyer
Douglas Miller
Denise Miller
Anita McBride Miller
Captain Frank Monaco
Wells Morrison
Kevin Nasypany
Steven O'Brien
Richard Paden
Stacey Taylor Parham
Eric Peterson
Paula Pluta
Tom Ridge
Thomas Rodgers
Norbert Rosenbaum
Michael Rosenbaum
Bob Schnarrenberger
Braden Shober
Ben Sliney
Corporal Louis Veitz
Clyde Ware
Robert Weaver
John Werth
Terry Yeazell
David Zacur

Here Is New York (New York City)

Available online at hereisnewyorkv911.org.

Ted Anderson
Sheila Denise Moody
Darrell Oliver
David Tarantino

High School for Leadership and Public Service (New York)

Available online at crafting-a-life.com/911.php

Keturah Bostick
Rosmaris Fernandez
Razvan Hotaranu
Heather Ordover
Robert Rosado

Historical Office of the Office of the Secretary of Defense (Pentagon, Virginia)

John Milton Brady, Jr.
Craig Bryan
Steven Carter
Victoria "Torie" Clarke
Chris Combs
Aubrey Davis
Lawrence Di Rita
Edmund Giambastiani
Randall Harper
William Haynes
John F. Irby
John Jester

Michael Nesbitt
Gilbert Oldach
James Phillips
Donald Rumsfeld
Dennis Smith
Joe Wassel

U.S. House of Representatives Historian's Office (Washington, D.C.)

Some of the work of the historians in the House of Representatives is available online at https://www.youtube.com/user/ushousehistory/playlists?view=50&sort=d-d&shelf_id=2

Eve Butler-Gee
Gerry Creedon
Steve Elmendorf
John Feehery
Mike Ferguson
Martin Frost
Brian Gaston
Brian Gunderson
Julia Rogers
Tyler Rogers
Tish Schwartz

StoryCorps — September 11th Initiative
Vaghn Allex
Beverly Eckert
Louise Rogers
John Yates

Interviews by the Author

John Anticev
Anthony Barnes
Ben Bell
Steve Bongardt
Emily Bouck
Monika Bravo
William "Buzz" Buzinski
Nic Calio
Andy Card
Linda Carpenter
Kat Cosgrove
Katie Couric
Scott Crogg
Mary Dettloff
Matt Dooley
Eric Draper
Ellen Eckert
Jason Fagone
Ari Fleischer
Lachlan Francis
Beau Garner
Steve Gaudin
Paul Germain
Porter Goss
Jenna Greene
Rick Greyson
Hillary Howard
Matthew Jellock
Gordon Johndroe
Nate Jones
Tom Keck

David Kelley
Richard Kolko
Robert Korn
B. Alexander "Sandy" Kress
Bill Kuchman
Dana Lark
Daphne Leigh
Rafael Lemaitre
Kathryn Mastandrea
Richard Mies
Rikki Miller
Brian Montgomery
Mike Morell
Matt Moyer
Rob O'Neill
Abby Perkins
Laura Petrou
Adam Putnam
Blake Richardson
Sonya Ross
Karl Rove
Dan Shuman
Preston Stone
Fred Stremmel
Michael Szwaja
Mark Tillman
Richard Tubb
Matthew Waxman
Dave Wilkinson
James "Sandy" Winnefeld, Jr.
Anne Worner
Natasha Wright

Cindy Wright
Julie Ziegenhorn

NOTES

Aboard the International Space Station

the only American off the planet: https://web
.archive.org/web/20090423055604/ https://
www.jsc.nasa.gov/Bios/htmlbios/culberts
.html.

*On September the 11th, 2001, I called the
ground:* Megan Gannon, "Astronaut Frank
Culbertson Reflects on Seeing 9/11 Attacks
from Space," *Space,* September 11, 2017,
at https://www.space.com/27117-nasa-
astronaut-saw-9-11-from-space.html.

September 10th

I'd been off most of the summer: Newseum,
Cathy Trost, and Alicia C. Shepard, *Running Toward Danger: Stories Behind the
Breaking News of 9/11* (Lanham, MD: Row-
man & Littlefield, 2002), 60.

I was on maternity leave: Mitchell Fink and
Lois Mathias, *Never Forget: An Oral History*

of September 11, 2001 (New York: William Morrow, 2002).

Tuesday Begins

My wife, Barbara, was supposed to travel: "Barbara Olson Remembered," CNN.com, December 25, 2001, at http://transcripts .cnn.com/TRANSCRIPTS/0112/25/ lkl.00.html.

I'd spent most of the morning going over the briefing: Smithsonian Channel, "9/11: Day That Changed the World — Laura Bush: Extended Interview," YouTube video, August 29, 2011, at https://www.youtube.com/ watch?v=ZEX32oeaCdI.

That was my first day on the job: "Aviation Officials Remember September 11, 2001," C-SPAN, September 11, 2010, at https:// www.c-span.org/video/?295417-1/aviation- officials-remember-september-11-2001.

One of the prettiest days: Leslie Filson, *Air War Over America: Sept. 11 Alters Face of Air Defense Mission* (Tyndall Air Force Base, FL: Headquarters 1st Air Force, Public Affairs Office, 2003), 60.

The bluest of blues: Mel Allen, "9/11 Started Here," *New England Today,* September 11, 2017, at https://newengland.com/today/ living/new-england-history/ticketagent/.

Checking In

Everybody was in a good mood: Jerry Harkavy, "Encounter Haunts Ex–Ticket Agent," *Press Herald* (Portland, ME), September 11, 2006, at https://www.pressherald.com/2011/08/25/michael-tuohey-september-11-hijackers-atta-alomari-portland-jetport-maine/.

These two guys came running: Ryan Hughes, "Va. Man Unintentionally Linked to 9/11 Still Works With His Feelings of Guilt," WJLA (Washington, D.C.), September 9, 2016, at https://wjla.com/news/local/va-man-unintentionally-linked-to-911-works-with-his-feelings-of-guilt.

I saw these two fellows standing there: "The Footnotes of 9/11," *CNN Presents,* September 11, 2011, at http://transcripts.cnn.com/TRANSCRIPTS/1109/11/cp.02.html.

We just finished the morning check-in: Ibid.

I said, "Mr. Atta, if you don't go now: Mel Allen, "9/11 Started Here," *New England Today,* September 11, 2017, at https://newengland.com/today/living/new-england-history/ticketagent/.

The Hijackings

Boston Center, good morning, American 11: Rutgers University Law Review, September 7, 2011, at http://www.rutgerslawreview.com/2011/ full-audio-transcript/.

Inside Air Traffic Control

I was the national operations manager on 9/11: C-SPAN, "Aviation Officials Remember September 11, 2001."

There was a huddle of people: Filson, *Air War Over America,* 55.

At this point our mind-set was the 1970s-vintage hijack: Ibid.

A scramble order was issued: C-SPAN, "Aviation Officials Remember September 11, 2001."

I left it in full afterburner: Filson, *Air War Over America,* 57; see also "Interview with Lt. Col. Tim Duffy and Leslie Filson" at https://www.scribd.com/document/18740499/T8-B22-Filson-Materials-Fdr-Lt-Col-Tim-Duffy-Interview-Typed-Notes-321.

At Mach One, it would take them: Filson, *Air War Over America,* 59.

The area was so congested: Ibid., 56.

We picked up a search track: Ibid.

The First Plane

In Manhattan, you rarely hear planes: Fink and Mathias, *Never Forget.*

I worked in One World Trade Center: Fink and Mathias, *Never Forget.*

I watched the fuselage disappear: Ibid.

Honestly, I think most people felt: Jessica Du-Long, *Dust to Deliverance: Untold Stories from the Maritime Evacuation on September 11th* (Camden, ME: Ragged Mountain Press, 2017), 15.

It looked like a ticker-tape parade: Richard Gray, *After the Fall: American Literature Since 9/11* (Hoboken, NJ: Wiley-Blackwell, 2011).

I told everybody to get in the rigs: Fink and Mathias, *Never Forget*.

Our office was on the 85th floor: Ibid.

I ran around the floor: Ibid.

The first thing that came to my mind: Ibid.

I saw two people out of the corner: Ibid.

It's a comedy of errors: Ibid.

I was on the corner of Church and Thomas: Ibid.

It was my son Kyle's first day: "CEO Howard Lutnick Remembers Sept. 11: How His Company Survived After Great Personal Loss," NPR, September 11, 2016, at https://www.npr.org/2016/09/11/493491879/ceo-howard-lutnick-remembers-sept-11-how-his-company-survived-after-great-person.

We had a clear shot from the 40s: Tom Barbash, *On Top of the World: Cantor Fitzgerald, Howard Lutnick, and 9/11: A Story of Loss and Renewal* (New York: HarperCollins, 2003), 18.

I was scheduled to host election night coverage: Oral history in the collection of the 9/11 Tribute Museum.

I was having breakfast at the Peninsula Hotel: Ibid.

I hailed a cab, jumped into it: Ibid.

As we approached Manhattan, we discussed: "Nigro," *New York Times,* undated, at http://www.nytimes.com/packages/html/nyregion/20050812_WTC_GRAPHIC/Nigro_Daniel.txt.

I'm a C5-C6 quadriplegic: Fink and Mathias, *Never Forget.*

I have known John for a long time: Ibid.

I had been there in 1993: Ibid.

He seemed to be in shock: Ibid.

They made it clear I was going with them: Ibid.

There were thousands of people running: Ibid.

I will never forget seeing an airplane engine: Oral history in the collection of the 9/11 Tribute Museum.

I ordered the cop at the desk: Fink and Mathias, *Never Forget.*

A lot of patients were coming out of the plaza: Gray, *After the Fall.*

All that morning, I don't think I really had: Fink and Mathias, *Never Forget.*

Nothing could have ever really prepared us: National Commission on Terrorist Attacks Upon the United States, "Testimony of the Former Commissioner of the New York City Fire Department Thomas Von Essen," May 18, 2004, http://govinfo.library.unt.edu/911/hearings/hearing11/essen_statement.pdf.

The Military Gears Up

We are looking at a host of potential problems: Filson, *Air War Over America,* 63.

The guy from the sector: Ibid.

I was the captain of the Midwest Express flight: C-SPAN, "Aviation Officials Remember September 11, 2001."

I was flying Milwaukee to New York: Ibid.

I was ordered to take evasive action: Ibid.

As we're watching the television: Filson, *Air War Over America,* 59.

As we are coming out of the right turn: C-SPAN, "Aviation Officials Remember September 11, 2001."

They say the second aircraft: Filson, *Air War Over America,* 60.

We were about 60 to 70 miles outside Manhattan: "Interview with Lt. Col. Tim Duffy and Leslie Filson."

At that point, we had to figure out: C-SPAN, "Aviation Officials Remember September 11, 2001."

They came back on and said: Filson, *Air War Over America,* 63.

Shortly after takeoff, they changed our heading: Ibid., 65.

The Second Plane

It was a fairly light news day: Covering Catastrophe: Broadcast Journalists Report Septem-

811

ber 11, ed. Allison Gilbert, Phil Hirshkorn, Melinda Murphy, Mitchell Stephens, and Robyn Walensky (Lanham, MD: Taylor Trade Publishing, 2003).

I was awakened: Fink and Mathias, *Never Forget.*

The first witnesses kept saying: Covering Catastrophe, Gilbert et al., 23.

The phone rang: Fink and Mathias, *Never Forget.*

We saw it live. As it rounded the corner: Covering Catastrophe, 31.

I simply put my hands in the air: Ibid., 34.

Our helicopter was on the southwest side: Fink and Mathias, *Never Forget.*

The second plane came in: Ibid.

It proceeded to fly right through the building: Ibid.

I was in my office in downtown Brooklyn: Ibid.

I'm scared: "9/11 stories: Stanley Praimnath and Brian Clark," BBC, September 5, 2011, at https://www.bbc.com/news/av/world-us-canada-14766882/9-11-stories-stanley-praimnath-and-brian-clark.

Debris and body parts and the plane: Fink and Mathias, *Never Forget.*

Mayor Giuliani made a comment to me: Ibid.

I remember seeing Ray Downey: Ibid.

We got on a truck and it seemed like: Ibid.

At Emma Booker Elementary School, Sarasota, Florida

Everyone had their hair done: Ely Brown, "Florida Students Witnessed the Moment Bush Learned of 9/11 Terror Attacks," ABC News, September 8, 2011, at https://abcnews.go.com/US/September_11/florida-students-witnessed-moment-bush-learned-911-terror/story?id=14474518.

Our principal introduced him to the children: Cullen Murphy and Todd S. Purdum, "Farewell to All That: An Oral History of the Bush White House," *Vanity Fair,* February 2009, at https://www.vanityfair.com/news/2009/02/bush-oral-history200902.

I remember him being all happy: "Florida Students Witnessed the Moment Bush Learned of 9/11 Terror Attacks."

I can remember seeing his expression change dramatically: Rob Shaw, "Students witnessed history," *Tampa Tribune,* September 11, 2011, at: http://www.charlesapple.com/2011/09/wednesdays-notable-911-anniversary-pages/.

I'll never forget the look on his face: Running Toward Danger, 60.

My notes say we took off: Ibid., 80.

First Reactions in D.C.

My Secret Service agent, the head of my detail: Smithsonian Channel, "9/11: Day That

Changed the World."

I thought, Well, that's a strange accident: University of Denver, "Recalling 9/11: Condoleezza Rice," YouTube video, 2:08, September 16, 2014, https://www.youtube.com/watch?v=RYRK-lKmvlY.

I heard of the disaster occurring: "Barbara Olsen Remembered," CNN.com, December 25, 2001, at http://transcripts.cnn.com/TRANSCRIPTS/0112/25/lkl.00.html.

It was the moment that changed everything: Evan Thomas, "The Day That Changed America," *Newsweek,* December 30, 2001, at https://www.newsweek.com/day-changed-america-148319.

Radar caught sight of an airliner: Jimmy Orr, "Nope, Dick Cheney Didn't Change His Mind . . . ," *Christian Science Monitor,* May 21, 2009, at https://www.csmonitor.com/USA/Politics/The-Vote/2009/0521/nope-dick-cheney-didnt-change-his-mind.

We learn that a plane is five miles out: Thomas, "The Day That Changed America."

My Secret Service agent said: "9/11: What Really Happened?," CNN.com, September 14, 2002, at http://transcripts.cnn.com/TRANSCRIPTS/0209/14/cp.00.html.

The Secret Service came in: Interview with Rice, at https://www.youtube.com/watch?v=0SDtt5QUMg4.

They practice this: Thomas, "The Day That Changed America."

The look on the faces of the Secret Service agents: Kate Anderson Brower, "Inside the White House on September 11," *Fortune,* September 11, 2016, at http://fortune.com/2016/09/11/the-residence-kate-andersen/.

A few moments later, I found myself: Orr, "Nope, Dick Cheney Didn't Change His Mind."

American Airlines Flight 77

One of the secretaries rushed in: "Barbara Olson Remembered," CNN.com, December 25, 2001, at http://transcripts.cnn.com/TRANSCRIPTS/0112/25/lkl.00.html.

We were trying to juggle big decisions: C-SPAN, "Aviation Officials Remember September 11, 2001."

I was in shock and horrified: CNN, "Barbara Olsen Remembered."

There had never been a situation where hijackers: C-SPAN, "Aviation Officials Remember September 11, 2001."

I'll never forget — it was a military transport: Ibid.

The pilot came right back: Ibid.

I called some people: CNN, "Barbara Olsen Remembered."

I noticed the aircraft: "Air Traffic Controllers Recall 9/11," ABC News, October 24, 2011, at https://web.archive.org/web/20130929181230/http://abcnews.go.com/2020/

story?id=123822&page=1.

I dreaded the realization: "On Sept. 11, Former Bush Solicitor General Remembers His Late Wife," NPR, September 11, 2016, at https://www.npr.org/2016/09/11/493491949/on-sept-11-former-bush-solicitor-general-remembers-his-late-wife.

I had the scope focused: Filson, *Air War Over America,* 65.

We waited, and we waited: "Air Traffic Controllers Recall 9/11," ABC News.

After the second phone call: "On Sept. 11, Former Bush Solicitor General Remembers His Late Wife," NPR.

The Washington National Airport controllers: "Air Traffic Controllers Recall 9/11."

The Third Plane

Instantly, 400,000 square feet of the Pentagon: Patrick Creed and Rick Newman, *Firefight: Inside the Battle to Save the Pentagon on 9/11* (New York: Presidio Press, 2008), 31.

I immediately ran down to the Operations Center: Oral history in the collection of the Historical Office of the Office of the Secretary of Defense (Pentagon, Arlington, Virginia).

People were told to get out — run: Oral history in the collection of the U.S. House of Representatives Historian's Office (Washington, D.C.).

Flight 93 in Peril

The first official report of trouble: Jane Pauley, "No Greater Love," NBC News, September 11, 2016, at http://www.nbcnews.com/id/14789502/ns/dateline_nbc/t/no-greater-love/#.W_GqmWRKjqI.

The phone rang: Fink and Mathias, *Never Forget.*

The call came in at 6:37 in the morning: Ibid. NOTE: Hoagland in Fink and Mathias's oral history says the call came in at 6:44 a.m., but according to the FBI reconstruction, the call happened at 6:37 a.m. PT, so I use that time here.

As I was explaining: Ibid.

I must have gotten up: Ibid.

A news reporter came on: Ibid.

Tom Burnett was in 4B: Ibid.

Then Jeremy started asking me: Ibid.

The phone rang again: Ibid.

Honey, are you there?: Pauley, "No Greater Love."

Jeremy said he didn't think: Fink and Mathias, *Never Forget.*

I asked the caller his name: Ibid.

We knew how bad things were: C-SPAN, "Aviation Officials Remember September 11, 2001."

We had a report from a small, private aircraft pilot: Ibid.

817

He called back: Fink and Mathias, *Never Forget.*

The World Trade Center Evacuation

Inside the [North Tower grand-floor] lobby, I think we knew less: Fink and Mathias, *Never Forget.*
We tried every possible means of communication: Ibid.
People saw the helicopter: Ibid.
Groups of firefighters were coming in: Ibid.
I crawled the entire length of the loans department: "9/11 Stories: Stanley Praimnath and Brian Clark," *BBC News,* September 5, 2011, at https://www.bbc.com/news/av/world-us-canada-14766882/9-11-stories-stanley-praimnath-and-brian-clark.
Our offices occupied the entire 84th floor: Ibid.
This man behind the wall: "9/11 stories: Ibid.
Suddenly he said, "Can you see my hand?": Ibid.
He said, "Come on, buddy": Ibid.
No, it's so hot I'm burning up: Exhibit P200016, *United States v. Zacarias Moussaoui,* Criminal No. 01-455-A, "Melissa Doi 911 tape," at http://www.vaed.uscourts.gov/notablecases/moussaoui/exhibits/prosecution/P200016.html.
We made it to the ninth floor: Fink and Mathias, *Never Forget.*

818

We encountered maybe 20 to 25 firemen: Ibid.

As they walked past us: Ibid.

We started to make our way down the staircase: Ibid.

We wanted to make time: Ibid.

We kept switching our team: Ibid.

The firemen cheered us on: Ibid.

I just kept climbing: Ibid.

The dumb sons of bitches: Michael Grunwald, "A Tower of Courage," *Washington Post,* October 28, 2001, at https://www.washingtonpost.com/archive/lifestyle/2001/10/28/a-tower-of-courage/c53e8244-3754-440f-84f8-51f841aff6c8/?utm_term=.7fb8b3cba7aa.

We walked toward Battery Park: Mike Magee, *All Available Boats: The Evacuation of Manhattan Island on September 11, 2001* (West Hartford, CT: Spencer Books, 2002), 128.

I have the greatest admiration for the private security officers: Fink and Mathias, *Never Forget.*

Jumping

It was a sight and sound that I'll never forget: 9/11 Tribute Center.

You'd hear this whoosh: Fink and Mathias, *Never Forget.*

The clothes of the jumpers: Edward Cone, "A New Beginning at Ground Zero," *EdCone,* June 30, 2002, at https://edcone.typepad

.com/wordup/2002/07/a_reluctant_her.ht
ml#more.
I did see one jumper actually hit a fireman: Fink
and Mathias, *Never Forget.*
I must've blessed myself: Ibid.
I've been in this business 26 years: Ibid.

The FAA Makes History

As soon as Flight 77 hit the Pentagon:
C-SPAN, "Aviation Officials Remember
September 11, 2001."
The controllers were telling the pilots: U.S.
Department of Transportation, "Ten Years
Later: Air Traffic Controllers Remember
9/11," YouTube video, 5:37, September 1,
2011, at https://www.youtube.com/watch?
v=i7vWcQZjEwM.
Every plane was considered a threat: C-SPAN,
"Aviation Officials Remember September
11, 2001."
When the order came out to land: Ibid.
To put 4,500 aircraft on the ground: Ibid.
To give some perspective, I believe 700 landed:
Ibid.
They did an incredible job: U.S. Department
of Transportation, "Ten Years Later: Air
Traffic Controllers Remember 9/11."
*I do not think the aviation industry got the
thanks:* C-SPAN, "Aviation Officials Re-
member September 11, 2001."
We were the next-to-last aircraft: Ibid.

820

The Trade Center Rescue Continues

Everyone from my company got out but one: Fink and Mathias, *Never Forget.*

I stood at the door off of Church Street: ABC News, "9/11 WTC Cantor Fitzgerald CEO and Chairman Howard Lutnick," YouTube video, 9:43, June 15, 2011, at https://www .youtube.com/watch?v=8rf35t4d214.

There was nothing we could do: Barbash, *On Top of the World,* 18.

I've known the mayor for about 11 or 12 years: Fink and Mathias, *Never Forget.*

She was a little hysterical: "Three Families Share Stories of Last Communications From Loved Ones on 9-11," CNN, September 8, 2002, at http://transcripts.cnn.com/ TRANSCRIPTS/0209/08/sm.18.html.

Minutes later, Melissa Harrington Hughes called her husband: "On September 11, Final Words of Love," CNN.com, September 10, 2002, at http://www.cnn.com/2002/US/09/ 03/ar911.phone.calls/.

Jan's normal shift was lunch: "The Long Good-Bye," *New York* magazine, undated, http://nymag.com/nymetro/news/sept11/ features/5788/.

We have speakerphones in each office: ABC News, "9/11 WTC Cantor Fitzgerald CEO and Chairman Howard Lutnick."

My brother, Gary, was in the building: NPR, "CEO Howard Lutnick Remembers Sept.

11: How His Company Survived After Great Personal Loss."

My husband called to let me know: Fink and Mathias, *Never Forget.*

The First Collapse

It was this rat-tat-tat-tat-tat-tat-tat-tat: Gray, *After the Fall.*

We're talking to [NYPD officer] Glen Pettit: Fink and Mathias, *Never Forget.*

I'm looking at the building, and Sean's facing me: Ibid.

I was looking away from the building: Ibid.

The loudest sound I'd ever heard: NPR, "CEO Howard Lutnick Remembers Sept. 11: How His Company Survived After Great Personal Loss."

I can't even give you an analogy: Fink and Mathias, *Never Forget.*

Like an incoming missile: Ibid.

Like an avalanche: Gray, *After the Fall.*

Like a giant chandelier: DuLong, *Dust to Deliverance,* 55.

Like a machine gun: Magee, *All Available Boats,* 108.

I suddenly heard this loud explosion: StoryCorps, "Beverly Eckert," Vimeo video, 2:45, at https://vimeo.com/180606992; "Sean Rooney's Last Goodbye," 9/11 Memorial & Museum, February 17, 2017, at https://www.911memorial.org/blog/sean-rooney

%E2%80%99s-last-goodbye.

I ran into a woman on the street: Fink and Mathias, *Never Forget.*

In seconds, it was gone: Ibid.

We went into silent mode: Covering Catastrophe, 84.

The hardest words I've ever spoken on TV: Ibid., 102.

We stood there for a minute: Fink and Mathias, *Never Forget.*

Inside the Cloud

The South Tower collapsed: Thomas W. Eagar and Christopher Musso, "Why Did the World Trade Center Collapse? Science, Engineering, and Speculation," *JOM: Journal of the Minerals, Metals, and Materials Society* 53, no. 12 (2001): 8–11, https://www.tms.org/pubs/journals/jom/0112/eagar/eagar-0112.html.

I looked over my shoulder: NPR, "CEO Howard Lutnick Remembers Sept. 11."

Your brain couldn't adjust: Fink and Mathias, *Never Forget.*

We were docked near the pier: Ibid.

We were yelling for people in the water: Ibid.

I heard all the crashing and the steel: Ibid.

The pummeling by debris: 9/11 Tribute Center.

I could feel stuff going up my legs: Fink and Mathias, *Never Forget.*

I've never heard screaming: Ibid.

After the building collapsed, there was a calmness: Ibid.

People I was standing with: Garrett Kling, "The Burdens of Prayer: FDNY Chaplains Remember 9/11 Every Day," *A Journey Through NYC Religions,* September 11, 2015, at https://www.nycreligion.info/bur dens-prayer-fdny-chaplains-remember-911-day/.

Picture taking a handful of flour: Fink and Mathias, *Never Forget.*

Inside the PEOC

In the years since: Orr, "Nope, Dick Cheney Didn't Change His Mind."

Many of us thought that we might not leave: Richard Clarke, "Cheney and Rice Remember 9/11: I Do, Too," *Washington Post,* May 31, 2009, at http://www.washingtonpost.com/wp-dyn/content/article/2009/05/29/AR2009052901560.html.

Norm Mineta, the transportation secretary: Interview with Rice at: https://www.youtube.com/watch?v=0SDtt5QUMg4.

My first thought was: Ibid.

We were in foreign territory: Filson, *Air War Over America,* 73.

Our chain of command: "Major Heather Penney on September 11, 2001," C-SPAN, August 8, 2011, at https://www.c-span.org/

video/?300959-1/major-heather-penney-september-11-2001.

I handed our wing commander: C-SPAN, "Pilots Remember September 11, 2001," at https://www.c-span.org/video/?295417-2/pilots-remember-september-11-2001.

It had to be done: Stephen Hayes, "Cheney Speaks," *The Weekly Standard,* July 23, 2007, at https://www.weeklystandard.com/stephen-f-hayes/cheney-speaks-14972.

Vice President Cheney was very steady: Ibid.

As bad as the events of 9/11 were: "In Cody, Cheney Reflects On 9/11," *Powell (WY) Tribune,* May 31, 2018, at http://www.powelltribune.com/stories/in-cody-cheney-reflects-on-911,14163.

He was a calming influence: Thomas, "The Day That Changed America."

There were times that day: Ibid.

The Military Responds

My translation of the rules: Filson, *Air War Over America,* 82.

As we're going out to the jets: Nicole Weisensee Egan, "Inside a Hero Fighter Pilot's Decision to Give His Life in Kamikaze Mission on 9/11: 'We Were Going to Do the Unthinkable,' " *People,* September 9, 2016, at https://people.com/celebrity/911-f-16-pilot-marc-sasseville-was-prepared-for-kamikaze-mission/.

We would be ramming the aircraft: "Major Heather Penney on September 11, 2001," C-SPAN, August 8, 2011.

We didn't have a whole lot of options: Filson, *Air War Over America,* 82.

I had never been trained: "Major Heather Penney on September 11, 2001," C-SPAN, August 8, 2011.

We did everything humanly possible: Steve Hendrix, "F-16 Pilot Was Ready to Give Her Life on Sept. 11," *Washington Post,* September 8, 2011, at https://www.washing tonpost.com/local/f-16-pilot-was-ready-to-give-her-life-on-sept-11/2015/09/06/7c8cddbc-d8ce-11e0-9dca-a4d231dfde50_story.html?utm_term=.2c051fdfcd6d.

I just got my radios up: "Major Heather Penney on September 11, 2001," C-SPAN, August 8, 2011.

I was thinking, Wow: Filson, *Air War over America,* 82.

Sass and I fully expected: "Major Heather Penney on September 11, 2001," C-SPAN, August 8, 2011.

I was going into this moral: Ibid.

I genuinely believed that was going to be: Hendrix, "F-16 Pilot Was Ready to Give Her Life on Sept. 11."

Seeing the Pentagon was surreal: "Major Heather Penney on September 11, 2001," C-SPAN, August 8, 2011.

There was all this smoke in my cockpit: Nicole

Weisensee Egan, "Inside a Hero Fighter Pilot's Decision to Give His Life in Kamikaze Mission on 9/11."

The real heroes are the passengers: Ibid.

They made the decision: Filson, *Air War over America,* 82.

I don't remember how many miles: "Major Heather Penney on September 11, 2001," C-SPAN, August 8, 2011.

The Fourth Crash

We talked about how much we loved each other: Andrew Alderson and Susan Bisset, "The Extraordinary Last Calls of Flight UA93," *Telegraph* (U.K.), October 21, 2001, at https://www.telegraph.co.uk/news/worldnews/northamerica/usa/1360088/The-extraordinary-last-calls-of-Flight-UA93.html.

I didn't want to listen: Fink and Mathias, *Never Forget.*

My dad stayed on the line: Ibid.

I kept waiting: Ibid.

Fear at the Pentagon

It was on track to D.C.: Oral history in the collection of the Historical Office of the Office of the Secretary of Defense (Pentagon, Arlington, Virginia).

We were outside and heard the fire trucks: Ibid.

We looked around and decided: Ibid.

It was about 10 minutes after: Ibid.

The First Casualty

It's fantastic how I can sometimes: Barbara Bradley Hagerty, "Memories of Sept. 11's First Recorded Casualty Endure," NPR, September 5, 2011, at https://www.npr.org/2011/09/05/140154885/memories-of-sept-11s-first-casualty-burn-bright.

Priests and firemen both enter people's lives: Jennifer Senior, "The Firemen's Friar," *New York* magazine, undated, at http://nymag.com/nymetro/news/sept11/features/5372/#print.

There's a very old postcard: Ibid.

On 9/11, one of our friars: Fr. Michael Duffy, "Homily Preached at Funeral Mass for Fr. Mychal Judge, OFM," September 15, 2001, Franciscan Friars Holy Name Province, at https://hnp.org/wp-content/uploads/2014/03/09-15-01-mjhomily.pdf.

I saw Mychal Judge: Fink and Mathias, *Never Forget.*

You could see it in his face: Anna Mehler Paperny, "For Five Men, Tragedy Remains Over Photo of 9/11's First Casualty," *Global and Mail* (Toronto), September 1, 2011, at https://www.theglobeandmail.com/news/world/for-five-men-tragedy-remains-over-

photo-of-911s-first-casualty/article5929
45/.

He was in the lobby with us: 9/11, directed by
Jules Naudet, Gédéon Naudet, and James
Hanlon, CBS, 2002.

That's when the whole building shook: Jennifer
Senior, "The Fireman Friar," *New York,*
November 12, 2001, at http://nymag.com/
nymetro/news/sept11/features/5372/.

One of the firefighters put the light on him: Ibid.

I took an arm: Ibid.

I saw the firemen carrying a man: "The Long
Good-Bye," *New York,* March 18, 2002,
http://nymag.com/nymetro/news/sept11/
features/5788/.

*I noticed some rescue workers carrying this
man in a chair: Running Toward Danger,* 99.

I remember looking up: "Bill Cosgrove," Story
Corps, September 9, 2011, at https://story
corps.org/listen/bill-cosgrove/.

At the time: "How 9/11 Changed Us," *New
York,* September 11, 2003, at http://nymag
.com/nymetro/news/sept11/2003/n_9196/.

We carried him to a street corner: Senior, "The
Firemen's Friar."

We knelt down: Fink and Mathias, *Never Forget,* 63.

The firemen took his body: Quoting Father
Duffy's homily, "No Greater Love: Chaplain Mychal Judge, OFM," at https://www
.franciscanmedia.org/no-greater-love-

chaplain-mychal-judge-ofm/.

Mychal Judge's body was the first one released: "Slain Priest: 'Bury His Heart, but Not His Love,' " NPR, September 9, 2011, at https://www.npr.org/2011/09/09/1402939 93/slain-priest-bury-his-heart-but-not-his-love.

The first official casualty of the attack: Naudet, Naudet, and Hanlon, *9/11.*

I think he wouldn't have had it any other way: Hagerty, "Memories of Sept. 11's First Recorded Casualty Endure."

After the Collapse

I can't tell you how long: Fink and Mathias, *Never Forget.*

I remember walking north on West Street: Ibid.

All of Lower Manhattan was covered: Ibid.

Maybe I'm exaggerating: Ibid.

We came across the marina: Ibid.

Aboard Air Force One, Somewhere over the Gulf of Mexico

I called the president: University of Denver, "Recalling 9/11: Condoleezza Rice."

Among Those Who Knew

"Does al-Qaeda have to hit the Pentagon: Matt Schudel, "Michael A. Sheehan, Counter-terrorism Expert Who Warned of bin La-

830

den, Dies at 63," *Washington Post,* August 1, 2018, at https://www.washingtonpost .com/local/obituaries/michael-a-sheehan-counterterrorism-expert-who-warned-of-bin-laden-dies-at-63/2018/08/01/5497830 c-959b-11e8-810c-5fa705927d54_story.ht ml?utm_term=.c6741c4bba85.

The first time I ever heard: "The Man Who Knew," *Frontline,* PBS, at: https://www.pbs .org/wgbh/frontline/film/showsknew/ transcript/.

In 1998, I sat with Osama bin Laden: John C. Miller, Michael Stone, and Chris Mitchell, *The Cell* (New York: Hachette Books, 2002), 4.

In June of 2001, the intelligence community: "The Man Who Knew," *Frontline,* PBS, at https://www.pbs.org/wgbh/frontline/film/ showsknew/transcript/.

John O'Neill was frustrated: "Fran Towsend," [*sic*] *Frontline,* PBS, October 3, 2002, at https://www.pbs.org/wgbh/frontline/article/ fran-towsend/.

The night of September 10th: "The Man Who Knew," *Frontline.*

The system was blinking red: U.S. National Commission on Terrorist Attacks upon the United States, "The System Was Blinking Red," chapter 8 in *9/11 Commission Report: The Official Report of the 9/11 Commission and Related Publications* (Washington, D.C.: GPO, 2004), at http://govinfo.library

.unt.edu/911/report/911Report_Ch8.pdf.

Time ran out: Ibid.

When the first plane hit: "Fran Towsend," [*sic*] *Frontline.*

John O'Neill had spent the better part of 10 years: Miller, Stone, and Mitchell, *The Cell,* 315.

Escaping the Pentagon

All the credit that public safety: Oral history in the Arlington County Public Library Oral History Project (Virginia), at https://library archives.arlingtonva.us/index.php/Detail/objects/195.

Among the responding units: Ibid.

The smoke was so bad: Oral history in the collection of the Historical Office of the Office of the Secretary of Defense (Pentagon, Arlington, Virginia).

Colonel Anderson and I went into the building: Fink and Mathias, *Never Forget.*

We were so jacked up on adrenaline: Ibid.

In Between Collapses

To understand all this: U.S. National Commission on Terrorist Attacks Upon the United States, "Testimony of the Former Commissioner of the New York City Fire Department Thomas Von Essen."

They told us to evacuate Tower One: Fink and

Mathias, *Never Forget.*
Billy and I coaxed the gentleman down: Ibid.
When we came upon Josephine: Ibid.
I started down with Josephine: Ibid.
Everybody was trying to push us along: Ibid.
The whole building started to rock: Ibid.
Then everything went black: Ibid.

The Second Collapse

Billy and I finally got Ralph to the lobby: Fink
  and Mathias, *Never Forget.*
I heard this sick cracking noise: Ibid.
This police officer came up next to me: CNN,
  Facebook post, September 11, 2016, at
  https://www.facebook.com/cnn/videos/
  10155290144326509.
We went over by Kennedy: "Interview with
  Lt. Col. Tim Duffy and Leslie Filson."
People are screaming: Fink and Mathias,
  Never Forget.
We were pushing people: Ibid.
I lived about nine blocks north: Jenny Pachucki,
  "The Actor: Robert De Niro," *9/11 Memo-*
  rial and Museum, March 24, 2016, at https://
  www.911memorial.org/blog/new-yorkers-
  tell-their-911-story-new-podcast-series.
I have no memory of any noise: Fink and
  Mathias, *Never Forget.*
You're choking, trying to breathe: Ibid.
Every time I'd breathe in: Ibid.

Trapped in the Ruins

I said to my sergeant: Fink and Mathias, *Never Forget.*

Nobody trained for this: "Last Man Out," *60 Minutes,* CBS News, November 23, 2004, at https://www.cbsnews.com/news/last-man-out/.

Immediately, you look at yourself: Ibid.

Somebody was watching over us: OWN, "The Angel of Ladder Company 6," YouTube video, 4:17, at https://www.youtube.com/watch?v=paffg3F83q4.

After the Collapse

I started crawling my way out of there: Fink and Mathias, *Never Forget.*

People started calling out: Ibid.

At the Waterfront

A makeshift, unorganized armada: "List from 2011 PortSide Exhibit 'Mariners Response to 9/11,' " *Portside New York,* undated, at https://static1.squarespace.com/static/50dc baa5e4b00220dc74e81f/t/57d559dcb3db2 b1e5a13a5c3/1473599965084/PortSide+ NewYork+list+of+9-11+boatlift+boats .pdf.

I heard a lady yell: Fink and Mathias, *Never Forget.*

He was a real cutie: Ibid.

I carried her down to the water: Ibid.

An NYPD harbor boat pulled up: Ibid.

There were one or two fireboats: Ibid.

It was like being the last lifeboat: DuLong, *Dust to Deliverance,* 45.

Mothers and nannies with infants: Magee, *All Available Boats,* 40.

There was a small boat: Boatlift: An Untold Tale of 9/11 Resilience, directed by Eddie Rosenstein, Brooklyn, NY: Eyepop Productions, 2011, at https://www.youtube.com/watch?time_continue=428&v=18lsxFcDrjo.

At any given time, Battery Park: Magee, *All Available Boats,* 58.

We went back and forth: Boatlift.

When we arrived at the pier: Magee, *All Available Boats,* 76.

We decided to make the call on the radio: Boatlift.

Tugboats — I've never seen so many: Ibid.

There were thousands and thousands of people: Magee, *All Available Boats,* 130.

A blue New York Waterway ferryboat: Ibid., 86.

There was dust all over the boat: Ibid., 66.

If we had injured people on board: Ibid., *52*

As we got off the boat in Jersey City: Ibid., 98.

I was told the command center: "Nigro," *New York Times.*

Midmorning at the Pentagon

I grabbed a DPS guy: Oral history in the collection of the Historical Office of the Office of the Secretary of Defense (Pentagon, Arlington, Virginia).

Very early I knew we didn't have enough people: Ibid.

We transported 94 people: Oral history in the collection of the Arlington County Public Library Oral History Project (Virginia), at https://libraryarchives. arlingtonva.us/ index.php/Detail/objects/195.

NEADS wanted to know: Filson, *Air War Over America,* 66.

With the Secretary of Defense

These Doomsday and Continuity of Government plans: C-SPAN, "Aviation Officials Remember September 11, 2001."

Midday in New York City

It was like the scene from The Ten Commandants: Gray, *After the Fall.*

We kept walking and wiping our faces: Barbash, *On Top of the World,* 4.

I thought my fiancé, Kevin: Fink and Mathias, *Never Forget.*

I got in the car and drove in: Ibid.

At a rally point in Cunningham Park: Ibid.

We couldn't even hear our own footsteps: Ibid.

As I got farther up into the East 50s: Gray, *After the Fall.*

I went to get the girls at school: Fink and Mathias, *Never Forget.*

I decided to go to my brother's firehouse: Ibid.

We had to break in: Ibid.

The boss [NYPD Commissioner Bernard Kerik]: Ibid.

I'll never forget one obviously homeless gentleman: Maury Thompson, "Pataki Looks Back at 9/11, and the Days That Followed," *Post Star* (Glens Falls, NY), September 10, 2011, at https://poststar.com/pataki-looks-back-at-and-the-days-that-followed/article_beae9b6a-dc23-11e0-9030-001cc4c03286.html.

Airborne, Somewhere over the Plains

In each cabin on board Air Force One: Covering Catastrophe, 190.

At Mount Weather

I was heading out to Andrews Air Force Base: C-SPAN, "Former House Speaker Dennis Hastert on September 11, 2011."

I ended up at an undisclosed location: Oral history in the collection of the U.S. House of Representatives Historian's Office (Washington, D.C.).

We didn't know what was facing us: Ibid.

At Ground Zero

As they were pulling the trucks out of the wreckage: Fink and Mathias, *Never Forget.*

At the Hospitals

I spent the rest of the day: Ibid.
I walked back to Saint Vincent's Hospital: Fink and Mathias, *Never Forget.*
We spent that day marshaling state resources: Oral history in the collection of the 9/11 Tribute Museum.

The 9/11 Generation

My son was going to turn one month old: Sheryl Meyer, post to Associated Press Facebook page, August 3, 2011, at https://www.facebook.com/APNews/posts/1015 0259303741623?comment_id=179602 49&comment_tracking =%7B%22tn%22% 3A%22R%2360%22%7D.
My mom worked at one of the high-rise buildings: "Reader Memories of 9/11: Jingqu," *Los Angeles Times,* 2012, at http://latimes .tumblr.com/post/9443823702/9-11-jingqu.
The sky was gray as my babysitter woke me up: "Reader Memories of 9/11: Katiewhy," *Los Angeles Times,* 2012, at http://latimes .tumblr.com/post/9520540790/9-11- katiewhy.

All the adults seemed weird: "Reader Memories of 9/11: Tumblingalma," *Los Angeles Times,* 2012, at http://latimes.tumblr.com/post/9491800730/9-11-tumblingalma.

There were Black Hawk helicopters: Monica Hesse and Caitlin Gibson, "This Was 9/11 If You Were a Kid," *Washington Post,* September 8, 2016, at https://www.washingtonpost.com/lifestyle/style/this-was-911-if-you-were-a-kid/2016/09/08/b3371eb6-754c-11e6-8149-b8d05321db62_story.html?utm_term=.cb662d2333ac.

I was a pretty shy and quiet child: Ibid.

My teacher walked me up the steps: Dan Reimold, " 'Why Is the Sky Dark on the TV?': Students Share 9/11 Memories," *USA Today,* September 11, 2014, at https://www.usatoday.com/story/college/2014/09/11/why-is-the-sky-dark-on-the-tv-students-share-911-memories/37395955/.

I was the new kid in school: Hesse and Gibson, "This Was 9/11 If You Were a Kid."

That was the first time I realized that truly awful things: "Reader Memories of 9/11: Barelyasleep," *Los Angeles Times,* 2012, at http://latimes.tumblr.com/post/9485063973/9-11-barelyasleep.

"Is your mom OK?": Reimold, " 'Why Is the Sky Dark on the TV?': Students Share 9/11 Memories."

The banner on the screen appeared: "Reader

Memories of 9/11: Undermyhijab," *Los Angeles Times,* 2012, at http://latimes.tumblr.com/post/9364021710/9-11-under myhijab.

Everyone was distraught: Dina Spector and Kevin Lincoln, "Here's What Celebrities Were Doing When They Heard About 9/11," *Business Insider,* September 10, 2011, at https://www.businessinsider.com/celebrities-remember-september-11-2011-9.

I was a figure skater: Karen Zhou, post to Associated Press Facebook page, August 3, 2011, at https://www.facebook.com/APNews/posts/10150259303741623?comment_id=18401186&comment_tracking=%7B%22tn%22%3A%22R%2328%22%7D.

I didn't know what the Twin Towers were: "Reader Memories of 9/11: Justliziam," *Los Angeles Times,* 2012, at http://latimes.tumblr.com/post/9655398573/9-11-justliziam.

I couldn't understand why anyone: "Reader Memories of 9/11: Kristincamillechez," *Los Angeles Times,* 2012, at http://latimes.tumblr.com/post/9694959141/9-11-kristincamillechez.

My mom told me that some planes had crashed: Hesse and Gibson, "This Was 9/11 If You Were a Kid."

It was the tradition in my elementary school: Ibid.

The events unfolded well before I got up: "Reader Memories of 9/11: Godinezzz," *Los Angeles Times,* 2012, at http://latimes.tumblr.com/post/9575583896/9-11-godinezzz.

When my siblings got ready for school: "Reader Memories of 9/11: Alterposer," *Los Angeles Times,* 2012, at http://latimes.tumblr.com/post/9573861880/9-11-alterposer.

I was looking up the World Trade Center: Hesse and Gibson, "This Was 9/11 If You Were a Kid."

I was trying something new that year: "Reader Memories of 9/11: Wastebaskets," *Los Angeles Times,* 2012, at http://latimes.tumblr.com/post/9532243332/9-11-wastebaskets.

It was the first time I completely understood: "Reader Memories of 9/11: Oocbear," *Los Angeles Times,* 2012, at http://latimes.tumblr.com/post/9515356892/9-11-oocbear.

At around seven in the morning: "Reader Memories of 9/11: jonmichaelkay," *Los Angeles Times,* 2012, at http://latimes.tumblr.com/post/9357751088/9-11-jonmichaelkay.

September 11th was also picture day: "Reader Memories of 9/11: notnadia," *Los Angeles*

Times, 2012, http://latimes.tumblr.com/post/9997558234/9-11-notnadia.

We were told we should leave school: Joanna Fischetti, post to Associated Press Facebook page, August 3, 2011, at https://www.facebook.com/APNews/posts/10150259303741623?comment_id=17959833&comment_tracking=%7B%22tn%22%3A%22R%2382%22%7D.

A long line of people waited: "Reader Memories of 9/11: Mallory," *Los Angeles Times,* 2012, at http://latimes.tumblr.com/post/9365066210/9-11-mallory.

It was my first real time living away: "Reader Memories of 9/11: Shortformblog," *Los Angeles Times,* 2012, at http://latimes.tumblr.com/post/9603515777/9-11-shortformblog.

Suddenly being out in the world: "Reader Memories of 9/11: Courtsomething," *Los Angeles Times,* 2012, at http://latimes.tumblr.com/post/9508426372/9-11-courtsomething.

At Offutt Air Force Base

We didn't know who was friend or foe: Oral history in the collection of the 9/11 Tribute Museum.

He said, "We're going to find out: CNN, "9/11: What Really Happened?"

The whole tenor of the presidency changed: Ibid.

The Secret Service thought the White House press room: Karen Hughes, "Karen Hughes Remembers the 9/11 Terror Attacks," Fox News, September 9, 2011, at https://www .foxnews.com/opinion/karen-hughes-remembers-the-9-11-terror-attacks.

Afternoon in America

My husband worked in the South Tower: Oral history in the collection of the Arlington County Public Library Oral History Project (Virginia), at https://libraryarchives.arling tonva.us/index.php/Detail/objects/195.

A melancholy silence crept in: Covering Catastrophe, 209.

I remember the silence of the sky: "Reader Memories of 9/11: Intellichick," *Los Angeles Times,* 2012, at http://latimes.tumblr.com/post/10006807702/9-11-intellichick.

The world seemed to have stopped: Anne Marie Reidy Borenstein, post to Associated Press Facebook page, August 3, 2011, at https://www.facebook.com/APNews/posts/10150259303741623?comment_id=17 959917&comment_tracking=%7B%22tn %22%3A%22R%2378%22%7D.

All I wanted to do: Fink and Mathias, *Never Forget.*

Searching

There was a "worst moment" for me: Covering Catastrophe, 165.

My brother was a pilot: Kimberly Archie, post to Associated Press Facebook page, August 3, 2011, at https://www.facebook.com/APNews/posts/10150259303741623?comment_id=17959995&comment_tracking=%7B%22tn%22%3A%22R%2372%22%7D.

Why did we get out?: Fink and Mathias, *Never Forget.*

It was a day of lefts and rights: Ibid.

Once you got to the top of the rubble pile: Oral history in the collection of the 9/11 Tribute Museum.

Evening in Washington

We walked across the East Front: C-SPAN, "Former House Speaker Dennis Hastert on September 11, 2011."

Daschle came up and spoke: Ibid.

I remember the chills: Ibid.

In the hours and days and weeks later: "Reader Memories of 9/11: Breakthecitysky," *Los Angeles Times,* 2012, at http://latimes.tumblr.com/post/10009875778/9-11-breakthecitysky.

The rest of the afternoon, I just ran: "Former Attorney General Recalls Sept. 11," NPR,

September 8, 2011, at https://www.npr.org/
2011/09/08/140291047/former-attorney-
general-recalls-sept-11.
By that night, the president: CNN, "9/11: What
Really Happened?"
I was nervous for the president: Ibid.

In the Oval Office

As we lifted off and headed up the Potomac:
"Cheney Recalls Taking Charge From
Bunker," CNN.com, September 11, 2002,
at http://edition.cnn.com/2002/ALLPOLI
TICS/09/11/ar911.king.cheney/.
I recall watching the vice president: Ibid.
The headquarters of the U.S. military: Ste-
phen F. Hayes, "Cheney Speaks," *Weekly
Standard,* July 23, 2017, at https://www
.weeklystandard.com/stephen-f-hayes/
cheney-speaks-14972.
I remember sitting in the living room: Ibid.

The Evening of 9/11

I had been dating someone: "Reader Memories of 9/11: Hystericalanduseless," *Los
Angeles Times,* 2012, at http://latimes
.tumblr.com/post/9613642001/9-11-
hystericalanduseless.
It was a depressed, dismal: Naudet, Naudet,
and Hanlon, *9/11.*
The race was on: "Last Man Out," *60 Minutes,*

CBS News, November 23, 2004, at https://www.cbsnews.com/news/last-man-out/.

We heard people, some excitement: Oral history in the collection of the 9/11 Tribute Museum.

The Day Ends

That night, a bunch of our friends: "Reader Memories of 9/11: Wholetheblogsout," *Los Angeles Times,* 2012, at http://latimes.tumblr.com/post/9341803302/9-11-wholetheblogsout.

I got home at 2:00 a.m.: Running Toward Danger, 242.

We met when we were only 16: StoryCorps, "Beverly Eckert."

Epilogue

All told, thousands of Pentagon workers had been displaced: Creed and Newman, *Firefight,* 261.

The morning after Jeremy had died: "Lyz Glick's Courage," NBC News, August 20, 2002, at http://www.nbcnews.com/id/3080114/ns/dateline_nbc-newsmakers/t/lyz-glicks-courage/#.XHwCU2RKgy4.

I didn't know what I had done: StoryCorps, "On Sept. 11, He Checked Hijackers Onto Flight 77. It's Haunted Him Ever Since," NPR, *Morning Edition,* September 9, 2016, at https://www.npr.org/2016/09/09/493 133084/on-sept-11-he-checked-hijackers-onto-flight-77-its-haunted-him-ever-since.

By Wednesday's end, the official death toll: Robert Lee Hotz, "Agonizing Search for Survivors," *Los Angeles Times,* September 13, 2001, at http://articles.latimes.com/2001/sep/13/news/mn-45260.

I called the 800 number: "September 11: Bearing Witness to History," Smithsonian Institution, at https://amhistory.si.edu/september11/collection/record.asp?ID=41.

I remember the day of the death certificates: Barbash, *On Top of the World,* 41.

We were ready to start receiving the dead: 9/11 Tribute Center oral history.

The city was plastered: "Reader Memories of 9/11: Yespleaseandthankyou," *Los Angeles Times,* 2012, at http://latimes.tumblr.com/post/9672897542/9-11-yespleaseandthankyou.

The most emotionally searing time: Jenny Pachucki, "The Couric Effect: Katie Couric," *9/11 Memorial & Museum,* September 7, 2016, at https://www.911memorial.org/our-city-our-story-podcast-series.

I was captain of the first aircraft: C-SPAN, "Aviation Officials Remember September 11, 2001."

The real change in the president: Murphy and Purdum, "Farewell to All That: An Oral

History of the Bush White House."

We kept working: "9/11 audio timeline," National September 11 Museum and Memorial, at https://timeline.911memorial.org/#Timeline/3/AudioEntry/656.

The Friday after September 11: "How 9/11 Changed Us," *New York* magazine, September 11, 2003, at http://nymag.com/nymetro/news/sept11/2003/n_9196/.

As much as obviously 9/11: "Stories of Flight 93," CNN, February 18, 2006, at http://transcripts.cnn.com/TRANSCRIPTS/0602/18/lkl.01.html.

The markets open tomorrow: Richard W. Stevenson and Jonathan Fuerbringer, "After the Attacks: The Economy; Nation Shifts Its Focus to Wall Street as a Major Test of Attack's Aftermaths," *New York Times,* September 17, 2001, at https://www.nytimes.com/2001/09/17/business/after-attacks-economy-nation-shifts-its-focus-wall-street-major-test-attack-s.html.

It was a wake one day: Fink and Mathias, *Never Forget.*

There were days we went to four [funerals]: Barbash, *On Top of the World,* 88.

Four days a week: Fink and Mathias, *Never Forget.*

The emptiness from the losses: National Commission on Terrorist Attacks Upon the United States, "Testimony of the Former Commissioner of the New York City Fire

Department Thomas Von Essen."

I stated over and over again: "The Tragedy Expert," *Without Fail* podcast, April 8, 2019, at https://gimletmedia.com/shows/without-fail/5who4m/the-tragedy-expert.

My birthday is 9/11: POLITICO Playbook, September 11, 2017, at https://www.politico.com/story/2017/09/11/playbook-birthday-jeh-johnson-242544.

The toll was great at the Pentagon as well: Creed and Newman, *Firefight,* 455; "Statistics From 9/11 and 15 Years Later," *Never Forget Project,* at http://neverforgetproject.com/statistics/.

9/11 tore through the department: Creed and Newman, *Firefight,* 455.

Due to the physical nature of their jobs: Dr. David Prezant, "FDNY World Trade Center Health Program Fact Sheet," July 20, 2015, at http://www.911healthwatch.org/files/WTC-Health-Program-911-FDNY-fact-sheet.pdf.

I had this wild thing in my mind: "On Sept. 11, He Checked Hijackers Onto Flight 77: It's Haunted Him Ever Since," NPR, September 9, 2016, at https://www.npr.org/2016/09/09/493133084/on-sept-11-he-checked-hijackers-onto-flight-77-its-haunted-him-ever-since.

You cannot say that something that happened: Alan Baker, "Mourning a Woman Who Shared a 9/11 Miracle," *New York Times,*

January 16, 2011, at https://www.nytimes.com/2011/01/17/nyregion/17harris.html.

The six firefighters made the request: "Farewell to the 'Guardian Angel of 9/11,' " reprinted from NFDA's *Memorial Business Journal,* April 7, 2011, at http://www.memorialsolutions.com/sitemaker/sites/Maryla1/images/WebsiteArticle-FarewelltotheGuardianAngelof9-11.pdf.

It was an honor to do this for her: Marla Diamond, "Firefighters Say Goodbye to Their 9/11 'Guardian Angel,' " CBS News, January 21, 2011, at https://newyork.cbslocal.com/2011/01/21/firefighters-say-goodbye-to-their-911-guardian-angel/.

IMAGE CREDITS

Insert 1

Page 1: Getty Images/Staff (top); Monika Bravo (bottom)

Page 2: Collection of the 9/11 Memorial Museum / Roberto Rabanne Archive / Photograph by Roberto Rabanne (top); Courtesy of the Ong family (bottom left); Collection 9/11 Memorial Museum, Gift of Richard D. Eichen (bottom right)

Page 3: Sean Adair / Reuters (top); Jesse Randall (bottom)

Page 4: Photo by Eric Draper, Courtesy of the George W. Bush Presidential Library (top); Photo by David Bohrer, Courtesy of the National Archives (bottom)

Page 5: Courtesy of the Department of Defense

Page 6: Collection 9/11 Memorial Museum, John Labriola Archive, Photograph © John Labriola (top and bottom)

Page 7: Richard Drew/AP

Page 8: Photograph by John O'Sullivan (top and bottom)

Page 9: Collection of the 9/11 Memorial Museum, Roberto Rabanne Archive, Photograph by Roberto Rabanne (top and bottom)

Page 10: Defense Department photo by Staff Sgt. Jim Varhegyi, USAF (top); Defense Department photo by Journalist Petty Officer 1st Class Mark D. Faram, USN (bottom)

Page 11: Department of Defense / Michael Garcia (top and bottom)

Page 12: Photo by David Bohrer, Courtesy of the National Archives (top and middle); Photo by Eric Draper, Courtesy of the George W. Bush Presidential Library (bottom)

Page 13: © 2001. Used with permission of the New York City Police Department (top and bottom)

Page 14: Department of Defense (top); Reuters/Tim Shaffer (bottom)

Page 15: AP Photo/Tribune-Democrat/David Lloyd (top); Reuters/Tim Shaffer (bottom)

Page 16: Department of Defense (top); NASA/Frank Culberston

Insert 2

Page 1: Photo by Eric Draper, Courtesy of the George W. Bush Presidential Library

(top left, top right, and bottom)

Page 2: Photo by Eric Draper, Courtesy of the George W. Bush Presidential Library (top and bottom)

Page 3: Photo by John O'Sullivan (top, middle, and bottom)

Page 4: Courtesy of U.S. National Archives (top); U.S. Coast Guard photo (bottom)

Page 5: Photo by John O'Sullivan (top and bottom)

Page 6: Photo by John O'Sullivan

Page 7: Photo by Eric Draper, Courtesy of the George W. Bush Presidential Library (top and bottom)

Page 8: Photo by David Bohrer, Courtesy of the National Archives (top); Photo by Eric Draper, Courtesy of the George W. Bush Presidential Library (middle and bottom)

Page 9: Screenshot courtesy of C-SPAN (top); Navy photo by Petty Officer 2nd Class Robert Houlihan (bottom)

Page 10: Photo by David Bohrer, Courtesy of the National Archives (top and bottom)

Page 11: US Air Force photograph by Lt. Col. Terry Moultrup (top); U.S. Navy photograph by Chief Photographer's Mate Eric Tilford (bottom)

Page 12: Courtesy of NYPD Detective David Brink (top); Photo Courtesy of Dr. Cynthia Otto (bottom)

Page 13: Roberto Rabanne Collection of the 9/11 Memorial Museum / Roberto Rabanne Archive / Photograph by Roberto Rabanne (top); Defense Department photo by Tech Sgt. Cedric Rudisill, USAF (bottom)

Page 14: Collection 9/11 Memorial Museum, Gift of Mickey Kross, Photograph by Matt Flynn (top); Collection 9/11 Memorial Museum, Gift of Retired Port Authority of NY&NJ Police Officer Sharon A. Miller, Photograph by Matt Flynn (middle); Collection 9/11 Memorial Museum, Gift of Alison and Jefferson Crowther and Family, Photograph by Michael Hnatov (bottom)

Page 15: Department of Defense / Michael Garcia (top); Photo by Geoffrey T. Chesman of Image Link Photography, provided by The Pentagon Memorial Fund, Inc. (bottom)

Page 16: National Park Service Photo/ Brenda T Schwartz (top); 9/11 Memorial & Museum, Photograph by Jin S. Lee (bottom)

Interior Images

Page 184: Photo by David Bohrer, Courtesy of the National Archives

Page 303: AP Photo/ Suzanne Plunkett

Page 350: Photo by Shannon Stapleton / Reuters

Page 363: Photo by Todd Maisel/New York Daily News.

ABOUT THE AUTHOR

Garrett M. Graff is a journalist and historian who has written for publications including *WIRED, Esquire, Rolling Stone,* and *The New York Times,* and edited two of Washington's most prestigious magazines, *Washingtonian* and *POLITICO Magazine.* Graff's previous books include *The Threat Matrix: Inside Robert Mueller's FBI* and the national bestseller *Raven Rock.* Today, he is a contributor to *WIRED* and CNN and works with the Aspen Institute's Cybersecurity & Technology Program. He lives in Vermont.

The employees of Thorndike Press hope you have enjoyed this Large Print book. All our Thorndike, Wheeler, and Kennebec Large Print titles are designed for easy reading, and all our books are made to last. Other Thorndike Press Large Print books are available at your library, through selected bookstores, or directly from us.

For information about titles, please call:
(800) 223-1244

or visit our website at:
gale.com/thorndike

To share your comments, please write:
Publisher
Thorndike Press
10 Water St., Suite 310
Waterville, ME 04901